D1158027

INFORMATION STORAGE AND RETRIEVAL

ROBERT R. KORFHAGE

WILEY COMPUTER PUBLISHING

John Wiley & Sons, Inc.
New York • Chichester • Weinheim • Brisbane • Singapore • Toronto

Executive Publisher: Katherine Schowalter
Editor: Marjorie Spencer
Managing Editor: Erin Singletary
Electronic Products, Associate Editor: Mike Green
Text Design & Composition: North Market Street Graphics

Designations used by companies to distinguish their products are often claimed as trademarks. In all instances where John Wiley & Sons, Inc., is aware of a claim, the product names appear in initial capital or ALL CAPITAL LETTERS. Readers, however, should contact the appropriate companies for more complete information regarding trademarks and registration.

This text is printed on acid-free paper.

This publication is designed to provide accurate and authoritative information in regard to the subject matter covered. It is sold with the understanding that the publisher is not engaged in rendering legal, accounting, or other professional service. If legal advice or other expert assistance is required, the services of a competent professional person should be sought.

Library of Congress Cataloging-in-Publication Data:
Korfhage, Robert R.
    Information storage and retrieval / Robert R. Korfhage.
        p.   cm.
    Includes index.
    ISBN 0-471-14338-3 (cloth : alk. paper)
    1. Database management.   2. Information storage and retrieval
systems.   I. Title.
QA76.9.D3K657   1997
025.04—dc21   96-49511
                                                         CIP

Printed in the United States of America
10 9 8 7 6 5 4 3 2 1

Contents

Preface   xi

Acknowledgments   xv

CHAPTER 1. OVERVIEW   1

1.1. ABSTRACTION   2

1.2. THE INFORMATION SYSTEM   4

1.3. MEASURES   6

1.4. FROM DATA TO WISDOM   8

1.5. TOWARD EFFECTIVE INFORMATION
RETRIEVAL SYSTEMS: A VIEW OF THE BOOK   11

REFERENCES   14

EXERCISES   16

CHAPTER 2. DOCUMENT AND QUERY FORMS   17

2.1. THE CONCEPT OF A DOCUMENT   17

2.2. DATA STRUCTURES IN THE LARGE   20

2.3. DOCUMENT SURROGATES   21

2.4. VOCABULARY CONTROL   24

2.5. THE FINE STRUCTURE OF DATA   25

2.6. DATA COMPRESSION   27

2.7. TEXT DOCUMENTS   38

2.8. IMAGES AND SOUND   39

   REFERENCES   42

   EXERCISES   47

CHAPTER 3. QUERY STRUCTURES   51

3.1. MATCHING CRITERIA   52

3.2. BOOLEAN QUERIES   53

3.3. VECTOR QUERIES   63

3.4. EXTENDED BOOLEAN QUERIES   65

3.5. FUZZY QUERIES   69

3.6. PROBABILISTIC QUERIES   71

3.7. NATURAL LANGUAGE QUERIES   71

3.8. INFORMATION RETRIEVAL AND DATABASE SYSTEMS   73

   REFERENCES   73

   EXERCISES   77

CHAPTER 4. THE MATCHING PROCESS   79

4.1.   RELEVANCE AND SIMILARITY MEASURES   80

4.2.   BOOLEAN-BASED MATCHING   81

4.3.   VECTOR-BASED MATCHING: METRICS   82

4.4.   VECTOR-BASED MATCHING: COSINE MEASURE   84

4.5.   MISSING TERMS AND TERM RELATIONSHIPS   86

4.6.   PROBABILISTIC MATCHING   88

4.7.   FUZZY MATCHING   92

4.8.   PROXIMITY MATCHING   93

4.9.   EFFECTS OF WEIGHTING   95

4.10.   EFFECTS OF SCALING   96

4.11.   DATA FUSION   97

4.12.   A USER-CENTERED VIEW   98

REFERENCES   99

EXERCISES   103

CHAPTER 5. TEXT ANALYSIS   105

5.1.   INDEXING   105

5.2.   MATRIX REPRESENTATIONS   110

5.3.   TERM EXTRACTION AND ANALYSIS   111

5.4.   TERM ASSOCIATION   113

5.5.   LEXICAL MEASURES OF TERM SIGNIFICANCE   114

5.6.   OTHER METHODS OF DOCUMENT ANALYSIS   123

5.7.   DOCUMENT SIMILARITY   125

5.8. STOP LISTS   133

5.9. STEMMING   135

5.10. MULTILINGUAL RETRIEVAL SYSTEMS   137

5.11. THESAURI   138

5.12. SUMMARY   139

REFERENCES   140

EXERCISES   142

CHAPTER 6. USER PROFILES AND THEIR USE   145

6.1. SIMPLE PROFILES   145

6.2. EXTENDED PROFILES   146

6.3. CURRENT AWARENESS SYSTEMS   147

6.4. RETROSPECTIVE SEARCH SYSTEMS   148

6.5. MODIFYING THE QUERY BY THE PROFILE   149

6.6. THE QUERY AND PROFILE AS SEPARATE
REFERENCE POINTS   153

6.7. THE ETHICS OF A USER PROFILE   158

REFERENCES   159

EXERCISES   159

CHAPTER 7. MULTIPLE REFERENCE POINT SYSTEMS   163

7.1. DEFINITIONS   163

7.2. DOCUMENTS AND DOCUMENT CLUSTERS   164

7.3. THE MATHEMATICAL BASIS   165

7.4. GUIDO   168

7.5. VIBE   173

7.6. BOOLEAN VIBE   179

7.7. BIRD   183

7.8. SUMMARY   185

REFERENCES   187

EXERCISES   188

CHAPTER 8. RETRIEVAL EFFECTIVENESS MEASURES   191

8.1. BINARY VERSUS *N*-ARY MEASURES   191

8.2. PRECISION AND RECALL, AND RELATED MEASURES   194

8.3. USER-ORIENTED MEASURES   198

8.4. AVERAGE PRECISION AND RECALL   199

8.5. OPERATING CURVES AND SINGLE MEASURES   203

8.6. EXPECTED SEARCH LENGTH   204

8.7. SATISFACTION AND FRUSTRATION,
AND RELATED MEASURES   208

REFERENCES   216

EXERCISES   216

CHAPTER 9. EFFECTIVENESS IMPROVEMENT TECHNIQUES   219

9.1. INFORMATION THE USER MAY FIND HELPFUL   219

9.2. RELEVANCE FEEDBACK   221

9.3. GENETIC ALGORITHMS   224

9.4.   GENETIC ALGORITHMS FOR RELEVANCE FEEDBACK   226

9.5.   GENETIC ALGORITHMS IN A REALISTIC SITUATION   231

9.6.   THE TREC EXPERIMENTS   232

REFERENCES   234

EXERCISES   235

CHAPTER 10. ALTERNATIVE RETRIEVAL TECHNIQUES   237

10.1.   NATURAL LANGUAGE PROCESSING   238

10.2.   CITATION PROCESSING   241

10.3.   HYPERTEXT LINKS   245

10.4.   INFORMATION FILTERING AND PASSAGE RETRIEVAL   246

10.5.   IMAGE PROCESSING   247

10.6.   SOUND PROCESSING   249

REFERENCES   251

EXERCISES   256

CHAPTER 11. OUTPUT PRESENTATION   257

11.1.   REFERENCE VERSUS SURROGATE VERSUS DOCUMENT   257

11.2.   GROUPING AND RANKING   260

11.3.   QUANTITY VERSUS QUALITY ISSUES   260

11.4.   MEDIA   261

11.5.   CRITIQUE   264

11.6.   VIRIs (VISUAL INFORMATION RETRIEVAL INTERFACES)   265

REFERENCES   267

EXERCISES   270

CHAPTER 12. DOCUMENT ACCESS   271

12.1. ELECTRONIC ACCESS   271

12.2. PROCESSING SCANNED DOCUMENTS   272

12.3. PROCESSING ELECTRONICALLY
       GENERATED DOCUMENTS   275

12.4. DISTRIBUTED DOCUMENT SYSTEMS   276

12.5. INTERNET AND WEB ACCESS   277

REFERENCES   278

EXERCISES   279

CHAPTER 13. THE ECTOSYSTEM AND POLICY ISSUES   281

13.1. THE USER   281

13.2. THE FUNDER   283

13.3. THE SERVER   285

13.4. COPYRIGHT ISSUES   286

13.5. PRIVACY ISSUES   288

13.6. SECURITY ISSUES   288

REFERENCES   289

EXERCISES   289

APPENDIX A. STRING MATCHING TECHNIQUES   291

A.1. KNUTH-MORRIS-PRATT MATCHING   291

A.2. BOYER-MOORE-GALIL MATCHING   297

A.3. AHO-CORASICK MATCHING   299

A.4. RABIN-KARP MATCHING   299

A.5. STRING DIFFERENCING   300

   REFERENCES   303

   EXERCISES   304

APPENDIX B. FILE STRUCTURES   **305**

   B.1. SEQUENTIAL FILES   307

   B.2. HASHED FILES   307

   B.3. INDEXED FILES   308

   B.4. TREE-STRUCTURED FILES   310

   B.5. CLUSTERED FILES   311

   B.6. NETTED FILES   312

      REFERENCES   312

Glossary   *313*

Index   *339*

Preface

People need information to solve problems, whether as simple as deciding on an evening's entertainment or as weighty as resolving a world crisis. To meet this need, people rely on a number of sources: their own backgrounds, friends and colleagues, experts, libraries, and public and private information sources. This book addresses the problem of providing a response to an information need through the use of computer- and telecommunications-based access to information sources.

Information storage and retrieval has been a focus of research and development efforts for 40 years or more. However, developments in technology during recent years have greatly changed the context within which this study takes place. We now have personal computers with gigabyte disk drives, reliable data transmission lines with capacities two orders of magnitude higher than those available a decade ago, full-text and multimedia databases, and worldwide access to distributed databases through the Internet and the World Wide Web. An approach to information storage and retrieval that would have been considered visionary a decade ago now reflects reality and may soon be replaced by still more sophisticated approaches.

This book attempts to provide an informative and critical bridge between the more customary approaches to information storage and retrieval and the newer approaches designed around present day technology and concepts. It covers most of the commonly accepted modes of storing and retrieving textual documents—and provides criticism of these techniques when warranted. It also discusses the modification of these techniques and concepts to fit the world of full-text and multimedia databases. The book introduces an approach using a genetic algorithm to enhance the retrieval capabilities of an information system, explores the use of current computer systems' graphic abilities for enhancing the interface that an information system presents to the user, and considers the problems and opportunities in information access that are provided by the Internet and the World Wide Web. Topics are examined in the context of both theory and some of the practicalities exemplified in existing information retrieval systems.

The book begins with a focus on the information need of an individual user. Satisfaction resulting from this individual need being met is the touchstone for truly effective system performance. Throughout the text, this focus is maintained; the discussion repeatedly returns to the question of how a given technique or concept relates to the end user. The book moves from expressing the information need as a query, to describing documents, to matching the documents to the query. It emphasizes that evaluation of an information retrieval system's effectiveness is critical to its success. Based on these fundamentals, the book turns to the more subtle problems arising from the new technological context, addressing the issues of full-text retrieval, image and sound retrieval, and access to distributed databases via a telecommunications network.

A particular emphasis in the book is on the interaction of the user with the system. User profiles are applied to enhance the retrieval capabilities of the system; multiple reference points are introduced to enhance the user's ability to define the information need and to browse the system. The development of visual information retrieval interfaces (VIRIs) represents a current effort to provide the user with a more structured and meaningful display of search results than is presented by the traditional ordered list of retrieved documents. The information retrieval system should provide complete and appropriate assistance to the user while leaving the user fully in charge of the information search. System functionality should be analogous to that of a fine 35-mm camera, providing a "point and shoot" capability for the novice user, while comprehensive overrides permit the sophisticated user to tailor a search closely to a specific need.

Even with the underlying concern for the user of an information retrieval system, the approach taken in this book is largely a "systems" approach in contrast to a "cognitive" one. That is, the book concentrates on data structures, algorithms, and quantitative measures that apply to information retrieval. In recent years there has been increasing interest in the cognitive side of information retrieval—studies focusing more on how users employ an information retrieval system to meet an information need. The measures used in such studies are of necessity more qualitative in nature than those used in the past. While the cognitive approach is discussed at several points in this book, to do it justice and to fully explore the methods and results of this approach requires another volume.

Because computers and algorithmic methods play a major role in the development of the theme of the text, the reader is assumed to have a certain facility with this technology. It is not required that the reader be a computer programmer; however, experience with using computers for text processing, database searches, financial calculations, or other "serious" purposes is a background that will stand the reader in good stead. In addition, mathematical models play a major role in the development of the theory of information storage and retrieval. Thus the reader is expected to have a fundamental background in sets, logic, vectors, probability or statistics, and geometry.

A quick scan of the references in this book shows that information retrieval papers are published in many different journals and conference proceedings. Thus to stay current the researcher or practitioner must follow many publications. However, four publications dominate the field. These include two journals—*JASIS, the Journal of the American Society for Information Science,* and *Information Processing & Management*—and the proceedings of two annual conferences—the International Conference on Research and Development in Information Storage and Retrieval, sponsored by the Special Interest Group on Information Retrieval (SIGIR) of the Association for Computing Machinery (together with information retrieval groups from other countries), and the annual conference of the American Society for Information Science. Of these publications, only the SIGIR proceedings focuses on information retrieval as a specialty within information science. It is anticipated, however, that a journal devoted entirely to information storage and retrieval will appear within a year or two.

Acknowledgments

The creation of a textbook is a substantial effort that includes input from many people and sources. While the author has the task of blending ideas together into a coherent whole, those ideas come from a wide variety of sources. In particular, the following people have contributed significantly to the present effort. Tefko Saracevic and Gary Marchionini both reviewed the manuscript and made many helpful suggestions. Josiane Mothe, a colleague in France, and Monika Schwartz, a graduate student at the University of Pittsburgh, both were extremely helpful in tracking down references that were hard to find. Anthony Debons spent many wonderful hours discussing with me the finer points of cognition and need with respect to information retrieval. Thanks must also go to the students who suffered through the class notes that were used in preparing the text. The fate of any author is in the hands of the editorial and production staff; the staff at Wiley has been highly cooperative and helpful. And finally, thanks must go to my wife, Ann, who has tolerated my odd working hours and kept me well-fed throughout the writing.

Overview

People depend on information to carry out the activities of daily life. Every task, from crossing the street to diagnosing complex medical problems, requires information. Some of this information, such as whether the traffic light is red or green, is readily available; other information requires extensive searching and the assembly of ideas from multiple sources. People learn at an early age to solve simple information needs; solving more complex information needs requires both education and experience.

In ancient times, recorded drawings and writings were an attempt to capture information believed important. The design of computer-based systems to aid in the search for information is a specialized task, requiring extensive knowledge of how information can be organized and how people search for information. Today's information systems are far beyond the cave wall or the cuneiform tablet, and frequently involve expensive and sophisticated computing and communications equipment. Although many people can learn to use a computer or a communications system for relatively simple tasks, the design and use of a system to handle complex information tasks efficiently is the work of a specialist.

This book addresses information storage and information retrieval—two sides of a coin: If a person is to be able to search for information, that information must have been stored in some form. The form in which information is often presented, text or images, makes it difficult or impossible to obtain clear and precise answers to many questions that a user might ask. Searching a document collection may be eased or made more complicated by the manner in which the collection is organized.

The focus of this book is on methods and technologies available for storing and retrieving information in the form of documents that contain text and that may also contain tables, mathematical or chemical formulas, charts, and images. Although the discussion will primarily cover the use of digital computers and electronic information processing equipment, the concepts and principles presented will be applicable to all means of storing and retrieving information, from the totally manual system to the totally automated system.

In this chapter, the distinctions among *data, information,* and *reality* are drawn. Information system organization is outlined, and the problem of measuring the quality of an information system, both in a given context and independently of any specific context or problem, is introduced.

1.1   ABSTRACTION

There is a *reality* independent of the individual human observer, that is, a reality that is basically the same for everyone. A portion of this reality corresponds to the physical world with which people interact every day. Another portion is more abstract, consisting of the concepts that underlie mathematics, music, art, and other areas of knowledge and study. The key point to make about reality is that it cannot be known in its entirety. Yet individual perceptions have enough in common that people can communicate and operate effectively.

Any information system has at its heart a collection of *data* about reality. Although this collection is always incomplete, new data are incorporated and existing data refined in an ongoing process to match reality more closely. It is this collection of data, not reality itself, that any information system uses. This exemplifies the first abstraction principle:

> *In any information system, the "real world" is represented by a collection of data abstracted from observations of the real world and made available to the system.*

Consider the user of an information system. A person uses an information system in two major ways: to store information (data) in anticipation of a future need, and to find information (data) in response to a current need. In either case, the user has some *information need* driving the use of the information system. This need must be expressed to the system (Debons, Horne, and Croenweth 1988). If the user is storing information, then the form in which the information is stored will reflect the anticipated need. That is, the user will try to store information that is expected to be useful, in a form that facilitates its retrieval at a later time. The form in which the information can be stored is, to a large extent, influenced by the information system. For example, information must be digitized to use it in a computer-based system. If the user is trying to retrieve information, then the need must be expressed in the form of a query that is interpretable by the system. Again, the system strongly influences the form that the information query can take. This exemplifies the second abstraction principle:

> **A user's information need, whether for production, storage, or retrieval of information, is abstracted into a form that is commensurate with the information system to be used.**

These two abstraction principles inform the fundamental problem facing information system developers. The user has an information need that should be filled by information from the real world. Yet the information system can only work at the abstracted level, matching data to query (Figure 1.1). Similarly, when the user is trying to store information, the problem for the system is to provide a format that minimizes the distortion caused by the abstraction process.

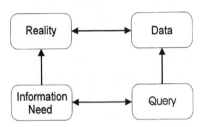

Figure 1.1 The abstractions and mappings of an information system.

1.2 THE INFORMATION SYSTEM

An information system is composed of two major portions, the ectosystem and the endosystem (Korfhage and DeLutis 1969). From the point of view of a system designer, the *ectosystem* consists of those system factors that are not under the control of the designer. These factors include the people who are involved with the system, the forms in which information is available, and the equipment and technology available for the system. The *endosystem* consists of those factors that the designer can specify and control, such as the equipment, algorithms, and procedures used.

The ectosystem has three main human components: the user, the funder, and the server (Nance 1967; Baker 1968). The *user* is the person who wishes either to store information in the system or to retrieve information from the system. Frequently, the user has little knowledge of the organization of the system or precisely how it works. Thus the user may judge system performance on the basis of partial knowledge. The user's judgments are strongly related to expectations vis-à-vis his or her information need. Most information systems have more than one user. The characteristics of the user group—the homogeneity or heterogeneity of the group members, their information interests, and their familiarity with the system—must be considered in developing and operating the endosystem.

The *funder* is the person (or organization) who underwrites the cost of operating the information system. No system is without cost, and the funder wishes to maintain a system in which the benefits outweigh the costs. The costs of the system may be funded in several ways. It is not uncommon for organizations to absorb these costs as overhead, thus providing "free information" to the users. Organizations can also charge users a fee for various services, recovering some or all of the costs. If the user is paying for services, then he or she must perceive the benefits of system use as being worth the cost. Similarly, the funder must be assured that the benefits from the system outweigh the net cost of operating the system, over and above any user fees. While costs can often be measured quite clearly, the benefits from a system, other than monetary gain, are much more difficult to measure. They may include ease of access to information, the time required to locate information, or, more generally, the perceived "good of the organization."

The *server* is the information professional who operates the system and provides service to the users. Many systems, such as large library systems or information services, have several servers on staff, each providing service in different ways. Some of the servers come into direct contact with the users, while others function behind the scenes, providing the support services necessary for successful operation of the information system. The technical staff—the system analysts, the system designers, and the operation and maintenance staff—are included in this group of servers, as are any library staff involved in system operation and use.

None of the three human components of the ectosystem is under the control of the system designer. Yet all must be taken into account in analyzing and designing an information system. All influence the success of the system. The three roles are not necessarily distinct, however. In a very small information system, such as a home recipe or budgeting system, the user, funder, and server are likely to be one and the same person. In larger systems, the boundaries between the roles may not be distinct. For example, if the user pays a fee for services, then to some extent the user is also the funder. For many personal information systems the user is also one of the servers, performing retrieval and other information processing tasks directly.

In contrast to the lack of control that he or she has over the ectosystem, the system designer has complete control of the endosystem. The endosystem has four components: the media used to store the information, the devices used to process the information, the algorithms by which the devices work, and the data structures used to organize the information.

The *media* include various forms of hard copy, such as printed text, art works, and maps, as well as machine-readable media, including microforms, magnetic tapes and disks, and CD-ROMs. The types of processing that can be done on the data are restricted by the media available in a system.

The *devices* available in an information system range from file drawers and book shelves to digital computers, optical scanners, and laser-based processing equipment. It is clearly important for the system designer to match the devices and media closely for optimal operation of the system. An improperly balanced system can be costly and ineffective.

Careful choice of the *algorithms* chosen for processing stored information, queries, and other data can make the difference between an efficient and effective information system and one that is too costly to operate or fails to provide adequate service. The user is generally interested in the services that the information system can provide. The capabilities presented to the user stem more from the algorithms chosen than from the devices or media.

The system designer can choose from many different *data structures* those structures that best match the algorithms and the applications. At times, the media or the devices constrain these structures. For example, if information is stored on magnetic tape, then access to the data is sequential, and any data organization other than sequential is largely wasted. Since random access to the data is important in most retrieval situations, magnetic tape is largely relegated to a backup role, with magnetic disks and CD-ROMs providing the primary mass storage. A good system designer carefully considers the interaction among devices, media, algorithms, and structure before making a firm commitment to a specific configuration.

1.3 MEASURES

The performance of an information system is largely dictated by the designer's choice of media, devices, algorithms, and structures—by the endosystem design, in other words. However, evaluation of that performance resides within the ectosystem: The user may or may not be satisfied with the responses to queries, the funder may feel that the system is not being run in an economically sound manner, or the server may believe that some of the system operations could be more efficiently carried out. If any of the user's, funder's, or server's needs and expectations are not met by the system, the potential for system failure exists (Meadow 1973; Kraft and Bookstein 1978; Blair and Maron 1985; McCain, White, and Griffith 1986; Shaw 1986; Tague and Schultz 1988; Losee 1991; Turtle and Croft 1991; Dumais 1994).

Each member of the ectosystem judges system performance from a distinct viewpoint. The user is primarily concerned with the *effectiveness* of the system—how well it meets the information need. Many things contribute to the user's perception of a system's effectiveness, to be discussed in detail later on. They include the speed with which the system can respond, the accuracy and thoroughness of the response to a query, and the amount of irrelevant information included in any response. The user who feels that a given system does not meet his or her needs will turn elsewhere. If many users do this, the endosystem design can be said to have failed (Bottle 1965; Hamilton and Chervany 1971; Heaps 1971; Eisenberg and Hu 1987; Frei and Schäuble 1991; Frei and Wyle 1991).

The server tends to be more aware of the *efficiency* of the system. He or she may ask: Is the system designed so that a user's information needs can be efficiently expressed? Does the system provide its response to a query in a highly efficient manner, or is there much wasted effort in responding to a user? Can the system, for example, locate a needed piece of information quickly, or must it make a lengthy search throughout the data? Are the algorithms and structures well chosen to minimize the effort needed for the major tasks? Is the time required to respond to an information need commensurate with the need and the characteristics of the data? The satisfaction that the servers feel as they work with the system is inversely related to the frustration that they feel while waiting for the system to finish one or another task (Lancaster and Climenson 1968).

The main concern of the funder is the *economy* of the system. While it is important that a system be effective and efficient, if it is not economical— that is, if it does not meet the economic goals of the funder—the system may be regarded as a failure, with the resultant loss of operating funds (Bourne and Ford 1964; Korfhage and DeLutis 1969; Lancaster 1971; Cooper 1972; Taylor 1986).

Thus the various people involved with an information system judge it in distinctly different ways. These judgments are interrelated. An inefficient endosystem may cause a lowering of user satisfaction despite producing reliable responses to information needs. Loss of users then results in lower income, hence making the endosystem uneconomical. In contrast, an efficient system, even one that provides relatively poor responses to information needs, may appear to be highly effective to users, and thereby be successful at attracting increased usage. This brightens the economic view of the system and may lead the funder to underwrite enhanced services.

There are thus three types of measures. All are important, but this book will concentrate primarily on effectiveness measures, examining sound and consistent ways to measure the system effectiveness. One problem in finding adequate system measurement methods is that different people have different criteria. "User satisfaction," for example, has as many meanings as there are users. Trying to meet or even define criteria that will satisfy a large, heterogeneous group of users is an impossible task; the system designer is forced to develop a compromise set of criteria that are acceptable to most users and still permit the development and implementation of a sound information system. These criteria should be established and fixed during the analysis and requirements definition phase of system design.

A second problem lies in the complexity of information systems and the difficulty in scaling any judgments to systems of different sizes. We expect many different services from an information system. The algorithms that provide these services are frequently nonlinear, so that as the volume of data to be handled grows, the efficiency of some operations deteriorates rapidly. Algorithms that perform well with megabytes of data may prove to be far too slow in handling gigabytes of data, or in handling data that are distributed across a network. Conversely, an algorithm that is very efficient for large quantities of data may involve sufficient processing overhead that other algorithms should be used for smaller quantities of data.

1.4   FROM DATA TO WISDOM

In the preceding pages, the words *data* and *information* have been used quite informally; now it is time to distinguish between them. The distinction described here may not be universally accepted, but is the usage in this book. *Data* are received, stored, and retrieved by an information endosystem. The data are impersonal; they are equally available to any users of the system. *Information,* in contrast, is a set of data that have been matched to a particular information need. That is, the concept of information has both personal and time-dependent components that are not present in the concept of data. For example, even if a system can provide to the user the list of ingredients in a certain breakfast cereal or the names of the signers of the Declaration of Independence, these data are not information if they are already known to the user or have no relevance to the user's need. In effect, these data become noise in the system, disrupting the user's awareness and concentration. In addition, they potentially dilute the system response to any information need.

Another way to distinguish between data and information is on the basis of organization. Although data can be organized independently of individual users, the organization of information is a more personal thing, requiring the active intervention of a user. All data have some organization, if only the organization imposed by the process of collecting and storing the data. Information, however, has a higher level of organization imposed by its relationship to a specific information need. In database systems where the same types of needs and questions arise repeatedly, much of the organization appropriate to these needs can be built into the storage system. Yet even here, designers and users speak of multiple *views* of data. In more general information retrieval systems, however, it may be impossible to anticipate fully the most appropriate organization until the various needs are expressed.

In addition to data and information, three more terms belong in this short hierarchy of increasing complexity: *signal, knowledge,* and *wisdom.* At one end, less complex than data, is the *signal* that must be transmitted from one place to another during information processing. This signal may be a bit stream, an electromagnetic wave form, or some other form. It is properly the concern of the transmission engineer, whose task it is to move the signal reliably from one location to another. Note that this task has nothing to do with the content of the signal. Properly speaking, this area of study and research should be called *transmission theory,* but Claude Shannon originally called it *communication theory* (Shannon 1948), and it is now commonly called *information theory.* Researchers in this area focus on the statistical properties of the signal to achieve reliable transmission. Use of these properties permits the development of transmission codes that can detect and correct errors during transmission. The term *noise* is used to identify transmission errors that corrupt the original signal. The signal received consists of data with a minimal amount of noise. Certain data are selected and organized by the user to constitute the information responsive to a need. The importance of signal processing in information storage and retrieval lies in the fact that some algorithms and measures used are based on concepts arising in information theory.

Beyond signal, data, and information lies *knowledge.* Knowledge builds upon information, integrating any new information with that previously known to form a large, coherent view of a portion of reality. Thus, while information is localized in response to a specific query, knowledge has a broader scope. Workers in artificial intelligence speak of *knowledge bases.* A knowledge base is typically constructed by attempting to incorporate into the stored data and algorithms various facts, concepts, and rules that are representative of one or more selected experts in a particular area. The system built on this knowledge base is called an *expert system.*

Finally, *wisdom* adds to this knowledge a broader view still, encompassing all of known reality, and governing the use of the information that has been obtained and the knowledge that has been developed. It involves the capacity to make balanced judgments in the light of certain value criteria (Kochen 1974; Debons, Horne, and Croenweth 1988). To the best of our knowledge, there has been no attempt to incorporate wisdom into the endosystem of any information system.

The chain that begins with signal and ends with wisdom is similar to that proposed by Kochen, who used the terms *data, information, knowledge, understanding,* and *wisdom* (Kochen 1974, 62).

Because information has personal aspects and an information system can only work with data, the term *information storage and retrieval* reflects aspirations rather than reality. One user generates and stores data representative of the information that he or she desires to retain. Another user retrieves these data; this user's aspiration is to retrieve information—that is, data that are well matched to his or her particular need. The information that the second user seeks is not necessarily that which the first user has tried to represent in the data. Knowledge and wisdom involve the individual user so strongly that they are beyond the scope of an information retrieval system. They involve the integration of information from many sources, most of which are not available to a given information system. Nevertheless, the development of knowledge and wisdom depends on access to good information; this development depends on efficient and effective information storage and retrieval systems.

The great variety of information needs that a system must handle makes development of the system a challenging task—particularly systems that are meant for public use, in contrast to those designed for a relatively small, homogeneous group of users. This development involves process, product, and feedback. The *process* of designing an information system leads to a *product,* the system itself. This in turn leads to another process, use of the system to meet an information need. The result of this process is another product, the list of documents retrieved in response to the need. Three different *feedback* loops are involved in the development and use cycle, leading to improved information systems (Figure 1.2).

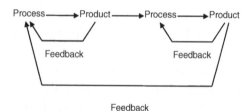

Figure 1.2 The process-product-feedback cycle for information systems.

1.5   TOWARD EFFECTIVE INFORMATION RETRIEVAL SYSTEMS: A VIEW OF THE BOOK

Whether designing a new information retrieval system, evaluating an existing system, or merely trying to use a system, it is important to understand the components of the system and the methods that can be used with the system. The types of tests used in information retrieval system design and evaluation include many that are common to all system design—formal modeling, analytical studies, simulations, laboratory tests, and finally, user tests. The user tests assume added significance for information retrieval systems, since it has thus far not been possible to model the user's concept of effectiveness completely in the formal operations of an information retrieval system.

While many different tasks may be carried out by the system, the ultimate goal is matching information to information need, through matching documents to queries. Thus the book begins by examining the forms that documents and queries can assume. It considers the ways in which documents and queries can be represented to allow both effective and efficient processing.

Most information retrieval research in the past has focused on textual documents. Hence the concepts and procedures discussed in this book come largely from that context. Nevertheless, image and sound data are also discussed in the book, together with the methods available to identify and retrieve them.

In contrast to the database documents, which generally are imported into an information retrieval system from external sources and thus have a predefined form, the form that queries take is under the control of the system designer. At least half a dozen query forms have been studied, ranging from forms that are efficient for computational processing but perhaps difficult for the user, to natural language queries that place a heavier computational load on the system but are easily stated by the user.

The discussion of query forms is followed by an examination of the matching process itself. The methods of matching a document to a query are closely related to the query form used. The results obtained vary in quality depending on many factors. These factors are discussed before the question of assessing retrieval quality is tackled.

Analyzing a document in preparation to matching it to queries involves several steps. Typically these steps begin at the lexical level, determining the number of occurrences of words and phrases in a document. These data can be used to compute term values for the matching process. The term value is a number that represents the importance of a term in a given document. In addition, linguistic, pragmatic, and heuristic techniques can be applied in an attempt to better determine the content and significance of a document, as well as its relationship to potential queries. Techniques that work across multiple languages are of increasing interest as electronic information covers the world.

The user is central to the success of an information retrieval system. Information about the individual user, neglected for many years, is increasingly forming a significant component of system design. Not only are user tests assuming increased importance, but also methods are being explored to introduce information about a user's preferences and background into the retrieval process.

Work with user interest and background profiles has led to the concept of using multiple reference points, rather than a single query, to control the retrieval process. Multiple reference points result in a more complex retrieval structure than the traditional list of documents. Representation of this complex structure has in turn provided a strong incentive for the development of visual information retrieval interfaces. Three such systems, with distinct purposes, are described in Chapter 7.

With this background, the book turns to the question of evaluating retrieval effectiveness. The traditional measures of precision and recall, while falling short in many ways, are still used in most retrieval system evaluations. Other measures that relate more directly to user preferences, or that take into account sequencing and other relational effects among the documents retrieved, have also been introduced. Qualitative assessments of user satisfaction are strongly advocated by some researchers; the direct impact of these on system design and use is still undetermined.

By most standard measures, information retrieval systems are not very effective. Once the performance of a system has been measured, the obvious next step is to try to improve its effectiveness. Researchers continue to experiment with new algorithms and data structures. However, a significant improvement in the performance of any information retrieval system can be gained by involving the user directly in the processing. The most commonly used process is *relevance feedback,* whereby the user evaluates a sample of retrieved documents and this evaluation is used to modify the retrieval process.

While the matching of words from the document to words in the query is the most common basis for retrieval, other techniques have been investigated and are available in some systems. Many attempts have been made to do a deeper analysis of the natural language of the document and the query, with some success. The use of bibliographic citations to link a document to similar ones has also been used in some retrieval systems. Hypertext links that point directly from a term or concept in a document to other related documents are becoming increasingly important in the context of the World Wide Web. With the large volume of data now readily available, *information filtering,* or *data mining,* is an important precursor to effective retrieval. In information retrieval, "information filtering" refers to rapid, inexpensive selection of a "rich ore" of documents to be processed in more detail for retrieval. Similarly, in database work the term "data mining" refers to extraction of a "rich ore" of data from the mass of data in the system, to be further processed into a view meeting the information need. As multimedia documents are integrated into information retrieval systems, the ability to process images and sound becomes as important as the ability to process text for retrieval.

A major factor in user acceptance of any retrieval system is the interface through which the user interacts with the system. The classical textual interfaces are still widely used, despite their shortcomings. However, many visual or graphical interfaces have been developed by research groups. User acceptance of such interfaces is now heavily studied.

The more limited computational resources of the past long made it acceptable for an information retrieval system to return a brief representation of the document and a reference to the complete document. It was assumed that the interested user would then manage to locate a copy of the document. However, with increased on-line storage and document access through the Internet and CD-ROMs, many new systems aim at returning the full document to the user. The penultimate chapter of the book examines both the advantages and the problems of full-text and Internet access to documents.

Finally, the more sophisticated information retrieval systems of today raise ethical and policy issues that could largely be ignored in the past. These include copyright, privacy, and security issues. Information professionals, funders, and users all need to be aware of these issues, the impact that they can have on retrieval performance, and the methods that are used to assure that everyone involved in the generation, storage, and retrieval of information is treated fairly.

REFERENCES

Baker, Norman R. 1968. A descriptive model of library/user/funder behavior in a university environment. *Drexel Library Quarterly* 4:16–30.

Blair, David C., and M.E. Maron. 1985. An evaluation of retrieval effectiveness for a full-text document-retrieval system. *Communications of the ACM* 28, no. 3:289–299.

Bottle, R.T. 1965. A user's assessment of current awareness services. *Journal of Documentation* 21:151–162.

Bourne, C.P., and D.F. Ford. 1964. Cost analysis and simulation procedures for the evaluation of large information systems. *American Documentation* 15, no. 2:142–149.

Cooper, Michael D. 1972. A cost model for evaluating information retrieval systems. *JASIS* 23, no. 5:306–312.

Debons, Anthony, Esther Horne, and Scott Croenweth. 1988. *Information science, an integrated view*. Boston: G.K. Hall.

Dumais, Susan. 1994. Evaluating interactive retrieval systems (panel abstract). In *Proceedings of the 17th Annual International ACM/SIGIR Conference on Research and Development in Information Retrieval,* Dublin, Ireland, p. 361.

Eisenberg, Michael B., and Xiulan Hu. 1987. Dichotomous relevance judgments and the evaluation of information systems. In *Proceedings of the 50th ASIS Annual Meeting,* Boston, pp. 66–70.

Frei, Hans-Peter, and Peter Schäuble. 1991. Determining the effectiveness of retrieval algorithms. *Information Processing & Management* 27, no. 2/3:153–164.

Frei, Hans-Peter, and M.F. Wyle. 1991. Retrieval algorithm effectiveness in a wide area network information filter. In *Proceedings of the 14th Annual International ACM/SIGIR Conference on Research and Design in Information Retrieval,* Chicago, pp. 114–122.

Hamilton, S., and N.L. Chervany. 1971. Evaluating information system effectiveness. *MIS Quarterly* 5, no. 4:649–652.

Heaps, H.S. 1971. Criteria for optimum effectiveness of information retrieval systems. *Information and Control* 18:156–167.

Kochen, Manfred. 1974. *Principles of information retrieval.* Los Angeles: Melville.

Korfhage, Robert R., and Thomas G. DeLutis. 1969. A basis for time and cost evaluation of information systems. In *The Information Bazaar. Proceedings of the Sixth Annual National Colloquium on Information Retrieval,* ed. Louise Schultz. Medical Documentation Service, The College of Physicians of Philadelphia, pp. 293–326.

Kraft, Donald H., and Abraham Bookstein. 1978. Evaluation of information retrieval systems: A decision theory approach. *JASIS* 29, no. 1:31–40.

Lancaster, F. Wilfrid. 1971. The cost-effectiveness analysis of information retrieval and dissemination systems. *JASIS* 22, no. 1:12–27.

Lancaster, F. Wilfrid, and W.D. Climenson. 1968. Evaluating the economic efficiency of a document retrieval system. *Journal of Documentation* 24, no. 1:16–40.

Losee, Robert M., Jr. 1991. An analytic measure predicting information retrieval system performance. *Information Processing & Management* 27, no. 1:1–13.

McCain, Kate W., Howard D. White, and Belver C. Griffith. 1986. Text retrieval as a measure of system performance: MEDLINE and the medical behavioral sciences. In *Proceedings of the 49th ASIS Annual Meeting,* pp. 199–203.

Meadow, Charles T. 1973. *Analysis of information systems,* 2d ed. New York: Wiley.

Nance, Richard E. 1967. Strategic simulation of a library/user/funder system. Ph.D. diss., Purdue University, West Lafayette, Indiana.

Shannon, Claud E. 1948. A mathematical theory of communication. *Bell Systems Technical Journal* 27:379–423, 623–656.

Shaw, W.M., Jr. 1986. On the foundation of evaluation. *JASIS* 37, no. 5:346–348.

Tague, Jean M., and R. Schultz. 1988. Some measures and procedures for evaluation of the user interface in an IR system. In *Proceedings of the 11th Annual International ACM/SIGIR Conference on Research and Development in Information Retrieval,* Grenoble, France, pp. 371–385.

Taylor, Robert S. 1986. *Value-added processes in information systems.* Norwood, New Jersey: Ablex.

Turtle, Howard R., and W. Bruce Croft. 1991. Evaluation of an inference net-
    work-based retrieval model. *ACM Transactions on Information Sys-
    tems 9*, no. 3:187–221.

EXERCISES

Answer the following questions. The answers themselves are not as important as how you find them, what difficulties you encounter, and how you
overcome the difficulties. What capabilities would a good information
retrieval system need to do likewise?

1. What is Donald Knuth's first published paper? (To maintain his
   peace of mind, *please* do not contact Donald Knuth for the answer!)
2. Who invented the water bed, and where was it first mentioned?
3. Produce a bibliography on American joinery in the 19th century.
4. Find the earliest documented instance of the collapse of a structure
   due to resonance.
5. Who wrote "A Dissertation Upon Roast Pig," and where did he or
   she get the idea?
6. What was the ruling of the Indiana legislature on the value of pi (π),
   and when did it occur?
7. What did John von Neumann have to say about common set
   transversals for three or more collections of sets?
8. Who chose the letters *K* and *W* as the first call letters of American
   radio and TV stations, and why?
9. How are the digits of a Social Security number determined?
10. Who invented cribbage?
11. What information is available on the toxicity of *Melongena*?
12. Who scored the last home run for the Pittsburgh Penguins?
13. Why was it customary to carve a crescent moon in the door of an
    outhouse?
14. Who was Joe Pye?
15. Who said, "If I were two-faced, would I be wearing this one?"
16. Who invented the ballpoint pen, and when?

CHAPTER 2

Document and Query Forms

The data within an information system include two major categories: the documents, or the data to be stored and retrieved, and the queries, or the expressions of information need. From an information retrieval viewpoint, the key problems are how to state an information need and how to identify documents that match that need. These processes are affected by the form in which the data are stored, both mentally and within the endosystem itself. In this chapter, the types of data structures that can be used to handle the data and the organization of these structures into coherent units for processing are examined.

2.1 THE CONCEPT OF A DOCUMENT

While many people think of a document merely as a printed paper or book, for purposes of information retrieval the concept of a document includes a much broader spectrum of things. A document is a stored data record in any form. This includes not only formally printed papers and books, but also informal writing such as letters or messages. For many purposes it is desirable to consider a large body of data (such as a book) not as a single document but as a collection of smaller documents. Thus a chapter, a section, or a paragraph can be considered as one document among the coordinated set of documents constituting the larger body of data (Salton, Allan, and Buckley

1993; Callan 1994; Mittendorf and Schäuble 1994; Knaus, Mittendorf, and Schäuble 1995; Melucci 1995). This is appropriate, for example, when searching an encyclopedia for information on a given topic. The document concept can also be extended to include computer programs, data files, e-mail messages, images and image collections, graphics of all kinds, and voice or sound recordings.

A point of contention within the research community is the relationship between queries and documents. Some researchers take the position that a query is sufficiently different from the documents being sought that it should not be considered a document (Bollmann-Sdorra and Raghavan 1993). They cite, for example, the fact that a query typically is much shorter than a document to be retrieved, that an individual term is likely to occur only once or twice in a query—so that word-frequency statistics are meaning-less—and that queries may not be as well formed linguistically as a document in a database. Other researchers take the opposite point of view, that a query, despite its difference from other documents, is still a document. There are counterarguments to each view. For example, in the TREC experiments (Harman 1993, 1994, 1995), the queries are presented in the form of *topics,* many of which are longer than some of the documents to be retrieved. These topic statements are constructed in a specific format, with the information needs clearly stated. Thus a topic statement has many of the characteristics that one would like in a document being sought. In contrast, the documents in the TREC collections to be searched do not generally have this explicit structure. Furthermore, some TREC documents are taken from news sources and have a relatively low standard of spelling and grammar. A more common reason for including query statements with other documents is that in many instances it is possible to identify a specific document as being of interest and to use that document as the model for the query (Olsen et al. 1993). The position taken in this book is that a query or statement of information need should be considered to be a document. It should be noted, however, that some retrieval systems, particularly Boolean systems, force the information need statement into a query structure that is quite alien to the usual document structure.

The distinction between considering a query to be a document and considering it to be different from a document affects the manner in which the retrieval process is modeled. If the query is considered to be a document, then retrieval is a process of *matching* one document to another. If, however, queries are considered to be distinct from documents, the retrieval process becomes one of *mapping* documents onto queries, and identifying those documents for which the mapping satisfies certain fitness criteria. "Mapping" involves transforming the document into a form or structure that can be directly matched to a query. Here's a crude analogy: It is easy to compare one recipe to another directly. But if I go to a bakery to find a pastry (the document) that is similar to a recipe I have (the query), I must transform the pastry into a list of ingredients (e.g., by asking the baker). Match/map is a theoretical distinction affecting the model but invisible to the IR system user.

A key concept underlying the storage, search, and retrieval process is that a document is stored in a recoverable form, for at least some period of time. Some documents are ephemeral: A stored query may be discarded once it has been answered; an e-mail message may be deleted once it has been read. Other documents change with time: A person's daily calendar of events is one example. Yet at any given time even ephemeral and changeable documents have a specific existence and can be accessed for purposes of analysis, organization, and retrieval.

Broadening the class of documents to include images, graphics, and sound pushes at the frontiers of what can be handled in an information retrieval system. While there is active research on the direct handling of images and sound, most commercial retrieval systems handle these documents only through textual representations of them, if at all. Active research is being done on the structural properties of these extended types of documents to develop data structures that allow for direct retrieval. At the other end of the spectrum, numeric and other fixed-field databases are sufficiently important that the techniques for organizing and querying them form a subject entire unto itself—database systems design. Hence, although the basic concepts of storage and retrieval apply to this broad spectrum of documents, the context for this book is largely that of text retrieval; many of the techniques and measures introduced focus specifically on text. However, analogous techniques and measures can be developed for other types of data (Gudivada and Raghavan 1993, 1994; Thompson and Kellogg 1993; Chakravarthy 1994; Lorenz and Monagan 1995; Meghini 1995; Rowe 1995; Schäuble and Wechsler 1995; Sparck Jones et al. 1995).

2.2   DATA STRUCTURES IN THE LARGE

Whatever the fine structure of a document, whether numbers, words, pixels, or something else, there is an overall gross structure. This gross structure affects both the storage format of the document and the modes of access. The main characteristic of the gross structure is the extent and type of formatting that the document exhibits.

At one end of the spectrum are fully formatted documents. The data found in relational, network, or hierarchical databases are typically of this type. Each document of this type consists of a predefined number of fields; each field has a predefined size and position within the document. As long as the data conform well to the specifications of the fields, this type of structure is excellent for exact retrieval of exact data and for retrieval of data falling within a specific range of values. Either the required data are in their proper fields, or they are not available in the database. This fully formatted structure is less appropriate for storage of imprecise data and for response to imprecise queries, where a more intuitive judgment must be made on the appropriateness of the data to the database field and the query.

At the other end of the spectrum are fully unformatted documents—documents for which the only structure is the order imposed by the process of recording them. Telemetry data, data from medical monitoring, sound and image data, and even some textual data display a lack of structure that affects both the storage and the retrieval processes. Storage of such data becomes almost trivial: Data are simply recorded in the order in which they are received. But the lack of further structure such as an abstract or section headings means that there are no guideposts for locating information within such a document. Retrieval depends essentially on complete scans of the document set.

Since the purpose of storing data is to retrieve them later in response to an information need, some structure is generally imposed on any document stored. At times the pace at which the data are received precludes much analysis and structural definition; at other times it is relatively simple to provide at least a skeleton structure. For most textual documents, this structure identifies the title, author, source, and perhaps an abstract or some other condensed data. Rarely, except in experimental situations, is there the luxury of being able to perform an in-depth analysis of each document. As a result, many documents are in an intermediate or mixed form, largely unformatted but including some formatted portions. This suggests that a two-stage retrieval process might be efficient—doing a rough retrieval based on the formatted portion of the data, then refining the "ore" generated by this process to locate the desired items.

Some of the structure available in a document may be unnoticed, or not directly available to the user, yet have a role to play in an information system. For example, a text document is divided into chapters, sections, paragraphs, sentences, and words. The user may take little notice of these divisions, particularly the smaller ones. Yet they are useful in organizing a document for information storage and retrieval. Electronic documents frequently have additional encoded information about the format, not normally available to the user. However, an information system can be designed to make use of these codes in analyzing and storing a document.

Finally, in addition to whatever explicit structure a document has, there is also some implicit structure. This implicit structure may be as simple as a document identifier that is automatically assigned or as complex as logical, graphical, or conceptual relationships among various portions of the document. In music, for example, certain structure is inherent in the form of the music. Sonatas, fugues, blues, bluegrass, and rock all have accepted formats enabling recognition, formats that are potentially useful in storage and retrieval. Classically these implicit structures have been used for error checking, such as assuring that the data in a given field fall within the limitations imposed on that field (for example, neither too large nor too small in value).

2.3   DOCUMENT SURROGATES

Despite the current research emphasis on full-text and image retrieval (Molto 1993; Rosengren 1994; Celentano 1995; Enser 1995), many data are presently stored either in relational (or other fully formatted) databases or as *document surrogates,* that is limited representations of full documents. Because of this, much information retrieval work focuses on these document surrogates—how to generate them and how to evaluate them in response to a stated information need. In a sense, the first challenging problems of information storage and retrieval are centered around the document surrogates, since the use of a surrogate potentially implies incomplete knowledge of the document itself. This poses the problem of making firm decisions on the basis of incomplete (and perhaps misleading) information. For example, if all that is known about a document is the title *Interdisciplinary Cooperation,* how can the document contents be judged accurately?

The first surrogate for any document is obviously a *document identifier.* Whatever else is done, some identifier is almost always appended to a document as a means of linking the surrogate to the document. This may be simple and have little significance to the user, such as the accession number that a library assigns to a book. Or it may be a more elaborate identifier that attempts to place the document within some structured set. Both the Dewey decimal and the Library of Congress classifications that libraries apply to books are identifiers of this sort. These classification schemes each apply some structure to the collection of documents within the library; the code assigned to an individual document provides the user with information for locating that document within the collection. However, the code provides little additional data about the document. Do you want to retrieve the book "T210 C37 1982" in response to your query? Even to those who know the coding, in the absence of other information the code does not provide adequate data for making a decision. Product numbers and bar codes are of a similar nature: If you feel hungry, do you really want some "200737 103146" for dinner?

Because of the lack of evident information within the identifier, an identifier by itself is not a useful response to most information needs. (Note, however, that the identifier by itself is excellent for some purposes, such as inventory control of stock in a store.) Typically other data are included within the document surrogate. Titles and names—author names, corporate names, publisher names—are generally considered useful to the inquirer. Dates associated with the document help the user to judge its timeliness and appropriateness. Important words and phrases, unit descriptors such as "Introduction," "Summary," and "Bibliography," abstracts, extracts, and reviews all provide additional data that can be useful both to the person with the information need and to the designer of an information system. If numeric or other specific data are included in the document, summaries of such data are appropriate for a document surrogate. Descriptions of images, whether figure captions or more elaborate descriptions, are also to be considered in developing a surrogate (Rowe 1995).

The key issue in developing a document surrogate is its usefulness (Kerner and Lindsley 1969; Fidel 1986; Molina 1995). Keywords and abstracts are considered sufficiently useful that many journals require one or both to be present in a published document. A *keyword* is one of a set of individual words chosen by the author or editor, or perhaps automatically, to represent the content of a document. Similarly, a *key phrase* is a phrase so chosen. Keywords (and key phrases) are frequently left to the author's discretion. Hence while these data elements should indicate the contents of a document, they are subject to a degree of variability. However, in some instances the keywords may be dictated by the publication medium. For example, the Association of Computing Machinery (ACM) publishes a review journal, *Computing Reviews*, that has a defined hierarchical structure for knowledge in computing. In its other journals, ACM follows the practice of requiring that each paper include the appropriate *Computing Reviews* categories, by number and by keyword or key phrase. The authors may then list additional keywords if they wish.

An *abstract* is a brief one- or two-paragraph description of the contents of a paper. A well-written abstract enables the reader to determine whether the entire paper should be retrieved. However, since abstracts are also left to the author's discretion (even when required), quality varies greatly, and some are merely copies of the opening paragraph of the paper. In some situations abstracts are written by someone other than the author. In such cases they bear the interpretation of the abstract writer rather than the author of the paper.

Extracts are artificially constructed surrogates created by someone other than the author of a paper. Various methods have been suggested for constructing an extract, which consists of sentences or phrases taken from the paper. For example, the first sentence of each paragraph might be used, or sentences that contain certain significant words and phrases. These are not necessarily the keywords that the author might list. A phrase like "we conclude that" might trigger inclusion of a sentence in an extract.

A *review* is similar to an abstract written by someone other than the author. However, whereas the abstract is merely descriptive, a review is meant to be critical, and to provide some indication of the value of the paper in the context of other works in that particular field. Thus a review does not provide direct access to a paper or book, but rather provides a commentary on the work being reviewed together with a pointer to it. The review itself is a separate document that may be worth retrieving.

If a document surrogate is to be used internally by the endosystem, then the data included in the surrogate must conform to the algorithms that the system uses to select documents in response to needs. If the surrogate is to be presented to the user, then it must contain data that the user can interpret and use in any decision. The identifier "T210 C37 1982" may be all that is needed if the user has great faith in the accuracy of the endosystem, or is sufficiently versed in the coding to know whether the class of the document (T210) or the age (1982) makes it appropriate or inappropriate. Generally, however, it must be assumed that the user is not that knowledgeable and needs further data to evaluate the significance of a given document.

2.4 VOCABULARY CONTROL

Just as researchers debate the distinction between queries and documents, so also have they long debated the issue of controlling the vocabulary that is available to the searcher. Obviously one cannot control the vocabulary that an author chooses to use in a document. At best, the editor of a journal may insist that any key terms specifically used to describe a document come from a controlled list of terms. Control on the searching process is more easily enforced, however, simply by designing the retrieval system to recognize only certain terms and informing the searcher that these terms must be used. The issue is the impact that this has on the retrieval process.

The strongest argument for a *controlled vocabulary* is that it enforces a uniformity throughout the retrieval system, making search and retrieval a more efficient process. The controlled vocabulary forces concepts that are similar but slightly different to be treated as one. Thus a query on any one of the concepts will return all of the documents identified by the corresponding controlled vocabulary term.

The counterargument raises two points. First, forcing the user to employ a controlled vocabulary eliminates any ability to describe the information need in fine detail. A second, related point is that while documents may be quickly retrieved, many of them are likely to be slightly wide of the mark. As an extreme example (a realistic retrieval system is unlikely to be this extreme), suppose that the only term allowed in describing documents about database research is "database." Someone interested in object-oriented databases could not describe this specific focus and would be faced with scanning and rejecting documents on network, hierarchical, and relational databases to find those on object-oriented databases.

Opponents of controlled vocabularies believe that the added complexity of search with a free or uncontrolled vocabulary is a small price to pay for added precision in retrieving documents focused on the information need.

Many commercial retrieval systems have opted for an uncontrolled vocabulary rather than have the user face the frustration of trying to select the best term to describe an information need. However, unless the system employs a sound internal thesaurus or other mechanism for bringing together related terms, the user may miss an important document simply because the author has used a different vocabulary.

2.5 THE FINE STRUCTURE OF DATA

Developments in data processing and communication technology have led to systems that handle databases of increasingly sophisticated documents. Historically the representation of *atomic data* items—that is, items that are not to be decomposed into parts—has gone through a period of standardization, and then expansion beyond the standards. Standards for the encoding of data provide the basis for easy integration and handling of data from multiple sources. At the same time, standards provide a straitjacket into which it may be difficult to fit newer forms of data. For example, United States standards that have been developed over the years in both the construction and the automotive industries have been strong deterrents to the introduction of metric measurements into those industries. Similarly, programming language and practice standards developed on the basis of such languages as FORTRAN, Pascal, and C may not be well suited to object-oriented programming languages. In document organization, the Dewey decimal system was developed in an earlier era, in a different social and technological context. As a result, it is at times difficult to fit documents about newer technologies into this classification code.

Early computing systems used a very limited set of characters, based on the coding that was available in punched cards. This character set included uppercase letters, numbers, and a small set of punctuation and other special characters: Obviously, it was inadequate for any significant text processing. Two major encoding systems (along with some variants) were developed to meet the text processing needs. Both EBCDIC (Extended Binary Coded Decimal Information Code) and ASCII (American Standard Code for Information Interchange) were based on the use of a byte to encode an atomic datum. A *byte* consists of eight *bits* of data. Since each bit can have two states, 0 and 1, or "off" and "on," a byte is capable of representing 2^8, or 256 characters. This enables the representation of both upper- and lowercase letters, numbers, and a goodly variety of functions and special characters, with plenty of codes to spare.

Over the years, ASCII gradually became the standard for text encoding. However, the common ASCII code set uses only seven bits of information, namely the codes 0 through 127. These codes include upper- and lowercase letters, numbers, punctuation, some special characters, and several non-printing control codes, such as carriage return and line feed. Standards for the remaining codes have been developed but not fully accepted. Microsoft Windows uses both the ANSI (American National Standards Institute) code, which is an extension of ASCII code, and the RTF (Rich Text Format) code. These both differ from the extended character set that IBM uses for its personal computers. Macintosh computers use the ANSI code (ANSI 1971).

At the same time, the limitations of the ASCII code, even extended to 256 characters, have become increasingly apparent as the sophistication of document processing increases. A typical document may include boldface and italic words in addition to the normal text font. Non-English languages introduce additional characters into the alphabet. Mathematical formulas and equations that may occur in the text include special symbols that would not occur in a literary text. One typical word processor, WordPerfect, has fifteen different character sets:

ASCII	95 characters, 32 control codes
Multinational	242 characters
Phonetic	145 characters
Box Drawing	88 characters
Typographic Symbols	102 characters
Iconic Symbols	255 characters
Math/Scientific	238 characters
Math/Scientific Extension	229 characters
Greek	219 characters
Hebrew	119 characters
Cyrillic	250 characters
Japanese (Hiragana and Katakana)	63 characters

Arabic	196 characters
Arabic Script	220 characters
User Defined	Up to 256 characters

While there is room to expand each character set except the Iconic Symbols, such expansion would still not meet the full need for characters. For example, various methods for encoding Chinese characters are based either on two bytes (65,536 possible characters) or on three bytes (16,777,216 possible characters). In this case, the two-byte code for Chinese characters is adequate for daily use, but more detailed work such as that done in a library requires the three-byte code.

In addition to several character sets, each word processing system has its own set of codes to indicate word processing functions, including spacing, line breaks, page breaks, hyphenation, font characteristics, and so forth. The lack of standardization here has resulted in a plethora of conversion programs, as the developers of each system strive for compatibility with other systems without giving up their own special codes. Most major word processing systems now provide two-way conversion between their codes and the standard ASCII code. Several also provide direct conversion between their own codes and those used by other word processors. These conversions may be less than perfect, omitting or misinterpreting some characters.

The advent of computer-controlled printing, in particular the introduction of laser printers into daily use in many offices, has further complicated the situation. It makes sense, in terms of efficiency, to capture documents for use in other information systems as they are formatted for printing, rather than to transfer them to paper and then return them to a machine-readable form. The formatting codes, called a *markup language,* are discussed in Section 2.7. They provide yet another set of codes that must be interpreted by the information system but that can be used to aid the retrieval of information.

2.6 DATA COMPRESSION

With the increased emphasis on full-text databases, the problem of handling the quantity of data becomes significant. A typical document surrogate may contain between 200 and 2000 bytes of data, but the text of a full book, say a novel, may contain one to three megabytes of data. The data handling problem is further complicated by the introduction of pictures and other figures, each of which may contain one megabyte of data or more. Since the time required to search a database is heavily dependent on the amount of data, for efficient operation of an information system it is necessary both to organize the data well and to find as efficient a representation for the data as is possible. Thus there is growing interest in *data compression*. Document surrogates may be regarded as a crude form of data compression, since they represent relatively large documents in a small number of bytes. Each of the surrogates represents a loss of data from the original document. Evidently this loss of data is not highly critical, since people do find the surrogates useful. However, the user may not be sure whether the document thus represented is relevant to a specific information need. Thus the loss of information does impact the effectiveness and efficiency of the information system. While some compression techniques are dictated in part by human readability considerations (ISO 1972, 1973), most work in this area assumes that the compressed data will be used entirely within the computer. Hence the compressed data can be totally incomprehensible to the human reader (Bentley et al. 1986; Choueka et al. 1986; Cheng, Iyengar, and Kashyap 1988; Choueka, Fraenkel, and Klein 1988; Klein, Bookstein, and Deerwester 1989; Bookstein and Klein 1990, 1991a, 1991b; Aalbersberg 1991; LeGall 1991; Liu and Yu 1991; Witten, Moffat, and Bell 1994).

One compressive technique that is widely used is *stemming,* or the removal of grammatical suffixes, converting a set of related words to a common root form (Frakes and Baeza-Yates 1992, chap. 8). While this has the effect of compressing text to some extent, its main purpose is to identify a set of related words so that the user will automatically retrieve documents containing any of them. Thus if the system uses the stem *comput,* the user who asks for documents about *computers* will automatically also receive documents containing any of the words *computer, computational, computing,* and so forth. Several different stemming algorithms exist. Most of those currently in use are *iterative affix removal* stemmers. That is, by a set of rules applied iteratively, they successively remove suffixes, and sometimes prefixes, from words to obtain a common root. The rules must be carefully crafted because of the many exceptions that arise in common spellings. For example, while we generally would remove the suffix *ed,* we clearly do not want to remove it from the word *bed.* Word length rules can cover many such situations, but others must be covered by rules handling individual cases. Suffix removal may also involve a change in the morphology of the word, such as changing both *knife* and *knives* to *knif.* Among the best-known stemmers are those developed by Lovins (1968) and Porter (1980). These have both been well tested in use and are widely accepted. A more recent stemming algorithm by Paice (1990) does not have the same history of use but seems to be equally good.

It might be thought that any representation other than the full document will involve a loss of data, but this is not the case. Natural languages are highly redundant, as can be demonstrated by a simple experiment in removing vowels: Ths sntnc cn b rd rthr qckly by mst ppl. Note that people use context to reduce ambiguities. For example, *rd* could have come from *arid, read, red, redo, rid, rod, road,* or *rude,* but in the given context only one of these makes sense. Similarly, most images are highly redundant. We easily recognize outline drawings for the objects they represent. When people familiar with a particular style of music hear a musical fragment, they can readily anticipate what notes will be played next. In everyday usage this redundancy is good: It enables us to identify and automatically correct errors in data transmission or representation. However, this redundancy also means that a database may be larger than necessary by 30 percent or more in terms of the information content. Thus we have the possibility of reducing the size of a database by eliminating the redundancy.

Three types of techniques for data compression provide an overall view of the field. A recent book on these and other compression techniques focuses specifically on techniques that relate well to information retrieval (Witten, Moffat, and Bell 1994). Many of the techniques are directed toward text compression, that is, text encoding requiring fewer bits than the standard ASCII codes. Different techniques are used for image compression, taking advantage of the two-dimensional and largely nontextual nature of images.

Two decisions must be made initially that strongly impact the effect of any data compression. One is the choice of *level of compression.* Compression can be done at either the character or the word level. That is, a compression method can be developed on the basis of the frequencies of individual characters and groups of characters, or on the basis of the frequencies of words and phrases. The advantage of compression at the character level is the relatively small set of possible characters to be handled, in contrast to a vocabulary of tens of thousands of words. The advantage of compression at the word level is that a speedier and more effective compression can possibly be achieved by focusing on entire words.

The second choice is the type of *data model* that is used. Essentially all text compression techniques are based on the statistical distribution of the objects being compressed, whether characters or words. The basic concept is that short and efficient compression codes should be used for frequently occurring symbols, while less efficient compression can be tolerated for symbols that occur more rarely. There are two broad classes of data models, static models and adaptive models. A *static model* is constructed by examining a sample of text and constructing statistical tables representing this sample. This model is then used for the entire body of text to be compressed. An *adaptive model* begins with an a priori statistical distribution for the text symbols but modifies this distribution as each character or word is encoded. Thus, as more text is encoded, an adaptive model should become an increasingly close representation of the statistical properties of the specific texts in the database.

A third type of model, the *semi-static model,* is a compromise between the two primary types. For this model a static data model is used, but the model is redefined periodically, perhaps with each document file encountered. Thus, to compress the text of a book, each chapter might be considered as a separate file. A static model of the first chapter would be developed. This would be modified to better fit the second chapter, then modified again for the third chapter, and so forth.

The different types of data models have several effects on compression. First, since the static models involve less computation, they generally provide faster compression and decompression. Second, since the adaptive models fit the actual text more closely, they generally provide higher compression. Third, since the functioning of adaptive models depends on a dynamic analysis of the text stream during compression, the interpretation of code, say, halfway through a compressed file depends on the encoding used for the entire earlier portion of the file. In effect, this means that one cannot interpret the code in the middle of an adaptively compressed file without decoding the entire earlier portion, since a given character or word may be represented quite differently in the two portions.

Adaptive compression thus involves a dilemma. This type of compression works best for encoding relatively large files; but random access of the compressed file, which is important for information retrieval, is impossible. A compromise solution to this problem is to introduce *synchronization points,* where the adaptive coding is stopped and restarted. This does not provide full random access but also does not require decoding a file from the very beginning. A semi-static model provides this type of mechanism at a rather coarse level. One might choose synchronization at a finer level, perhaps at the level of the section or paragraph within a text.

Three types of codes exemplify those used for text compression: Huffman codes, Ziv-Lempel codes, and arithmetic codes. *Huffman code* is by far the oldest of these methods. It was developed in the 1950s by David Huffman (1952) and is sufficiently good that it is still in wide use today. Huffman codes can be quite effective in compressing data files but can also be relatively ineffective. In a series of tests, Huffman encoding resulted in a code of roughly five bits per character whereas adaptive coding techniques produced codes of less than three bits per character (Witten, Moffat, and Bell 1994, 67). This is a static code (and hence can be used in semi-static compression models). The model behind a Huffman code is the frequency distribution of the symbols to be encoded, whether characters or words. A binary tree is then constructed recursively. Initially each symbol is considered as a separate (trivial) binary tree. Two trees with the lowest frequencies are chosen and combined into a single binary tree whose assigned frequency is the sum of the two given frequencies. The chosen trees (initially the characters or words, later the constructed trees) form the two branches of the new tree. This process is then repeated until only a single binary tree remains. At that point the original symbols occupy the leaves of the tree. When the two branches from each node in the tree are assigned values 0 and 1, the code for each symbol can be read by following the branch from the root to the symbol.

Example 2.1   Suppose that the 10 characters *a, b, . . . ,j* have associated frequencies 7, 4, 10, 5, 2, 11, 15, 3, 7, and 8 (Table 2.1). Here is the process.

Choose *e* and *h*, with frequencies 2 and 3; form the *eh* tree with frequency 5.

Choose *b* and *d*, with frequencies 4 and 5; form the *bd* tree with frequency 9.

Choose *a* and *eh*, with frequencies 7 and 5; form the *a(eh)* tree with frequency 12.

Choose *i* and *j*, with frequencies 7 and 8; form the *ij* tree with frequency 15.

Choose *c* and *bd*, with frequencies 10 and 9; form the *c(bd)* tree with frequency 19.

Choose *f* and *a(eh)*, with frequencies 11 and 12; form the *f(a(eh))* tree with frequency 23.

Table 2.1
The Character-Frequency
Table

Symbol	Frequency
a	7
b	4
c	10
d	5
e	2
f	11
g	15
h	3
i	7
j	8

At this point, most of the individual characters and character combinations have combined into larger combinations. This is indicated by the term "used" in the extended Table 2.2.

Table 2.2
The Updated
Character-Frequency Table

Symbol	Frequency
a	(used) 7
b	(used) 4
c	(used) 10
d	(used) 5
e	(used) 2
f	(used) 11
g	15
h	(used) 3
i	(used) 7
j	(used) 8
eh	(used) 5
bd	(used) 9
a(eh)	(used) 12
ij	15
c(bd)	19
f(a(eh))	23

Choose *g* and *ij*, with frequencies 15 and 15; form the *g(ij)* tree with frequency 30.

Choose *c(bd)* and *f(a(eh))*, with frequencies 19 and 23; form the *(c(bd))(f(a(eh)))* tree with frequency 42.

Finally, choose the tree just constructed and *g(ij)*, with frequencies 42 and 30; form the final tree with frequency 72.

The resulting tree is shown in Figure 2.1, where the value 0 has been assigned to the left-hand edge from each node and 1 to the right-hand edge.

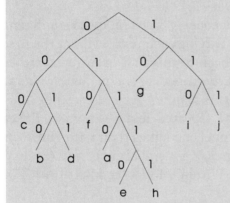

Figure 2.1 A Huffman tree corresponding to Table 2.1.

The corresponding codes are given in Table 2.3.

Table 2.3
A Huffman Code
Corresponding to Table 2.1

Symbol	Code
a	0110
b	0010
c	000
d	0011
e	01110
f	010
g	10
h	01111
i	110
j	111

Huffman code is a variable-length code, with the more frequent symbols being assigned shorter codes. The result is a static code of minimal average length (see Exercise 2.10). In addition it has the *prefix property:* no code is the prefix of any other code. This has two interesting effects. First, any bit stream is uniquely decodable with a given Huffman code; second, data transmission errors, such as adding, dropping, or switching a bit, are almost always automatically filtered out. While the transmission error results in erroneous decoding, within a very few characters the decoding has adjusted itself and is once again representing the text accurately. (See Exercise 2.11.) There is, however, always one code sequence for which certain errors will not self-correct, but will repeat. (See Exercise 2.12.)

Ziv-Lempel code (also called Lempel-Ziv code) is based on quite a different principle (Ziv and Lempel 1977, 1978): identifying each text segment the first time it appears and then simply pointing back to this first occurrence rather than repeating the segment. This is an adaptive model of coding, with increasingly long text segments encoded as the text is scanned. As a result, the pointers ultimately require less space than the repeated text segments. Higher compression can be achieved with Ziv-Lempel encodings than with Huffman codes. In the same tests previously mentioned, Ziv-Lempel encodings resulted in codes of roughly four bits per character (Witten, Moffat, and Bell 1994, 67).

Example 2.2   There are two major types of Ziv-Lempel encodings, plus variants. This example illustrates the type known as LZ77, which is the basis for the GZip encoding. The code consists of a set of triples $<a,b,c>$, where a identifies how far back in the decoded text to look for the upcoming text segment, b tells how many characters to copy for the upcoming segment, and c is a new character to add to complete the next segment. This example begins with the four triples $<0,0,p>$, $<0,0,e>$, $<0,0,t>$, $<2,1,r>$. The triples beginning with 0 identify new characters, not previously seen. The last of these triples directs the decoding to look back two characters, pick up one character, and add a new character. Here is the entire decoding process, involving 20 triples.

$<0,0,p>$	p
$<0,0,e>$	pe
$<0,0,t>$	pet

<2,1,r>	peter
<0,0,_>	peter_
<6,1,i>	peter_pi
<8,2,r>	peter_piper
<6,3,c>	peter_piper_pic
<0,0,k>	peter_piper_pick
<7,1,d>	peter_piper_picked
<7,1,a>	peter_piper_picked_a
<9,2,e>	peter_piper_picked_a_pe
<9,2,_>	peter_piper_picked_a_peck_
<0,0,o>	peter_piper_picked_a_peck_o
<0,0,f>	peter_piper_picked_a_peck_of
<17,5,l>	peter_piper_picked_a_peck_of_pickl
<12,1,d>	peter_piper_picked_a_peck_of_pickled
<16,3,p>	peter_piper_picked_a_peck_of_pickled_pep
<3,2,r>	peter_piper_picked_a_peck_of_pickled_pepper
<0,0,s>	peter_piper_picked_a_peck_of_pickled_peppers

Table 2.4 shows the number of characters encoded per triple in this example. That number must rise above three characters per triple before any compression is achieved. This occurs in longer texts, resulting in the compression figures cited previously.

Table 2.4
Ziv–Lempel Compression

No. of code triples	Average text length	No. of code triples	Average text length
1	1.00	11	1.82
2	1.00	12	1.92
3	1.00	13	2.00
4	1.25	14	1.93
5	1.20	15	1.87
6	1.33	16	2.13
7	1.57	17	2.12
8	1.88	18	2.22
9	1.78	19	2.26
10	1.80	20	2.20

The final type of compression to be examined is *arithmetic coding*. In this method, the text stream is represented by a number whose digits (or bits) reflect the statistical frequency distribution of the symbols. This is also an adaptive code. Often the initial distribution is chosen to be uniform, although a different distribution can be used if information about the data supports it. The distribution statistics are then modified as the text is encoded. The distribution drives calculation of the number that is to represent the text. The encoding is usually chosen so that the final number lies between 0 and 1, but this is not necessary.

Example 2.3   Suppose the problem is to encode the character string *abacus*. The five distinct characters involved are each initially assigned one-fifth of the interval between 0 and 1 (Figure 2.2a).

The first *a* encountered restricts the interval to [0.000 . . . , 0.200 . . .), the portion of the initial interval assigned to *a*. (The "[. . .)" notation indicates that 0.000 . . . is included in this interval, but 0.200 . . . is not.) At the same time, the frequencies are recomputed. The initial assumption was that each letter occurred one time out of five. Now that one letter has been processed, there are six letter occurrences (counting the assumed five occurrences), two of which are *a*. Hence *a* now has two-sixths of the restricted interval, with one-sixth assigned to each of the other letters (Figure 2.2b). The next symbol met, *b*, reduces the interval further, to that portion assigned to *b*, [0.0666 . . . , 0.1000 . . .). Each subsequent letter extends the process, further reducing the interval (Table 2.5).

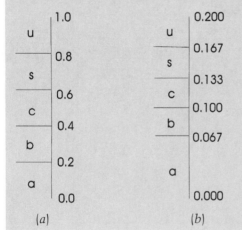

(a)   (b)

Figure 2.2   Arithmetic coding for abacus.

Table 2.5
Full Arithmetic Coding for *abacus*

	PROBABILITIES						
Symbol	initial	after *a*	after *ab*	after *aba*	after *abac*	after *abacu*	after *abacus*
a	1/5	2/6	2/7	3/8	3/9	3/10	3/11
b	1/5	1/6	2/7	2/8	2/9	2/10	2/11
c	1/5	1/6	1/7	1/8	2/9	2/10	2/11
s	1/5	1/6	1/7	1/8	1/9	1/10	2/11
u	1/5	1/6	1/7	1/8	1/9	2/10	2/11
Upper bound	1.000	0.200	0.1000	0.076190	0.073809	0.073809	0.073795
Lower bound	0.000	0.000	0.0666	0.066666	0.072619	0.073767	0.073781

Any number in the final interval, for example, 0.07379, now represents the word *abacus* and will decode to that word. In the decoding, the "0.0" indicates that the number lies within the *a* segment of the interval, so that the first letter is *a*. Proceeding, the "0.07" shows that the number lies in the *b* portion of the *a* interval, since it is between 0.0666 . . . and 0.1000. . . . Hence the second letter is *b*. The decoding process follows the same narrowing of the interval that the encoding process did. The compression that can be achieved through arithmetic coding is not evident in this small example. However, for a typical data file the compressed code can be about 2.5 bits per character (Witten, Moffat, and Bell 1994, 67).

Note that as the encoding proceeds the first digits (or bits, if using binary arithmetic) become fixed from one iteration to the next. Thus they can be moved to the output stream and the interval renormalized to the remaining digits. This alleviates the need for increased accuracy in later arithmetic computations.

Other models and coding methods exist, each with its merits and faults. While arithmetic coding produces very high compression, one evident problem with it is that a single mistake—a bit or digit out of place—can result in a completely inaccurate decoding. An amusing tale of extremely high data compression is the short story "Ms Fnd in a Lbry," by Hal Draper (Mowshowitz 1977).

Arithmetic coding can result in much higher compression than a Huffman code, since the latter requires at least one bit for each symbol encoded. For example, in an arithmetic code, a symbol whose probability of occurrence is 0.99 (admittedly, extraordinarily high) can be encoded with just 0.015 bits. Although arithmetic encoding provides very high rates of data compression, the fact that random access into a document is difficult or impossible makes this a poor choice for encoding text. If, however, random access into a document is not needed, then the arithmetic code is well worth considering. This is usually the case when the document is a photograph or line drawing, for example. Thus in documents containing both text and images it is often desirable to segment the document—to identify text portions and image portions—and adopt a compression scheme that works to the best advantage for each type of segment.

2.7   TEXT DOCUMENTS

The largest portion of data in most documents consists of statements or text written in some natural language. The basic representation of such text is a string of characters, including punctuation, spacing, and writing conventions that provide more structure to the text. In using text, people quite naturally use these additional structural conventions to aid interpretation. Thus a reader mentally follows the author's segmentation of the document into paragraphs, sections, and chapters to aid in understanding the document. The syntax and semantics of a sentence or paragraph are used to help determine whether it matches our information need. The reader also applies pragmatic criteria, trying to relate the text more closely to the perceived information need. Information retrieval systems now frequently incorporate some linguistic cues into their data processing for the same purpose—better matching of the text to the query.

Markup languages constitute one class of tools available for the interpretation of a text document. Arising from the system of marks used by editors and printers in preparing a document for printing, the principal aim of a markup language is to provide a set of instructions—a program—for computer-based formatting, organization, and typesetting of a text. However, when the markup language is kept with the document, it provides a valuable set of clues for information retrieval as well. The most widely used markup language today is SGML, the Standard Generalized Markup Language (Bradley

1992). Among other things, it identifies within the document the title, author, section titles, paragraph boundaries, and the location of nontextual elements. It also includes formatting codes, such as those that specify indentation, boldface, and italic characters. A subset of SGML is HTML, the Hyper-Text Markup Language (Aronson 1994), which is used to compose Web pages for the World Wide Web. It follows the conventions of SGML closely, with added codes for hypertext links and other elements related to network communication. Thus not only can HTML code tell the user (or the retrieval system) much about the organization of a given document, it can also label pointers to related documents.

Documents that exist on paper are frequently scanned into a computer to create or augment a database. When scanned documents are processed, *segmentation* is frequently invoked. Segmentation is the identification of the various pieces, textual and nontextual, of a document. In addition to text, many documents contain graphical elements such as figures and tables. In interpreting the document it is important to identify these nontextual elements and isolate them from the text. It is also important to properly identify and organize portions of the text. For example, when figures interrupt the flow of text or the text is written in multiple columns, the text segments must be reassembled in the proper sequence. Similarly, figure captions and footnotes constitute pieces of text that should be isolated from the main body and treated separately. Segmentation is the first step in this process (Krishnamoorthy et al. 1993). Techniques used in segmentation include locating indentations and white space, and using graphical characteristics to help distinguish text from tables and figures. Syntactic and semantic methods are helpful in piecing together text that has been separated by a figure or table. Once this has been done, the text can be treated as a whole, with pointers to the tables and figures. In addition, a long text such as a book can readily be broken into chapters or sections.

2.8   IMAGES AND SOUND

With the ability of computer systems to store and manipulate extremely large quantities of data, images and sound are becoming more important in the definition of a document and in its processing. Images have been used in paper documents since the earliest days; now they are being incorporated into electronic documents as well. Sound is presently less important, but a major thrust in computing today is toward *multimedia* systems (or, more accurately, *integrated media* systems), incorporating sound and animation as well as text and still images.

Unfortunately, the development of computer-based retrieval systems to handle images and sound is in its infancy. Most if not all commercially available image databases rely on textual descriptions of the images. Thus they are really text databases with attached images. A true image database would enable the user to query and retrieve documents through direct use of images, in addition to textual descriptions. Experimental developments in this direction are appearing with increasing frequency. One such is QBIC, Query By Image Content, being developed by IBM (Niblack et al. 1993; Faloutsos et al. 1994). This system uses basic graphic properties such as color and shapes to define an image, and permits the user to query the system by relatively crude sketches of the image elements desired. Other projects along this line have been initiated in the United States, Japan, and elsewhere (Thompson and Kellogg 1993; Gudivada and Raghavan 1993, 1994, 1995; Ogle and Stonebraker 1995; Papadias and Sellis 1995). One driving force behind the development of image retrieval systems is the rising interest in *geographic information systems* (Mainguenaud and Portier 1990; Calcinelli and Mainguenaud 1994). Geographic information systems are systems with data related to a geographic region, such as a city, state, or country. They frequently include maps showing roads, topographic data, or demographic data, and may also include satellite images, either raw or color-coded.

Four standards have been developed for image compression. CCITT has promulgated a fax standard that relies on *run length encoding* (Hunter and Robinson 1980). This is particularly good with text and other bilevel (black and white) images. Run length encoding divides a scan line across an image into black and white segments, and reports the number of pixels in each segment. For example, assuming that a line begins with a white pixel, an encoding 10, 2, 5, 3, 17, 9, . . . would represent a sequence of ten white pixels, two black pixels, five white pixels, three black pixels, and so forth. The CCITT standard uses both this one-dimensional encoding and a two-dimensional version, whereby a given scan line is described by its difference from the preceding line. While this provides higher compression, one problem with the two-dimensional encoding is that an error in one line is propagated to succeeding lines. Thus the typical encoding scheme will rely primarily on a two-dimensional scheme but periodically start over with a fresh one-dimensional encoding. This limits the spread of any error. The run lengths can be encoded using an arithmetic coding. Since black and white pixels often have very different run length distributions in text, for example, separate arithmetic codes are used.

The remaining three standards are based on *context encoding.* These codes focus more on continuous-tone images. Based on the fact that abrupt changes in such images are relatively rare (for example, when an object edge is encountered), these encodings use a small neighborhood of pixels that have already been seen to predict and encode the value of a target pixel. A basic neighborhood might be the five pixels in the preceding line, immediately above the target pixel, together with the two pixels preceding it in the same scan line as the target pixel. Other neighborhoods can also be used. In any case, the values of the neighborhood pixels determine the encoding of the target pixel. JBIG, the Joint Bilevel Image Experts Group standard, was developed for bilevel (black and white) images but can also be used with grayscale images (CCITT 1993; Witten, Moffat, and Bell 1994, 229–236). It is useful for fax documents and the images often published in scientific and technical journals. JPEG, the Joint Photographic Experts Group standard, applies to continuous-tone images, both grayscale and color. Thus JPEG is a more general-purpose encoding standard than JBIG (Pennebaker and Mitchell 1993; Wallace 1991; Witten, Moffat, and Bell 1994, 236–242). The third standard, MPEG, the Moving Picture Experts Group standard, is, as the name implies, well adapted to the needs of the emerging multimedia document world. It includes standards for the encoding of animation and other motion, along with associated sound information (LeGall 1991).

These methods produce extremely high levels of compression. In addition, a certain amount of information loss can be tolerated in pictorial data for all except the most precise work. As a result, an encoding using 0.25–0.5 bit per pixel is sufficient for some applications, and an encoding using 0.75–1.5 bits per pixel is sufficient for most work. The most demanding applications may require as much as 1.5–2 bits per pixel to represent a full continuous-tone image.

Sound databases are still in their infancy and are even less well developed than image databases. Telephone companies, focusing more on sound transmission than retrieval, have long used both time and frequency compression to increase the number of messages that a telephone line can carry. High frequencies, which are important for fine music and some scientific applications, are of little value for ordinary conversation and are typically cut out of the transmitted signal. In addition, a certain amount of time can be eliminated from a transmitted signal without affecting its understandability. These methods, however, may not be appropriate for information retrieval applications. Musical Instrument Digital Interface (MIDI) is an emerging standard for sound encoding. To the extent that images and sound are handled through textual surrogates, textual data structures and processing techniques are appropriate. The situation is comparable to the early days of bibliographic information retrieval, when a document was represented by its title, author, and citation. Just as bibliographic retrieval systems have become more sophisticated and capable, image and sound retrieval systems can be expected to make similar progress.

REFERENCES

Aalbersberg, IJsbrand Jan. 1991. Posting compression in dynamic retrieval environments. In *Proceedings of the 14th Annual International ACM/ SIGIR Conference on Research and Development in Information Retrieval*, Chicago, pp. 72–81.

ANSI (American National Standards Institute, Inc.). 1971. *American National Standard for Bibliographic Information Interchange on Magnetic Tape.* Report ANSI Z39.2-1971.

Aronson, Larry. 1994. *HTML manual of style.* Emeryville, California: Ziff-Davis.

Bentley, Jon Louis, Daniel D. Sleator, Robert E. Tarjan, and Victor K. Wei. 1986. A locally adaptive data compression scheme. *Communications of the ACM* 29, no. 4:320–330.

Bollmann-Sdorra, Peter, and Vijay V. Raghavan. 1993. On the delusiveness of adopting a common space for modeling IR objects: Are queries documents? *JASIS* 44, no. 10:579–587.

Bookstein, Abraham, and Shmuel T. Klein. 1990. Optimal graphs for bit-vector compression. In *Proceedings of the 13th Annual International ACM/SIGIR Conference on Research and Development in Information Retrieval*, Brussels, pp. 327–342.

Bookstein, Abraham, and Shmuel T. Klein. 1991a. Compression of a set of correlated bitmaps. In *Proceedings of the 14th Annual International*

ACM/SIGIR Conference on Research and Development in Information Retrieval, Chicago, pp. 63–71.

Bookstein, Abraham, and Shmuel T. Klein. 1991b. Flexible compression for bitmap sets. In *Proceedings of the Data Compression Conference,* Snowbird, Utah, pp. 402–410.

Bradley, Neil. 1992. SGML concepts. *Aslib Proc.* 44, no. 7/8:271–274.

Calcinelli D., and M. Mainguenaud. 1994. Cigales, a visual query language for a geographical information system: The user interface. *Journal of Visual Languages and Computing* 5:113–132.

Callan, James P. 1994. Passage-level evidence in document retrieval. In *Proceedings of the 17th Annual International ACM/SIGIR Conference on Research and Development in Information Retrieval,* Dublin, pp. 302–310.

CCITT. 1993. Draft recommendation T.82 & ISO DIS 11544: Coded representation of picture and audio information—progressive bi-level image compression.

Celentano, Augusto. 1995. Query and retrieval in multimedia databases: A new perspective. In *Fourth Annual Symposium on Document Analysis and Information Retrieval,* pp. 503–512.

Chakravarthy, A.S. 1994. Toward semantic retrieval of pictures and video. In *Proceedings of RIAO 94,* pp. 676–686.

Cheng, Y., S.S. Iyengar, and R.L. Kashyap. 1988. A new method of image compression using irreducible covers of maximal rectangles. *IEEE Transactions on Software Engineering* 14, no. 5:651–658.

Choueka, Yaacov, Aviezri S. Fraenkel, and Shmuel T. Klein. 1988. Compression of concordances in full-text retrieval systems. In *Proceedings of the 11th Annual International ACM/SIGIR Conference on Research and Development in Information Retrieval,* Grenoble, France, pp. 597–612.

Choueka, Yaacov, Aviezri S. Fraenkel, Shmuel T. Klein, and E. Segal. 1986. Improved hierarchical bit-vector compression in document retrieval systems. In *Proceedings of the 9th Annual International ACM/SIGIR Conference on Research and Development in Information Retrieval,* Pisa, Italy, pp. 88–97.

Enser, Peter. 1995. Image databases for multimedia projects. *JASIS* 46, no. 1:60–64.

Faloutsos, C., R. Barber, M. Flickner, J. Hafner, W. Niblack, D. Petrovic, and W. Equitz. 1994. Efficient and effective querying by image content. *Journal of Intelligent Information Systems* 3:231–262.

Fidel, Raya. 1986. The possible effect of abstracting guidelines on retrieval performance of free-text searching. *Information Processing & Management* 22, no. 4:1309–1316.

Frakes, William B., and Ricardo Baeza-Yates, eds. 1992. *Information retrieval—data structures and algorithms.* Englewood Cliffs, New Jersey: Prentice-Hall.

Gudivada, Venkat Naidu, and Vijay V. Raghavan. 1993. Spatial similarity based retrieval in image databases. In *Second Annual Symposium on Document Analysis and Information Retrieval,* pp. 255–270.

Gudivada, Venkat Naidu, and Vijay V. Raghavan. 1994. A system for retrieving images by content. In *Proceedings of RIAO 94,* pp. 418–436.

Gudivada, Venkat Naidu, and Vijay V. Raghavan. 1995. Design and evaluation of algorithms for image retrieval by spatial similarity. *ACM Transactions on Information Systems* 13, no. 2:115–144.

Harman, Donna K., ed. 1993. *The First Text REtrieval Conference (TREC-1).* Washington, D.C.: NIST Special Publication 500–207.

Harman, Donna K., ed. 1994. *The Second Text REtrieval Conference (TREC-2).* Washington, D.C.: NIST Special Publication 500–215.

Harman, Donna K., ed. 1995. *Overview of the Third Text REtrieval Conference (TREC-3).* Washington, D.C.: NIST Special Publication 500–225.

Huffman, David A. 1952. A method for the construction of minimum redundancy codes. *Proceedings of IRE* 40, no. 9:1098–1101.

Hunter, R., and A.H. Robinson. 1980. International digital facsimile coding standards. *Proceedings of IEEE* 68, no. 7:854–867.

ISO (International Organization for Standardization). 1972. *Documentation—International Code for the Abbreviation of Titles of Periodicals.* ISO 4-1972(E).

ISO (International Organization for Standardization). 1973. *Documentation—International list of periodic title word abbreviations.* ISO 833-1973(E).

Kerner, Carol J., and Thomas F. Lindsley. 1969. The value of abstracts in normal text searching. In *The information bazaar. Proceedings of the*

Sixth Annual National Colloquium on Information Retrieval, Philadelphia, pp. 437–440.

Klein, Shmuel T., Abraham Bookstein, and Scott C. Deerwester. 1989. Storing text retrieval systems on CD-ROM: Compression and encryption considerations. In *Proceedings of the 12th Annual International ACM/SIGIR Conference on Research and Development in Information Retrieval,* Cambridge, Massachusetts, pp. 160–167.

Knaus, Daniel, Elke Mittendorf, and Peter Schäuble. 1995. Improving a basic retrieval method by links and passage level evidence. In *Overview of the Third Text REtrieval Conference (TREC-3),* ed. Donna K. Harman. Washington, D.C.: NIST Special Publication 500-225, pp. 241–246.

Krishnamoorthy, M., George Nagy, Sharad Seth, and Mahesh Viswanathan. 1993. Syntactic segmentation and labeling of digitized pages from technical journals. *IEEE Transactions on Pattern Analysis and Machine Intelligence* 15, no. 7:737–747.

LeGall, Didier J. 1991. MPEG: A video compression standard for multimedia applications. *Communications of the ACM* 34, no. 4:46–58.

Liu, Chengwen, and Clement T. Yu. 1991. Data compression using word encoding with Huffman code. *JASIS* 42, no. 9:685–698.

Lorenz, Oliver, and Gladys Monagan. 1995. A retrieval system for graphical documents. In *Fourth Annual Symposium on Document Analysis and Information Retrieval,* pp. 291–300.

Lovins, J.B. 1968. Development of a stemming algorithm. *Mechanical Translation and Computational Linguistics* 11, no. 1-2:11–31.

Mainguenaud, M., and M.-A. Portier. 1990. Cigales: A graphical query language for geographical information systems. In *Fourth International Symposium on Spatial Data Handling,* ed. K. Brassel and H. Kishimoto, Zurich, Switzerland, pp. 393–404.

Meghini, Carlo. 1995. An image retrieval model based on classical logic. In *Proceedings of the 18th Annual International ACM/SIGIR Conference on Research and Development in Information Retrieval,* Seattle, Washington, pp. 300–308.

Melucci, Massimo. 1995. Navigation-based passage retrieval (poster abstract). In *Proceedings of the 18th Annual International ACM/SIGIR Conference on Research and Development in Information Retrieval,* Seattle, Washington, p. 373.

Mittendorf, Elke, and Peter Schäuble. 1994. Passage retrieval based on hidden Markov models. In *Proceedings of the 17th Annual International ACM/SIGIR Conference on Research and Development in Information Retrieval,* Dublin, pp. 318–327.

Molina, Maria Pinto. 1995. Documentary abstracting: Toward a methodological model. *JASIS* 46, no. 3:225–234.

Molto, Mavis. 1993. Improving full text search performance through textual analysis. *Information Processing & Management* 29, no. 5:615–632.

Mowshowitz, Abbe. 1977. *Inside Information. Computers in Fiction.* Reading, Massachusetts: Addison-Wesley.

Niblack, Wayne, R. Barber, W. Equitz, M. Flickner, E. Glasman, D. Petkovic, P. Yanker, C. Faloutsos, and G. Taubin. 1993. The QBIC project: Querying images by content using color, texture and shape. In *SPIE Storage and Retrieval for Image and Video Databases,* ed. Wayne Niblack, Bellingham, Washington, pp. 173–187.

Ogle, V., and Michael Stonebraker. 1995. Chabot: Retrieval from a relational database of images. *IEEE Computer* 28, no. 9:40–48.

Olsen, Kai A., Robert R. Korfhage, Kenneth M. Sochats, Michael B. Spring, and James G. Williams. 1993. Visualization of a document collection with implicit and explicit links: The VIBE system. *Scandinavian Journal of Information Systems* 5:79–95.

Paice, Chris. 1990. Another stemmer. *SIGIR Forum* 24, no. 3:56–61.

Papadias, D., and T. Sellis. 1995. A pictorial query-by-example language. *Journal of Visual Languages and Computing* 6, no. 1:53–72.

Pennebaker, W.B., and J.L. Mitchell. 1993. *JPEG still image data compression standard.* New York: Van Nostrand Reinhold.

Porter, M.F. 1980. An algorithm for suffix stripping. *Program* 14:130–137.

Rosengren, P. 1994. Applying conceptual models to multimedia information retrieval. In *Proceedings of RIAO 94,* pp. 328–337.

Rowe, Neil C. 1995. Retrieving captioned pictures using statistical correlations and a theory of caption-picture co-reference. In *Fourth Annual Symposium on Document Analysis and Information Retrieval,* pp. 525–534.

Salton, Gerard, James Allan, and Chris Buckley. 1993. Approaches to passage retrieval in full text information systems. In *Proceedings of the 16th Annual International ACM/SIGIR Conference on Research and Development in Information Retrieval,* Pittsburgh, pp. 49–58.

Schäuble, Peter, and Martin Wechsler. 1995. First experiences with a speech retrieval system (poster abstract). In *Proceedings of the 18th Annual International ACM/SIGIR Conference on Research and Development in Information Retrieval*, Seattle, Washington, p. 375.

Sparck Jones, Karen, J.T. Foote, G.J.F. Jones, and S.J. Young. 1995. Spoken document retrieval—a multimedia tool. In *Fourth Annual Symposium on Document Analysis and Information Retrieval*, pp. 1–12.

Thompson, Paul, and Robert Kellogg. 1993. ADIIR: A testbed for experiments in document/image indexing and retrieval. In *Second Annual Symposium on Document Analysis and Information Retrieval*, pp. 157–168.

Wallace, G.K. 1991. The JPEG still picture compression standard. *Communications of the ACM* 34, no. 4:30–44.

Witten, Ian H., Alistair Moffat, and Timothy C. Bell. 1994. *Managing gigabytes: compressing and indexing documents and images.* New York: Van Nostrand Reinhold.

Ziv, J., and A. Lempel. 1977. A universal algorithm for sequential data compression. *IEEE Transactions on Information Theory* IT-23:337–343.

Ziv, J., and A. Lempel. 1978. Compression of individual sequences via variable rate coding. *IEEE Transactions on Information Theory* IT-24:530–536.

EXERCISES

1. Write a computer program (any language) that will provide a sorted list of all the words in a given text, together with a count of how many times each word occurs. Note that you will have to account for several anomalies in usage, such as the fact that periods and commas may be used as grammatical sentence or phrase terminators, or in numbers and abbreviations. You will need also to distinguish between hyphens that occur as part of a word, as in *twenty-two,* and those that occur because a word is broken at the end of a line. In addition, you must deal with capitalization—the fact that *The* and *the* are the same word but that *brown* as a color (which may occur capitalized) is different from *Brown* as a name, for example.

2. Determine the extensions to your program of Exercise 1 that are needed to handle text containing font changes, such as **boldface** or

italic characters, or even characters in a totally different font. (In text generated on a word processor, these may be indicated by inserted control characters.)

3. Determine the extensions to your program of Exercise 1 that are needed to handle text containing Greek or Cyrillic characters.

4. Determine the extensions to your program of Exercise 1 that are needed to handle text containing mathematical symbols and equations.

5. Determine the extensions to your program of Exercise 1 that are needed to handle text containing chemical formulas and names.

6. Determine the extensions to your program of Exercise 1 that are needed to handle text containing typesetting marks, such as those used by SGML.

7. Discuss the problem of handling the structure diagrams that are frequently used in chemistry. What tools do you think would help in identifying all or part of such diagrams? (Some chemists consider these diagrams to be more important for retrieval purposes than the text itself.)

8. Discuss the problems of handling a language constructed on a nonalphabetic basis, such as Chinese, or Egyptian hieroglyphics.

9. Discuss the problems of handling a "language" that is completely different from our normal concept. For example, consider a database of musical scores. The keywords of a textual document might become the themes of a piece of music. How would one identify (and count) these musical elements?

10. Using either the symbols and frequencies of Example 2.1 or symbols and frequencies of your choosing, determine the number of bits necessary to represent each symbol in a flat binary code, that is, a code that uses the same number of bits per symbol. Then, based on the frequencies of occurrence, find the weighted average number of bits in a Huffman code for the same symbol set.

11. Consider the following bit string:

    0110110111100010011000111010011100011010110101101011101

    Use the Huffman code developed in Example 2.1 to decode this bit string. (You can ignore any partial code left at the end.) Then try each of the following experiments three times and determine how soon the decoding returns to the correct values. In each case, choosing a location toward the left end of the string will best demonstrate the effect.

Insert a bit (either 0 or 1) at a randomly chosen location in the bit string.

Delete a bit from a randomly chosen location in the bit string.

Switch a bit (0 to 1, or 1 to 0) at a randomly chosen location in the bit string.

12. Determine a character string and error condition that will result in a non-self-correcting sequence using the Huffman code of Example 2.1. *Hint:* Fixed length codes will not self-correct if the initial decoding point is wrong.

13. Assuming that the alphabet consists of *a*, *b*, and *c*, develop arithmetic encoding for the following strings:

aaa	*aab*
aba	*baa*
abc	*cab*
cba	*bac*

14. Assuming that the alphabet consists of *a*, *b*, and *c*, decode each of the following numbers into a three-character string, and into a four-character string.

0.175	0.456
0.692	0.913

15. List six characteristics that could be used to distinguish among English text, tables, and figures when they are scanned into a computer.

16. Implement the Paice stemming algorithm and test it against either the Lovins or Porter stemmers on a reasonably large body of text, say, 10,000 words.

Query Structures

Although a query can be considered to be yet another document that an information system must handle, in many ways a query is distinct from the types of documents that the user is typically trying to retrieve. Most queries are relatively brief. The language of the query may be quite constrained; indeed, a query may not satisfy the normal rules of syntax. Both the terms used in a query and the manner in which they can be used may be subject to rigorous rules of the system. Word frequency counts, which are useful in processing longer documents, are of little or no use in queries, since each keyword or phrase tends to appear at most once. Ultimately, the goal is to define a match between a given query and those documents that the user would like to retrieve in response to the query. The matching process is complicated by the fact that the query and the documents may have quite different forms. After examining briefly the types of matches that can be defined, this chapter covers the various structures that have been proposed and used for queries to a retrieval system.

The document and the query undergo parallel processes within the retrieval system. On the document side, someone generates or gathers some data and formulates it into a document. This happens within the ectosystem. Within the endosystem the document is transformed into an internal representation, which must then be further transformed into a format that can be used in the matching process. Similarly, on the query side someone begins with an information need, using it to generate a query. Again, this happens in the ectosystem. Within the endosystem the query is given an internal representation, which must also be further transformed into a format that can be matched to the documents. A good system design will make these transformations as simple and automatic as possible, largely transparent to the user.

3.1   MATCHING CRITERIA

The user would always like an exact and perfect answer to the query posed to the system. This, however, is only possible when the query is exactly posed and the data in the database can be definitely identified as responding to the query or not. The most obvious *exact match* situations arise with numerical or business databases. The terms in such databases are organized into definite fields, and it is possible to determine exactly whether the value of a given term matches the value specified in the query. Any datum whose term values all match the values specified in the query will be retrieved; all other data will be rejected.

An immediate extension of the exact match is the *range match*. In this type of matching a range of acceptable values is given for each term. For example, the match may require ages or salaries within a given range, or names that fall within a given alphabetical range. Range matches are possible on terms that have a natural order (for example, numerical or alphabetical), so that it is meaningful to specify that a term be greater than some minimum value or less than some maximum value. These matches are also possible whenever there is a clearly defined set of acceptable term values, so that the system can determine whether a given value is or is not in this set. Range match queries work well with numerical or business databases, where the user can pose reasonably exact queries and the data are organized into clearly defined fields.

Most text and image databases are not well adapted to exact or range matching. The data are not that well organized, and the types of queries posed are not that precise. Hence the aim is to develop a good *approximate match* to a query. This requires some way to measure how well a given document, as described within an information system, matches the query. The goal is to satisfy an information need exactly; the user must settle for approximately matching a query. The ability to succeed in this task rests on the form of the query and on the evaluation functions that are used.

As systems become capable of processing full-text documents, the boundaries between the above types of queries blur. The system may be called upon to respond to a query that has mixed characteristics. It is not unreasonable to frame a query that calls for an approximate match, but then to limit the query by specifying exact or range values that must be satisfied. For example, a user might request information on federal funding for energy development projects, but then specify that the funding must be at least $1,000,000 and that the funding must have been awarded in the fiscal year 1995. Retrieval systems that are oriented toward approximate matches based on text must thus be modified to include components that can handle exact and range matches.

3.2 BOOLEAN QUERIES

A user often thinks of a query in one of two forms—either as a question in everyday English or some other natural language, or as a list of terms. The first of these forms will be discussed toward the end of the chapter. The second, a list of terms, seems simple enough but presents some ambiguity. When asked, many users are rather vague about exactly what they mean by the list of terms in a query. Although they would often prefer to have all listed terms present in any answer, they may be satisfied if some of the terms are found. They may even have clear, but unstated, preferences among the terms.

One standard model of a query developed from a term list is a *Boolean query*. The Boolean query is based on concepts from logic, or *Boolean algebra*, with its terms joined together by logical connectives. Typically the connectives permitted are AND, OR, and NOT. These are sufficient, together with grouping of terms, to express any logical combination of terms. Thus a typical query might be for documents related to *restaurants* AND (*Mideastern* OR *vegetarian*) AND *inexpensive.* The appropriate response to this query is to retrieve any document having the three words *restaurants, Mideastern,* and *inexpensive,* or the three words *restaurants, vegetarian,* and *inexpensive.* If a document contains all four words, that's fine but not important.

This search may be expanded by stemming, or the reduction of a word to its root form. The given query might be replaced by *restaurant* AND (*Mideast* OR *veget*) AND *inexpens,* for example. Another expansion technique is to use a thesaurus, or list of related terms. The term *Mideastern* could be expanded with a list of specific countries. Other cuisines such as

Indian could be included in expanding the term *vegetarian,* even though the country is not considered to be Mideastern.

In a Boolean query the use of AND requires that both terms this connects be present in the retrieved document, whereas the use of OR requires that at least one of the terms be present. Note that this is an *inclusive* use of OR, meaning that it is acceptable for both of the terms to be present. If an *exclusive* use of OR is desired—one term or the other, but not both—the construction is more complex: (*A* AND NOT *B*) OR (*B* AND NOT *A*), or (*A* OR *B*) AND NOT (*A* AND *B*). NOT, obviously, requires that the specified term be absent from any retrieved document.

Many commercially available retrieval systems are based on Boolean queries. One of the best known of these is Dialog. Others include search services provided by newspapers such as *The New York Times,* and even newer systems such as Visual Recall, developed by the XSort division of Xerox Corporation. Some of these systems add *proximity operators,* so that the user can specify "icing within three words of chocolate," and a few may permit conditional queries ("if icing then chocolate"). Such operators permit more-easily defined queries, but are not absolutely necessary.

Another type of operator that some Boolean query systems permit allows the user to specify how many terms in a list must be present if it is not necessary to have the full list. For example, a user may specify three terms in a query but be satisfied if any two of them are present. This can be specified with standard Boolean operators:

$$(A \text{ AND } B) \text{ OR } (A \text{ AND } C) \text{ OR } (B \text{ AND } C),$$

but it is simpler to specify

$$2 \text{ OF } (A, B, C).$$

This capability is particularly useful when the user will be satisfied with a small number of a larger choice of terms, such as four out of seven terms. In particular, it enables the user to bring related terms into the query explicitly without requiring that all of them be present. For example, in designing a garden, the user might ask for information about

$$4 \text{ OF } (peony, daisy, dahlia, lily, hosta, zinnia, marigold).$$

Without this ability the user would need to specify many different floral combinations. See Exercise 3.1.

Despite the simplicity and appeal of Boolean queries, they present a number of significant problems. First, in a pure Boolean query there is no good way to weight terms for significance. Either a term is present or it is absent. Thus the user has little control over how important a given term is to the query. The user of a music database, for example, cannot easily frame a Boolean request for "music by Beethoven, preferably a sonata." The simplest Boolean queries related to this would be *Beethoven* AND *sonata*, which eliminates any of Beethoven's other music, and *Beethoven* OR *sonata*, which includes sonatas by other composers. The request (*Beethoven* AND *sonata*) OR *Beethoven* would achieve the desired result, but most Boolean systems would not distinguish between the Beethoven sonatas and other Beethoven music. In other words, the simple query *Beethoven* would achieve a similar result. (Weighted Boolean query systems, which are discussed in Section 3.4, attempt to remove this constraint.)

While the lack of an adequate weighting mechanism results in queries that are less than optimal, the second problem with Boolean queries can result in retrieval results that are wrong because of a misstated query. This problem involves incorrect interpretation of the Boolean connectives AND and OR. People who are not fully conversant with logical conventions, having used these connectives only informally, tend to misuse them in certain situations. For example, a person seeking Saturday night entertainment may specify an interest in

dinner AND sports AND symphony.

The choice of events that are simultaneously dinner and sports and symphony is limited; most probably the person means

dinner OR sports OR symphony,

or perhaps

dinner AND (sports OR symphony).

A Boolean retrieval system does not know this, however, and will misinterpret the query.

The third problem with Boolean retrieval systems lies in the *order of precedence* for the logical connectives. Two different standards for order of precedence are followed. Both rely on parentheses to group terms together: The combination within parentheses is evaluated as a unit before being combined with the terms outside the parentheses. In one type of system, NOT is applied first within the parentheses, followed by AND, followed by OR, with a left-to-right precedence among operators of the same kind. Other systems, however, follow a strict left-to-right order of precedence without regard to the operators. Thus the query

A OR B AND C

would be interpreted as

A OR (B AND C)

in the first type of system, but as

(A OR B) AND C

in the second type of system. In either case, parentheses are required if one wishes an interpretation other than the one that the system automatically assumes. Note that in this example, the first interpretation will retrieve a document containing only the term A, but the second will not, since it requires term C to be present. One interesting study (Avrahami and Kareev 1993) shows that people tend to interpret this ambiguity one way or another, depending on the semantic relationships among the three terms. For example people interpret the request *"coffee AND croissant OR muffin"* differently from the request *"raincoat AND umbrella OR sunglasses."*

The operator NOT introduces another problem, but one that is more easily resolved. Since NOT retrieves every document that does *not* contain a specific term, a query such as NOT *aardvark* runs the risk of retrieving virtually the entire database. One way to resolve this is to restrict the use of NOT to situations where it is applied only to an already small set of documents. For example, suppose that the query is

(NOT A) AND B AND C.

Rather than begin the interpretation of the query with NOT A, which will retrieve every document not containing the term A, begin with B AND C. Then the condition NOT A is applied to the much smaller set of documents that results, namely only those that contain both B and C.

Most users of information systems are not well trained in Boolean algebra. The problem of learning the correct interpretations of the Boolean operators and their rules of precedence, combined with the fact that many users do not access an information retrieval system on a regular basis, presents a major barrier to the effective use of Boolean retrieval systems.

A fourth potential source of difficulty in processing a Boolean query is that the user is free to construct a highly complex query that requires the development of many partial responses to be assembled into the final response to the query. However, every Boolean query can be recast into either *disjunctive normal form* (DNF), or *conjunctive normal form* (CNF), each of which provides a standard form that is easy to process. This can be done automatically, without requiring the user to carry out the process. The value of the DNF or CNF for a query is the same as that for the original query, and the same set of documents is retrieved in response to the query.

There are three levels of expressions in a *disjunctive normal form:*

- *Terms*, which are individual words or phrases that occur either *naturally* or *negated*. For example, *concert* and NOT *play* are two valid terms;
- *Conjuncts*, which are terms joined by AND. For example, *dinner* AND *concert* AND NOT *play* is a valid conjunct;
- *Disjuncts*, which are conjuncts joined by OR. A query in DNF is constructed from one or more disjuncts. For example,

$$(\textit{concert} \text{ AND } \textit{dinner} \text{ AND NOT } \textit{play}) \text{ OR}$$
$$(\textit{swimming} \text{ AND } \textit{tennis}) \text{ OR}$$
$$(\textit{baseball} \text{ AND NOT } \textit{football})$$

is a valid DNF query. Observe that one advantage of the DNF is that a query in this form can be split into smaller queries, each consisting of one of the conjuncts. Thus the query in the example can be treated as three separate queries, and the results merged to produce the response to the original query. Some authors insist that each conjunct contain all of the possible terms in an expression. Thus in place of

$$(A \text{ AND } B) \text{ OR } (A \text{ AND NOT } C),$$

these authors would expand each term, resulting in the form

$$(A \text{ AND } B \text{ AND } C) \text{ OR } (A \text{ AND } B \text{ AND NOT } C)$$
$$\text{OR } (A \text{ AND NOT } B \text{ AND NOT } C).$$

The completely expanded form is called the *full disjunctive normal form.*

A *conjunctive normal form* query is similarly defined, with the roles of AND and OR interchanged. Terms are joined together by OR to form disjuncts, and these are joined by AND to form the conjuncts. A typical query in this form might be

(*concert* OR *dinner* OR NOT *play*) AND

(*swimming* OR *tennis*) AND

(*baseball* OR NOT *football*).

(Note that this is *not* a different form of the DNF query given above: it is a totally different query and will retrieve quite a different set.)

The process of transforming a Boolean query into either DNF or CNF is called *normalization*. Normalization of an arbitrary Boolean query is most easily accomplished through use of a *truth table*. In a truth table, each row has a value of either *true* or *false*. To construct the full DNF for a query only the true rows of the table are used. These constitute precisely the terms in the full disjunctive normal form for the expression. As an example, consider the query

(*A* OR *B*) AND (*C* OR NOT *D*) AND (*D* OR *B*),

and expand it into a truth table (Table 3.1).

The full DNF for the query is formed by taking the truth table rows that are true and combining them with OR:

Row 1:   *A* AND *B* AND *C* AND *D*

Row 2:   *A* AND *B* AND *C* AND (NOT *D*)

Row 4:   *A* AND *B* AND (NOT *C*) AND (NOT *D*)

Row 5:   *A* AND (NOT *B*) AND *C* AND *D*

Row 9:   (NOT *A*) AND *B* AND *C* AND *D*

Row 10: (NOT *A*) AND *B* AND *C* AND (NOT *D*)

Row 12: (NOT *A*) AND *B* AND (NOT *C*) AND (NOT *D*)

Each of these conjuncts can be processed separately, or they can be combined into the full DNF for the original query,

Table 3.1
Truth Table for Full Disjunctive Normal Form

Row	A	B	C	D	A OR B	C OR NOT D	D OR B	Expression
1	T	T	T	T	T	T	T	T
2	T	T	T	F	T	T	T	T
3	T	T	F	T	T	F	T	F
4	T	T	F	F	T	T	T	T
5	T	F	T	T	T	T	T	T
6	T	F	T	F	T	T	F	F
7	T	F	F	T	T	F	T	F
8	T	F	F	F	T	T	F	F
9	F	T	T	T	T	T	T	T
10	F	T	T	F	T	T	T	T
11	F	T	F	T	T	F	T	F
12	F	T	F	F	T	T	T	T
13	F	F	T	T	F	T	T	F
14	F	F	T	F	F	T	F	F
15	F	F	F	T	F	F	T	F
16	F	F	F	F	F	T	F	F

$(A$ AND B AND C AND $D)$

OR $(A$ AND B AND C AND (NOT D))

OR $(A$ AND B AND (NOT C) AND (NOT D))

OR $(A$ AND (NOT B) AND C AND D)

OR ((NOT A) AND B AND C AND D)

OR ((NOT A) AND B AND C AND (NOT D))

OR ((NOT A) AND B AND (NOT C) AND (NOT D)).

The full DNF for a query often involves quite a few phrases (conjuncts), some of which can be combined. In this example, since Row 1 and Row 2 are both included, it is clear that for these rows it does not matter whether D or NOT D holds. In both of these rows A, B, and C are true. Thus the expression A AND B AND C is true for these two rows and for no other. This single expression covers both rows and can be substituted for the two expressions involving D and NOT D. Several techniques exist for *minimizing* a Boolean expression, that is, reducing it to the simplest possible form (Korfhage 1984). Applied to this example, these techniques yield the simpler DNF expression

$$(A \text{ AND } C \text{ AND } D) \text{ OR } (B \text{ AND } C) \text{ OR } (B \text{ AND } (\text{NOT } D)).$$

The three conjuncts cover all true rows (and none of the false rows) of the table:

Row 1: $(A \text{ AND } C \text{ AND } D)$, $(B \text{ AND } C)$

Row 2: $(B \text{ AND } C)$, $(B \text{ AND } (\text{NOT } D))$

Row 4: $(B \text{ AND } (\text{NOT } D))$

Row 5: $(A \text{ AND } C \text{ AND } D)$

Row 9: $(B \text{ AND } C)$

Row 10: $(B \text{ AND } C)$, $(B \text{ AND } (\text{NOT } D))$

Row 12: $(B \text{ AND } (\text{NOT } D))$

The full CNF for a query can be similarly obtained. Begin by forming the full DNF using the false rows of the table. This is clearly the DNF for the negation of the query. By negating this and applying *DeMorgan's Laws*, it is converted to the CNF for the original query. DeMorgan's Laws move negation to individual terms, interchanging AND and OR in the process:

$$\text{NOT } (A \text{ AND } B) = (\text{NOT } A) \text{ OR } (\text{NOT } B),$$
$$\text{NOT } (A \text{ OR } B) = (\text{NOT } A) \text{ AND } (\text{NOT } B).$$

Also used in the process is the *Law of Double Negation:*

$$\text{NOT } (\text{NOT } A) = A.$$

Using a shorter example, if the DNF for the negation of a query is

$$(A \text{ AND } B \text{ AND NOT } C) \text{ OR } (\text{NOT } A \text{ AND } C) \text{ OR } (B \text{ AND } C),$$

then the CNF for the query is determined by negating this expression and expanding it:

NOT ((*A* AND *B* AND NOT *C*) OR (NOT *A* AND *C*) OR (*B* AND *C*))

= NOT (*A* AND *B* AND NOT *C*)

AND NOT (NOT *A* AND *C*)

AND NOT (*B* AND *C*)

= (NOT *A* OR NOT *B* OR NOT (NOT *C*))

AND (NOT (NOT *A*) OR NOT *C*)

AND (NOT *B* OR NOT *C*).

The final result is the CNF expression

(NOT *A* OR NOT *B* OR *C*) AND (*A* OR NOT *C*) AND (NOT *B* OR NOT *C*).

Each disjunct in a DNF produces a set of answers to the query, which are then merged to develop the full set. This is not so with the CNF. While each conjunct produces a set of candidates responding to the query, these candidates must still be validated by satisfying the other conjuncts. Thus in our example any document satisfying NOT *A* OR NOT *B* OR *C* must also satisfy *A* OR NOT *C* and NOT *B* OR NOT *C*. However, think of the CNF form as basically a conjunctive query,

A AND *B* AND *C* AND *D*,

where each of the conjuncts *A*, *B*, *C*, and *D* has been replaced by a list of synonyms or alternative terms. Thus the use of a thesaurus can easily expand a given CNF query to a broader CNF query. Reference librarians, who are familiar with the terms used in a particular literature collection, often use a CNF query for this reason.

The amount of processing for a Boolean query can be reduced with a little knowledge of the database. Beginning with a given set of documents, processing each conjunction (AND) reduces the size of the set, since it eliminates those documents not satisfying the conjunction. Thus the number of documents retrieved in response to the query *A* AND *B* must be at most the smaller of the number of documents containing *A* and the number of those containing *B*, and will probably be smaller than either. Hence if the sizes of the various sets satisfying the terms in a query are known, processing the sets in order of increasing size will result in handling the smallest possible document sets.

The fifth problem associated with Boolean retrieval systems is in controlling the size and composition of the retrieved set. Technically, the system should return all documents satisfying the query. This may, however, be either a very small number or a very large one. In the latter case, the system may present the user with several hundred documents to examine, in no particular order. One solution to this is to begin again with a more restrictive query. The user can frame a new query, either immediately or after examining the first few documents, by adding more terms to the original query or by constructing an entirely new set of terms. Many systems automatically restrict the number of documents returned to the user. This number may be set by the system or may be user-specifiable. However, unless the endosystem sorts the documents by the number of query terms that they match, such an arbitrary cutoff may retain relatively weak documents while discarding the best of those found.

Sorting the documents by the number of matching query terms provides a rough ranking of the documents. This can be enhanced in a Boolean system that uses a thesaurus to expand the query terms (Lee, Kim, and Lee 1993). However, this still does not address the problem of the relative importance of the individual terms in the query.

There is one final, philosophical problem with Boolean queries. The object of performing a retrieval is to match a document to a query. A document can easily be represented by a list of the terms that it contains. But since this is a list, not a Boolean expression, the introduction of Boolean connectives into a query seems to produce a query form that is less like the document than a query in the form of a list of terms would be. Because of this structural difference between the query and the document, it is better to think of Boolean retrieval as a mapping process rather than a matching process.

Having said all this, the fact remains that Boolean retrieval systems are highly popular and reasonably effective. Ease of use is certainly a factor in this. The user specifies a list of terms combined with AND, OR, and NOT, perhaps augmented by proximity or other operators. There is no need to think about how important a given term may be. The difficulties of framing the query with logical precision, while very real, have little practical impact: People tend to use only two or three terms at a time, not trying to assemble complex queries. The results of a search may not be very good (see Chapter 8), but they are often better and more quickly obtained than the user could achieve by a manual search. Finally, other retrieval models that may be more interesting theoretically have not, in practice, achieved results that are distinctly superior to those of Boolean retrieval systems. Whether this will remain true as retrieval systems shift to full-text and multimedia documents remains to be seen.

3.3 VECTOR QUERIES

Boolean queries are based on a set of terms. Although a set is inherently unordered, for ease of processing, the terms are normally considered in alphabetical or some other fixed order. In a Boolean query, the order in which the terms are considered is determined, at least partially, by the logical operations in the query. In a *vector model*, each document is represented by a *vector*, or ordered list of terms, rather than by a set of terms. The underlying set of terms is the same for both models. (Note that the system can easily sort the terms, so the user does not need to worry about that.) Differences between the Boolean model and the vector model arise when the individual term representations and the methods of determining the similarity between a document and the query are considered.

In the Boolean model of retrieval, the similarity between a document and a query (or between any two documents) is based on the presence of terms in both the query and the document. Thus the basis is essentially a contingency table (Table 3.2).

In contrast, the vector model of similarity and retrieval uses more sophisticated similarity calculations. Evaluation methods can be based on a *0,1-vector*, where each component is either 0 if the corresponding term is absent or 1 if the corresponding term is present in the document or query being rep-

Table 3.2
Contingency Table for Document-Query Match

		DOCUMENT	
		Term in	Term not in
Query	Term in	Match	No match
	Term not in	No match	No match

resented. Alternatively, evaluation methods can be based on a *weight vector* whose components are the weights or values assigned to each term in the document.

The vector model in its pure form is an impractical ideal, however. In any vector representing a document, the vast majority of the components will be 0. (Of perhaps 10,000 or more components representing the vocabulary terms, a given document is likely to contain only a few hundred.) Thus while the vector is a good model for the mathematical theory behind similarity and retrieval, in practice a more compact representation is used, consisting only of the weights for terms actually present in the document or its surrogate. The key to success in using this model is to maintain *dimensional compatibility*. That is, the system must be designed to ensure that the comparison of two documents (or a document and a query) is always based on comparing the same terms in each document. This means that some (implicit) expansion of the compact representation must take place, to account for terms that occur in one but not the other document.

Assigning weights to document terms in a vector is a complex process. Weights can be assigned automatically in a document, based on the frequency counts of terms. It is reasonable to assume that the more frequently a term occurs in a document, the more important it is to the document. (Obvious exceptions must be made for the "glue" words such as *the, a, of, and*, and so forth, which occur frequently because of the structure of the language.) However, when a user is asked to assign weights in a *query*, the frequency data are both not present and not relevant. The weights assigned by a user reflect the importance of a term to the perceived information need and hence do not relate directly to term frequencies in documents. Asking a user to assign weights representing relative values raises an interesting problem. For the sake of uniformity the user may be asked to assign weights within a given range of values, say 0.0 to 1.0. This raises the *judging dilemma:* What should the user do if one term has been assigned a weight of 1.0 and she then discovers a more significant term? Either she assigns the weight 1.0 to the new term, hiding its real significance, or she must reevaluate all previously assigned weights. An alternative to this is to give the user free rein in selecting weights. While the user may begin with a conception of weights being within a given range, there is still the freedom to assign weights outside of that range should certain index terms warrant such treatment.

If the user can assign weights freely, then some sort of normalization is necessary to ensure that the weights used are compatible with those assigned to documents by the system. Letting s denote system weights and u denote user weights, a linear transformation that accomplishes this is

$$s = \frac{s_{\max}(u - u_{\min}) + s_{\min}(u_{\max} - u)}{u_{\max} - u_{\min}}.$$

This transforms $u_{\min}$ into $s_{\min}$ and $u_{\max}$ into $s_{\max}$, thus making the user's range of values correspond to the system's range. To do this the maximum and minimum user weight values must be determined, either by asking the user or by analyzing the query.

Retrieval on the basis of a similarity function raises the question of which documents should be retrieved and which should be rejected. Note that each document in a collection receives a similarity value with respect to a given query. Hence the documents can be ordered for retrieval by decreasing similarity. There are then two bases upon which to decide on the specific set to retrieve: Either retrieve a fixed number of documents (perhaps specified by the user) or retrieve all documents whose similarity value is above a certain threshold value (again, perhaps specified by the user). Coupling the similarity value calculation with the control that the user has over either the threshold or the number of documents retrieved provides some assurance that those documents best matching the query are the ones that the user sees.

3.4 EXTENDED BOOLEAN QUERIES

Whereas Boolean models have the disadvantage of not incorporating term weights, vector models have the disadvantage of not being capable of expressing logical connectives easily. Various attempts have been made to mediate between Boolean and vector queries by the introduction of *weighted,* or *extended, Boolean queries.* In the method studied by Salton and others, terms are assigned weights between 0.0 and 1.0 (Bookstein 1978, 1980; Waller and Kraft 1979; Salton, Fox, and Wu 1983; Lee et al. 1993; Lee 1994). Consider the query

$$A_{w_1} \star B_{w_2},$$

where A and B are query terms, w_1 and w_2 are the weights, and $\star$ represents a Boolean or logical operation. The weighting operation depends on a concept of *distance* between the document sets **A** and **B** corresponding to the terms A and B. The distance between sets is usually defined as the minimum of the distances between a pair of elements, one from each set. Thus if d_A is a document in set **A** and d_B is a document in set **B**, they are represented by term vectors and the distance between them is calculated. Usually ordinary Euclidean (straight line) distance is used. This computation must be repeated for all possible choices of the two documents. If **A** contains m documents and **B** contains n documents, this requires mn distance computations before choosing the minimum.

To explain weighting, take $w_1 = 1.0$, thereby including all of set **A** in consideration. Now consider the changes in the represented set as w_2 increases from 0.0 to 1.0. A set **S** derived from **A** and **B** is considered, the specific set depending on the operation *. The general philosophy is that if B is given a weight of 0.0, then it is not considered at all—the result of the operation is simply A. But if B is given a weight of 1.0, then the result of the operation is the standard Boolean operation. Intermediate values of w_2 represent the proportion of the elements in **S** to be considered.

CASE 1: * *denotes OR.* The set **S** is defined to be **B** − **A**. The items in **S** that are closest to **A** and have not yet been included are successively added to **A**. In the extreme cases,

$$A \text{ OR } B_0 = A \quad \text{and}$$
$$A \text{ OR } B_1 = A \text{ OR } B.$$

Since the OR operation corresponds to a set union, normally including all items in both sets **A** and **B**, it seems reasonable to gradually include more and more of the elements of **B**, beginning with those closest to the set **A**. Of course, all of the elements in the intersection of these sets are included automatically beginning with set **A**. See Figure 3.1.

A

B

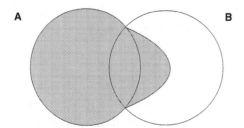

Figure 3.1   Weighted OR of two sets.

CASE 2:   * *denotes AND*. The set **S** is defined to be **A** − **B**. The items in **S** farthest from **A** ∩ **B** are successively deleted from **A**. In the extreme cases,

$$A \text{ AND } B_0 = A \quad \text{and}$$
$$A \text{ AND } B_1 = A \text{ AND } B.$$

This operation begins with the set **A** (for B_0) and ends up with the set **A** ∩ **B** (for B_1). Thus it is reasonable to gradually delete those elements of **A** that are farthest from the intersection. See Figure 3.2.

CASE 3:   * *denotes AND NOT.* The set **S** is defined to be **A** ∩ **B**. The items in **S** farthest from **A** − **B** are successively deleted from **A**. In the extreme cases,

$$A \text{ AND NOT } B_0 = A \quad \text{and}$$
$$A \text{ AND NOT } B_1 = A \text{ AND NOT } B.$$

Here the type of deletion reasoning used for the AND case holds, beginning with the set **A** and ending with **A** − **B**. See Figure 3.3.

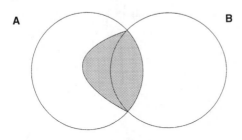

A   **B**

Figure 3.2   Weighted AND of two sets.

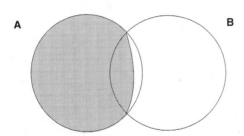

A   **B**

Figure 3.3   Weighted AND NOT of two sets.

This method extends directly to weights on all terms in a query. For example, to evaluate the query

$$A_{0.2} \text{ OR } B_{0.6},$$

include the two-tenths of the documents in **A** − **B** that are closest to **B** and the six-tenths of the documents in **B** − **A** that are closest to **A**. Remember that the documents in both sets are automatically included.

Example 3.1   Consider two document sets

$$\mathbf{A} = \{1, 4, 5, 10, 11, 15, 17, 18, 19, 23\}$$
$$\mathbf{B} = \{1, 2, 4, 5, 7, 8, 10, 13, 17, 22\},$$

corresponding to terms A and B and the query $(A_{0.8} \text{ OR } B_{0.4})$. Suppose also that the distance measure used is simply the absolute value of the numerical differences.

Begin by holding the A part fixed, and focus on "OR B." Since the operation is OR, if the weight on B were 0 only **A** would be retrieved, and if the weight on B were 1 the set **A** ∪ **B** corresponding to A OR B, the normal Boolean set, would be retrieved. Thus the set **S** is **B** − **A**, and the 0.4 of the elements of **S** closest to **A** are to be added to **A**. (Remember that the next step is to turn things around and look at A itself.) Thus

$$\mathbf{S} = \{2, 7, 8, 13, 22\};$$

for each element of **S**, compute the distance to the closest element of **A** (in the order of the elements of **S**):

$$1, 2, 2, 2, 1.$$

Keep the two closest elements, 2 and 22, from **S** as part of the OR, removing 7, 8, and 13.

Now do the same thing, using **B** and **S** = **A** − **B**. Thus

$$\mathbf{S} = \{11, 15, 18, 19, 23\},$$

and the respective distances are

$$1, 2, 1, 1, 1.$$

In this case keep the four closest, 11, 18, 19, and 23. To this add the elements in **A** ∩ **B,** 1, 4, 5, 10, and 17, since they will be included in both of the sets **A.** Thus the weighted OR becomes the set

$$\{1, 2, 4, 5, 10, 11, 17, 18, 19, 22, 23\}.$$

In this example the number of elements to be kept was always an integer. When this is not the case, some adjustment obviously must be made to handle only entire documents, not fractions of them. If the calculation indicates that 1.7 or 1.4 elements should be kept, round up or down to the nearest integer, as is appropriate. In some cases, more than enough elements may qualify for inclusion or removal. For example, if the weight on A had been 0.6, only three of the four elements at distance 1 would have been kept. In this situation the method by which the elements are chosen affects the results; if they are chosen at random, repeated applications of the same query can yield different results.

A final observation on the example is that the resulting set is the intersection **A** ∩ **B,** {1, 4, 5, 10, 17}, plus some additional elements from **A** (11, 18, 19, 23) and **B** (2, 22). More elements were added from **A** than from **B** because of the larger weight given to A.

While much research has been done on the extended Boolean query model (Lee et al. 1993; Lee 1994), it is not clear that this model results in significantly better retrieval system performance than do other models. Furthermore, it suffers from the flaw that logically equivalent queries may fail to produce the same results when weights are applied. (See Exercise 6.) In part because of this flaw, it is difficult to predict the effect of any specific weighting. Perhaps because of this difficulty, extended Boolean query systems have not become very popular.

3.5 FUZZY QUERIES

Another solution to the problem of presenting a query that accurately represents an information need is the *fuzzy query,* based on the concept of a *fuzzy set* (Kandel 1986; Zadeh 1988). In ordinary set theory a set has "sharp edges," that is, an element is either in a given set or it is not. There is no question about it. In fuzzy set theory each element has an associated *membership grade* with respect to a given set, which represents, in some sense, the strength or degree of belief in its membership in the set. The membership grades are usually given values ranging from 0.0 to 1.0.

Consider, for example, the "set of tall people." In ordinary set theory the concept of "tall" must be exactly defined. If "tall" is chosen to mean at least 6 feet tall, then anyone that tall is in the set, and anyone shorter, even a person of height 5' 11.995", is not in the set. In fuzzy set theory, this clear distinction does not hold. Rather, each person has a membership grade, or "degree of tallness," that indicates the likelihood that the person is in the set. A person of height 4'5" would have a membership grade very close to 0.0, while a person of height 6'10" would have a membership grade close to 1.0. Persons of intermediate height, say 5'8" or 6'2", would have intermediate membership grades, perhaps something like 0.45 and 0.52, to show the degree of belief that these people should be included in the set of tall people. If the task is to retrieve the set of tall people, the first person would undoubtedly be omitted and the second one included, but the decision on people of intermediate height could go either way.

Suppose U is a universal set, that is, the set of all entities to be considered. The fuzzy set S is defined as $\{<x, \mu_s(x)> \mid \mu_s > 0\}$, where x is any element of U and μ_s is the membership grade function. By this definition, every element of U for which $\mu_s > 0$ is an element of S to some extent. The classical set operations are modified to include the membership function. Thus if $x \in A \cap B$, the membership function for x with respect to this intersection can be computed as the minimum of $\mu_A(x)$ and $\mu_B(x)$. Similarly, the membership function for the union of two sets is the maximum of the two membership functions, and that for x in the complement of A is $1.0 - \mu_A(x)$.

The argument for fuzzy information retrieval is that the system (and often the user) cannot accurately tell whether a given document will meet the information need. This uncertainty is modeled in a "fuzzy" evaluation of the document with respect to the query. Thus fuzzy information retrieval is closely related to classical retrieval systems that compute some measure of relevance for a document and present the documents retrieved to the user in decreasing order of relevance, perhaps with the calculated measure. The concept of fuzzy information retrieval allows for both fuzzy document evaluations and fuzzy queries. Indeed, one makes little sense without the other (Bookstein 1980; Kerre et al. 1986; Kamel, Hadfield, and Ismail 1990; Lucarella 1990; Lucarella and Morara 1991).

3.6 PROBABILISTIC QUERIES

The fuzzy query approach to retrieval assumes that a membership grade function has somehow been defined. Other than the requirement that the values of this function are all between 0 and 1, and the rules about how membership functions combine under logical or set operators, there are no requirements placed on these functions. *Probabilistic queries* are similar in nature to fuzzy queries but impose the additional requirement that the membership or judgment functions used be probabilities. Specifically, in a probabilistic retrieval system, the set returned for any query is supposed to consist of documents which satisfy that query with a probability higher than a specified threshold.

This sounds much like the requirement that the response to a fuzzy query consist of documents whose membership function is above a certain threshold, and it is. The difference is that there are fixed rules that probabilities must satisfy. One requirement, that the probability that a given document *does* satisfy a query and the probability that it *does not* must add up to 1, is the same as the computation of the membership function with respect to a set and the complement of the set. Other rules specify exactly how probabilities for individual terms can combine to yield the probability that a document satisfies a query.

The advantage of probabilistic queries over fuzzy queries is that there is a well-established body of methods for computing probabilities from frequency data. Thus the term frequency data can be used to estimate the probability that a document containing a given set of terms will satisfy a query. In an extension of this concept, system usage can be monitored and the data gathered can be used to improve the probability estimates on the usefulness of a given document for a given type of query (Maron and Kuhns 1960; Bookstein 1985; Losee and Bookstein 1988; Fuhr 1989; Wong and Yao 1989; Cooper 1991; Gordon and Lenk 1991).

3.7 NATURAL LANGUAGE QUERIES

All of the query models that have been discussed thus far begin with the query either as a Boolean combination of terms or as a vector of terms. These may be terms provided directly by the user or terms developed by applying stemming or other techniques to user-supplied terms. While it is not difficult for a user to supply such a list of terms, many people feel more comfortable with a *natural language query,* presented as an ordinary question. Indeed, most systems that use an information professional as an intermediary are based on the assumption that the end user will ask a natural language query. The information professional's task includes casting the query into a suitable form for processing.

The natural language query is easiest for a user to formulate. However, it is typically imprecise and inaccurate, and frequently ungrammatical. The user may even ask a question that relates to the information need but does not express it directly. For example, in conversation, the person who asks, "Do you know the time?" does not really expect the answer to be the strictly proper "yes" or "no." The trained professional intermediary has relatively little trouble coping with a natural language query, particularly when the opportunity for a clarifying dialogue with the user exists.

There is increasing interest in processing natural language queries automatically. A crude processing of a natural language query consists of developing a list of words by extracting and stemming words in the query. However, this type of processing really undermines the idea that the way in which words are used in the query provides some information to guide the search. Thus the processing of a natural language query should bring to bear all of the syntactic, semantic, and pragmatic knowledge that is available. Because a query is typically brief, imprecise, and possibly ungrammatical, obtaining an accurate interpretation is a more difficult task than obtaining an accurate interpretation of a longer piece of text, say a story or a technical paper.

Natural language processing is an active area of information research, but thus far the ability of a computer to "understand" natural language is severely limited. The most successful systems restrict the discourse to a narrowly defined domain. A broad area such as medicine creates problems for computer-based language understanding systems. The more restricted domain of diagnosis of illness is narrow enough that some success has been achieved. In any case, most computer-based natural language systems rely heavily on a dialogue with the user, as do the information professionals such as reference librarians (Harris 1958; Swanson 1960; Climenson, Hardwick, and Jacobson 1961; De Heer 1974; Jacobs and Rau 1988; Lewis 1988; Smeaton 1989; Anick et al. 1990; Blair 1990; Harman and Candela 1990).

3.8 Information Retrieval and Database Systems

As previously mentioned, the advent of full-text retrieval systems has given increasing importance to queries that combine imprecise textual elements with precise numerical or other limits. Many of the topics used in the TREC series of experiments, for example, involve such explicit limits as "funding of at least $1,000,000," "any second country except Japan," or "after April 1993" (Harman 1993). Because of this there have been research efforts at constructing retrieval systems that have aspects of both traditional text-retrieval systems and database systems. Many of these focus on the relational database model (Fuhr 1993, 1994; DeFazio et al. 1995; Driscoll, Theis, and Billings 1995; Grossman, Holmes, and Frieder 1995; Järvelin and Niemi 1995). These approaches have been criticized by Macleod (1991), on the grounds that neither the textual component nor the relational database component adequately meets the needs of a combined system. While the merits of the two components are largely complementary, integrating them into a single system is not, in Macleod's view, highly successful.

Recent research has addressed this criticism and extended the usability of merged text-retrieval and database systems by building on an object-oriented database model (Croft, Smith, and Turtle 1992; McLean 1995). Since this approach treats each document as an object with its own set of defined properties, it is possible for a given document to include both textual portions accessible by traditional text-retrieval methods, and numeric or other fixed field portions accessible by database methods. In addition, a document can also have image components, with access methods appropriate to that type of data. While such a system theoretically meets the criticisms of Macleod, it remains to be seen if this approach will result in commercially viable information systems.

References

Anick, Peter G., J.D. Brennan, Rex A. Flynn, David R. Hanssen, B. Alvey, and J.M. Robbins. 1990. A direct manipulation interface for Boolean information retrieval via natural language query. In *Proceedings of the 13th Annual International ACM/SIGIR Conference on Research and Development in Information Retrieval*, Brussels, pp. 135–150.

Avrahami, Judith, and Yaakov Kareev. 1993. What do you expect to get when you ask for "a cup of coffee and a muffin or a croissant"? On the interpretation of sentences containing multiple connectives. *International Journal of Man-Machine Studies* 38:429–434.

Blair, David C. 1990. *Language and representation in information retrieval.* New York: Elsevier.

Bookstein, Abraham. 1978. On the perils of merging Boolean and weighted retrieval systems. *JASIS* 29, no. 3:156–158.

Bookstein, Abraham. 1980. Fuzzy requests: An approach to weighted Boolean searches. *JASIS* 31, no. 4:240–247.

Bookstein, Abraham. 1985. Probability and fuzzy set applications to information retrieval. *Annual Review of Information Science and Technology* 20:117–152.

Climenson, W.D., N.H. Hardwick, and S.N. Jacobson. 1961. Automatic syntax analysis in machine indexing and abstracting. *American Documentation* 12, no. 3:178–183.

Cooper, William. 1991. Probability theory as the basis of text retrieval. In *Proceedings of ASIS 91,* pp. 366–369.

Croft, W. Bruce, Lisa A. Smith, and Howard R. Turtle. 1992. A loosely-coupled integration of a text retrieval system and an object-oriented database system. In *Proceedings of the 15th Annual International ACM/SIGIR Conference on Research and Development in Information Retrieval,* Copenhagen, pp. 223–232.

De Heer, T. 1974. The application of the concept of homeosemy to natural language information retrieval. *Information Processing & Management* 18, no. 5:229–236.

DeFazio, Samuel, Amjad Daoud, Lisa Ann Smith, and Jagannathan Srinivasan. 1995. Integrating IR and RDBMS using cooperative indexing. In *Proceedings of the 18th Annual International ACM/SIGIR Conference on Research and Development in Information Retrieval,* Seattle, Washington, pp. 84–91.

Driscoll, J., G. Theis, and G. Billings. 1995. Using database schemas to detect relevant information. In *Overview of the Third Text REtrieval Conference (TREC-3),* ed. Donna K. Harman. Washington, D.C.: NIST Special Publication 500-225, pp. 373–383.

Fuhr, Norbert. 1989. Models for retrieval with probabilistic indexing. *Information Processing & Management* 25:55–72.

Fuhr, Norbert. 1993. A probabilistic relational model for the integration of IR and databases. In *Proceedings of the 16th Annual International ACM/SIGIR Conference on Research and Development in Information Retrieval*, Pittsburgh, pp. 309–317.

Fuhr, Norbert. 1994. Integration of information retrieval and database systems. In *Proceedings of the 17th Annual International ACM/SIGIR Conference on Research and Development in Information Retrieval*, Dublin, p. 360.

Gordon, Michael D., and P. Lenk. 1991. A utility theoretic examination of the probability ranking principle in information retrieval. *JASIS* 42, no. 10:703–714.

Grossman, D.A., D.O. Holmes, and Ophir Frieder. 1995. A parallel DBMS approach to IR in TREC-3. In *Overview of the Third Text REtrieval Conference (TREC-3)*, ed. Donna K. Harman. Washington, D.C.: NIST Special Publication 500-225, pp. 279–288.

Harman, Donna K., ed. 1993. The First Text REtrieval Conference (*TREC-1*). Washington, D.C.: NIST Special Publication 500-207.

Harman, Donna K., and Gerald Candela. 1990. Bringing natural language information retrieval out of the closet. *SIGCHI Bulletin* 22, no. 1:42–48.

Harris, Z.S. 1958. Linguistic transformation for information retrieval. In *Proceedings of International Conference on Scientific Information* 2:937–950.

Jacobs, Paul S., and Lisa F. Rau. 1988. Natural language techniques for intelligent information retrieval. In *Proceedings of the 11th Annual International ACM/SIGIR Conference on Research and Development in Information Retrieval*, Grenoble, France, pp. 85–99.

Järvelin, Kalervo, and Timo Niemi. 1995. An NF2 relational interface for document retrieval, restructuring and aggregation. In *Proceedings of the 18th Annual International ACM/SIGIR Conference on Research and Development in Information Retrieval*, Seattle, Washington, pp. 102–110.

Kamel, M., B. Hadfield, and M. Ismail. 1990. Fuzzy query processing using clustering techniques. *Information Processing & Management* 26, no. 2:279–293.

Kandel, Abraham. 1986. *Fuzzy mathematical techniques with applications*. Reading, Massachusetts: Addison-Wesley.

Kerre, Etienne E., Rembrand B.R.C. Zenner, and Rita M.M. De Caluwe. 1986. The use of fuzzy set theory in information retrieval and databases: A survey. *JASIS* 37, no. 5:341–345.

Korfhage, Robert R. 1984. *Discrete computational structures*, 2d ed. New York: Academic Press.

Lee, Joon Ho. 1994. Properties of extended Boolean models in information retrieval. In *Proceedings of the 17th Annual International ACM/SIGIR Conference on Research and Development in Information Retrieval,* Dublin, pp. 182–190.

Lee, Joon Ho, Myoung Ho Kim, and Yoon Hoon Lee. 1993. Ranking documents in thesaurus-based Boolean retrieval systems. *Information Processing & Management* 30, no. 1:79–91.

Lee, Joon Ho, Won Yong Kim, Myoung Ho Kim, and Yoon Joon Lee. 1993. On the evaluation of Boolean operators in the extended Boolean retrieval framework. In *Proceedings of the 16th Annual International ACM/SIGIR Conference on Research and Development in Information Retrieval,* Pittsburgh, pp. 291–297.

Lewis, David D. 1988. Natural language and information retrieval interfaces. Abstract in *Proceedings of the 51st ASIS Annual Meeting,* Atlanta, p. 216.

Losee, Robert M., Jr., and Abraham Bookstein. 1988. Integrating Boolean queries in conjunctive normal form with probabilistic retrieval models. *Information Processing & Management* 24, no. 3:315–321.

Lucarella, D. 1990. Uncertainty in information retrieval: An approach based on fuzzy sets. In *Proceedings of the Ninth Annual IEEE Conference on Computers and Communications,* Scottsdale, Arizona, pp. 809–814.

Lucarella, D., and R. Morara. 1991. FIRST: Fuzzy information retrieval system. *Journal of Information Systems* 17:81–91.

Macleod, Ian A. 1991. Text retrieval and the relational model. *JASIS* 42, no. 3:155–165.

Maron, M.E., and J.L. Kuhns. 1960. On relevance, probabilistic indexing and information retrieval. *Journal of ACM* 7, no. 3:216–244.

McLean, Stuart A. 1995. Reconsidering text retrieval: Accessing semi-structured text through an object-oriented query language. Ph.D. diss., University of Pittsburgh.

Salton, Gerard, Edward A. Fox, and Harry Wu. 1983. Extended Boolean information retrieval. *Communications of the ACM* 26, no. 11:1022–1036.

Smeaton, Alan F. 1989. Information retrieval and natural language processing. *Informatics* 10:1–14.

Swanson, Donald R. 1960. Searching natural language text by computer. *Science* 132, no. 3434:1099–1104.

Waller, W.G., and Donald H. Kraft. 1979. A mathematical model of a weighted Boolean retrieval system. *Information Processing & Management* 15, no. 5:235–245.

Wong, S.A. Michael, and A. Yao. 1989. A probability distribution model for information retrieval. *Information Processing & Management* 25:39–53.

Zadeh, Loft. 1988. Fuzzy logic. *Computer* 21, no. 4:83–93.

EXERCISES

1. Suppose that a user wishes to request information on four out of seven given terms. How many quadruples of terms does this involve? In other words, determine the length of the fully explicit query

(*A* AND *B* AND *C* AND *D*) OR (*A* AND *B* AND *C* AND *E*) OR. . . .

2. Determine those combinations of *A*, *B*, and *C* (for example, *A* present, *B* and *C* absent) that will be retrieved by each of the expressions *A* OR (*B* AND *C*) and (*A* OR *B*) AND *C*.

3. Show that the Boolean query (*A* AND *B*) OR (*A* AND *C*) is the DNF of the query *A* AND (*B* OR *C*) and hence is logically equivalent to it.

4. Show that the set retrieved by (*A* AND *B*) OR (*A* AND *C*) differs from the set retrieved by (*A* OR *B*) AND (*A* OR *C*).

5. Suppose that we have the sets

$$A = \{5, 7, 8, 11, 12, 20, 22, 23, 25, 26\},$$
$$B = \{1, 2, 3, 4, 6, 8, 13, 16, 18, 19, 22, 25\}, \quad \text{and}$$
$$C = \{1, 4, 5, 6, 8, 10, 11, 13, 15, 17, 18, 20, 21, 24, 28\}.$$

Using the absolute value of the difference as a measure of the distance between two numbers, compute the sets corresponding to the following expressions.

$(A_{0.4}$ OR $B_{0.2})$ AND NOT $C_{0.3}$

$A_{0.7}$ AND $(B_{0.3}$ OR $C_{0.6})$

$(A_{0.6}$ AND NOT $B_{0.4})_{0.5}$ OR $(C_{0.8}$ AND NOT $B_{0.6})_{0.2}$

6. Show that weights on A, B, and C can be chosen so that the two queries of Exercise 3, in weighted form, produce different results.

The Matching Process

Matching one term or phrase against another is the fundamental underlying process in information retrieval. However, the fact that a string in a document has been matched to a term in a query does not automatically mean that the document should be retrieved in response to the query. In the first place, the query probably contains more than one term, so the success or failure in matching each of the query terms must be considered. In the second place, the fact that a document contains a given term does not mean that the document is strongly related to the term. The term may merely have been mentioned in passing, or may be in the document in a context not appropriate to the query. As an extreme case, the term may be mentioned only in the context of denying its importance in the document, "This document is not about . . ." or, stated more positively, "The effect of . . . will only be considered in a subsequent paper." Finally, a document may match a query very well yet not be suitable for retrieval simply because of its age or because the user already knows about it.

This chapter focuses on evaluating a match between a document and a query. The basic premise of the chapter is that document D has tentatively been identified as relating to query Q. The problem is to determine whether the relationship is strong enough to warrant retrieving the document. In this chapter, only the *topicality* of the document—how well the topic of the document matches the topic of the query—is discussed. Integrating the user's knowledge, background, and preferences into the process is postponed until Chapter 6.

For this chapter, assume that the document consists only of text, although many of the ideas and remarks apply to documents in general. Images will be considered in Chapter 10.

4.1   RELEVANCE AND SIMILARITY MEASURES

The set of documents to be searched is organized in some specific manner: Without such organization, retrieval of more than a few documents from any set becomes prohibitively expensive. This organized set of documents is called a *document space.* Whether the document space contains queries and user profiles is, as discussed in Chapter 2, dependent on the document space model used and, to some extent, on personal taste.

In some models the structure of the query (or profile) largely precludes it from inclusion in the document space. This is the case, for example, in Boolean retrieval systems. Such systems cast the query in the form of a logical statement or expression, whereas the documents themselves are straight text. In this situation, retrieval can best be viewed as a mapping from the document space into the query space. Each document is mapped, or transformed, into a representation compatible with that of the query. The system then determines whether the transformed document meets the query requirements.

If the query cannot be included in the document space, another way to view it is as an evaluation function on the document space. In the simplest case, this is a *characteristic function,* that is, a function having the value 1 on documents relevant to the query and 0 on documents that are not relevant. In more complex models the function is a mapping into a range of values, such as the range from 0 to 1, denoted by [0,1], representing degrees of relevance to the query.

When the query and the document representations are similar, the query can be considered as a point in the document space. In such cases, the mental image is that of relevant documents being clustered near the query point ("near" may be interpreted either in terms of being close in distance or in terms of lying in a similar direction from the origin of the document space). The evaluation function defines a contour that separates the relevant documents from the irrelevant ones, or a series of contours corresponding, as they broaden, to documents of increasingly less relevance to the query.

Whatever mental model is used, to apply a computer to the task of retrieving documents in response to a query, the process must ultimately be reduced to an evaluation of each document on the basis of some computable function, or *measure.* The determination for each document is whether it is relevant to a given query, that is, whether it is an appropriate document to retrieve in response to the information need expressed in the query. As relevance is ultimately in the mind of the user, it is difficult to measure directly. Retrieval systems must rely primarily on measurements that can be made within the system on the basis of the document and query representations. At their cores, most retrieval systems equate relevance, in the form of topicality, with *lexical similarity.* It can be argued that even when the retrieval process is overlaid with sophisticated semantic and other artificial intelligence techniques, the basis must be lexical similarity, or the matching of words, since the text as it stands is fundamental to all relevance judgments.

Many different measures of similarity have been proposed (see Section 5.7). Many are calculated as values within some closed interval, say [0,1], with the interpretation that the high value in the interval (1) represents the greatest similarity and the low value (0) represents the least similarity. There is, however, no reason why the scale must be so chosen. A similarity scale can be chosen to be open-ended, or to have 0 as the measure of greatest similarity.

4.2   BOOLEAN-BASED MATCHING

Boolean retrieval systems arose when the technology included punched cards and edge-notched cards. With this technology, separating the documents containing a given term from those that do not is the most obvious methodology. This operation translates easily into the logic of Boolean retrieval. In such a system, the design of queries forces the viewpoint that they are not points in the document space. Each query is a logical function of given words; a document, in the conventional sense, is not so defined. As there is no structural similarity between document and query, the query is regarded as an entity apart, and retrieval with respect to a given query is regarded as a characteristic function defined on the document space.

Difficulties with Boolean retrieval systems were recognized shortly after they came into existence (Verhoeff, Goffman, and Belzer 1961). Lancaster (1972) wrote, "The use of Boolean algebra for querying computer-based retrieval systems may have been a mistake. . . ."

A purely Boolean retrieval system provides no basis for the development of significant similarity judgments. By definition, a given document either satisfies the Boolean query or it does not. Since the mapping defined by a query is a characteristic function, it divides the document space into two distinct sets: those documents that satisfy the query and those that do not.

Various modifications of Boolean query systems permit some finer grading of the set of retrieved documents. Consider, for example, the query *A* OR *B* OR *C*. This is satisfied by any document containing at least one of the three terms. Some of these documents will contain only one of the terms, while others will contain two or all three. Thus the retrieved set can be graded by how many of the three terms each document contains and even by the specific terms, thus separating the documents with the terms *A* and *B* but not *C* from those with the terms *A* and *C* but not *B*, and both of these sets from the documents that contain all three terms. If the system permits proximity judgments (see Section 4.8), then gradations of the retrieved set can be made on that basis. Since Boolean systems operate on the basis of the presence or absence of terms, many such systems do not include the term frequency data. Hence organization of the retrieved set on the basis of similarity measures depending on frequency cannot be done. However some visual interfaces for retrieval systems, including VIBE and InfoCrytsal, automatically provide full separation of the documents according to the specific Boolean criteria satisfied. These are discussed in Chapter 7.

4.3 VECTOR-BASED MATCHING: METRICS

As deficiencies in Boolean retrieval systems became apparent, alternative models of retrieval were developed. Among the earliest successful systems built on the vector model was the SMART system, originally developed at Harvard University (Lesk 1964; Salton 1964, 1971). Continued development of this system by Salton and his students at Cornell University has kept it a vital force in experimental information retrieval today.

When the vector model of retrieval is used, similarity measurements can be associated either with the idea of distance, following the philosophy that documents close together in the vector space are likely to be highly similar, or with an angular measure, based on the idea that documents "in the same direction" are closely related. The SMART system uses primarily an angular measure, to be discussed in the next section.

Metrics, or *distance measures*, are described more fully in Section 5.7, where several different metrics are defined. All metrics have the property that the measure of a document with respect to itself (its distance from itself) is 0. In this respect, metrics are not directly suitable as similarity measures in which high values represent closely similar documents. For this reason, some people refer to metrics as *dissimilarity* measures. However, a transformation can be applied to turn a metric into a measure for which high values represent high similarity. (Note that this is not needed if one is willing to accept 0 as a measure of maximum similarity.) A linear conversion from a metric to a similarity measure is generally not desirable. Suppose, for example, that the transformation of a metric, μ, into a similarity measure, σ, is defined by the equation $\sigma = k - \mu$, for some fixed value of k. Then when two documents are identical ($\mu = 0$) the similarity value is k. But no matter how k is chosen, σ becomes negative for documents at a distance greater than k from the query. This might be interpreted as indicating that documents with a positive similarity to the query are relevant and those with a negative similarity are not relevant. However, the measure then becomes dependent on the value of k chosen, and must be recomputed for different values of k.

It is better to choose an inversion transform that maps the distance into some fixed positive range of numbers, such as (0,1], that is, values greater than 0 and less than or equal to 1. A simple transform that does this is

$$\sigma = b^{-\mu}$$

for some fixed value of $b > 1$, such as $b = 2$ or $b = e$, the base of the natural logarithms. This transform provides a measure with a sharp peak at $\mu = 0$, gradually sloping away toward 0 as μ becomes larger (Figure 4.1a).

More complex transforms with different properties include

$$\sigma = b^{-\mu^2}$$

and

$$\sigma = b^{-P(\mu)},$$

where $P(\mu)$ is a monotone nondecreasing function of μ such that $P(0) = 0$ (Chavarria Garza and Korfhage 1982). (A *monotone nondecreasing function* f has the property that for any $x_2 > x_1$, $f(x_2) \geq f(x_1)$.) These transforms provide a measure that is flat at $\mu = 0$ and gradually decreases toward 0 as μ increases (Figure 4.1b).

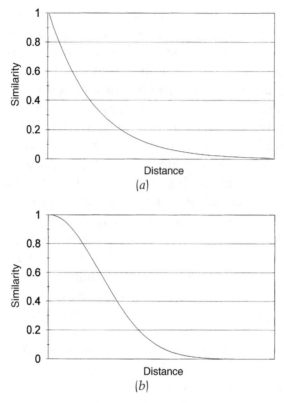

Figure 4.1   Similarity calculated from (a) distance, $\sigma = b^{-\mu}$, and (b) distance-squared, $\sigma = b^{-\mu^2}$.

4.4 VECTOR-BASED MATCHING: COSINE MEASURE

Another measure that is widely used is the *cosine measure* (van Rijsbergen 1979; Wilkinson and Hingston 1991). This is not a distance measure, but rather is developed from the cosine of the angle between the vectors representing the document and the query (or two documents, for document-to-document similarity). Its definition is

$$\sigma(D,Q) = \frac{\sum_k (t_k \times q_k)}{\sqrt{\sum_k (t_k)^2} \times \sqrt{\sum_k (q_k)^2}},$$

where t_k is the value of term k in the document and q_k is its value in the query. (In mathematical terms this is the *inner product* of the document and query vectors, normalized by their lengths.) A straightforward angular measure of similarity is like a metric in the sense that 0 represents the highest similarity. Using the cosine transforms the angular measure into a measure ranging from 1 for the highest similarity to 0 for the lowest.

The distance and angular measures represent two distinct approaches to the judgment of similarity. Distance measures are *intrinsic*, based solely on the group of documents under consideration. From a given point in the document space all directions are considered equal: Similarity depends only on how far a given document is from the point.

Angular measures, however, are *extrinsic*, representing a view of the document space from a fixed point, the *origin*. If this point were changed significantly (for example, if someone indexed the documents quite differently), the viewing point would change, and hence the angle between the document and the query might change significantly. In addition, an angular measure does not consider the distance of each document from the origin, but only the direction. Hence two documents that lie along the same vector from the origin will be judged identically, despite the fact that they may be far apart in the document space. This means that a one-paragraph announcement and an extensive, detailed paper about a topic might be judged to be equally relevant to a query. For example, suppose there are three documents, each described by the same two terms, with document vectors

$$D_1 = \text{<1, 3>},$$

$$D_2 = \text{<100, 300>}, \quad \text{and}$$

$$D_3 = \text{<3, 1>}.$$

By the cosine measure, $\sigma(D_1, D_2) = 1.0$ and $\sigma(D_1, D_3) = 0.6$. Using Euclidean distance, we see that $\mu(D_1, D_2) = 314.96$ and $\mu(D_1, D_3) = 2.83$ (to two decimal places). The cosine measure views D_2 as more similar to D_1 than is D_3; the distance measure reverses this assessment. It can be argued that in D_1 and D_2 the two terms have the same relative importance; that is, that the ratio of their values is the same. However, D_3 is much closer to D_1 than is D_2. Should the ratio or the distance be the significant measure? This is perhaps not a major problem in the simplest vector space model, where the only permissible values for a term are 0 and 1; but it can be significant when a full range of term weights is permitted.

The cosine measure (or any angular measure), in effect, projects the entire document space onto an n-dimensional sphere of fixed radius around the origin, where n is the dimensionality of the document space, usually related to the size of the vocabulary. This, however, eliminates any distinction between D_1, which is mildly "about" a set of terms, and D_2, which is much more strongly "about" the same terms. In practice, distance and angular measures seem to give results of similar quality. This may be because any distance-based cluster of documents under consideration is sufficiently far from the origin of the document space that the documents in the cluster all lie roughly in the same direction.

4.5 MISSING TERMS AND TERM RELATIONSHIPS

One problem with the vector space model arises when we consider missing terms. (Actually, this is a problem in all models but is perhaps more significant in this context.) By convention, the value 0 is assigned to any term that is missing in a query or a document description. But it may be that a term is missing from a document description because an indexer did not think it significant, rather than because it does not occur in the document. Similarly, a term may be missing from a query because the user did not think of it or because the user missed its significance, rather than because of an active decision by the user not to use the term. Thus the conventional 0 value is really used in two ways: to indicate terms that are truly missing and to indicate terms about which there is no information.

To be completely proper, the value for any term not specifically included in or excluded from the query should be left undefined. However, if this is done, a document (or query) is no longer a point in the vector model, but rather a very high dimensional subset of the space. Here is a very simple example. Suppose that two terms, A and B, are being used, and that the description of a document includes a value of 3 for term A. Conventionally, if B is not mentioned in the description, it is assigned a value 0, thus representing the document by <3, 0>. Suppose that a user presents a query consisting of term B with a weight of 4. Again, conventionally this is represented by <0, 4>. The document and query thus become two definite points with a clearly defined distance separating them—7 in the L_1 (city block) metric, 5 in the L_2 (Euclidean) metric, or 4 in the L_∞ (maximal direction) metric. (See Section 5.7 for definitions of specific metrics.) The cosine measure for this document and query has value 0, indicating that they are unrelated. However, given the view that nothing is known about the missing terms, the representations for the document and query become the lines <3, –> and <–, 4>, respectively (Figure 4.2). The distance between the document and the query becomes undefined, with the possibilities ranging from 0 (for the document/query <3, 4>) to extremely large values. The cosine measure is also undefined, with the full range of values possible. This model thus introduces an uncertainty about the distance or similarity of a document and a query, which should be considered in determining the set of retrieved documents. Assigning the value 0 to any terms that are not explicitly given nonzero values simplifies the mathematics greatly. At the same time, it reflects an assumption that if a relationship between two documents vis-à-vis a given term is not known, then there is none.

Another problem with the vector model arises from the relationships among the terms in a document or query. On the one hand, one of the major advantages of the vector model arises from the ability to bring to bear known results from vector algebra and vector calculus. Many of these results, however, are based on having a vector space defined from a *linearly independent* set of *basis vectors*. In the document context, this would mean defining a document by means of terms that have no relationships among themselves. On the other hand, the terms that *are* used to define the vector model for information retrieval are clearly not independent: a *digital computer*, for example, is much more common than a *digital canary*. There is a strong relationship between the words *digital* and *computer*. Some research has

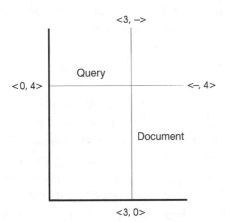

Figure 4.2   *Missing term effect.*

been done on defining a set of linearly independent basis vectors for the vector space model, but the results are not yet widely accepted (Wong and Ziarko 1985; Raghavan and Wong 1986; Wong et al. 1987). It is possible, of course, that there are enough sources of inaccuracies in the retrieval process that the failure to use independent terms has little or no effect on retrieval. In any case, few researchers even investigate the effect that this has on retrieval.

Finally, one should note that while the distance and angular measures are symmetrical with respect to query and document, in practice they are used asymmetrically. The user is interested in matching documents to queries, not queries to documents. As an extreme case, the user hopes that the encyclopedia contains the answer to the query, not that the query asks all possible questions that can be answered by the encyclopedia. The document in this situation is guaranteed to contain many terms that are missing from, and not relevant to, the query.

4.6   PROBABILISTIC MATCHING

One concern about both Boolean- and vector-based matching is that they are based on "hard" criteria. In Boolean-based matching, either a document meets the logical conditions or it does not; in vector-based matching, a similarity threshold is set, and either a document falls above that threshold or it does not. The ability to define various similarity measures and thresholds in the vector case softens the impact of the threshold value to some extent. However, a number of researchers, believing that even this does not adequately represent the uncertainties that abound in text retrieval, focus their attention on models that include uncertainties more directly. In this section, the more classical of these models, probabilistic matching, is discussed; in the following section, a more innovative model, fuzzy matching, is examined.

The basic tenet of *probabilistic matching* is that given a document and a query it should be possible to calculate the probability that the document is relevant to the query. The concept was first introduced by Maron and Kuhns (1960) and has more recently been explored by an increasing number of researchers (Robertson, Maron, and Cooper 1982; Bookstein 1983, 1985a, 1985b; Kwok 1984, 1985, 1989, 1990; Losee 1987; Fuhr 1989a, 1989b, 1992, 1995; Lee and Kantor 1991; Wong and Yao 1991; Cooper, Gey, and Dabney 1992; Cooper, Gey, and Chen 1993; Fuhr and Buckley 1993; Cooper 1994;

Gey 1994, 1995; Robertson and Walker 1994; Sebastiani 1994; Taghva, Borsack, and Condit 1994; Cooper, Chen, and Gey 1995; Crestani and van Rijsbergen 1995; Dumais 1995a; Rajashekar and Croft 1995).

Discussing probabilistic matching requires some notation and concepts from probability theory. The assumption is that at any given time a single query is being used. Thus all of the probabilities discussed are to be taken in the context of that query. It is also assumed, for purposes of discussion, that the number of documents within the database that are relevant to the query is known. If a document is selected at random from the database there is a certain probability that it will be relevant to the query. If the database contains N documents, n of which are relevant, then this probability is estimated by

$$P(rel) = \frac{n}{N} \, .$$

In accordance with probability theory, the probability that a document is not relevant to the query is then given by

$$P(\neg rel) = 1 - P(rel) = \frac{N - n}{N} \, .$$

Obviously documents are not picked at random, but rather chosen on the basis of how well they match the query—based on an analysis of the terms contained in both (and possibly other syntactic, semantic, and pragmatic cues). Thus the idea of relevance is related to the terms (from the query) occurring in the document.

In probability theory, the conditional probability of event A occurring given that event B has occurred is denoted by $P(A|B)$. Knowledge of B can affect the perception of the probability of A. For example, if a word is picked at random from some text, there is a certain probability that the word is *computer*. However, it seems reasonable that the word following *digital* has a substantially higher probability of being the word *computer* than the randomly chosen word. This perception can be checked by counting the relative number of occurrences of *computer* in the text, to estimate $P(computer)$, and the relative number of occurrences of *computer* immediately following the word *digital*, to estimate $P(computer|digital)$.

A given query divides the document collection into two sets—those that are selected in response to the query and those that are not. Not all of the documents selected are truly relevant. Therefore the probabilities that a document is relevant or not relevant, given that it has been selected, should be considered. These are defined by $P(rel|selected)$ and $P(\neg rel|selected)$. This specifically ignores the documents that have not been selected.

Suppose that a set S of documents within the database has been selected in response to a query. The question is whether this is the set that should have been selected in response to the query. One criterion might be to select the set if it is more probable that a document in the set is relevant than that it is not, that is,

$$P(rel|selected) > P(\neg rel|selected)$$

for any document in S.

Since the sum of these two probabilities is one, this implies that

$$P(rel|selected) > 0.5.$$

This leads to a *discriminant function* on the set,

$$dis(selected) = \frac{P(rel|selected)}{P(\neg rel|selected)}.$$

Retrieve the given set if and only if $dis(selected) > 1$ for every document in the set. This criterion can be modified by weighting the two probabilities. For example, if the probability of nonrelevance is given three times the weight of relevance, the balance point shifts to 0.75:

$$P(rel|selected) > 3\ P(\neg rel|selected),$$

$$P(rel|selected) > 3\ (1 - P(rel|selected)),$$

$$P(rel|selected) + 3\ P(rel|selected) > 3,$$

$$P(rel|selected) > 0.75.$$

The discrimination function criterion is then $dis(selected) > 3$.

Since judgment of a document depends on the terms it contains, these probabilities must be related to term occurrences within the documents. Bayes's theorem from probability theory allows us to "invert" conditional probabilities:

$$P(A|B) = \frac{P(B|A)P(A)}{P(B)}.$$

Applying that to the discriminant function yields

$$dis(selected) = \frac{P(rel|selected)}{P(\neg rel|selected)} = \frac{P(selected|rel)P(rel)}{P(selected|\neg rel)P(\neg rel)}.$$

The numerator of this fraction is the probability that a document is selected, given that it is relevant, multiplied by the probability that an arbitrary document from the collection is relevant. The denominator is a similar product, for nonrelevant documents. Observe that the last portion of this formula, $P(rel)/P(\neg rel)$, is constant for a given query and document database, independent of any particular document. Although this transformation may seem only to complicate matters, it permits a focus on which terms are likely to occur in relevant documents.

Assume that a document is represented by terms $t_1, \ldots, t_n$, and that these terms are statistically independent, that is, that an occurrence of one term does not depend on the occurrence of any other term. (This is not really the case—recall *digital* and *computer*—but it is extremely complicated to consider terms that are not statistically independent.) Under this assumption, the document probabilities can be represented as a product of the term probabilities:

$$P(selected|rel) = P(t_1|rel)P(t_2|rel) \ldots P(t_n|rel),$$

and similarly for $P(selected|\neg rel)$.

The discussion has thus arrived at the following point: If estimates for the probability of occurrence of various terms in relevant documents and in nonrelevant documents can be obtained, then the probabilities that a document will be retrieved, given that it is relevant, or that it is not, can be estimated. If there are also estimates for the probability that a document chosen at random is relevant or not, the discriminant function for a given set of documents can be computed, and the decision made whether to retrieve that set in response to a query.

Example 4.1 Suppose a given query and database, with the probability that any document in the database is relevant to the query being 0.1. Thus the constant factor in this situation is $P(rel)/P(\neg rel) = 0.1/0.9 = 0.111\ldots.$ Now consider a specific document, D. Suppose that this document is represented by four terms, and that the probabilities of these terms occurring in relevant or nonrelevant documents in this database is given by Table 4.1. Using this information, compute the discriminant function for D:

Table 4.1
Term Probabilities for Probabilistic Retrieval

Term	$P(t|rel)$	$P(t|\neg rel)$
t_1	0.8	0.4
t_2	0.6	0.1
t_3	0.2	0.9
t_4	0.9	0.6

$$dis(D) = \frac{0.8 \times 0.6 \times 0.2 \times 0.9 \times 0.1}{0.4 \times 0.1 \times 0.9 \times 0.6 \times 0.9} = \frac{0.00784}{0.01944} = 0.403.$$

Since this value is less than one, D should not be retrieved.

Obviously probabilistic retrieval involves much calculation and many assumptions. Numerous experiments demonstrate that probabilistic retrieval procedures yield good results. However, the results have not been sufficiently better than those obtained using Boolean or vector techniques to convince system developers to move heavily in this direction. It may be that the new context of full-text retrieval from heterogeneous databases available over the Internet is complex enough that probabilistic retrieval techniques will become better established in practice.

4.7   FUZZY MATCHING

The problem with probability matching is, of course, in estimating the probabilities. *Fuzzy matching* appears similar to probability matching but replaces the need to estimate probabilities by a need to estimate a sense of belief about a document being relevant. Thus the strict rules that govern the use of probabilities do not apply. The idea of a fuzzy query was introduced in Section 3.5. The natural counterpart, a fuzzy document, does not exist: Authors do not assign membership grades to the terms and concepts in their documents. However, a fuzzy judgment can be made about whether a document should be in the set matching the query. This is done on the basis of the set of terms describing the document or the terms used in the document. Recall that in probability matching the calculation ultimately devolved onto the probabilities that terms in the documents targeted as potentially relevant to a query are contained in relevant or nonrelevant documents. In fuzzy matching the calculation is based on defined membership grades for terms. The question becomes one of the degree of confidence that a document containing a given term is relevant. If this is used to define the membership grades, then—using the arithmetic of fuzzy sets—the membership grade with respect to the set of relevant documents can be computed for any document. This computation is simpler than that for probabilistic retrieval, since it involves simple functions of the membership grades for each document.

Different approaches can be taken to the concept of fuzziness. In considering semantically related terms, one might consider how well a related term matches a given term. For example, if the query is about *cocker spaniel*, a document containing the term *springer spaniel* does not match, but the two breeds of dog are related closely enough that the document may still contain useful information. Another document about dogs in general may also contain useful information but is perhaps less likely to do so. This depends, of course, on how specific the query is to cocker spaniels—a fuzzy judgment.

Another approach is to look for modifiers or descriptors that give some indication of the value of the information in a document. These descriptors may be either qualitative or quantitative (Kamel, Hadfield, and Ismail 1990). The qualitative descriptors include both numerical ones, such as *small*, *high*, and *tall*, and nonnumeric ones, such as *nice* and *colorful*. Fuzzy quantitative descriptors include words such as *few* and *most of*. The use of a term in a document may also be described in a fuzzy manner, such as *fairly important* or *very significant*, and the results of the retrieval described as *highly relevant* or *partially relevant*. The problem then becomes one of deciding how such terms translate into the membership functions associated with fuzzy retrieval. A fuzzy matching process can also be combined with other matching processes, such as a weighted Boolean approach (Bordogna and Pasi 1993).

4.8 PROXIMITY MATCHING

A much older and more widely used matching method involves the proximity of terms in a text. Two terms that are associated in a query may occur in unrelated roles in a document. This is particularly true in long documents such as books. Thus many retrieval systems permit the user to apply proximity criteria in the retrieval process. That is, the user may be able to specify that terms *A* and *B* occur within three words of each other, within the same sentence, or some similar criterion.

Proximity criteria have nothing directly to do with any of the various matching models that have been discussed, each of which is based solely on the occurrence or nonoccurrence of terms. It is possible to introduce concepts like the conditional probability that term *B* occurs given that term *A* has occurred, but these are generally based on simple co-occurrence, not on a proximity measure. Thus proximity criteria can be used independently of any other criteria. Frequently proximity measures are used as additional criteria to further refine the set of documents identified by one of the other matching methods.

Modifications of proximity criteria can increase their effectiveness. One such modification is to use *phrases* rather than simple word proximity. The incorporation of phrases into the similarity judgment process requires that a given set of words occur in a highly specific sequence. This focuses the search criteria more sharply but has the negative effect of discounting expressions that are equivalent to, but different from, the specified phrase. For example, if the phrase *information retrieval* is required, then a document referring to the *retrieval of information* will be rejected. A solution to this difficulty is to include standard proximity criteria but give added weight to documents having the specified phrase.

Another modification, less strict than the use of phrases, is the use of *ordered proximity* to aid in the retrieval decision. Very clearly, the order in which words occur affects their interpretation. One classic example with a clear distinction in interpretation is *junior college* versus *college junior.* Although ordered proximity will distinguish between these two phrases, selecting only documents with the desired interpretation, it will sometimes cause relevant documents to be missed: for example, in a document on a student in her *junior year in college* and in one on the *retrieval of information.* A decision to use either phrase or ordered proximity techniques depends on knowledge not generally available to a computer system and thus must be made by the user or a trained information professional.

Many systems that permit proximity judgments rely on a simple matching of the proximity criteria: Either a given criterion is matched or it is not. It is possible, however, to extend the use of proximity criteria by introducing a measure on the proximity. For example, when using simple proximity (no order of the words implied), the value of any proximity could be calculated on the basis of the number of intervening words. Thus *information retrieval* might rate highly, *retrieval of information* somewhat less highly, and *retrieval of stored documentary information* still lower. The variety of such measures that could be introduced is great; the value of any such measure needs to be tested for each retrieval system and database.

4.9 EFFECTS OF WEIGHTING

Not all terms are equally important in a query. Thus it is important to allow the user to indicate the relative importance of various terms by weighting them. *Weighting of terms* modifies the calculations upon which relevance judgments are made. However, the modification has only a slight impact on system efficiency. The more important impact of weighting is its effect on the entire set of retrieved documents. Changing weights on terms can change the membership in this set, sometimes causing a dramatic change in the size of the set. In the vector space model, for example, using term weights shifts the location of a document or query point. This changes both the distance and angular relationships to other documents in the space.

Weighting can also be applied at a broader level than individual terms. Suppose, for example, that a dinner party is being planned and the hostess has decided to use beef and broccoli (perhaps because they are in the refrigerator) as elements in the menu. Thus she is interested in retrieving documents (recipes) containing the terms *beef* and *broccoli*. She might also have some other possibilities in mind, such as *noodles, snow peas,* and *water chestnuts* to create a Chinese dish. However, since creating a Chinese dish is only of secondary importance she gives the terms *beef* and *broccoli* added weight. On top of that, she might decide to give added weight to any recipe that mentions both, or to any menu plan that contains both words. Her final query might then look like

(*beef* and *broccoli*): 5; (*beef* but not *broccoli*): 2; (*broccoli* but not *beef*): 2; *noodles*: 1; *snow peas*: 1, *water chestnuts*: 1,

where the numbers are the weights given to the terms. Thus a recipe or menu mentioning all five ingredients would receive a score of 8, while one that contained everything but broccoli would have a score of 5, and a recipe lacking both beef and broccoli but having the other ingredients would receive a score of 3. If these terms had also been assigned weights indicating their importance in each recipe, then those recipes most similar to the query would be relatively close to it in the vector model, and thus retrieved. In other models, the query weights could be used as multipliers on the document term weights. Requiring a minimum score of 4 would eliminate any recipe containing only noodles, snow peas, and water chestnuts, thus assuring that either beef or broccoli is included. Note, however, that this would also exclude a recipe containing beef and noodles but none of the other ingredients.

Weighting at this broader, multiterm level can add to the time required to respond to a query. However, the amount of added time should be small if the process is considered as one of successive filters: First isolate a set of documents based on the individual terms, then examine only this isolated set for term combinations, modifying the values assigned to the documents by the weights for combinations. Done in this way, the more complex calculations will be confined to a relatively small set of documents.

4.10   EFFECTS OF SCALING

The *scaling effect,* or impact of the size of the document collection, can be major. A substantial document collection can contain a thousand times as many documents as a test collection. In such a collection it will take roughly a thousand times as long to match each individual document against a query, and it will take much longer if the interest is in document-to-document matches. In a test collection that has K documents, there are $K(K - 1)/2$ document pairs to match; the expanded collection with $1000K$ documents will have $1000K(1000K - 1)/2$ document pairs, just under half a million times as many. The time needed to perform other operations such as sorting also grows rapidly with an increase in collection size. For this reason, a serious concern about any experimental technique is whether it will be feasible to apply it to real document collections. It thus becomes particularly important to organize the matching process to reduce the work involved as much as possible. Ideally, simple techniques should be used to extract from a large collection a relatively small set of candidate documents. More complex techniques can then be applied to refine that small set. The analogy to mining is an apt one—separate the ore from the earth by relatively simple and inexpensive means, then refine only the extracted ore using more expensive techniques.

There is, however, another effect of scaling that may not be so apparent. Large collections by their very nature tend to be more general than small collections. Thus the relative proportion of documents appropriate to a given query will likely be smaller. In addition, false drops—documents that appear to match the query but are not appropriate—become more likely. For example, if one is searching a computer and information science collection for papers on *object-oriented programming,* the likelihood of a false drop is small. But in a more general collection one might also retrieve documents about television programs that deal with objects. The user may thus be faced with searching a much more extensive collection that is likely to contain few, if any, additional relevant documents.

The term *information filtering* has been introduced to describe the process of reducing a large document collection to a reasonably sized set of potentially retrievable documents (Belkin and Croft 1992; Foltz and Dumais 1992; Morita and Shinoda 1994; Persin 1994; Dumais 1995b). Although filtering is closely related to retrieval, the goal is not to determine a specific set of documents to be retrieved. Rather, the goal is to produce a relatively small set containing a high proportion of relevant documents. Then, either more precise techniques can be applied to identify the relevant documents within this set, or the user can browse through the set to locate interesting documents. In either case the amount of effort required for the filtering can be significantly less than that required for retrieval directly from a very large document collection. For example, suppose that retrieval from a set of n documents requires n^2 steps and filtering requires only n steps, and that a collection contains 10,000 documents. Whereas straight retrieval from this set would require 100,000,000 steps, filtering down to a set of 1000 documents, followed by retrieval from that set, would require only $10,000 + 1000^2 = 1,010,000$ steps. (These numbers are completely artificial; for any given filtering and retrieval system, realistic values would be determined and substituted into this kind of calculation.)

4.11 DATA FUSION

As databases from multiple sources become more readily accessible, particularly over the World Wide Web, the importance of being able to effectively access all data sources has risen. The fact that no single retrieval technique will work equally well in all situations has led to *data fusion,* the study of techniques for merging the results of multiple search techniques on multiple databases to produce the best possible response to a query.

One problem in data fusion stems from a lack of standardization among databases. The structure, the available statistics, and the vocabulary may differ widely from one database to another. The first problem for the system designer is to develop a retrieval technique that can adapt to the style, format, and content of any database that might be searched. The second problem is to determine a method to fairly combine the search results arising from the different databases.

This development of a package of multiple search engines leads naturally to the use of the various search techniques even on a single database. If, say, Boolean, vector, and probabilistic techniques all produce reasonable but not perfect results, and if these results differ depending on the search engine used, why not employ all of the techniques, then merge the results? In doing so it becomes necessary to combine the scores that a given document obtains using each of the techniques into a final score that better approximates its true value in response to the query.

4.12   A USER-CENTERED VIEW

While it is relatively easy to match words and phrases between documents, or between a document and a query, relying on this as a basis for retrieval has not proven to be extremely successful. Each user has an individual vocabulary that may not match that of the author, editor, or indexer. As a result, retrieval systems commonly miss some documents that might have been informative to the user and retrieve others that the user does not find helpful. Some of the more sophisticated techniques discussed in later chapters attempt to correct this. Thus far, success has been mixed. Still lacking is a good way to describe the user's mental model—how he or she sees the information need—along with the methods to interpret this model and match the available documents to it automatically.

Several cognitive difficulties hinder development in this direction. It is common for authors to assume more subject familiarity than the typical user has. The user may have difficulty in describing the information need accurately. A feeling of "I'll know it when I see it" is at times the best description that a user can give of the desired documents. This does little to inform system design, except to suggest that an iterative retrieval method designed to capture and capitalize on any identification the user can make may be more effective than a design that blocks the user from direct interaction with the system.

REFERENCES

Belkin, Nicholas J., and W. Bruce Croft. 1992. Information filtering and information retrieval: Two sides of the same coin? *Communications of the ACM* 35, no. 12:29–38.

Bookstein, Abraham. 1983. Outline of a general probabilistic retrieval model. *Journal of Documentation* 39:63–72.

Bookstein, Abraham. 1985a. Implication of Boolean structure for probabilistic retrieval. In *Proceedings of the Eighth Annual International ACM/SIGIR Conference on Research and Development in Information Retrieval*, Montreal, pp. 11–17.

Bookstein, Abraham. 1985b. Probability and fuzzy set applications to information retrieval. *Annual Review of Information Science and Technology* 20:117–152.

Bordogna, Gloria, and Gabriella Pasi. 1993. A fuzzy linguistic approach generalizing Boolean information retrieval: A model and its evaluation. *JASIS* 44, no. 2:70–82.

Chavarria Garza, Hector, and Robert R. Korfhage. 1982. Retrieval improvement by interaction of queries and user profiles. In *Proceedings of COMPSAC '82, the Sixth International Conference on Computer Software and Applications*, Chicago, pp. 470–475.

Cooper, William S. 1994. The formalism of probability theory in IR: A foundation for an encumbrance? In *Proceedings of the 17th Annual International ACM/SIGIR Conference on Research and Development in Information Retrieval*, Dublin, pp. 242–247.

Cooper, William S., A. Chen, and Frederic C. Gey. 1995. Experiments in the probabilistic retrieval of full text documents. In *Overview of the Third Text REtrieval Conference (TREC-3)*, ed. Donna K. Harman. Washington, D.C.: NIST Special Publication 500–225, pp. 127–134.

Cooper, William S., Frederic C. Gey, and A. Chen. 1993. Probabilistic retrieval in the TIPSTER collections: An application of staged logistic regression. In *Overview of the First Text REtrieval Conference (TREC-1)*, ed. Donna K. Harman. Washington, D.C.: NIST Special Publication 500-207, pp. 73–88.

Cooper, William S., Frederic C. Gey, and Daniel P. Dabney. 1992. Probabilistic retrieval based on staged logistic regression. In *Proceedings of the 15th Annual International ACM/SIGIR Conference on Research and Development in Information Retrieval*, Copenhagen, pp. 198–210.

Crestani, F., and C.J. van Rijsbergen. 1995. Probability kinematics in information retrieval. In *Proceedings of the 18th Annual International ACM/SIGIR Conference on Research and Development in Information Retrieval*, Seattle, Washington, pp. 291–299.

Dumais, Susan T. 1995a. Latent semantic indexing (LSI): TREC-3 report. In *Overview of the Third Text REtrieval Conference (TREC-3)*, ed. Donna K. Harman. Washington, D.C.: NIST Special Publication 500-225, pp. 219–230.

Dumais, Susan T. 1995b. What you see is what you want: Combining evidence for effective information filtering. Poster abstract in *Proceedings of the 18th Annual International ACM/SIGIR Conference on Research and Development in Information Retrieval*, Seattle, Washington, p. 369.

Foltz, P.W., and Susan T. Dumais. 1992. Personalized information delivery: An analysis of information-filtering methods. *Communications of the ACM* 35, no. 12:51–60.

Fuhr, Norbert. 1989a. Models for retrieval with probabilistic indexing. *Information Processing & Management* 25:55–72.

Fuhr, Norbert. 1989b. Optimum polynomial retrieval functions based on the probability ranking principle. *ACM Transactions on Information Systems* 7, no. 3:183–204.

Fuhr, Norbert. 1992. Integration of probabilistic fact and text retrieval. In *Proceedings of the 15th Annual International ACM/SIGIR Conference on Research and Development in Information Retrieval*, Copenhagen, pp. 211–222.

Fuhr, Norbert. 1995. Probabilistic datalog—A logic for powerful retrieval methods. In *Proceedings of the 18th Annual International ACM/SIGIR Conference on Research and Development in Information Retrieval*, Seattle, Washington, pp. 282–290.

Fuhr, Norbert, and Chris Buckley. 1993. Optimizing document indexing and search term weighting based on probabilistic models. In *Overview of the First Text REtrieval Conference (TREC-1)*, ed. Donna K. Harman. Washington, D.C.: NIST Special Publication 500-207, 89–100.

Gey, Frederic C. 1994. Inferring probability of relevance using the method of logistic regression. In *Proceedings of the 17th Annual International ACM/SIGIR Conference on Research and Development in Information Retrieval*, Dublin, pp. 222–231.

Gey, Frederic C. 1995. Evaluation of probabilistic retrieval methods. Poster abstract in *Proceedings of the 18th Annual International ACM/SIGIR Conference on Research and Development in Information Retrieval*, Seattle, Washington, p. 370.

Kamel, M., B. Hadfield, and M. Ismail. 1990. Fuzzy query processing using clustering techniques. *Information Processing & Management* 26:279–293.

Kwok, K.L. 1984. A document-document similarity measure based on cited titles and probability theory, and its application to relevance feedback retrieval. In *Research and Development in Information Retrieval: Proceedings of the Third Joint British Computer Society/ACM Symposium*, Cambridge, England, pp. 221–231.

Kwok, K.L. 1985. Experiments with cited titles for automatic document indexing and similarity measure in a probabilistic context. In *Proceedings of the Eighth Annual International ACM/SIGIR Conference on Research and Development in Information Retrieval*, Montreal, pp. 165–178.

Kwok, K.L. 1989. A neural network for probabilistic information retrieval. In *Proceedings of the 12th Annual International ACM/SIGIR Conference on Research and Development in Information Retrieval*, Cambridge, Massachusetts, pp. 21–30.

Kwok, K.L. 1990. Experiments with a component theory of probabilistic information retrieval based on single terms as document components. *ACM Transactions on Information Systems* 8:363–386.

Lancaster, F. Wilfrid. 1972. Evaluation of on-line searching in Medlars (AIM-TWX) by biomedical practitioners. Report No. 101. Graduate School of Library Science, University of Illinois, Urbana, Illinois.

Lee, Jung Jin, and Paul Kantor. 1991. A study of probabilistic information retrieval systems in the case of inconsistent expert judgments. *JASIS* 42, no. 3:166–172.

Lesk, Michael E. 1964. The SMART automatic text processing and document retrieval system. Report ISR-8, sec. II. Harvard Computation Laboratory, Cambridge, Massachusetts.

Losee, Robert M., Jr. 1987. Probabilistic retrieval and coordination level matching. *JASIS* 38, no. 4:239–244.

Maron, M.E., and J.L. Kuhns. 1960. On relevance, probabilistic indexing and information retrieval. *Journal of ACM* 7, no. 3:216–244.

Morita, Masahiro, and Yoichi Shinoda. 1994. Information filtering based on user behaviour analysis and best match text retrieval. In *Proceedings of the 17th Annual International ACM/SIGIR Conference on Research and Development in Information Retrieval*, Dublin, pp. 272–281.

Persin, Michael. 1994. Document filtering for fast ranking. In *Proceedings of the 17th Annual International ACM/SIGIR Conference on Research and Development in Information Retrieval*, Dublin, pp. 339–348.

Raghavan, Vijay V., and S.K.M. Wong. 1986. A critical analysis of vector space model for information retrieval. *JASIS* 37, no. 5:279–287.

Rajashekar, T.B., and W. Bruce Croft. 1995. Combining automatic and manual index representations in probabilistic retrieval. *JASIS* 46, no. 4:272–283.

Robertson, Stephen E., M.E. Maron, and William S. Cooper. 1982. Probability of relevance: A unification of two competing models for document retrieval. *Information Technology: Research and Development* 1, no. 1:121.

Robertson, Stephen E., and S. Walker. 1994. Some simple effective approximations to the 2-Poisson model for probabilistic weighted retrieval. In *Proceedings of the 17th Annual International ACM/SIGIR Conference on Research and Development in Information Retrieval*, Dublin, pp. 232–241.

Salton, Gerard. 1964. A flexible automatic system for the organization, storage, and retrieval of language data (SMART). Report ISR-5, sec. I. Harvard Computation Laboratory, Cambridge, Massachusetts.

Salton, Gerard, ed. 1971. *The SMART retrieval system—Experiments in automatic document processing.* Englewood Cliffs, New Jersey: Prentice-Hall.

Sebastiani, Fabrizio. 1994. A probabilistic terminological logic for modelling information retrieval. In *Proceedings of the 17th Annual International ACM/SIGIR Conference on Research and Development in Information Retrieval*, Dublin, pp. 122–130.

Taghva, Kazem, Julie Borsack, and Allen Condit. 1994. Results of applying probabilistic IR to OCR text. In *Proceedings of the 17th Annual Inter-*

national *ACM/SIGIR Conference on Research and Development in Information Retrieval*, Dublin, pp. 202–211.

van Rijsbergen, C.J. 1979. *Information retrieval*, 2d ed. London: Butterworths.

Verhoeff, J., William Goffman, and Jack Belzer. 1961. Inefficiency of the use of Boolean functions for information retrieval systems. *Communications of the ACM* 4:557–558, 594.

Wilkinson, Ross, and Philip Hingston. 1991. Using the cosine measure in a neural network for document retrieval. In *Proceedings of the 14th Annual International ACM/SIGIR Conference on Research and Development in Information Retrieval*, Chicago, pp. 202–210.

Wong, S.K.M., and Y.Y. Yao. 1991. A probabilistic inference model for information retrieval. *Information Systems*, 16, no. 3:301–321.

Wong, S.K.M., and W. Ziarko. 1985. On generalized vector space model in information retrieval. *Annals of the Society of Mathematics of Poland, Series IV: Fundamentals of Information* 8, no. 2:253–267.

Wong, S.K.M., W. Ziarko, Vijay V. Raghavan, and P.C.N. Wong. 1987. On modeling of information retrieval concepts in vector spaces. *ACM Transactions on Database Systems* 12, no. 2:299–321.

EXERCISES

1. Determine the slope at $x = 0$ of the function

$$f(x) = b^{-x^n}$$

   for $n = 1, 2, 3, \ldots$ (Any $b > 1$ will do.)

2. Investigate the behavior of each of the following functions for $x \geq 0$. In particular, determine whether the functions are monotone and for which values of x they have slope zero.

$$b^{-(x^2 + x^4 + x^6)}$$

$$b^{-(x^2 + 4x^4 + 4x^6)}$$

$$b^{-(x^2 + x^4 + 0.25x^6)}$$

$$b^{-(x^3 + 0.5x^2 - 4x + 3)}$$

$$b^{-(2x^3 + x^2 + 2x - 4)}$$

3. One model of a similarity function includes a "terraced" effect, with the value dropping off rather sharply at several points. In this

model, each drop-off then indicates a clear difference in the similarity values for documents on one side of the drop-off as compared with those on the other side. On the basis of your investigation for Exercise 2, suggest a technique for defining such a similarity function with drop-offs at prespecified points k_1, k_2, k_3, ... Is there any way to control the heights of the drop-offs?

4. In the recipe example in Section 4.9, using the given weights a recipe containing beef, noodles, and snow peas would be retrieved but a recipe containing only beef and none of the other listed ingredients would be missed. Determine a set of weights and a minimum score that will retrieve *any* recipe that contains either beef or broccoli, while giving an enhanced score to recipes mentioning both of these or any of the other listed ingredients.

CHAPTER 5

Text Analysis

Most textual databases do not permit inclusion of the full document text. Even when full text is permitted, the inclusion of only the raw text in the database generally results in inefficient operation due to the need to access the text linearly. One key to efficient retrieval of documents is the creation of a set of document surrogates, to be used either in place of or in conjunction with the original documents. This chapter examines the problems of creating surrogates for textual documents, leaving aside the problems of creating surrogates for images and sound. The creation of a document surrogate requires analysis of the original document. This might be as simple as identifying the author and title or as complex as a thorough linguistic analysis of the document contents.

5.1 INDEXING

One major product of document analysis is an *index* into the database, permitting more efficient access to individual documents or document subsets. When writing a book or other large document, the author frequently creates an index. The index contains selected terms, with the principal locations where these terms occur. In addition, special indexes may be used that locate occurrences of figures, theorems in a mathematics text, plant names in a gardening book, author citations, and so forth. Thus the retrieval system has these readily available, particularly if one is using the full document text. However, such an index is idiosyncratic and may vary in quality from minimal to excellent. When many documents are collected in a database, the variation in indexing quality is detrimental to efficient and effective retrieval.

While many nonfiction books have indexes, shorter documents such as research reports and journal papers are rarely indexed. Furthermore, indexes rarely exist for a large body of literature, including virtually all fiction, drama, and poetry. Thus, whatever documents are included in a textual database, there is often a need for the information system designer or manager to create an index.

An index is constructed on the basis of an *indexing language,* or *vocabulary,* consisting of a set of index terms. These terms may be single words, longer phrases, or both. For consistency throughout a database, decisions on the characteristics of the indexing language should be made before any index terms are assigned.

Indexing, the act of assigning index terms to a document, may be carried out either manually or automatically. In either situation the indexing language may be *controlled,* that is, limited to a predefined set of index terms, or *uncontrolled,* allowing use of any term that fits some broad criteria. One source of problems with author-developed indexes is that the process is generally manual, with an uncontrolled vocabulary and no predefined inclusion rules. There is no reason to expect consistency of indexing done in this manner across a document collection.

Indexing has three primary purposes in information retrieval:

- to permit easy location of documents by topic,
- to define topic areas, and hence relate one document to another, and
- to predict relevance of a given document to a specified information need.

Any index created for retrieval purposes must be judged by how well it fulfills these three purposes.

Manual indexing involves some intellectual effort to identify and describe the content of a document. For manual indexing, an uncontrolled indexing language is generally used. This permits the indexer more flexibility in document description but presents some problems for an automatic retrieval system, even when the indexing is done by trained indexers. One problem is a *lack of consistency*. Creation of indexes for documents in a large collection is a major undertaking, generally requiring the use of several indexers. Even among professional indexers there is a lack of consistency. Various studies have established that different indexers will not always assign the same index terms to a given document. In fact, the agreement in index term assignment may be as little as 20%. Even a single indexer finds it difficult to maintain consistency over a period of time (Jacoby and Slamecka 1962; Cooper 1969; Salton 1969; Preschel 1972; Borko 1979).

Two characteristics of an indexing language are its exhaustivity and specificity. *Exhaustivity* refers to the breadth of coverage of the index terms—the extent to which all topics and concepts met in a document set are covered. *Specificity* refers to the depth of coverage—the extent to which specific topic ideas are indexed in detail. An indexing language that permits only reference to the topic *dogs* is less specific than one that permits reference to individual breeds of dogs, whereas an indexing language that permits reference to various breeds of dogs but does not include all breeds is more specific but less exhaustive. Manual indexing is likely to produce varying levels of exhaustivity and specificity in the document surrogates as different indexers are employed, or even as an individual indexer works through the collection. In addition, an indexer brings his or her own perspectives to a document collection and may bias the index accordingly. For example, one cookbook indexer may deem it sufficient to create an index category *meats* and include all types of meats under that term. Another may feel that it is correct to break this group of foods down into *meats, poultry,* and *fish,* including under *meats* only those products derived from nonflying land animals.

The imposition of a controlled vocabulary alleviates this problem to some extent, but at the cost of introducing another problem. If the indexer is restricted to a controlled vocabulary, he or she may find it difficult to represent the document content accurately. This is particularly true in a rapidly evolving field, where new terms are continually introduced into the written documents and the meanings of terms become modified over time. To introduce a new term into a controlled vocabulary requires a decision on the part of the person or persons controlling the vocabulary. Such a decision, however, cannot be made until the proposed new term becomes rather widely used. By that time a number of documents containing the term will have been indexed without using it.

Another problem, particularly with manual indexing, is *indexer-user mismatch.* Both common experience and experimental evidence show that the user and the indexer are likely to represent the same concept by quite different terms (Weinberg 1987). It is not clear that the terms used by the indexer to describe a document will match those used in a query that should retrieve that document. A controlled vocabulary may do little to solve this problem. While it forces both indexer and user to adhere to a common set of terms, it does not guarantee that the indexer and user will choose the same terms from the controlled list at all times. In fact, the more tightly controlled the vocabulary is, the more likely it is that indexer and user will choose the same terms—but the more difficulty they may have in finding terms that properly describe the documents. This imposes on the user the intellectual task, for example, of accepting both a symphony orchestra and rock band as similar *musical groups.*

Manual indexing rules developed by publishers and others impose some degree of control on the indexing language, even when the specific terms are left open and flexible. Many manual indexing languages are *precoordinated.* That is, subsets of terms are identified, each represented in the indexing language by a single term. For example, an indexing language that is not highly specific might require that *coal, gas, oil,* and *peat* all be represented by the single term *fuel.*

Manual indexing rules frequently specify the form that an index entry can take. The rules may require, for example, that the term *digital computer* be used in the form *computer, digital* in the index to a document. (Although this serves to emphasize the noun, is this really the best way to list the term, from the user's viewpoint?) The person seeking information who is unfamiliar with such rules may have difficulty in locating a relevant document thus indexed.

The concepts of *links* and *roles* are sometimes used to characterize the occurrence of terms in an indexing language. Two terms are *linked* if they occur together (for example, *digital* and *computer*) or if there is some semantic relationship between them. A term in an index may occur in one or more *roles,* indicating its function or usage. A *shovel,* for example, may play the role of an object being described or the role of an agent used to carry out a certain task. In a garden book index, the name of a flower may refer to a botanical description of the flower or to its use in a garden or flower arrangement.

Prepositional phrases may identify the roles that a given word assumes. Similarly, conjunctions can be used to form explicit links between terms.

Cross-referencing is used to enhance the usability of an indexing language. By this technique, reference to one index term automatically produces references to related terms. The most common cross-referencing types are

- *See* references, which point to the standard (controlled) vocabulary entry. For example, "coal, *see* fuel."
- *See also,* or *related term (RT),* references, which point to related entries. For example, "microcomputer, *see also* personal computer (PC)."
- *Broader term (BT)* references, which refer to more generic terms. For example, "poodle, *BT* dog."
- *Narrower term (NT)* references, which refer to more specific terms. For example, "dog, *NT* poodle, cocker spaniel, pointer."

In automatic indexing, an algorithm is used to decide which index terms shall be used to represent a document. The index is thus free from the bias that a manual indexer might introduce. It includes, however, whatever bias the system programmer built into the algorithm. Almost all automatic indexing algorithms are based in some way on the frequency of occurrence of words within a document. The guiding principles are

- The set of words can be divided into two subsets—words that occur largely for grammatical and relational reasons, and words that are *content-bearing.*
- Among the content-bearing words, the more frequently a word occurs within a document, the more likely it is to be of importance in that document.
- A word can be used to distinguish a document whenever its occurrence in that document differs significantly from its average occurrence throughout the document collection.

In practical terms it appears likely that automatic indexing will play an ever-increasing role in the development of textual and multimedia databases due to the volume of work involved. This does not, however, settle the issue of a controlled vocabulary versus an uncontrolled one, which is still subject to much debate (Rowley 1994).

Recent trends in indexing research have followed two distinct paths. One is the idea of developing indexes on the basis of a deeper linguistic knowledge of the document than is obtained from word frequency counts. Some of these approaches focus on the syntactic structure of the document (Smeaton, O'Donnel, and Kelledy 1995). Others develop indexes on the basis of the semantics and concepts within a document collection (Bartell, Cottreel, and Belew 1992; Hersh, Hickam, and Leone 1992; Di Nubila et al. 1994; Hull 1994; Collantes 1995). One such effort, DR-LINK, uses both syntactic and content analysis to produce a list of the proper names, common terms and phrases, and other distinguishing characteristics that can serve to identify and index the document (Liddy and Myaeng 1993). Still other research efforts try to apply inferencing techniques to develop an index (Tzeras and Hartmann 1993).

A major use of the index is to create an *inverted file* of documents. Suppose that the user wishes to find documents containing a given term, such as *Napoleon*. Without an index, the system must examine each document to determine whether it contains that term. However, once an index has been developed, the document collection can be represented by an inverted file that lists the documents containing each term rather than the terms contained in each document. Thus there would be one entry in the inverted file for the word *Napoleon*. This entry would consist of identifiers for each document containing that term. Retrieval is then a simple matter of using this line to identify and retrieve the desired documents. The work of matching terms to documents must still be done, but it is done once, before any queries are presented, and the results are used for all queries.

5.2   MATRIX REPRESENTATIONS

There is a "many-to-many" relationship between terms and documents: Each term occurs in many documents and each document contains many terms. Three matrices are used to clarify this relationship. A *matrix* is a rectangular array of cells holding information. A *term-document matrix*, A, is a matrix whose rows represent vocabulary terms and whose columns represent documents. The value in cell A_{ij} is 0 if the ith term does not occur in the *j*th document. If the term does occur in the document, then the value may be either 1, indicating simply that the term occurs, or a count of the number of occurrences.

A *term-term matrix, T,* is a square matrix whose rows and columns each represent the vocabulary terms. For this matrix, a nonzero value in cell T_{ij} means that the *i*th and *j*th terms occur together in some document or have some other defined relationship. Similarly to the term-document matrix, the nonzero value can be either 1, simply representing co-occurrence, or a count of the number of documents which contain both terms.

A *document-document matrix, D,* is a matrix whose rows and columns represent documents. In this matrix, a nonzero value in cell D_{ij} would indicate that the documents have some terms in common or have some other defined relationship, such as an author in common.

The idea behind each of these matrices is to identify and quantify a relationship between the entities represented as rows and those represented as columns. However, the matrices cannot be used directly due to their size. For example, suppose that a library has a collection of 3,000,000 documents with a total vocabulary of 50,000 terms. The document-document matrix then has 9×10^{12} cells, the term-document matrix 15×10^{10} cells, and the term-term matrix 25×10^8 cells. Fortunately, these matrices are *sparse*—that is, most of the cells contain zeroes. To avoid storing and processing the empty cells, other representations equivalent to the matrices are used. For example, the term-document matrix is replaced by a list of terms, each of which has its own attached list of documents that contain that term. If only the presence or absence of a term in a document is of interest, the document identifiers are sufficient. If, however, the frequency of a term in a document is important, then the list entries are pairs consisting of a document identifier and the term frequency in that document (or some function computed from the term frequency). This greatly speeds up processing and causes no difficulties unless one wishes to perform matrix arithmetic, which is little used in information retrieval work.

5.3   TERM EXTRACTION AND ANALYSIS

One characteristic of a language is that its basic units occur with different frequencies. This is true whether one considers the basic units (in English) to be letters, letter combinations, words, or word phrases. (Sentences and larger units are sufficiently complex that they each essentially occur with a frequency of 1.) This frequency variation is one basis for selection of words and phrases as automatic indexing terms. Numerous studies of documents show that if the words in a text are ranked in order of decreasing frequency, they follow a relationship known as *Zipf's law* (Zipf 1949):

$$\text{rank} \times \text{frequency} \approx \text{constant}.$$

This law is, of course, only approximate for any given document or document collection. The law implies that the frequency of words in a text falls off very rapidly for the most frequently occurring words, then more and more gradually as words occur more rarely. If the law were to hold strictly (which it does not), the second most frequent word would occur only half as often as the most frequent one, and the tenth most frequent word would occur only one-tenth as often as the most frequent one.

The most frequently occurring words are those included by grammatical necessity, such as *the, of, and,* and *a.* This type of word so dominates text that it has been estimated that up to half of any given text is made up of approximately 250 distinct words (Watters 1992). Such words are generally considered poor index terms for two reasons. First, they occur so frequently that almost every document contains many of them. (Think of a document that does not have any of the four example words.) Second, the words generally have little or no specific relationship to the ideas in a paper or book.

The words at the other end of the frequency scale, which may occur only once or twice within a document collection, also tend to be considered poor index terms. The problem in this case is not in the significance of the words, since they often relate strongly to the ideas in a paper. The problem, rather, is that since they occur so infrequently, very few documents will be retrieved when indexed by these terms. In fact, if several such terms are used together then it is almost certain that no documents will be found containing all of them.

These two observations suggest that two thresholds be established for defining index terms. The high-frequency terms are not desirable because they are so common, so an upper threshold on frequency should be established. The rare words are not desirable because of their inability to retrieve many documents, so a lower threshold should also be set. Only terms whose frequency of occurrence in a document collection falls between the two limits should be considered as candidates for index terms.

We make two observations about Zipf's law. First, the most common words have little specific relationship to the content (topic) of documents within a given collection. Hence one should expect their frequency of occurrence to depend only on the size of a document collection and not on its specific orientation or topic. Second, there will likely be a large number of words that occur only once, twice, or three times within a document collection. In terms of Zipf's law, these will be words of high rank. Clearly the law breaks down for such terms, which requires that 100 words that each occur only once have 100 different ranks. Thus Zipf's law should be used only as a general guideline.

Zipf's law is sometimes lightly used to support such statements as "the most frequent 20% of the text words account for 70% of term usage." Careful analysis shows that this may not be so. Consider three cases:

1. $f = kr^{-1}$. This is the "pure" Zipf's law, where f, r, and k denote the frequency, rank, and a constant, respectively. The total collection frequency is approximately the area under this curve. (Here we are approximating a discrete distribution by a continuous one.) The area under the curve, which can be determined by integration, will be found to be infinite! Hence no finite portion of the area is "70% of term occurrences." The most frequently used 20% of the terms may account for many term occurrences, but not 70% of them.

2. $f = kr^{-(1-\epsilon)}$, where $\epsilon > 0$. In this case, no matter how small ϵ is, the area is still infinite, and no finite portion of the terms accounts for "70% of term occurrences."

3. $f = kr^{-(1+\epsilon)}$, where $\epsilon > 0$. In this case, no matter how small ϵ is, the area is finite. Hence a claim such as that made above can be true.

Because of the sensitivity of Zipf's law to the value of ϵ, it is unwise to base any system decision on statements relating to the proportion of term occurrences carried by certain terms.

5.4 TERM ASSOCIATION

One of the aspects that must be considered in developing an indexing language is the association that words may have with one another. If certain word pairs and phrases occur sufficiently often, then they should probably be included in the indexing vocabulary.

This association is expanded with the concept of word proximity, at some risk of improperly associating words. Consider the sentence "The felon's information assured retrieval of the money." Here the words *information* and *retrieval* are used in the same sentence but not in the sense of *information retrieval*. Within a longer document such as a full paper or a book, it is entirely reasonable to expect the co-occurrence of words where they have nothing to do with each other. On the other hand, the phrase *retrieval of information* should be flagged when the search term is *information retrieval*. Hence many retrieval systems include a measure of word proximity. These measures may depend on a given number of intervening words, on the words appearing in the same sentence, or on some other criterion. The word order is sometimes included along with proximity measures. Whatever the measure, it is not foolproof. Punctuation is also significant in term association: "Based on the felon's information, retrieval of the body was easy."

One must also consider the association of words with document collections. Words (and phrases) that are significant in one document collection may not be important in a different collection. The term *digital computer* might be considered significant in a medical literature collection or a music literature collection, but in a computer science collection it would probably occur too frequently to be a good index term. Similarly, in a philosophy collection the term *digital computer* might be very rare, and hence rejected as a potential index term.

5.5 LEXICAL MEASURES OF TERM SIGNIFICANCE

Development of an indexing language begins with analysis of the words and phrases occurring in a document collection. This analysis relies largely on frequency-based methods. These begin with the raw frequency counts of words in documents. It is good practice when using these methods to keep the frequency counts by document. From these individual frequency counts one can develop frequency counts over the entire document collection and at the same time have the individual counts for use in the various techniques that can be applied. For more detailed work, it may even be reasonable to keep the counts by document section or paragraph. *Text tiling* (Hearst and Plaunt 1993; Hearst 1995) is one retrieval technique that makes use of this finer analysis of documents.

It is convenient to think of the data as arranged in an *array* matching terms against documents. Considering each row of the array to represent a term and each column a document, the entry in row i and column j represents the frequency of term i in document j. This is the term-document matrix previously defined. Although this is a convenient model, it cannot be practically represented directly in a computer because of the sparsity of the matrix; instead, a data structure that carries the term-document relationship information in a more compact form, based on a term list, is used.

Observe that although the frequencies of word phrases cannot be determined directly from the word frequency counts, they are clearly related to the frequencies of individual words. Suppose that there is a two-word phrase, *AB*. If f represents the frequency count, we know that

$$f(AB) \leq \min(f(A), f(B)),$$

that is, that the phrase *AB* cannot occur more frequently than the rarer of A and B. Furthermore, the phrase *AB* can occur only in those documents that contain both of these words. This knowledge simplifies the hunt for the phrase *AB* and may rule it out as a potential index term simply because of the low bound on its frequency. The data in the term-document matrix provides a better, but still inaccurate, approximation to $f(AB)$. Consider position j in rows A and B of the matrix. Document j contains both of these words if and only if the elements in positions $<j, A>$ and $<j, B>$ are both positive. In that case the maximum possible number of occurrences of the phrase *AB* in this particular document is the smaller of the two frequency counts. An upper bound on the frequency of the phrase *AB* in the document collection is obtained by summing these estimates.

Use of *absolute term frequency* (the raw counts) can be very misleading, primarily because documents and document collections both vary in size. It is reasonable to expect that a given term is likely to occur more frequently in a long document within a collection than in a short one in the same collection. At the same time, it is not reasonable to expect the frequency of a given term to be roughly the same in all documents of a given length, since it may be a common term for documents in one collection and a rare one for documents in another collection.

Thus *relative term frequency*, that is, term frequency counts that have been adjusted to take into account the document and collection sizes and characteristics, is often used in retrieval computations. There are several ways to make this adjustment. The simplest method of defining relative term frequency is to divide the raw frequency count for each document by the length of the document. While this normalizes the frequency for document length, it does not take into account anything beyond the single document: The characteristics of the document collection do not influence this number. Frequency counts over an entire document collection can be adjusted either by dividing the total frequency count of a term by the total number of words in the documents of the collection or by dividing the number of documents containing a term by the total number of documents in the collection. These two methods naturally yield different numbers; the choice of method depends on the intended use of the relative frequencies.

Inverse Document Frequency Weight

Since the objective of determining term frequencies is to determine likely index terms, it is important to view the frequencies in the context of a specific document collection. One fundamental way of doing this is to use the *inverse document frequency weight*. In this method, the frequency of occurrence of a term in a document is weighted by the number of documents in the collection that contain the term. If the term occurs in many of the documents in the collection, then it does not serve well as a document identifier and should be given a low weight as a potential index term. Calculation begins with the definition of four variables:

N: the number of documents in the collection,

d_k: the number of documents containing the term k,

f_{ik}: the absolute frequency of term k in document i, and

w_{ik}: the weight of term k in document i.

Assume that $d_k \neq 0$—that is, that term k occurs in at least one document. With this assumption, define the inverse document frequency (idf) to be

$$\log_2(N/d_k) + 1 = \log_2 N - \log_2 d_k + 1.$$

The ratio d_k/N is the fraction of documents in the collection that contain the term. Note that the idf measure decreases as d_k increases, from $\log_2 N + 1$ for $d_k = 1$, to 1 for $d_k = N$. The inverse document frequency weight, tf.idf, of term k in document i is defined by multiplying the term frequency by the inverse document frequency:

$$w_{ik} = f_{ik}[\log_2 N - \log_2 d_k + 1].$$

Thus the weight of a term in a document is its frequency multiplied by a factor that depends logarithmically on the proportion of the documents in the collection that contain the term. The importance (weight) of a term in a document increases with the frequency of the term in the document and decreases with the number of documents containing the term. Note that the formula uses the logarithm of the ratio N/d_k rather than the ratio itself. This moderates the effect of increasing the collection size: Doubling the size of the collection only adds one to the value of the inverse document frequency. It is generally felt that this produces a reasonably accurate measure of the effect of collection size changes.

Signal-to-Noise Ratio

A different measure of the value of a term for indexing and retrieval is based on information theory. Information theory was developed by Claude Shannon (1948) with the motivation of providing a theoretical foundation for work on the transmission of signals or messages. The basis of the theory is the definition of the *information content* of a given signal or (for text) sequence of words. In the sense that Shannon used the word, *information* has nothing to do with meaning but refers instead to the unexpectedness of a message. Suppose that there is a set of n events (messages) and that message i has probability p_i of occurring, $i = 1, \ldots, n$. From probability theory, the n probabilities are all nonnegative, and they total to 1. The goal is to measure the information content, $H(p_1, \ldots, p_n)$, of the choice of a message from this set of messages. In the simplest case, the messages are single words and the value p_i is the probability that the ith word is chosen from the set of words being considered. Common words such as *the* and *also* occur frequently and thus have a high probability of occurrence. Intuitively, finding one of these words does not tell much about a text. However, words like *paleontology, medieval,* and *impressionism* are much less frequent and tell more about the text. This suggests that the latter words carry more information than the former ones.

The basic assumptions made in defining the information content H are

- H is a continuous function of the p_i; that is, as each p_i is changed slightly, H changes only slightly as well. (This can be defined precisely.)

- If all of the p_i are equal, $p_i = 1/n$, then H is a monotone increasing function of n. That is, the information content is greater if there are more possible messages from which to choose.
- If the choice of a message is broken down into two successive choices, the original H should be a weighted sum of the resulting values of H.

To illustrate the third assumption, suppose there are three messages with probabilities $p_1 = \frac{1}{2}$, $p_2 = \frac{1}{3}$, and $p_3 = \frac{1}{6}$. (As required, the probabilities are non-negative and add to 1.) The information content in a direct choice of one of the three messages is $H(p_1, p_2, p_3) = H(\frac{1}{2}, \frac{1}{3}, \frac{1}{6})$. However, rather than choosing one of the messages directly, a person might choose initially between the first message and the other two, and then if the first message was not chosen, choose between the other two. Now the first choice is between two events (message 1 or some other message) of equal probability, so its information content is $H(\frac{1}{2}, \frac{1}{2})$. The second choice is between two events, one of which (message 2) is twice as likely to be chosen as the other. Its information content is thus $H(\frac{2}{3}, \frac{1}{3})$. The third assumption says that

$$H\left(\frac{1}{2}, \frac{1}{3}, \frac{1}{6}\right) = H\left(\frac{1}{2}, \frac{1}{2}\right) + \frac{1}{2} H\left(\frac{2}{3}, \frac{1}{3}\right),$$

where the last term is divided by 2, since that choice only occurs one-half of the time. Similarly, if the first choice were between the second message (with probability $\frac{1}{3}$) and the other two (with combined probability $\frac{2}{3}$), then the information content of the second choice would be $H(\frac{3}{4}, \frac{1}{4})$. This is because the first message has a probability that is three times as large as that of the third message. The equation relating these would be

$$H\left(\frac{1}{2}, \frac{1}{3}, \frac{1}{6}\right) = H\left(\frac{2}{3}, \frac{1}{3}\right) + \frac{2}{3} H\left(\frac{3}{4}, \frac{1}{4}\right).$$

Figure 5.1 shows these relationships.

It can be shown that the only function satisfying the three basic assumptions is H, the entropy function from physics, of the form

$$H = -K \sum_i p_i \log_2 p_i,$$

where K is a positive scaling constant and the sum is for $i = 1, \ldots, n$. For present purposes we may set $K = 1$. In the example, the value of H would be

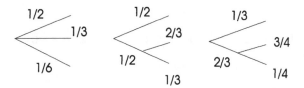

Figure 5.1   Combining entropy values.

$$-\left(\frac{1}{2}\log_2\frac{1}{2}+\frac{1}{3}\log_2\frac{1}{3}+\frac{1}{6}\log_2\frac{1}{6}\right)$$

$$=\frac{1}{2}\log_2 2+\frac{1}{3}\log_2 3+\frac{1}{6}\log_2 6$$

$$=\frac{1}{2}+\frac{1.585}{3}+\frac{2.585}{6}=1.46.$$

It is convenient to absorb the negative sign into the logarithm and write the function in the form

$$H=\sum_i p_i \log_2\left(\frac{1}{p_i}\right).$$

The information content of a single message (for these purposes a word or phrase) is then $\log_2(1/p_i)$, where p_i is the probability of occurrence of the message. This agrees with the intuition that the more frequent or probable a word is, the less information it carries. In the definition of H, this value is multiplied by the probability that the message occurs. Thus the function H represents the *average information content* of the set of messages.

   A measure of the value of an index term can also be defined from the information theoretic value. This is called the *signal-to-noise ratio*. The noise, n_k, of index term k for a collection of N documents is defined as

$$n_k=\sum_i \left(\frac{f_{ik}}{t_k}\right)\log_2\left(\frac{t_k}{f_{ik}}\right),$$

where t_k is the total frequency of term k in the collection $(t_k = \Sigma\, f_{ik})$, and the sum is for $i = 1, \ldots, N$. (By definition, if a term does not occur in document i, that term in the sum has the value 0.) This is simply the information content of term k. The signal, s_k, of term k is then defined by

$$s_k = \log_2 t_k - n_k,$$

and the weight, w_{ik}, of term k in document i is defined by

$$w_{ik} = f_{ik}s_k.$$

The noise can also be written in the form

$$n_k = \sum_i \log_2[(t_k/f_{ik})^{(f_{ik}/t_k)}]$$

$$= \log_2 \prod_i [(t_k/f_{ik})^{(f_{ik}/t_k)}].$$

Thus the signal can also be expressed as

$$s_k = \log_2\left(\frac{t_k}{\prod_i[(t_k/f_{ik})^{(f_{ik}/t_k)}]}\right).$$

Term Discrimination Value

A major use of index terms is to identify sets of documents that are relevant to the user's information need. An index term provides a means of separating documents into two sets—those to be retrieved and those to be ignored. Presumably the retrieved set is to be of "reasonable" size—large enough to give the user a choice but not large enough to overwhelm her. The *term discrimination value* is a measure of how well a term will distinguish one document from another. This requires first a way to measure the *similarity* of two documents.

A common way to define document similarity is to relate it to the key terms that two documents have. In this view, two documents are highly similar if they have exactly the same key terms. (Note that the documents need not be identical.) Two documents are highly dissimilar if they have no key terms in common. Similarity measures will be discussed in Section 5.7. For now it suffices to know that a measure of document similarity, σ, can be defined and that such measures can be based either on the presence or absence of terms in each document, or on the frequencies of occurrence. In either case the similarity measure can be *normalized* so that $\sigma(D_1, D_2) = 1$ if D_1 and D_2 are highly similar and $\sigma(D_1, D_2) = 0$ if D_1 and D_2 are highly dissimilar. (See Section 5.7.)

An *average similarity* for documents in a given collection can be computed by summing $\sigma(D_1, D_2)$ over all document pairs, D_1 different from D_2, and multiplying by a suitable constant. Typically the value $1/(N(N-1))$ is chosen for this constant, where N is the size of the document collection. (Note that there are $N(N-1)/2$ pairs of distinct documents included in the calculation, and that each pair occurs twice in the sum.)

Computation of the average similarity by direct document comparison in this way is an $O(N^2)$ process and hence quite time consuming for large document collections. A simpler computation is achieved by defining an artificial centroid document, $D^\star$, with the characteristic that the frequency of each term in $D^\star$ is the average frequency of that term in the document collection,

$$f^\star{}_k = \frac{\sum_i f_{ik}}{N} = \frac{t_k}{N}.$$

This is an $O(N)$ computation for each term. The average similarity for documents in a collection can then be computed in $O(N)$ time by comparing each document to $D^\star$,

$$\sigma^\star = c \sum_i \sigma(D^\star, D_i),$$

for a suitable constant c.

In the same way, the *deleted average similarity* for term k, $\sigma^\star{}_k$, can be computed by carrying out the computation with the term k dropped from consideration. Finally, the *discrimination value* of term k in the collection is defined as

$$\delta_k = \sigma^\star{}_k - \sigma^\star.$$

The discrimination value measures the difference in similarity when the term k is considered, $\sigma^\star$, from that when it is not considered, $\sigma^\star{}_k$. If $\delta_k > 0$, then removing term k from consideration makes the documents appear more similar. That is, the presence of term k *increases the dissimilarity* of documents in the collection. Similarly, if $\delta_k < 0$, then removing term k from consideration makes the documents appear less similar. That is, the presence of term k *decreases the dissimilarity* of the documents. This enables grouping the terms into three broad classes:

- Good discriminators have high positive values of δ_k.
- Poor discriminators have high negative values of δ_k.
- Indifferent discriminators have values of δ_k near zero.

Finally, the discrimination value can be used to define the weight, w_{ik}, of term k in document i,

$$w_{ik} = f_{ik}\, \delta_k.$$

Phrases and Proximity

Although the fundamental counts on a document are of word occurrences, these counts do not pick up the relationships that occur among words. Word *phrases* are obviously important. When the word *information* occurs in a phrase such as *information structure, information retrieval,* or *information system,* the phrase as a whole becomes meaningful, whether the individual words in the phrase are meaningful or not. Similarly, the phrase *Gang of Four* has a specific meaning in political history, although the individual words in the phrase are most probably not significant. Thus it is important also to recognize and account for significant phrases in a document.

Phrase frequency can be counted in the same way that individual word frequency can be, and the same sort of weighting can be applied. However, since the inherent frequency of a phrase is relatively low, perhaps a different weighting scheme should be used. Suppose, for example, that the word *information* occurs 172 times in a document, and the word *retrieval* occurs 57 times. It follows that the phrase *information retrieval* can occur at most 57 times, and most probably occurs less frequently than that. Thus if the same weighting scheme is applied to both words and phrases, the inherently lower frequency of the phrase influences its weight vis-à-vis the weights of the individual words. One scheme is to count both the individual words (if they are significant) and the phrase. Thus *information retrieval* and *retrieval of information* would each have a count of 3. A closely related scheme that can be used to counter the bias against phrases is to introduce a multiplicative factor, such as the number of words in a phrase, or one plus the logarithm of the number of words.

Phrases are often broken up in a text. For example, if the user is interested in the phrase *information retrieval,* he is probably also interested in the phrase *information storage and retrieval.* Yet these are different phrases, and quite possibly the latter phrase will be so infrequent as to lose any significance. It is reasonable, however, to suggest that *information storage and retrieval* should be included in the *information retrieval* count. One way to do this is to introduce a measure of word proximity. Thus, by counting the combination *information* and *retrieval* whenever these two words occur in the same sentence with at most two separating words, the count would include *information retrieval, information storage and retrieval,* and *retrieval of information.* Many commercial information retrieval systems do not use proximity as a criterion in determining index terms or measuring document content, but allow the user to specify proximity criteria in a query. The basic retrieval is then done without considering proximity (for example, by use of an inverted index of individual words), and the retrieved documents are judged by the proximity criteria before they are finally accepted or rejected.

To be most effective, lexical indexing and analysis methods should be applied to the collection of documents being used by a retrieval system. However, this is expensive for large document collections. Furthermore, as the collection changes by addition of new documents and the deletion of older ones, the lexical indexing may become increasingly out of tune with the characteristics of the collection. Unfortunately, there is often no serious attempt to keep the indexing current.

One alternative to a direct analysis of a document collection is to use a standard vocabulary analysis. While this is admittedly not as accurate, it is far less expensive and often just as effective, because inaccuracies elsewhere within the indexing and retrieval system may mask any inaccuracies introduced through the use of a standard vocabulary. Several standard vocabularies are available, the most well-known being the *Brown corpus,* developed in 1967 by Kučera and Francis at Brown University (Kučera and Francis 1967). This is a detailed analysis of American English in several categories of literature (newspaper stories, legal briefs, Westerns, and so forth), including word frequency counts, sentence length counts, and other data.

5.6   OTHER METHODS OF DOCUMENT ANALYSIS

The indexing and analysis methods discussed thus far depend only on word counts within a document. The only concession that they make to structure is the very minimal one of including phrases and proximity criteria in the judgment. However, the language of a document is clearly much richer than any structure revealed in this way. Although the results of a thorough statistical analysis of a document can be very revealing, most people believe that the way in which a document is written conveys its meaning far better than mere word counts can ever do. Hence there is a strong incentive to try to develop information retrieval systems based on a more detailed analysis of the individual documents. This analysis involving techniques for processing natural language is discussed in Chapter 10.

Pragmatic Factors

Another approach to the design of retrieval systems is to introduce *pragmatic factors* derived from either the specific characteristics of the database or the characteristics of its use. Among the simplest of these techniques is the identification of *trigger phrases* that signal particular types of information within the document. In a text with figures and tables, the words *figure* and *table* often identify either the location of one of these objects or a reference to one. The words *for example* serve to introduce material that expands on and explains material just previously discussed. Words such as *conclusion* or *finding* may identify key points and ideas in a document. Most of these words would be rejected in a lexical analysis as not being significant key words. They are too general and do not relate to the specific content of a document. Yet they serve a function that may be significant in designing a better information retrieval system.

Another pragmatic technique is to predicate the retrieval evaluation partially on the source of a document. Certain authors may be well known as leaders in their field, whose works could be given extra weight. Some journals publish material of a highly theoretical nature, others focus on applications, and still others have a more popular slant. The type of journal in which a paper appears can influence the user's perception of a document and may be used as a pragmatic factor in the design of an information retrieval system. Papers in a conference proceedings may be less comprehensive than those appearing in an archival journal, but they generally refer to more current work, simply because of the time required for writing, accepting, and publishing papers.

Finally, and of greatest complexity, one could introduce pragmatic factors related to the user. Is the user a high school student or a Ph.D.? Is the user well-versed in the subject area or seeking to enter a new area of study? Does the user have ready access to a given document, and if so, will she already have read it? These factors and others depend on the individual user and must generally be used dynamically. Only when the users constitute a small homogeneous group can such factors be built into the system as constants.

As the technology develops and interactive retrieval systems become the focus of activity, an increasing amount of research addresses the issue of properly and adequately representing the user as a component in the full information retrieval system. A significant group of researchers are studying the users of information retrieval systems, particularly on-line systems, in an effort to provide better user models that will improve retrieval system performance (Siegfried, Bates, and Wilde 1993; Fidel 1994; Spink 1996).

5.7   DOCUMENT SIMILARITY

Probably the single key concept behind information storage and retrieval is similarity. The aim is to retrieve documents whose contents are in some sense similar to the information need as expressed by the query. To aid in this process, catalogers and indexers try to organize the document collection so that similar documents are in some sense close together and can be retrieved as a group with little effort. Thus a firmer definition is needed of what is meant by saying that two documents are similar.

Unfortunately, there are many different definitions of similarity. Fortunately, they arise as variations on a few simple themes, many of which are lexically based. These variations all produce normalized similarity measures, which attempt to correct for differences in document length and other characteristics.

Any lexically based measure begins with word and term counts. Immediately there is a split into two distinct types of measures: those depending only on the presence or absence of a term and those depending on frequency of occurrence. Any document can be represented by a vector or list of terms that occur in it. In order to handle the documents within a collection, it is assumed that the vector represents all terms in the vocabulary of the collection, and that the vocabulary terms are in some fixed order, say, alphabetical order. Thus the *base representation* of any document is a vector of the form

$$D = <t_1, t_2, \ldots, t_N>,$$

where the *component* t_i relates to the ith term in the vocabulary. If this term does not occur in document D, then $t_i = 0$. If the term does occur, then t_i is either 1 (if the interest is only in occurrence or nonoccurrence of the term) or the frequency count for the term in the document (if the interest is in frequency of occurrence). In either case, t_i is a number related to term i, not the term itself. The occurrence-oriented vectors, called *0-1 vectors,* are simplest to use.

Let D_1 and D_2 be two document vectors, with components t_{1i} and t_{2i}, respectively, for $i = 1, \ldots, N$. We define the following notation:

w = the number of terms for which $t_{1i} = t_{2i} = 1$,

x = the number of terms for which $t_{1i} = 1$ and $t_{2i} = 0$,

y = the number of terms for which $t_{1i} = 0$ and $t_{2i} = 1$,

z = the number of terms for which $t_{1i} = t_{2i} = 0$,

$n_1 = w + x$,

$n_2 = w + y$,

$N = w + x + y + z$.

The relationships among these values can be shown in a *contingency table* (Table 5.1).

Since most of the vocabulary will not be used in any one document, z will generally be a relatively large number, independent of the similarity of the documents. If the two documents being compared in the table are quite similar, w can be expected to be large, and x and y relatively small. However, if the documents are quite different, that difference will be reflected in a small w and large x and y. Define the basic comparison unit by

$$\delta(D_1, D_2) = w - \frac{n_1 n_2}{N} .$$

Table 5.1
Contingency Table for Document-Document Match

		D_2		
		$t_{2i} = 1$	$t_{2i} = 0$	
D_1	$t_{1i} = 1$	w	x	n_1
	$t_{1i} = 0$	y	z	$N - n_1$
		n_2	$N - n_2$	N

Observe that δ can assume both positive and negative values. The value of w for which δ is 0, namely $n_1 n_2 / N$, is called the *independence value* of w. This was first defined for term-term similarity in Yule (1912) and is derived from assumptions about the statistical independence of the two terms or documents. Note also that δ is symmetric,

$$\delta(D_1, D_2) = \delta(D_2, D_1).$$

Researchers have held a variety of opinions on how to measure the similarity between two documents. Many of these can be defined as modifications of one basic measure, δ.

The comparison unit δ can be used as a measure of similarity or association between D_1 and D_2, defining a *coefficient of association* as

$$C_\alpha(D_1, D_2) = \frac{\delta(D_1, D_2)}{\alpha},$$

for some α (Kuhns 1965). The choice of α is determined by the definition of similarity. For example, representing the use of terms in two documents by the Venn diagram in Figure 5.2, one reasonable measure of similarity is the extent to which the circles representing D_1 and D_2 are separated. A measure of this separation is the fraction of the document set that contains one or the other of the terms, but not both:

$$\frac{x + y}{N} = \frac{n_1 + n_2 - 2w}{N} = 1 - \frac{w + z}{N}.$$

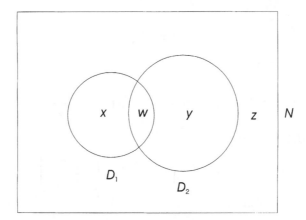

Figure 5.2 *Venn diagram for document separation.*

Observe that if there is no separation between D_1 and D_2, then $x + y = 0$ and $w + z = N$, so that the separation measure has the value 0. If, however, D_1 and D_2 are completely separate, then $w = 0$, so that the separation measure has the value $1 - z/N$, a positive number. The maximum value of this is 1, when D_1 and D_2 together contain all of the vocabulary terms. Relate this to δ by substituting the independence value for w into the measure, and subtracting the original measure from this. Use the second form given for the measure, obtaining

$$\frac{n_1 + n_2 - \dfrac{2n_1n_2}{N}}{N} - \frac{n_1 + n_2 - 2w}{N} = \frac{2\delta(D_1, D_2)}{N}.$$

Hence the factor associated with the *Separation Coefficient* is $\alpha(S) = N/2$.

Eleven other coefficients can be similarly defined. For each there is a reasonable argument that it should be the coefficient of association. Each of them is characterized by the factor α.

- *Rectangular Distance:*

$$\alpha(R) = \max(n_1, n_2)$$

- *Conditional Probability:*

$$\alpha(W) = \min(n_1, n_2)$$

- *Vector Angle:*

$$\alpha(G) = (n_1 n_2)^{1/2}$$

- *Arithmetic Mean:*

$$\alpha(E) = \frac{n_1 + n_2}{2}$$

- *Proportion of Overlap:*

$$\alpha(P) = \left(n_1 + n_2 - \frac{n_1 n_2}{N}\right)\left(1 - \frac{w}{n_1 + n_2}\right)$$

- *Probability Difference I:*

$$\alpha(U) = \max\left[n_1\left(1 - \frac{n_1}{N}\right), n_2\left(1 - \frac{n_2}{N}\right)\right]$$

- *Probability Difference II:*

$$\alpha(V) = \min\left[n_1\left(1 - \frac{n_1}{N}\right), n_2\left(1 - \frac{n_2}{N}\right)\right]$$

- *Linear Correlation:*

$$\alpha(L) = \left[n_1\left(1 - \frac{n_1}{N}\right)n_2\left(1 - \frac{n_2}{N}\right) \right]^{1/2}$$

- *Yule Coefficient of Colligation:*

$$\alpha(Y) = \frac{[(wz)^{1/2} + (xy)^{1/2}]^2}{N}$$

- *Yule Auxiliary Quantity:*

$$\alpha(Q) = \frac{wz + xy}{N}$$

- *Index of Independence:*

$$\alpha(I) = \frac{n_1 n_2}{N}$$

The relationships among these various coefficients of association are not straightforward. Obviously the maximum of a given quantity is at least as large as the minimum of the same quantity. This can be used to compare the Rectangular Distance to the Conditional Probability, for example. (Note that since α is a divisor, this means that the coefficient associated with rectangular distance is smaller.) In other cases the relationship is not so easy to define, and in several cases the relative sizes of the coefficients change depending on the values of n_1 and n_2. In Table 5.2, showing the relationships among the values of α, the symbol > in the *i,j* position indicates that $\alpha(i) \geq \alpha(j)$, and "s" in that position indicates that the inequality switches depending on the parameter values.

The relationships among the various values of α can also be shown in a graph where the largest α values are at the top and lines joining two values mean that the larger one is always greater than the smaller one (Figure 5.3). Where no line exists (for example between G and U), the relationship between the α values is not fixed, but switches depending on the parameter values. In this figure, the transitive relationships among the various measures are easily seen. For example, the left chain shows $\alpha(R) \geq \alpha(E) \geq \alpha(G) \geq \alpha(W) \geq \alpha(I)$. Using transitivity, these inequalities imply six other inequalities shown in the table. The remaining inequalities in the table are similarly deduced from this diagram.

Table 5.2
Comparison of Coefficients of Similarity

	S	P	R	U	E	G	L	W	V	Y	Q	I
S	—	s	s	>	s	s	>	s	>	>	>	s
P		—	s	>	s	s	>	s	>	>	>	s
R			—	>	>	>	>	>	>	>	>	>
U				—	s	s	>	s	>	>	>	s
E					—	>	>	>	>	>	>	>
G						—	>	>	>	>	>	>
L							—	s	>	>	>	s
W								—	>	>	>	>
V									—	>	>	s
Y										—	>	s
Q											—	s
I												—

Closely related to these coefficients are several others that are often used in information retrieval work. Basically, these are defined using only w rather than the independence value, and modifying that. *Dice's Coefficient*, for example, is defined as

$$\frac{2w}{n_1 + n_2}.$$

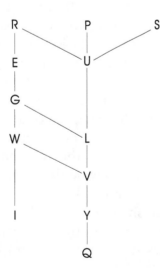

Figure 5.3   Order relationships among similarity measures.

This uses the arithmetic mean and is thus closely related to the Arithmetic Mean coefficient given above. Similar statements hold for the *Cosine Coefficient* (related to Vector Angle)

$$\frac{w}{\sqrt{n_1 n_2}}$$

and the *Overlap Coefficient* (related to Conditional Probability)

$$\frac{w}{\min(n_1, n_2)}.$$

Included with this same group is *Jaccard's Coefficient* (see Exercise 9)

$$\frac{w}{N - z}.$$

The wide variety of coefficients given here reflects the different concepts that have been proposed for document association or similarity. No one of these is "correct" in the sense that it provides the best measurement. Users of an information retrieval system have their own concepts of similarity, usually not precisely articulated. Based on the interactions of the user with the system, it may be possible to select one of these coefficients as best representing the views of a given user.

Similarity measures that depend on the frequency with which terms occur in documents can also be based on a metric, or distance measure, with the concept that the greater the distance between documents, the less similar they are. A metric has three defining properties:

- Its values are nonnegative, with the distance between two points being 0 if and only if the points are identical.
- It is symmetric: The distance from A to B is the same as the distance from B to A.
- It satisfies the *triangle inequality:* The distance from A to C is no greater than the sum of the distances from A to B and from B to C, for any points A, B, and C.

Some researchers prefer to work with a *pseudo-metric*, which allows the distance between two nonidentical points to be 0. It is certainly the case that when documents are represented by lists of key terms, two nonidentical documents may have identical representations and hence zero distance by any measure based on these representations. Whether one considers this using a pseudo-metric on the documents or a metric on the representations is largely a matter of personal preference. A pseudo-metric seems more appropriate when working with full-text documents. A document that meets all of the query terms and conditions should have the highest possible similarity to the query (that is, distance 0 from the query), even though the texts of the document and the query are distinct.

Any function satisfying the above three conditions qualifies as a metric. Similarity is then taken to be some function whose values are inversely proportional to the distance. For example, if d is the distance, an exponential function e^{-d} can be used as the similarity measure. Then a document at distance 0 from a given document or query would have a similarity of 1, and all other documents would have smaller similarity values.

Among the metrics that have been defined, the L_p *metrics* have been widely used. These are defined by the equation

$$L_p(D_1, D_2) = \left[\sum_i |d_{1i} - d_{2i}|^p \right]^{1/p}.$$

Commonly used values for p include $p = 1$ (*city block distance*, or *Manhattan distance*), $p = 2$ (*Euclidean distance*), and $p = \infty$ (*maximal direction distance*). Euclidean distance is the best known of these, corresponding to ordinary straight-line distance. City block distance is defined by

$$L_1(D_1, D_2) = \sum_i |d_{1i} - d_{2i}|.$$

It corresponds to the measure of the number of blocks from one point to another in a city with streets on a rectangular grid. Both the city block distance and the maximal direction distance have the advantage that they are simple to compute. The latter is defined by

$$L_\infty(D_1, D_2) = \max_i (|d_{1i} - d_{2i}|).$$

While Euclidean distance is most commonly used, L_1, L_∞, and other metrics all provide viable models for document similarity. The appropriate metric for a given situation is a matter of careful study.

Example 5.1   Suppose there are four documents whose representations are based on four different key terms, with term weights defined as follows:

$$D_1 = <2, 0, 3, 5>$$

$$D_2 = <0, 4, 0, 1>$$

$$D_3 = <3, 1, 1, 2>$$

$$D_4 = <2, 4, 1, 0>.$$

For the three different metrics, the distances between pairs of documents are given in Table 5.3.

Table 5.3
Comparison of Metrics

	L_1	L_2	L_∞
D_1, D_2	13	6.71	4
D_1, D_3	7	3.87	3
D_1, D_4	11	6.71	5
D_2, D_3	8	4.47	3
D_2, D_4	4	2.45	2
D_3, D_4	6	3.74	3

Study of this table brings out some interesting relationships between the metrics. For example, observe that the relative distances of D_2 and D_4 from D_1 change according to the metric used. This change shows that the variation of distance with metric is not always straightforward but must be considered carefully in selecting a metric.

5.8   STOP LISTS

Despite the use of various weighting schemes to modify word frequency counts and hence to indicate the importance of a word or term in a document, use of an uncontrolled vocabulary still presents several problems. In the remainder of this chapter, three of these are discussed: the impact of very common terms, variants of a given term, and the use of different terms with similar meanings.

Many studies have shown that the most common 250 to 300 words in English may account for 50% or more of any given text. For example, in studying one million words of general English text, Kučera and Francis (1967) found that the two most common words, *the* and *of*, account for 10% of the word occurrences. The next four words, *and, to, a,* and *in,* account for another 10%. Fully 30% of the running text was made up of only eighteen distinct words.

These very common words have two impacts on information retrieval systems. First, in any measurements depending on word frequencies, the very high frequencies of these words tend to diminish the impact of frequency differences among less common words. Second, as these words carry little meaning by themselves, they may result in a large amount of unproductive processing if left in the text. For these reasons, it is common to define a *stop list,* or *negative dictionary,* consisting of such words. Stop lists vary in size from around 15 words to over 500, with most containing around 250 to 300 words. When a text is initially processed, each word occurrence is checked against the stop list. If the word is found there, it is ignored in any further processing and may even be eliminated from the text representation.

One may wish to add a second stop list, more subject dependent, to this general one. Any well-defined field of study or work develops its own jargon. Some of these words and phrases may occur frequently enough that they are more characteristic of a particular document collection than of individual documents within the collection. Frequency weighting schemes may identify these words as being ill-suited for retrieval purposes. One may then choose to include them in a subject-dependent stop list to further reduce the processing required during document comparison and retrieval.

Quite clearly, each query that is used with an information retrieval system should also be processed against the system's stop lists. Failure to do this might result in effort wasted hunting for documents containing a query word that is on the stop list.

In organizing a retrieval system that uses phrases, the use of stop words must be carefully considered, as these are frequently the words that identify significant phrases. For example, one of the best known phrases in English literature, "To be, or not to be," consists entirely of words that would normally be considered stop words. Eliminating these four stop words would eliminate any reference to this phrase unless special measures were taken to retain the phrase.

Clearly it takes time in the initial processing to check each word against a stop list. Since the list is small and known ahead of time, this is not usually a problem. A binary search of eight steps will determine whether a text word is on a stop list of at most 256 words. If this amount of processing seems excessive, other techniques can be considered. For example, *hashing techniques* are focused on being able to determine whether a word is on a stop list with just one computation and one comparison. For a known list of stop words a *perfect hash function* can be developed, so that each stop word hashes to a different value. If a text word hashes to one of these values, then it is either the given stop word or not a stop word—a difference that needs but one comparison to check.

Another alternative to binary search is to structure the stop list as a *trie*. In this technique, each word is checked character by character against the stop list. For example, although words starting with *t* will be on the stop list (the, then, to, and so on), if none of these begins with *te*, two comparisons suffice to determine that *technology* is not a stop word. Binary search, perfect hashing, and trie structures are all simple to construct; a few tests with some sample text should determine which is best—or whether there is no significant difference in performance.

5.9 STEMMING

The second major problem with an uncontrolled vocabulary arises from the fact that a given word may occur in many different forms. For example, *computer, computers, computing, compute, computes, computed, computational, computationally, computable,* and various other words all have the same basic form and all deal with a set of closely related concepts. Conceivably, a user who asks for documents on *computers* may miss relevant documents just because they use other forms of the word and have low frequency counts for the specific form *computers*. This is clearly undesirable.

One way to address this problem is to introduce a *stemming algorithm*, which strips off word endings, reducing them to a common core or stem. In the above example, that stem might be *comput*. For a given document this will bring together the various forms of the word, resulting in a higher frequency count and thus in greater significance for the term. In a query, application of stemming assures that the user is not penalized for using one specific word form that does not occur frequently.

A number of stemming algorithms have been developed over the years. Three of the better known of these are by Lovins (1968), Porter (1980), and Paice (1990). These algorithms iteratively strip off multiple endings on a word to arrive at the stem. For example, *computationally* would be stripped to *computational*, then to *computation*, then to *computa*, and finally to *comput*. This iterative approach to stemming requires either multiple passes over a given word or an algorithm that looks for the longest suffix first but does not require a priori knowledge of all possible combinations of endings. The principal distinctions among these algorithms lie in the efficiency of their code and in the choice of suffixes to identify and strip. One study indicates that the performance of the Lovins stemmer may not match that of the other two, but the results are not fully conclusive (Paice 1996).

There is no theoretical reason why stemmers could not strip word prefixes as well. Common prefixes such as *de, im, in, non,* and *re* are certainly candidates for stripping. However, most stemming algorithms in use today to not strip prefixes. One reason for this might lie in the more difficult task of deciding whether a letter sequence is really a prefix or part of the word. For example, while *in* is frequently a negative prefix, this is not the case in words such as *inner, interior,* and *into.* There may be enough such exceptions to make prefix stripping computationally unattractive (see Exercise 10). Another concern is that stripping prefixes would frequently change the meaning of the word substantially. This is certainly the case with negative prefixes. Whether prefix stripping would be beneficial in retrieval is unclear.

There are two problems that any stemming algorithm must solve. One is the stripping of letter sequences that falsely appear to be endings. For example, while *ed* is normally striped from words, it should not be stripped from *bed.* This problem can be largely avoided by having a minimum acceptable stem length and by having a small list of exceptional words. If it were required that the stem contain at least three letters, then *bed* would not be stripped—but *breed* would be. Thus *breed* might be included on an exception list. Alternatively, there might be a rule that *eed* is not stripped, overriding the normal stripping of *ed.*

The other problem that a stemming algorithm must solve is that of stem changes in various word forms. This is most common in plurals, as in the change from *knife* to *knives.* While these morphological changes are exceptions to the general rule, there are relatively few of them, and checking for them is quite simple. A good stemming algorithm is designed to handle these changes as well.

Stemming on a large, full-text database is a very time-consuming operation. Recent studies indicate that the effort may not be worth it (Harman and Candela 1990). The length of the document representation may be changed by only 5 percent or so, and methods based on frequency counts seem to be little impacted by stemming or a lack thereof when applied to full-text documents. One compromise is to stem only the queries and then use wild cards in matching the query to the document. Thus if the word *computational* appears in a query, the system might stem and then match *comput** to the document, where the asterisk is used in its common role of an unrestricted wild card. The stemming algorithm used in this way would be slightly different. For example, if *knife* appears in the query, then the algorithm could either generate two possible stems, *knif* and *kniv*, or use the shorter stem *kni* and then verify the match.

5.10   MULTILINGUAL RETRIEVAL SYSTEMS

Almost all early work on computer-based information retrieval systems centered on English language texts. As computers have become more common throughout the world, and particularly as the Internet and the World Wide Web have developed, there has been a substantial effort to develop retrieval systems in other languages, and systems that can handle multiple languages. There are now retrieval systems in every major language and some in languages of more localized use. Among non-European languages, Arabic and Chinese are attracting much research interest (Wu and Tseng 1993; Al-Kharashi and Evens 1994).

Many of the techniques used are direct adaptations of classical information retrieval techniques. Yet every language has its own characteristics that must be accommodated. German, for example, has many *separable verbs,* with the property that the prefix that determines the specific meaning of the verb generally appears at the end of the sentence. Turkish is an example of an *agglutinative language,* in which syntactic relationships may be expressed by distinct suffixes. This results in a complex morphology requiring detailed analysis before stemming (Solak and Can 1994). Hebrew and Arabic are commonly printed without the diacritical marks indicating vowels. Chinese sentences are customarily printed as a string of characters, without breaks between words. Thus a given string of symbols may properly be interpreted in three or four different ways. In Arabic, the characters used in a word may change depending on the syntactic situation, in a manner analogous to the stem changes in English. Even within English, British and American spellings (*colour* vs. *color*) and usage (British *boot* = American *car trunk*; American *boot* = British *Wellington*) imply that retrieval systems must be adapted to a specific usage or made sufficiently sophisticated to handle both.

Several research groups are focusing on developing multilingual information retrieval systems, to enable queries in one language to retrieve documents in other languages (Hull and Greffenstette 1996). The results of such studies are promising. In one study, for example, a cross-language retrieval system was able to retrieve Italian documents in response to German queries as well as a standard all-Italian system could do from Italian queries—although not as well as an experimental Italian system could do (Sheridan and Ballerini 1996).

The utility of a multilingual retrieval system may depend heavily on the intended body of users. Many potential users of information retrieval systems cannot read a second language well enough to benefit from a multilingual system. However, within diplomatic circles or in certain research communities, for example, a multilingual system could be highly useful.

5.11 THESAURI

The final major problem to be considered here is the use of similar or related terms. These cannot be handled by a simple algorithm the way variant word forms are, since frequently the words are quite distinct. For example, one may *post* a letter or *mail* a letter, with exactly the same result. *Thesauri* are used to address this problem. A good thesaurus may contain both synonyms and antonyms for each word, together with broader and narrower terms, and closely related terms. A thesaurus can be used during document storage processing to control the vocabulary. This is done by replacing each term variant with a standard term chosen on the basis of the thesaurus. Alternatively, a thesaurus can be used during the query process to broaden a query and ensure that relevant documents are not missed because of a narrow query vocabulary.

The converse of this problem arises when *homographs,* two words with distinct meanings but identical spellings, are used. Syntactic, semantic, and pragmatic analysis all come into use in determining the equivalences and differences between such words. An extreme challenge to such analysis is the sentence,

> Mrs. Post decided to post a letter to the post office box of Sheriff Post post-haste, in order to meet the four p.m. post, about her intention to post a no trespassing notice on the lamp post on her property on Post Street.

As retrieval systems capable of handling multimedia documents are developed, a similar problem will arise with respect to *homonyms,* words that sound alike but have distinct meanings. The problem becomes quite complex. The word *bore,* for example, has several distinct meanings; in a verbal document this may be complicated by the introduction of the word *boar* as well.

Finally, while thesauri traditionally focus on terms with related meaning, it is possible to develop a thesaurus based solely on term co-occurrence. Such a thesaurus would be more heavily dependent on a particular document collection than would a thesaurus based on semantic properties. However, it might be useful to know, for example, that in one particular collection *cereal* frequently occurs in conjunction with *music.* This provides new and unanticipated ways of broadening a search. Thesauri based on term co-occurrence can be generated automatically, with little or no human intervention.

5.12 SUMMARY

When considering measures of document similarity based on term occurrence, the choice of which terms to count and how to count them can make a significant difference in the similarity measure. There are at least six basic positions from which to start, shown in Table 5.4.

Table 5.4
Term Use and Control Positions

	Term presence	Frequency count
Actual term occurrence		
Stemmed term		
Use of thesaurus		

The basic position and the measures used should be carefully chosen to conform as nearly as possible to the users' perceptions of similarity among the documents in the database.

REFERENCES

Al-Kharashi, Ibrahim A., and Martha W. Evens. 1994. Comparing words, stems, and roots as index terms in an Arabic information retrieval system. *JASIS* 45, no. 8:548–560.

Bartell, Brian T., Garrison W. Cottreel, and Richard K. Belew. 1992. Latent semantic indexing is an optimal special case of multidimensional scaling. In *Proceedings of the 15th Annual International ACM/SIGIR Conference on Research and Development in Information Retrieval*, Copenhagen, pp. 161–167.

Borko, Harold. 1979. Inter-indexer consistency. *Cranfield Conference.*

Collantes, Lourdes Y. 1995. Degree of agreement in naming objects and concepts for information retrieval. *JASIS* 46, no. 2:116–132.

Cooper, William S. 1969. Is interindexer consistency a hobgoblin? *American Documentation* 20, no. 3:268–278.

Di Nubila, B., I. Gagliardi, D. Macchi, L. Milanesi, M. Padula, and R. Pagani. 1994. Concept-based indexing and retrieval of multimedia documents. *Journal of Information Science* 20, no. 3:185–196.

Fidel, Raya. 1994. User-centered indexing. *JASIS* 45, no. 8:572–576.

Harman, Donna K., and G. Candela. 1990. Retrieving records from a gigabyte of text on a minicomputer using statistical ranking. *JASIS* 41, no. 8:581–589.

Hearst, Marti A. 1995. TileBars: Visualization of term distribution information in full text information access. *Proceedings of CHI '95 Human Factors in Computing Systems*, Denver, pp. 59–66.

Hearst, Marti A., and Christian Plaunt. 1993. Subtopic structuring for full-length document access. *Proceedings of the 16th Annual International ACM/SIGIR Conference on Research and Development in Information Retrieval*, Pittsburgh, pp. 59–68.

Hersh, W.R., David H. Hickam, and T.J. Leone. 1992. Words, concepts, or both: Optimal indexing units for automated information retrieval. In *Proceedings of the 16th Annual Symposium on Computer Applications in Medical Care* 16, pp. 644–648.

Hull, David A. 1994. Improving text retrieval for the routing problem using latent semantic indexing. In *Proceedings of the 17th Annual International ACM/SIGIR Conference on Research and Development in Information Retrieval*, Dublin, pp. 282–291.

Hull, David A., and Gregory Greffenstette. 1996. Querying across languages: A dictionary-based approach to multilingual information retrieved. In *Proceedings of the 19th Annual International ACM/SIGIR Conference on Research and Development in Information Retrieval*, Zurich, Switzerland, pp. 49–57.

Jacoby, J., and Vladimir Slamecka. 1962. Indexer consistency under minimal conditions. Report no. RADC TR 62-426. Documentation, Inc., Bethesda, Maryland, AD-288 087.

Kučera, H., and W.N. Francis. 1967. *Computational Analysis of Present-Day American English.* Providence, Rhode Island: Brown University Press.

Kuhns, J.L. 1965. The continuum of coefficients of association. In *Statistical association methods for mechanized documentation*, ed. Mary Elizabeth Stevens, Vincent E. Giuliano, and Laurence B. Heilprin. Symposium Proceedings, Washington, D.C., 1964. National Bureau of Standards Miscellaneous Publication 269, pp. 33–39.

Liddy, Elizabeth D., and Sung H. Myaeng. 1993. DR-LINK's linguistic-conceptual approach to document detection. In *The First Text REtrieval Conference (TREC-1)*, ed. Donna K. Harman. Washington, D.C.: NIST Special Publication 500-207, pp. 113–130.

Lovins, Julie Beth. 1968. Development of a stemming algorithm. *Mechanical Translation and Computational Linguistics* 11, no. 1–2:22–31.

Paice, Chris D. 1990. Another stemmer. *SIGIR Forum* 24, no. 3:56–61.

Paice, Chris D. 1996. Method for evaluation of stemming algorithms based on error counting. *JASIS* 47, no. 8:632–649.

Porter, M.F. 1980. An algorithm for suffix stripping. *Program* 14:130–137.

Preschel, B.M. 1972. Indexer consistency in perception of concepts and choice of terminology. Final report. School of Library Science, Columbia University.

Rowley, Jennifer. 1994. The controlled versus natural indexing languages debate revisited: A perspective on information retrieval practice and research. *Journal of Information Science* 20, no. 2:108–119.

Salton, Gerard. 1969. A comparison between manual and automatic indexing methods. *American Documentation* 20, no. 1:61–71.

Shannon, Claude E. 1948. A mathematical theory of communication. *Bell Systems Technical Journal* 27:379–423, 623–656.

Sheridan, Páraic, and Jean Paul Ballerini. 1996. Experiments in multilingual information retrieval using the SPIDER system. In *Proceedings of the 19th Annual International ACM/SIGIR Conference on Research and Development in Information Retrieval,* Zurich, Switzerland, pp. 58–65.

Siegfried, Susan, Marcia J. Bates, and Deborah N. Wilde. 1993. A profile of end-user searching behavior by humanities scholars: The Getty online searching project report no. 2. *JASIS* 44, no. 5:273–291.

Smeaton, Alan F., R. O'Donnel, and F. Kelledy. 1995. Indexing structures derived from syntax in TREC-3: System description. In *Overview of the Third Text REtrieval Conference (TREC-3),* ed. Donna K. Harman. Washington, D.C.: NIST Special Publication 500-225, pp. 55–67.

Solak, Ayşin, and Fazli Can. 1994. Effects of stemming on Turkish text retrieval. In *Proceedings of the Ninth International Symposium on Computer and Information Sciences,* Ankara, Turkey, pp. 49–56.

Spink, Amanda. 1996. Multiple search sessions model of end-user behavior: An exploratory study. *JASIS* 47, no. 8:603–609.

Tzeras, Kostas, and Stephan Hartmann. 1993. Automatic indexing based on Bayesian inference networks. In *Proceedings of the 16th Annual International ACM/SIGIR Conference on Research and Development in Information Retrieval,* Pittsburgh, pp. 22–34.

Watters, Carolyn. 1992. *Dictionary of information science and technology.* San Diego, California: Academic Press.

Weinberg, Bella Hass. 1987. Why indexing fails the researcher. In *Proceedings of the 50th ASIS Annual Meeting,* Boston, pp. 241–244.

Wu, Zimin, and Gwyneth Tseng. 1993. Chinese text segmentation for text retrieval: Achievements and problems. *JASIS* 44, no. 9:532–542.

Yule, George Udny. 1912. On measuring association between attributes. *Journal of the Royal Statistical Society* 75:579–642.

Zipf, George Kinglsey. 1949. *Human behavior and the principle of least effort.* Cambridge, Massachusetts: Addison-Wesley.

EXERCISES

1. Calculate $H(\frac{1}{2}, \frac{1}{3}, \frac{1}{6})$ by each of the two alternative formulas on page 118, thus demonstrating the validity of splitting up the computation.

2. Prove that the signal s_k is given by the formula

$$\left(\sum_i f_{ik} \log_2 f_{ik} \right) \bigg/ t_k,$$

where the sum is over all i such that $f_{ik} > 1$.

3. Prove that $s_k = 0$ for any term k that occurs at most once in any document in the collection.

4. When will two terms be given the same weighting factor:

Under inverse document frequency weighting?

Under signal-to-noise weighting?

Under term discrimination value weighting?

5. Prove or disprove: If two terms have the same signal-to-noise weighting factor, then they have the same inverse document frequency weighting factor, but not conversely.

6. Establish each of the inequalities shown in Table 5.2 among the coefficients of association.

7. For each switching pair identified in Table 5.2 of coefficients of association, find values of the parameters that show the inequality can go either way.

8. For each switching pair identified in Table 5.2 of coefficients of association, find values of the parameters for which the two coefficients are equal.

9. Show how Jaccard's Coefficient relates to the defined table of coefficients of association by defining a new coefficient, J, with $\alpha(J) = N - z$, and determining its relationship with the 12 defined coefficients.

10. Using your favorite dictionary, determine for each of the strings *de*, *im*, *in*, and *re* the proportion of words beginning with these letters in which the string is really a prefix that could be stripped from the words.

11. Group the occurrences of the word *post* in the example sentence in Section 5.11 into semantically related sets. Be sure to include the *post* in *p.m.*

CHAPTER 6

User Profiles and Their Use

A *user profile* consists of information about the user that has bearing on the user's information needs. Profiles have been used as a surrogate for queries from the early days of information retrieval. Recently, efforts have been made to integrate the use of profiles and queries into a more satisfactory system.

6.1 SIMPLE PROFILES

A simple user profile is much like a query. It consists of a set of key terms, often with given weights. Such profiles were originally developed for use in *current awareness* (CA), or *selective dissemination of information* (SDI), systems (Hensley et al. 1962). These systems are commonly used where there is a relatively fixed body of users with persistent interests. For example, many organizations use a current awareness system to help their research staff keep up with current developments in their areas. An investor or stockbroker might use this type of system to alert her to the latest developments in the corporations that she is following. In such a system, the user is typically asked to file an interest profile and to update it periodically, perhaps every six months, or as needed. In the meantime, the profile acts as a standard query that can be run periodically against updates to the database. The term *routing query* has recently been introduced to describe a persistent query such as a profile, in contrast to an *ad hoc query*, which typically is asked just once (Harman 1993).

The simple user profile, by its nature, is relatively easy to match against the document database. However, it is limited in its ability to portray the types of documents that the user can best use, since it is restricted to key-words and key phrases that would occur in the text.

6.2   EXTENDED PROFILES

In contrast to the simple user profile, an extended user profile contains information that is more difficult to correlate with documentary information but may still influence retrieval. The information included in such a profile relates to the user as a person rather than to any specific information need. In particular, it focuses on the person's use of information and on background information about the user that can be of help in determining which documents to include in the retrieved set. This is the type of information that might be elicited by a reference librarian in a client interview. Included in this type of profile we might find the following information:

- *Educational level.* A high school student and a Ph.D. will probably want different sets of documents in response to similar queries.

- *Familiarity with the area of inquiry.* A researcher familiar with a subject and wishing to stay current will look for different documents than will a person seeking to enter an area of study for the first time.

- *Language capabilities.* Papers written in a foreign language are of diminished utility if the user cannot read the language.

- *Journal subscriptions.* A journal to which the user subscribes is readily accessible and hence a good reference source.

- *Reading habits.* If the user regularly reads a certain journal, he probably knows about any important article in that journal. Thus any such references should probably be given at the end of the list, more as a reminder that the user has undoubtedly already seen them. If, however, the user does not read the journals to which he subscribes, then these become prime sources for new references.

- *Specific preferences.* The user may wish to follow the work of certain authors or have a preference for certain journals. Similarly, there may be some category of reference material that the user explicitly does not want to see, such as papers that she has written herself.

This type of information clearly is not directly comparable with that found in a book or a journal paper. Thus much of this information cannot be used directly in the retrieval process, but must be applied to the retrieved set to organize it in a way most compatible with the user's interests, and possibly to eliminate some documents that are unsuitable.

6.3   CURRENT AWARENESS SYSTEMS

A current awareness system is designed to keep its users informed concerning the state of the art in their areas of interest. Thus a basic premise behind such a system is that the user is adequately aware of past work and needs only to be kept abreast of current developments. The system is designed to take the burden of doing this away from the user, thus permitting the user to spend more time directly on research or other work. In this context, the system should operate automatically, without the user needing to intervene. Thus there are two requirements for the design of a current awareness system:

1. Only the current literature needs to be searched.
2. Searches should be made automatically, without the user needing to query the system actively.

With these requirements in mind, the user is asked to specify a user interest profile, which is kept on file. New documents arriving in the library or other information system are accumulated over a brief period of time, perhaps a week or two. Then all user profiles are run as routing queries against this set of documents, and the results are disseminated to appropriate users. The users have several options, ranging from requesting full copies of various documents, through filing the reports that they receive, to discarding the results. The user may redefine a profile at any time, and many systems will periodically remind users to review their profiles.

Most current awareness systems rely on the simple form of a user profile. This is certainly easier to match with incoming literature than any extended form, and it eliminates the need for either the user or the system to define a sophisticated profile. The current awareness system is most effective in situations where the literature is dynamic and changing rapidly. This is the case in many research settings and in organizations concerned with the daily flow of business, finance, and governmental and political changes. A similar situation arises in medical and other time-critical situations, where the "literature" includes records directly pertinent to the current situation. The term *pretrieval* has been suggested for a system that would automatically alert a clinical physician to the one or two documents most relevant to the case he is attending (Wagner 1995). The database for such a highly dynamic current awareness system would be updated continually.

Because the user is largely a passive participant in a current awareness system, it can be difficult to judge the system's effectiveness. If the results are given to the user on-line, then it is possible—with the user's consent—to monitor what the user does with these results. However, this is of limited value, for the user may simply download the entire set of documents presented and subsequently treat them off-line. This monitoring is of real value only if the user is willing to examine the document set on-line and to be selective about what is kept and discarded. If the results are not presented on-line, explicit cooperation by the user is necessary to obtain satisfactory measures of effectiveness. The only sure measure is a user's explicit request for a particular document.

6.4   RETROSPECTIVE SEARCH SYSTEMS

Retrospective search systems are designed to search the entire body of literature available to the information system in response to an ad hoc query. The typical retrospective search system has a relatively large and stable database of documents and a small, rapidly changing stock of queries, provided anew each time the user approaches the system. In contrast, the current awareness system has a relatively large and stable database of user profiles and a stock of documents that changes continually as new documents such as journal issues and technical reports arrive. Whereas a retrospective search system can be thought of as examining a database of documents to locate matches to a query, a current awareness system can be thought of as examining a database of user profiles to locate matches to a document.

Virtually all existing retrospective search systems, other than some experimental ones, treat the users monolithically. That is, all users appear to the system to be the same, and no effort is made to differentiate users on the basis of background or ability to use the information that the system provides. Although the system is easier to design and operate under this assumption than it would be if individual users were more differentiated, the result is that any such system is inherently limited in its ability to meet a user's information needs consistently and completely. The larger and more heterogeneous the user group, the more significant this problem becomes. An information system catering to a well-defined homogeneous group of users can operate on the basis of a "standard user" with relatively high effectiveness. But there is no standard user that is really adequate for use by a general system that must handle users with all levels of educational and experiential backgrounds and a great diversity of interests.

6.5 MODIFYING THE QUERY BY THE PROFILE

One tactic that a reference librarian uses in trying to help a person with a request is to learn something more about the person's background and level of knowledge. Obviously, this effort can be more successful in a library where there are many repeat users, as in a business or industrial environment, than in a library accessible to the general public. The reference librarian can become increasingly familiar with the individual users over time, noting their patterns of usage and their reactions to the materials provided to them. In effect, the reference librarian is constructing an informal mental profile of each user.

It makes sense intuitively to postulate that better knowledge of the individual user will enable the system to provide information that more accurately addresses the user's information needs. For example, if the user requests information on the *theory of groups*, a sociologist is likely to be referring to the behavior of a set of people, while a mathematician is more likely to be referring to a particular type of algebraic structure. The information system that knows the background of the user can make this distinction and focus the query on the appropriate set of documents. Similarly, the undergraduate mathematics student with this question is likely to be asking for basic material, whereas the experienced algebraist knows the basic material and is more likely looking for the latest research developments. With this in mind, it is appropriate to consider an information system that can make use of a query and a user profile simultaneously, using the latter to modify and interpret the former.

There are a number of ways to use the profile to modify the query or its interpretation. The first is to use the profile as a *post-filter* on the query. That is, the query is processed normally, then the results are organized on the basis of information in the profile. This modification may result in a reordering of the responses to the query. For example, we may design the system to list first those documents that are most accessible to the user, even if some of them have lower potential value than other, less accessible documents. It may also result in the elimination of some of the retrieved documents, or at least relegate them to a list that is not presented to the user unless specifically requested. Thus the latest research results might be withheld from the response given to an undergraduate student unless they are specifically requested, while more general documents providing a level of response appropriate to the typical student are presented.

Using the profile as a post-filter does not reduce the amount of effort required to retrieve and assemble the documents. Indeed, it adds an extra step to the processing. While the results may be good, other methods of using the profile may produce improved retrieval with less work by eliminating some documents from retrieval.

A second way to use the user profile is as a *pre-filter* on the query. That is, the profile can be used to modify the query before retrieval is attempted. The concept of a *document space* underlies this method of profile use. Begin with the vector model of the document. Recall that in this model the document is represented by either a 0,1-vector or a term weight vector. In a 0,1-vector, the ith component of the vector has the value 1 if term t_i is included in the document, or 0 if it is not. In a term weight vector the ith component has a value that reflects the significance of that term in the document. In either case we may consider each document vector as representing a point in the document space. For example, if a food document were represented by only two terms, say *calories* and *spiciness*, then a document about ice cream might have these terms at weights 8 and 0, respectively, since most ice cream has quite a few calories but is not at all spicy (Figure 6.1). This document is located at the point <8, 0> in a two-dimensional space. A document about fried chicken might have these terms at weights 10 and 3, respectively, as it has many calories and some spiciness. In a document about

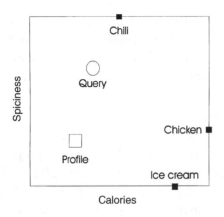

Figure 6.1   Sample food documents.

"three-alarm" chili, these terms might have weights 5 and 10. Thus the fried chicken document would be at the point <10, 3> and the chili document at <5, 10>. A food query would be located at another point in this space, perhaps at <3, 7>. If the user is a person who does not usually eat heavy, spicy foods, his user profile point might be at yet a different place, perhaps <2, 2>. Normally, food documents that are near the query point <3, 7> would be retrieved. However, applying the profile as a pre-filter might change the query, in effect moving it to the point <2.8, 6> or some other point. The interpretation would be that since the user normally likes light, mild food, perhaps he has overstated his query a little.

Of course in reality the situation is not as simple as this. The vectors representing the documents have many more terms, as they must account for all vocabulary terms. Thus we should think of the documents as points in a space of many thousands of dimensions. It is difficult to picture such a space, but mathematically this is no more difficult to handle than a two-dimensional space—there are just many more terms to include in any calculation.

Among the various formulas that can be used to modify the query, two are particularly simple (Myaeng and Korfhage 1985). One is a *simple linear transformation*. In effect this moves the query point directly toward the profile point. Suppose that the query and profile are represented by the vectors $<q_1, q_2, \ldots, q_n>$ and $<p_1, p_2, \ldots, p_n>$, respectively. Choose a value k, $0 \leq k \leq 1$, and replace each q_i by

$$q'_i = kp_i + (1 - k)q_i.$$

Observe that if $k = 0$ this leaves each q_i in its original location, while if $k = 1$ each q_i is replaced by the corresponding p_i, in effect replacing the query by the profile. Intermediate values for k place the modified query somewhere along the line between the original query and the profile. Another way to write the modification equation is

$$q'_i = q_i + k(p_i - q_i),$$

which shows more clearly that each q_i is modified by an amount proportional to the difference in the profile and query component values. The modified query in the food example was obtained by choosing $k = 0.2$. The transformation is called *linear* because a linear (first-degree) equation governs the modification of the query components.

A slightly more complex process is *piecewise linear transformation* of the query. In this, individual term weights are modified in different ways, depending on how they occur in the query and profile. There are four cases:

1. A term occurs in both the query and the profile. In this case, the type of modification suggested for the simple linear case seems most appropriate.

2. A term occurs in the query but not the profile. In this case, the term may be left unmodified or perhaps modified only slightly, perhaps reducing its value by 5%, on the grounds that the user normally is not interested in this term.

3. A term occurs in the profile but not the query. One option in this case is to not introduce the term; another is to introduce it with somewhat less weight than it has in the profile, on the grounds that the user normally is interested in this term.

4. A term occurs in neither the profile nor the query. In this case, the term has value 0 in both the query and the profile, and any modification of the types discussed above will leave the value at 0.

This potentially applies a different linear transformation to each of the terms in the query, hence the name *piecewise* linear transformation. Because each component is modified differently, there is no guarantee that the modified query will lie on the line joining the original query and the profile.

Example 6.1 Suppose that the user profile is <5, 0, 0, 3> and the query is <0, 2, 0, 7>. Since the first term is in the profile but not the query, add it to the query with half of its profile weight. The second term, in the query but not the profile, should probably be reduced a little, perhaps by 10%. The third term is in neither query nor profile. For the fourth term, which is in both, the user may decide that the query is three times as important as the profile. Hence its new value should be computed using $k = 0.25$. The modified query <2.5, 1.8, 0, 6> results. Observe that a simple linear modification with the given k value would have yielded the modified query <1.25, 1.5, 0, 6>.

Pre-filtering the query processes the query to arrive at a potentially better one before beginning retrieval. The amount of work to retrieve the documents is the same as with the unmodified query; the hope is that the retrieved set is of better quality.

6.6 THE QUERY AND PROFILE AS SEPARATE REFERENCE POINTS

Although pre-filtering the query moves the query point, it does not basically change the retrieval process. The paradigm is to retrieve all documents that lie within a given range from the query point and hence have a given similarity to it. A third way to use the profile is to treat it as a separate reference point in addition to the query. For purposes of this discussion, assume that similarity is measured by distance (a parallel development can be made using angle as the similarity measure). When these two reference points are used, a document must be judged for retrieval not only on its distance from the query point but also on its distance from the profile point. Judgments are based on these two distances, using the query and profile as *co-filters*. Two major problems arise: How should the two judgments be combined, and how should the query and profile distances be weighted? Should the query distance be given more weight, should both distances be weighted equally, or should the profile distance count more heavily?

There are four simple ways to combine the query and profile distances. Recall that the standard interpretation (using only the query) is to retrieve all documents lying within a fixed distance d from the query. Each method generalizes the standard interpretation in a reasonable way. Represent the distance between a document and a query, for example, by $\|D, Q\|$.

The first method is to require that a document be within distance d of either the query or the profile,

$$\|D, Q\| \leq d \quad \text{or} \quad \|D, P\| \leq d.$$

This is the least restrictive of the four methods, requiring only that the document be similar to one or the other reference point. Even if the query and profile have little to do with each other, this method will retrieve the set union of documents relating to both points. This is a *disjunctive model* of query-profile interaction.

An alternative definition of the disjunctive model is to require that

$$\min(\|D, Q\|, \|D, P\|) \leq d.$$

This definition produces precisely the same set of retrieved documents, and may be easier to handle in a retrieval system.

The second method is more restrictive, requiring that the distances from a document to both the query and the profile be within the limit d,

$$\|D, Q\| \leq d \quad \text{and} \quad \|D, P\| \leq d.$$

The retrieved set for this model is the intersection of the sets of documents related to the query and those related to the profile. Thus if the query and profile have little to do with each other, this method is likely to retrieve few, if any, documents. This is a *conjunctive model* of interaction.

An alternative definition of the conjunctive model is to require that

$$\max(\|D, Q\|, \|D, P\|) \leq d.$$

As is the case with the disjunctive model, this definition may be easier to handle in a retrieval system.

The third method, the *ellipsoidal model*, requires that the sum of the two distances be within the prescribed limit,

$$\|D, Q\| + \|D, P\| \leq d.$$

If retrieval from the query alone picks up documents within an n-dimensional sphere of radius d about the query point, this generalizes the sphere to an n-dimensional ellipsoid with foci Q and P (Chavarria Garza and Korfhage 1982).

The value of *d* defines a *contour* bounding the set of documents to be retrieved. If *Q* and *P* are close together, this model appears intuitively to work well (Figure 6.2). But if *Q* and *P* are far apart—that is, unrelated—many documents between the two reference points are picked up that are not really related to either point (Figure 6.3).

Because of this behavior when the query and profile are unrelated, the ellipsoidal model seems weak for general use. A fourth model, the *Cassini oval model*, seems to provide contours that have more intuitive appeal (Liu 1982). The basis for this model is the requirement that the product—rather than the sum—of the distances from *Q* and *P* be within the prescribed limit,

$$\|D,\, Q\| \times \|D,\, P\| \le d.$$

This equation results in contours that change their basic shape depending on the relationship between *Q* and *P*. When the query and profile are closely related, the contour resembles a slightly fat ellipse; with the query and profile located farther apart, the contour takes on the shape of a peanut (Figure 6.4a). The contour narrows still further with increased distance between *Q* and *P*, until at a critical point it becomes a lemniscate, or figure-eight shaped; beyond that point, the contour breaks into two pieces, one around the query and one around the profile (Figure 6.4b). This can be interpreted as showing that the query and the profile have nothing to do with each other. (For example, a user with a profile showing a usual interest in computing asks a question about mushrooms.)

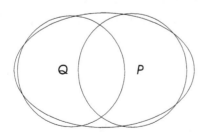

Figure 6.2   *Ellipsoidal model, Q and P close together.*

Figure 6.3   *Elliptical model, Q and P far apart.*

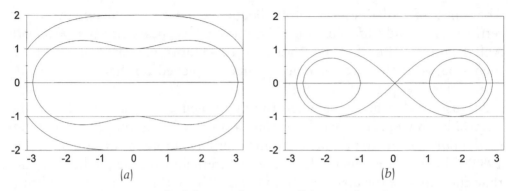

Figure 6.4   *Cassini ovals (a)* a = 2; k = 5, 8; *(b)* a = 2; k = 3, 4.

These models are interesting theoretically, but the question is whether they work in practice and, if they do, which is better. Before considering that aspect, however, there are other theoretical questions to consider. First, distance has been used as a measure of similarity, but the specific distance measure has not been defined. Different distance measures result in different similarity measures. The *unit circles* for L_1, L_2, and L_∞, three typical metrics, have the shapes shown in Figure 6.5. Thus if a point is at distance 1 from the origin by Euclidean distance, it is farther away by the city block distance and nearer by the maximal direction distance.

Another issue to consider is how the profile and query should be weighted. The user may feel that the query is more important and wish to place more emphasis on it. In the defining inequalities, weights can be applied as multipliers for the disjunctive, conjunctive, and ellipsoidal models,

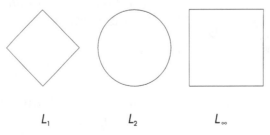

L_1 L_2 L_∞

Figure 6.5   *Unit circles for* L$_1$, L$_2$, *and* L$_\infty$.

$$\min(w_1\|D,\,Q\|,\,w_2\|D,\,P\|) \le d$$

$$\max(w_1\|D,\,Q\|,\,w_2\|D,\,P\|) \le d$$

$$w_1\|D,\,Q\| + w_2\|D,\,P\| \le d.$$

However, since the Cassini oval model is defined by a product, applying weights as factors is not effective. They would combine into a single weight affecting the entire product, rather than influencing the two distances separately. This is addressed by applying the weights as exponents in the Cassini oval model:

$$\|D,\,Q\|^{w_1} \times \|D,\,P\|^{w_2} \le d.$$

The final modification to be considered here is made possible by the fact that a modified query can be introduced by using the profile as a pre-filter. This raises the possibility of using the modified query as one of the two reference points, in combination with either the original query or the profile, or including it as a third point of reference.

There are a large number of possibilities. If the profile is used as a pre-filter, the choice involved is between the simple linear transformation or the piecewise linear transformation (or some other, as yet undefined, transformation). In the linear transformation, the value of one parameter must be chosen; for the piecewise transformation, parameter values for each of the three types of transformations involving terms that occur in either the query or the profile must be chosen. If the profile is used as a second reference point—a co-filter—then one of the four models must be selected as most appropriate, and the weights must be chosen. In any case, the metric to use in measuring distance must be selected (one of the three that have been discussed or some other one). And finally there is the choice of which combination of reference points to use.

All of this results in a large number of models of query-profile interaction to consider. Nothing in the theory would lead to the conclusion that one of these methods of interaction is more effective than another, or indeed, that any are effective at all. Thus it is necessary to provide experimental evidence of the effectiveness. This was done by Sung Myaeng in his doctoral dissertation (Myaeng 1987; Myaeng and Korfhage 1990). Myaeng tested 395 query-profile combinations against the query alone, for 30 different queries, using a database of documents from *Communications of the ACM*. For roughly

30% of the combinations, there was a small but statistically significant improvement in retrieval performance, confirming the intuition that information about the user can improve retrieval performance.

6.7   THE ETHICS OF A USER PROFILE

A user profile, even in its simplest form, provides a model of the user. In the more extended forms of the profile, this model can become quite detailed. The development and use of the profile thus raises two ethical questions.

The first arises from the use of a profile to limit or tailor the output to a given user. This rests on the presumption that any such modification is "right" for the user, and is what the user would want. The validity of this presumption is a matter of legitimate concern; however, the typical information retrieval system of today makes a similar presumption, albeit for the entire group of users. By limiting the output, whether to a specific number of documents or on the basis of a threshold value, the retrieval system implicitly declares that the documents not presented are not wanted by the user. Ordering the documents by any measure of significance, or similarity to the query, in effect declares that the system's measures are those that the user would apply if asked. Using the profile as part of this limiting process makes the process more complex but does not change its fundamental character—it still selects certain documents and presents them in an order considered best for the user.

The second question concerns the invasion of the user's privacy, particularly with the extended form of the profile. People are generally poor at self-description, so it has been suggested that the profile be monitored for effectiveness and adjusted to improve its effect. Conceivably this modification could take the form of adjusting weights of terms and factors (education, experience, and so forth) in the profile, and of adding new terms and factors. The presumed end of this would be a profile that quite accurately mirrors the information habits of the user. It could contain information-related facets of the user's behavior that the user does not want known or may not even recognize.

As building this profile model constitutes an invasion of the user's privacy, questions relating to the development, control, and use of the profile should be addressed. What control, for example, should the user have over profile modification? Should any modification be hidden from the user, or should all modifications be open to user control? If the latter, when should the control take effect—before the new profile is introduced to the system (when its effect is still unknown) or after the profile has been introduced and used for at least one query (so that the user can see the effect)? Should the user be able to veto any and all profile monitoring and adjustment, and potentially suffer the consequence of lower quality retrieval?

REFERENCES

Chavarria Garza, Hector, and Robert R. Korfhage. 1982. Retrieval improvement by interaction of queries and user profiles. *Proceedings of COMP-SAC '82, Sixth International Conference on Computer Software and Applications*, Chicago, pp. 470–475.

Harman, Donna K. 1993. *The First Text REtrieval Conference (TREC-1)*. Washington, D.C.: NIST Special Publication 500-207.

Hensley, C.B., T.R. Savage, A.J. Sowarby, and A. Resnick. 1962. Selective dissemination of information—A new approach to effective communication. *IRE Transactions of the Professional Group on Engineering Management*, EM-9:2.

Liu, Jung. 1982. A distance approach toward an ideal information retrieval system. M.S. thesis, Southern Methodist University, Dallas, Texas.

Myaeng, Sung Hyon. 1987. *The roles of user profiles in information retrieval*. Ph.D. diss., Southern Methodist University, Dallas, Texas.

Myaeng, Sung H., and Robert R. Korfhage. 1985. Dynamic user profiles. Technical Report No. 85-CSE-4, Department of Computer Science and Engineering, Southern Methodist University. (Presented at ACM Computer Science Conference, New Orleans, March 1985.)

Myaeng, Sung H., and Robert R. Korfhage. 1990. Integration of user profiles: Models and experiments in information retrieval. *Information Processing & Management* 26, no. 6:719–738.

Wagner, Michael M. 1995. *Decision-theoretic clinical information systems*. Ph.D. diss., University of Pittsburgh.

EXERCISES

1. Suppose that a retrieval system has developed a potential list of documents for retrieval in response to a query. Determine how each element of an extended user profile can be used to modify this list.

Which elements of the extended user profile are of most value in this process?

2. Determine what shape an ellipse (in two dimensions) has in the L_1 metric. Assume that the foci are at <2, 0> and at <0, 2>.

3. Determine what shape an ellipse (in two dimensions) has in the L_∞ metric. Assume that the foci are at <2, 0> and at <0, 2>.

4. Determine what shapes a Cassini oval (in two dimensions) has in the L_1 metric. Assume that the foci are at <2, 0> and at <0, 2>.

5. Determine what shapes a Cassini oval (in two dimensions) has in the L_∞ metric. Assume that the foci are at <2, 0> and at <0, 2>.

6. Determine the shape a conjunctive combination of query and profile can have in each of the three metrics.

7. Determine the shape a disjunctive combination of query and profile can have in each of the three metrics.

8. Investigate the effect of weighting on the shape of an ellipse by giving the query a weight of 2 and the profile a weight of 1. Use your choice of a metric.

9. Investigate the effect of weighting on the shape of a Cassini oval by giving the query a weight of 2 and the profile a weight of 1. Use your choice of a metric.

10. Investigate the effect of weighting on the shape of a conjunctive model by giving the query a weight of 2 and the profile a weight of 1. Use your choice of a metric.

11. Investigate the effect of weighting on the shape of a disjunctive model by giving the query a weight of 2 and the profile a weight of 1. Use your choice of a metric.

12. It has been suggested that the original query, the modified query, and the user profile be used together as three reference points. Determine the shape of an ellipse with three foci at <0, 0>, <1, 5>, and <6, 0>.

13. It has been suggested that the original query, the modified query, and the user profile be used together as three reference points. Determine the shape of a "Cassini oval" with three foci at <0, 0>, <1, 5>, and <6, 0>. Is it possible, with these or other foci, to develop

a "Cassini oval" with a hole in the middle? (This would indicate that there may be documents "in the middle" of all reference points, but sufficiently far away not to be of interest.)

14. Investigate and interpret the four given retrieval models when an angle measure such as the cosine is used in place of a metric.

15. Privacy issues are of concern not only in information retrieval systems, but also when handling highly sensitive material such as medical, credit, or police records. Determine what laws exist to protect the privacy of such records, and how they are enforced.

16. Open accessibility to the Internet and the World Wide Web has raised many questions of control of the material available to users through these sources. Investigate the controls that exist (or might exist) on such availability, and suggest ways in which user profiles could be effective in such control. Discuss the control of the user profiles themselves in this context.

CHAPTER 7

Multiple Reference Point Systems

Chapter 6 introduced the concept of applying the user profile as a second reference point, in addition to the query, when processing a query. At the same time, a modified query point was introduced, suggesting the possibility of using this in place of either the original query or the profile, or as a third reference point. This chapter generalizes the concept of a reference point and discusses the use of such points in retrieval. Specifically, four models that use visual interfaces to enable users to work with two or more reference points simultaneously are discussed.

7.1 DEFINITIONS

The term *reference point* means any defined point or concept against which a document can be judged. The query and the user profile are obvious examples. A known document is another example—a point against which any document can be judged for similarity. Other kinds of reference points correspond less directly to documents but may still be used as measuring points, as they pertain to characteristics of the documents. These include known authors, known journals, periods of time, and so forth. A known paper or book is a particularly important reference point. This can lead directly to other documents, either through similarity of theme or through citation links (see Chapter 10). An alternative name for a reference point is a *point of interest* (POI). This term is perhaps more appropriate for these more general types of reference points. Observe that once general reference points are introduced, a specific query need not be given. Rather, the user can specify a number of reference points and ask for documents similar to these points.

Weights and metrics may be applied to general reference points, as was done in Chapter 6. Specifically, the terminology $R_1, R_2, \ldots, R_n$ denotes n reference points, with corresponding weights $w_1, w_2, \ldots, w_n$. The query, when one is present, is identified with R_1. The weights are assumed to be nonnegative and are normalized to total to 1, $w_1 + w_2 + \ldots + w_n = 1$. A metric is indicated by double bars, $\| \ldots \|$. The ideas developed in this chapter are independent of the particular metric used, so any of the L_p family of metrics or any other metric can be used. The specific results depend, of course, on the metric chosen.

7.2   DOCUMENTS AND DOCUMENT CLUSTERS

If an individual document is to be used as a reference point, it must be represented in a way that is compatible with the system. Usually this means representing the document as a list of weighted or unweighted key terms, presenting no significant problem to the system designer.

It is also possible to define a reference point from a group of related documents. The user might have identified several documents on poverty in urban America. Rather than use the terms *poverty, urban,* and *America* (or perhaps in addition to these terms), and rather than single out one of the documents, the user might feel that the entire group forms a focus for search and retrieval. This can be done by defining a *document cluster* and determining one or more *cluster points* that represent this cluster.

Many methods of defining clusters have been proposed and implemented in software packages. Some are based on statistical techniques; others use graph theory as their basis. Some generate clusters that are distinct, that is, each object is in only one cluster; others generate overlapping clusters. Some techniques are decompositional in nature. That is, they begin with everything in one large cluster, then successively break this into smaller but more tightly defined clusters. Other techniques work in the opposite direction. They begin by assuming that each entity is a separate cluster, then, to define larger clusters, seek to bring together entities that are in some sense close.

Cluster methods can be computationally intensive. For example, if clustering is based on a similarity measure, then for a set of n documents there are $n(n-1)/2$ pairwise similarity measures to be computed. The situation, however, is not as bleak as this implies. In the first place, techniques developed in computational geometry can be used to reduce this from an $O(n^2)$ process to an $O(n)$ process. In the second place, the number of documents used to define a reference point is small, typically about 10 or 20, so that the complexity of the computation is not a major problem.

When a cluster of documents has been identified, the problem of representing the cluster arises. This can be solved by computing an artificial "centroid" document, having the terms associated with the individual documents, with weights that are the average of the weights in the individual documents. This becomes the cluster point representing that cluster. It may be desirable to define more than one cluster point for a given group of documents. In this situation, a decompositional clustering technique is appropriate, as it will break the group of documents into as many clusters as are desired.

There is one caution in using document cluster points as reference points. The techniques used to define the cluster points frequently result in a definition in which a large number of terms have nonzero values. This can significantly slow down computations involving the cluster points, such as computing the similarity of a document to a cluster point. If this happens, it may be desirable to artificially modify the cluster points by setting a threshold value, reducing any weight below that threshold to 0. This results in an insignificant shift in the cluster point, and much reduced computational time.

7.3   THE MATHEMATICAL BASIS

Recall the weighted disjunctive, conjunctive, ellipsoidal, and Cassini oval models from Chapter 6:

$$\min(w_1\|D, Q\|, w_2\|D, P\|) \leq d$$

$$\max(w_1\|D, Q\|, w_2\|D, P\|) \leq d$$

$$w_1\|D, Q\| + w_2\|D, P\| \leq d$$

$$\|D, Q\|^{w_1} \times \|D, P\|^{w_2} \leq d$$

These four functions of the weighted distances—the minimum, maximum, sum, and product—clearly generalize to an arbitrary finite number of distances. Development of the general ellipsoidal model illustrates the process; the remaining three are left as exercises. Assume n reference points with normalized weights, and note that

$$w_1 = 1 - (w_2 + \ldots + w_n).$$

The general condition for the ellipsoidal distance is

$$(1 - (w_2 + \ldots + w_n)) \, \|D, R_1\| + w_2\|D, R_2\| + \ldots + w_n\|D, R_n\| \leq d.$$

Rewrite this condition, grouping terms by the weights and factoring out the distance to R_1:

$$\|D, R_1\| + w_2(\|D, R_2\| - \|D, R_1\|) + \ldots w_n(\|D, R_n\| - \|D, R_1\|)$$

$$= \|D, R_1\| \left[1 + w_2\left(\frac{\|D, R_2\|}{\|D, R_1\|} - 1\right) + \ldots w_n\left(\frac{\|D, R_n\|}{\|D, R_1\|} - 1\right) \right] \leq d.$$

Recall that if there is only a single reference point, the query, the condition for retrieval is $\|D, R_1\| \leq d$. Thus for the ellipsoidal model of retrieval with n reference points, the effect is that of

> normal (query only) retrieval, with the distance multiplied by a function depending on the ratios of the distances from the document to each of the reference points, compared to the distance from the document to the first reference point (query).

The same statement applies to the Cassini oval model of retrieval, with only the specific modifying function changed. The situation is less clear for the disjunctive and conjunctive models, as these emphasize individual reference point effects. (See Exercises 1–3.) Note that the distance to the first reference point occurs in the modifying function as the initial term, 1. This leads to the following postulate:

> For any reference points $R_1, \ldots, R_n$, corresponding weights $w_1, \ldots, w_n$, with $w_1 + \ldots + w_n = 1$, and any functions $f, g_2, \ldots, g_n$, the inequality
>
> $$\|D, R_1\| f\left(1, g_2\left(\frac{\|D, R_2\|}{\|D, R_1\|}, w_2\right), \ldots, g_n\left(\frac{\|D, R_n\|}{\|D, R_1\|}, w_n\right)\right) \leq d$$

represents the retrieval of all documents within a threshold "distance" of d (Korfhage 1988, 1991a).

In this most general form, there are no restrictions on the functions f and $g_2, \ldots, g_n$. (The functions g_i explicitly tie the weights to the corresponding reference points.) Nor is there any restriction on the metric or distance function used. Thus the level d contour specified by the inequality can assume an arbitrary shape. There can theoretically be holes within the contour, or isolated groups of documents outside the main contour. It is a matter of open research to determine which functions and metrics correspond most closely to the goal of retrieving exactly and only those documents that meet a given information need.

Example 7.1 Suppose that there are four reference points. If the ellipsoidal model is used, the functions g_i are multiplications and the function f is addition:

$$\|D, R_1\|\left(1 + w_2 \frac{\|D, R_2\|}{\|D, R_1\|} + w_3 \frac{\|D, R_3\|}{\|D, R_1\|} + w_4 \frac{\|D, R_4\|}{\|D, R_1\|}\right) \leq d,$$

or

$$w_1\|D, R_1\| + w_2\|D, R_2\| + w_3\|D, R_3\| + w_4\|D, R_4\| \leq d.$$

In a Cassini oval model for the same four reference points, the g_i would be exponentiation and f would be multiplication:

$$\|D, R_1\|\left(\frac{\|D, R_2\|}{\|D, R_1\|}\right)^{w_2}\left(\frac{\|D, R_3\|}{\|D, R_1\|}\right)^{w_3}\left(\frac{\|D, R_4\|}{\|D, R_1\|}\right)^{w_4} \leq d,$$

or

$$\|D, R_1\|^{w_1}\|D, R_2\|^{w_2}\|D, R_3\|^{w_3}\|D, R_4\|^{w_4} \leq d.$$

A user could even, for some strange reason, decide to combine various models into one overall model. For example, he might want to use the disjunctive model with reference to R_2 and R_3, combining that with the Cassini oval model with reference to R_4, and finally use the ellipsoidal model to combine that result with the reference point R_1:

$$w_1\|D, R_1\| + w_{234}((\min(w_2\|D, R_2\|, w_3\|D, R_3\|))^{w_{23}}\|D, R_4\|^{w_4}) \leq d.$$

That such a combination as the last one in the example would be used is highly unlikely. The point is that the postulated general form for multiple reference points is extremely flexible, permitting models in which the "sphere" around R_1 is highly distorted, and may even have holes in it or isolated pieces. Thus this model apparently has the power to match a user's information need very accurately—if only a highly accurate description of that need could be determined. Unfortunately, the document space contours that enclose the retrieved set become extremely complex and difficult to understand. Thus simpler models of the retrieval process are required.

7.4   GUIDO

Two general conclusions arise from the above discussion—first, that distances are significant, and second, that the ratios of distances are also significant, since these ratios figure in the definition of the general model. These conclusions lead to more readily understandable models of the retrieval process.

The general vector model is based on the entire search vocabulary for a database. Hence it corresponds to a document space with many thousands of dimensions, one for each vocabulary term. Recall the practical difficulty that for any given document or query most of the terms in the vector representation are zero. This leads to using a reduced representation, consisting of only the nonzero terms. There is also another difficulty, that of visualizing this general document space. When several reference points are involved, the contours corresponding to various levels of retrieval become quite complex and difficult to predict.

However, the observation that distance is used as a measure of similarity leads to the conclusion that distance alone matters. In fact, this is precisely the model used for retrieval against a query alone: The documents are presented in order of decreasing similarity to (increasing distance from) the query point. In effect, the usual list presented in response to a query is a one-dimensional *distance space*. This can easily be generalized to multiple reference points. This model, called GUIDO (Graphical User Interface for Document Organization), results in a relatively low dimensional space, independent of the dimensionality of the document space (Korfhage 1991b; Nuchprayoon and Korfhage 1994).

Suppose that there are only two reference points—say, the query, Q, and the user profile, P. Then regardless of the dimensionality of the document space, the model presented by GUIDO is two-dimensional, with a document being located at a point whose coordinates are its distances from Q and P. Let $\mu = \|Q, P\|$. Then P is located at $<\mu, 0>$ and Q is located at $<0, \mu>$. The entire document space is mapped into an image anchored by these two points.

Consider now the line through Q and P in the document space, and let D be any document on this line. The two reference points divide this line into three segments; the distances from D to Q and P are related in various ways, depending on which segment contains D (Figure 7.1).

If D is in the Q end,

$$\|D, P\| = \|D, Q\| + \mu;$$

if D is between Q and P,

$$\|D, Q\| + \|D, P\| = \mu;$$

if D is in the P end,

$$\|D, P\| = \|D, Q\| - \mu.$$

Finally, by the triangle inequality, for any point not on this line three inequalities hold:

$$\|D, P\| + \|D, Q\| > \mu,$$

$$\|D, P\| + \mu > \|D, Q\|, \quad \text{and}$$

$$\|D, Q\| + \mu > \|D, P\|,$$

since the three distances involved are the lengths of the edges of the triangle formed by D, P, and Q. Thus the entire document space is represented within the semi-infinite plank bounded by the images of the three segments of the line through Q and P (Figure 7.2).

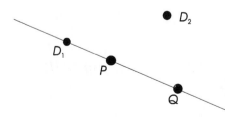

Figure 7.1 *The anchoring* P-Q *line for GUIDO.*

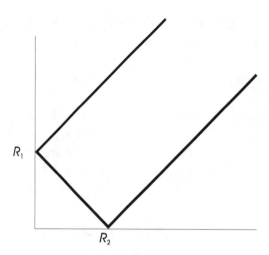

Figure 7.2   The distance space for GUIDO, with two reference points.

There are three effects of this mapping from the document space into the distance space. First, multiple document points are mapped onto the same point in the distance space. Specifically, if the document space has N dimensions, then the locus of all points with given distances from Q and P is an $N - 1$-dimensional ring whose axis is the Q-P line. Hence all of these points map onto one point in the GUIDO model. For example, using L_2 in a three-dimensional space, the spheres at distances d_Q from Q and d_P from P would intersect (if at all) in a circle. All points on this circle would map into the single point $<d_Q, d_P>$ in the distance space. This seeming ambiguity is actually in accordance with the retrieval criterion of retrieving (or not retrieving) all points having the same distances from Q and P (Figure 7.3).

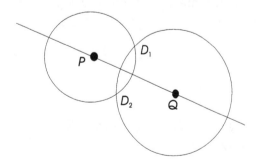

Figure 7.3   Ambiguity in GUIDO.

The second effect of the mapping is that potentially complex boundary contours for retrieval criteria become simpler. For example, in the ellipsoidal model the retrieval boundary is defined by an equation of the type $d_Q + d_P = k$. In the distance space this becomes a straight line parallel to the Q-P line (Figure 7.4). The documents to be retrieved are those between the base of the plank and the retrieval cap. If the distances are weighted, the line is still straight, but at an angle.

The third effect arises from the importance of the distance ratios in the retrieval models. The general model is stated in terms of these distance ratios. Specializing this to two reference points yields

$$\|D,\, Q\| f\left(1,\, \frac{\|D,\, P\|}{\|D,\, Q\|},\, w_2\right) \le d.$$

(Note that Q and P have been used in place of R_1 and R_2.) In other words, when the ratio of the distances from the document to the profile and query is constant, the distance inequality becomes

$$\|D,\, Q\| \le \frac{d}{f_r},$$

where f_r is the value of f for the given ratio and weight. In the document space, the locus of points having a given fixed distance ratio, k, is an $N - 1$-

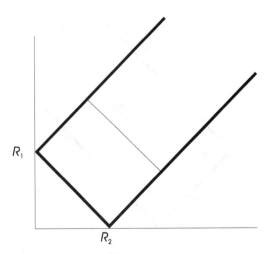

Figure 7.4   Elliptical retrieval cap in GUIDO.

dimensional ellipsoid. In GUIDO this becomes a straight line through the origin,

$$\|D,\, P\| = k\|D,\, Q\|.$$

See Figure 7.5. The limits on $\|D,\, Q\|$ are the values for which this line cuts the boundary of the half-infinite plank.

Thus the overall effect of the GUIDO model is to present a simpler, more understandable picture of the document locations with respect to the query and profile points. A similar statement holds for more than two reference points, although the surfaces bounding the distance space become somewhat more complex. For example, three reference points in the document space define a plane, with three lines through the pairs of points. Observe that this plane is divided into seven segments by the lines joining the three reference points (Figure 7.6). The GUIDO model corresponding to this becomes a three-dimensional semi-infinite prism whose sides are slightly bowed. The base of this prism corresponds to the triangle formed by the three points in the document space, and the sides of this prism are the images of the plane segments defined by the lines through the three reference points in the document space. Thus the prism has a triangular base and six sides. It can be shown that neither the base nor any of the sides are planar (flat).

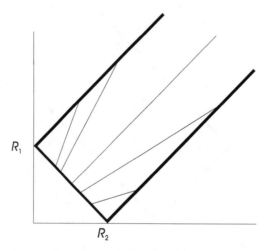

Figure 7.5   Loci of constant distance ratios in GUIDO.

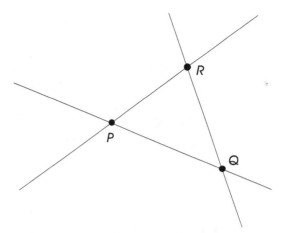

Figure 7.6   The anchoring P-Q-R *plane for GUIDO.*

Finally, note that throughout this discussion the exact metric used has not been specified. Thus the discussion applies to any metric. The size of the distance space and the location of documents within it will change as different metrics result in different distance measurements. But the basic shape of the distance space is invariant with respect to the choice of metric.

7.5 VIBE

Another model, VIBE (Visual Information Browsing Environment), focuses directly on the similarity ratios. In this model, the user chooses the reference points (POIs) and places circular icons representing them arbitrarily on the computer screen. Each document is automatically located at a position representing the ratios of its similarities to the reference points. The documents are each represented by a rectangular icon whose size relates to the importance of the document with respect to the reference points (Korfhage and Olsen 1991; Olsen et al. 1993a, 1993b). See Figure 7.7.

If there is only a single reference point (the query), the GUIDO model becomes a one-dimensional space. All of the documents are arrayed according to their distances from the reference point. Thus the model is of some, although minimal, utility. In contrast, since the VIBE model depends on the *ratio* of similarities, with only one similarity involved, the ratio is always 1.

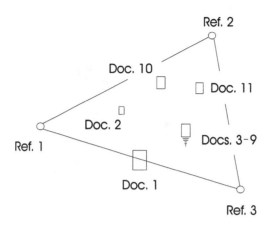

Figure 7.7   The VIBE display space.

In practice, all documents are located directly on top of that reference point. Thus the VIBE model is useless in this situation. The only information that it provides is the number of documents related to the given reference point.

Hence this discussion begins by examining the two-point model. In this example, *america* and *panama* are the POIs. The user applies the model by choosing locations (on the display screen) representing the two reference points. Once points representing *america* and *panama* have been chosen, each document D is positioned along the *america-panama* line segment at a point determined by the ratio of its similarities to the two reference points. Thus if D_1 is three times as similar to *panama* as it is to *america*, its position in the VIBE model will be three-fourths of the way from *america* to *panama*. If D_2 is equally similar to *america* and *panama*, it will be represented at the midpoint of the *america-panama* line segment (Figure 7.8). Documents related to only one of the reference points appear as icons on top of that POI, while documents related to neither do not appear. In the example, only 32 of 215 documents are related to *america* or *panama*. (See the upper right corner of Figure 7.8.) In order to achieve the clearest display, the user should position the two reference points as far apart as possible.

Similarly, if three reference points are used, the display will consist of a triangular region bounded by the line segments joining these three points. The icon for any document that is related to only one of the points will be positioned on top of that reference point. Documents related to two reference points but not the third will lie on the side of the triangle formed by

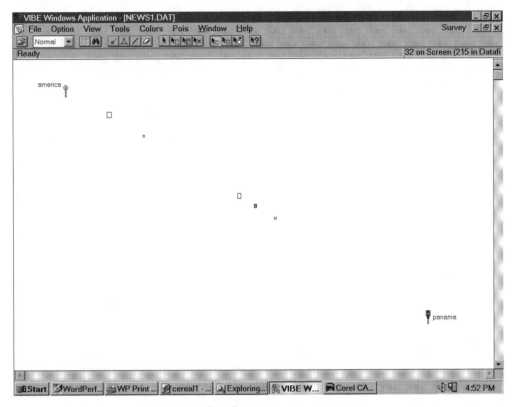

Figure 7.8   A two-POI VIBE display.

those two points. Finally, documents related to all three reference points will be positioned somewhere in the middle of the triangle (Figure 7.9).

As with two reference points, the user can achieve a clearer display by spreading the three reference points out widely on the display screen. VIBE gives the user dynamic control over the positions of these points, so that their locations can be adjusted for the most informative display.

The same display principle can be extended to more than three reference points. Suppose that there are n reference points. Let $s_1, s_2, \ldots, s_n$ be the similarities that a given document d has to each of these points. Since only the ratios of similarities are of concern, these similarities can either be taken to be in the interval [0, 1] or multiplied by some positive integer to place them in a broader range, for example [0, 10]. If p_i is the position vector of reference point R_i, then the position of d is determined by the equation

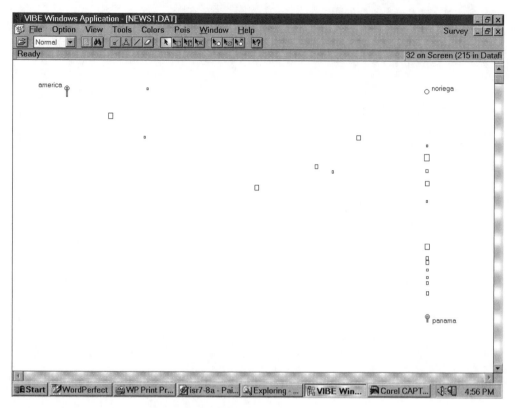

Figure 7.9   A three-POI VIBE display.

$$p_d = \frac{\sum_i s_i p_i}{\sum_i s_i} .$$

Example 7.2   Suppose that a document D has similarities 0.7, 0.3, and 0.2 to three given reference points A, B, and C. The position of D is then given by the equation

$$p_D = \frac{7p_A + 3p_B + 2p_C}{12} .$$

(Note that for convenience the similarities have been multiplied by 10.) If the reference points and the document are displayed in two dimensions, then the x and y coordinates of D can be determined from this equation by substituting in the x and y coordinates of the three reference points. Suppose the reference points are located at <0, 50>, <75, 100>, and <120, 10>, respectively. Then

$$x_D = \frac{0 + 225 + 240}{12} = \frac{465}{12},$$

$$y_D = \frac{350 + 300 + 20}{12} = \frac{670}{12}.$$

Moving any of the reference points will change these values. For example, if the second reference point were shifted to position <100, 90>, the new document position would be

$$x_D = \frac{0 + 300 + 240}{12} = \frac{540}{12},$$

$$y_D = \frac{350 + 270 + 20}{12} = \frac{640}{12}.$$

Similarly, the position of D in a higher dimensional "display" would be determined by substituting in each of the coordinate values for each reference point.

Moreover, the reference points need not be key terms, queries, or profiles. For example, if the user is interested in a term having a natural numerical range—to locate documents within a given period of years or salaries within a given range of values—she can specify two reference points, a high and low value, place them on opposite sides of the display, and have the documents spread out according to their positions within that range of values. A reference point can also be a known document or a known author. Any entity with the property that a document can be evaluated numerically with respect to that entity can be a reference point.

Consider now the placement of a document point with respect to the given reference points. The most obvious difference between this model and GUIDO is that similarity ratios are used in VIBE in contrast to the distances used in GUIDO. Recall the assumption that similarity is inversely related to distance. There are many ways in which this relationship can be expressed. Using the simplest relationship,

$$s = \frac{1}{d},$$

the similarity becomes very large for documents very close to the reference point. In fact, for a document identical to the reference point, the similarity is infinite. This can be avoided by setting some maximum limit on the similarity value. This action would have the effect of using the inverse distance as a similarity measure outside of a given contour, and declaring that all documents within that contour have the same (maximum) similarity to the reference point. If this simple inversion is used, a fixed ratio of similarities corresponds to a fixed ratio of distances:

$$c = \frac{s_1}{s_2} = \frac{1/d_1}{1/d_2} = \frac{d_2}{d_1}.$$

However, this is only true outside of the maximum similarity contour.

If, instead, the exponential type of inversion discussed in Section 4.3 is used, then the similarity value of 1 corresponds to a distance of 0, and the similarity value of 0 corresponds to an infinite distance. To implement this, any of the functions

$$s = k^{-d}$$

can be used, where s is the similarity, d the distance, and k a positive constant. (See Section 4.3.) Observe that a fixed ratio of similarities does not correspond to a fixed ratio of distances. If $s_1/s_2 = c$, then

$$c = \frac{k^{-d_1}}{k^{-d_2}} = k^{d_2 - d_1}.$$

Thus a fixed *ratio* of similarities corresponds, with these similarity functions, to a fixed *difference* of distances. Hence there is a further compression of the data, with all points having the same fixed difference of distances (independent of what those distances are) mapping onto the same point. Thus each point of the VIBE display has the potential to represent a large set of documents. To aid the user, VIBE represents multiple documents at a point by a tail on the rectangular icon, with the length of the tail proportional to the number of documents represented at a point.

Still other similarity functions can be chosen that map document points appropriately into the defined range of similarities. For each such choice, all documents lying on some high dimensional surface within the document space will map onto a single point in the VIBE display.

Showing the user all of the documents associated with a given set of reference points has the advantage that nothing is hidden from the user. However, it also has the disadvantage that the user may be presented with hundreds or thousands of documents of minor significance. One way to handle this is to give the user the ability to control the similarity value above which documents are visible. By controlling this threshold the user can begin with a display of several hundred documents and narrow it down to show only the 25 or 50 most significant ones, or even only the one or two most significant. If the user then believes that seeing more documents can be beneficial, she can lower the threshold to redisplay some of those that have been hidden.

7.6   BOOLEAN VIBE

While VIBE has a vector space basis, it also provides a display implementing full Boolean retrieval capabilities. This section begins by introducing a term from topology. An *n-simplex* is an *n*-dimensional polyhedron based on a set of $n + 1$ vertices. With this definition a 0-simplex is a single point, a 1-simplex is the line segment joining two points, a 2-simplex is the triangle bounded by three points, a 3-simplex is a tetrahedron, and so forth. Suppose that a VIBE display is developed using POIs A, B, and C. In the document space, these three reference points define a 2-simplex, or triangle. Documents whose icons appear directly on top of one of the POIs contain only the terms of that POI. (Note that each document in the display will also contain terms not represented by any of the POIs.) Documents appearing on the line joining two POIs, say A and B, contain the terms for both POIs and thus in some sense correspond to A AND B. If the display also contains the POI C, then these documents do not contain the C terms, just as those documents on top of the A POI contain neither the B nor the C terms. The documents correspond to the following representations:

on A: A AND NOT B AND NOT C,

on the A-B line: A AND B AND NOT C,

and similarly for the other POIs and POI lines. Extending this concept, documents appearing within the *A-B-C* triangle are those satisfying

$$A \text{ AND } B \text{ AND } C.$$

When the fourth POI, *D*, is introduced, the same concept extends readily. The topology is now that of a 3-simplex or tetrahedron. The phrase "AND NOT *D*" is added to each of the above phrases, while documents within the tetrahedron determined by the four POIs satisfy the Boolean expression

$$A \text{ AND } B \text{ AND } C \text{ AND } D.$$

Now, suppose that the weights assigned to a document for the given POIs are all 1 or 0, indicating only the presence or absence of the POI terms. Then all document icons not directly on top of a POI will migrate to the center of the simplex (line, triangle, tetrahedron, . . .) containing them. Figure 7.10 is the Boolean equivalent of Figure 7.9. The number beneath a document icon indicates the number of documents represented, if there are more than one. The resulting document points are called the *Boolean points* for VIBE. For *n* POIs, the resulting display consists of $2^n - 1$ Boolean points, representing all of the Boolean combinations of the POIs except that one which is completely negated,

$$\text{NOT } A \text{ AND NOT } B \text{ AND NOT } C \text{ AND NOT. . . .}$$

Thus VIBE can be used to effect Boolean classification and retrieval, as well as vector-based classification and retrieval.

It will be noted that this display is oriented toward conjunctive (AND) queries, and that disjunctive (OR) queries are apparently not represented. However, the disjunctive query *is* represented. The Boolean VIBE display explicitly shows every Boolean combination of the reference points except the fully negated one. Recall that through the use of DeMorgan's Laws, a disjunction

$$A \text{ OR } B \text{ OR } C \text{ OR . . . OR } D$$

is equivalent to

$$\text{NOT(NOT } A \text{ AND NOT } B \text{ AND NOT } C \text{ AND NOT . . . AND NOT } D).$$

Thus the full disjunctive normal form of a disjunctive query contains every Boolean combination except the fully negated one. But this is precisely what

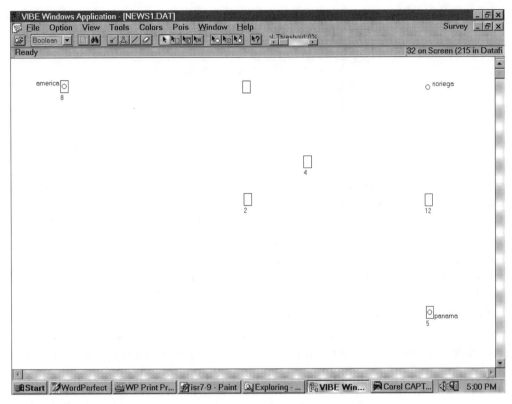

Figure 7.10   A three-POI Boolean VIBE display.

Boolean VIBE shows. Thus the disjunctive query *A* OR *B* OR *C* OR . . . OR *D* is represented by the totality of the documents shown in the display.

Boolean VIBE is sensitive to two threshold operations. It is linked to the normal vector VIBE, so that the number of documents shown is determined by the vector threshold, discussed in the previous section. The second threshold operates within Boolean VIBE to determine the location of each document. In converting from the vector representation of a document to a Boolean representation, each similarity value must be converted to 0 or 1. The threshold at which this decision is made is set by default at 50% of the maximum similarity, but the user can change this. Suppose, for example, that the range of similarity values is 0 to 10, and that a given document has similarity values of 10, 2, 4, and 7 with respect to POIs *A*, *B*, *C*, and *D*, respectively. The Boolean representation of this document at various threshold values is shown in Table 7.1.

Table 7.1
The Effect of the Boolean Threshold

Threshold	A	B	C	D	Document position
0%	1	1	1	1	A AND B AND C AND D
25%	1	0	1	1	A AND NOT B AND C AND D
50%	1	0	0	1	A AND NOT B AND NOT C AND D
75%	1	0	0	0	A AND NOT B AND NOT C AND NOT D
99%	1	0	0	0	A AND NOT B AND NOT C AND NOT D

The document thus always appears in the Boolean display, but at different Boolean points depending on the threshold setting. If the threshold is near 0, then every occurrence of a word counts, and most or all of the possible Boolean points have associated documents. If, on the other hand, the threshold is near the maximum, then only the most significant POI term (or occasionally two terms) counts, and documents migrate to the individual POI points.

One problem with any display, including VIBE, that maps a high-dimensional space into the plane is that there are likely to be false correspondences due to the mapping. That is, two points (documents) that are well separated in the document space may appear close together or even coincide due to the mapping. In general, the various functionalities of VIBE can be used to address this problem and to determine which "similar" documents really are similar, and which are those whose icons have been brought together by the mapping.

In the case of Boolean VIBE, however, it is possible to guarantee that no two of the points representing Boolean combinations of the POIs coincide, and this guarantee occurs almost without effort or cost. The reasoning is this. Two of the Boolean points will coincide in the display if and only if the points (in n-space) map onto the same point in the plane. But if they do, the mapping must have been along the direction of the line joining the points. There are only a finite number of these points, hence only a finite number of pairs of points. The "forbidden" directions are determined by these pairs of points; hence there are only a finite number of directions that must be avoided. *Almost any direction chosen at random will avoid the forbidden directions.* Hence almost any mapping (placement of the POIs) will guarantee that the Boolean points are all distinct. If the user is unfortunate enough to have two Boolean points coincide, shifting one of the POIs will solve the problem (Figure 7.11). The lines in the figure are available to the user to indicate which POIs relate to each document set.

7.7 BIRD

Another approach to the design of a multiple reference point retrieval system is to base it on an array determined by the reference points. This approach is exemplified by BIRD, a Browsing Interface for Retrieval of Documents (Kim and Korfhage 1994). The BIRD display consists of two major parts, with supporting functionalities. The underlying concept is to organize the documents within a data set on the basis of their similarity to two reference points at a time. A text window at the left of the display shows either the search terms the user may choose (the vocabulary) or document infor-

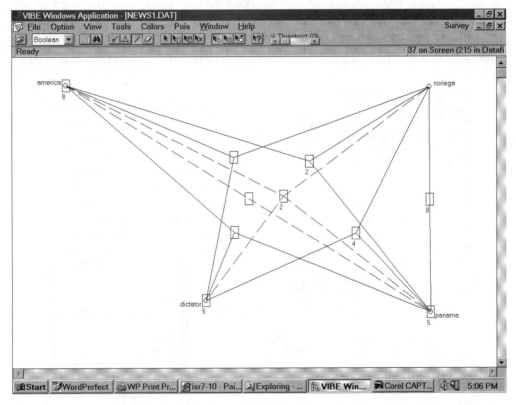

Figure 7.11   A four-POI Boolean VIBE display.

mation (Figure 7.12). The primary portion of the display is a *separator array* of four *cells*. Documents are distributed among these cells according to their relationship to two chosen reference points. The second portion of the display consists of a series of *classification bins*. The user isolates desired documents by moving them to these bins. To create Figure 7.12, the user has identified five cereal components—almonds, bran, oats, raisins, and rice—by color, then separated the cereals on the basis of manufacturer, General Mills or Kellogg's. Those cereals not made by either company have been moved to bin 1, and the General Mills cereals have been selected for display.

Initially, all documents are loaded into one of the classification bins. The vocabulary of the document set is listed for the user, along with a measure of the significance of each term, such as the count of the number of documents in which each term appears. After choosing two reference points, the user moves the document set to the origin of the array by depositing the documents on the funnel icon. The chosen reference terms define the axes of the array. Documents related to these terms are distributed throughout the array according to their relationships to the chosen reference terms. The user can open any cell to view the documents that it contains. The terms can also be

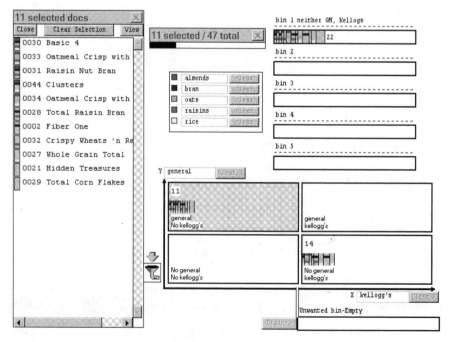

Figure 7.12   The BIRD display.

changed to modify the document distribution. The user can select the documents in any cell or combination of cells and move them into one of the bins, labeling that bin as she chooses. Bins can also be combined and relabeled.

A special classification list is the "unwanted" bin. Documents that are no longer of interest, such as those remaining in the origin cell, can be assigned to the unwanted bin. The terms that relate only to documents in the unwanted bin are then "hidden," or removed from the list of available terms. Thus the vocabulary can be narrowed to only those terms used in the desired documents.

At any time, the user can pick up one or more of the bins, including the unwanted bin, and reassign the documents to the separator array. Typically, the user then chooses new terms, thus refining the distribution of the selected documents. For example, if the user initially used terms A and B, then redistributed the documents using terms C and D, each of the separator cells would then contain documents with some specific combination of relationships to the four terms. In this way the user can create lists of documents having the characteristics that meet various information needs.

BIRD permits the user to construct a Boolean query iteratively. Suppose that the two chosen terms are A and B. The documents remaining in the origin cell are those not related to these terms. Thus they correspond to NOT A AND NOT B. The documents in the other three cells correspond to the Boolean expressions A AND NOT B, NOT A AND B, and A AND B. By choosing the documents in the A AND NOT B cell, for example, and redistributing these according to terms C and D the user creates the following four sets of documents:

$$A \text{ AND (NOT } B) \text{ AND (NOT } C) \text{ AND (NOT } D),$$

$$A \text{ AND (NOT } B) \text{ AND (NOT } C) \text{ AND } D,$$

$$A \text{ AND (NOT } B) \text{ AND } C \text{ AND (NOT } D),$$

$$A \text{ AND (NOT } B) \text{ AND } C \text{ AND } D.$$

7.8 SUMMARY

The point of graphical displays like GUIDO, VIBE, and BIRD is to present more information to the user in a more usable form. The traditional information system presents a limited list of documents to the user. Such a list is often unsatisfactory for a number of reasons. First, a retrieval system frequently presents a fixed number of documents, regardless of either the number of relevant documents or the number of documents the user really would like. Second, the ordering of the list is determined by the system, not the user. At worst this is an "as found" ordering, with no reference to the relevance of the individual documents; at best the ordering is made on a basis unknown to the user. Third, the linear nature of the list hides any relationships that exist among the documents. The second and third documents may be quite similar to each other, but the fourteenth and fifteenth may be quite different from each other, although they are ranked similarly with respect to the query. Fourth, if the documents on the list are unsatisfactory, the system provides the user little or no help in redefining the query. And fifth, the system typically does not provide a browsing capability.

GUIDO and VIBE (in both the vector and Boolean forms) are designed to overcome these limitations by allowing the user to approach the system with several different points of view in mind, by presenting to the user all documents that are in any way related to these points of view, and by providing a structured display of these documents through which the user can browse freely. In addition, these systems give the user dynamic control over the definitions of the reference points. Thus the user can see all of the documents of potential interest, identify those of greatest interest, and reorganize the display focusing attention on those documents. The one drawback to "bare" GUIDO and VIBE is that the documents are represented by icons. However, this limitation is overcome by providing a window in which the full contents of any document can be displayed. Coupled with other user-oriented enhancements, such as the use of color and lines relating to document placement, these systems seem to provide the user with greatly enhanced access to any database.

BIRD provides a similar, but more limited approach to meeting information needs. It should be noted that each of these three systems emphasizes a different aspect of information processing. GUIDO, with its defined retrieval caps, focuses on the problem of retrieving document sets. VIBE does not have this focus. Indeed, the use of similarity ratios in VIBE reduces its effectiveness as a retrieval tool. However, it is superior to GUIDO in its focal area, that of classifying and organizing a set of documents. BIRD is perhaps the interface most directly tied to the ultimate information need, as it focuses on constructing bibliographic lists of documents.

Interest in the development of visual interfaces is increasing. More than 50 different interface systems have been proposed and studied, using a variety of different retrieval and display models. Some of these systems are discussed in Chapter 11. It should be noted that these systems are still largely experimental, and thus their effectiveness in actual use remains to be demonstrated.

REFERENCES

Kim, Hanhwe, and Robert R. Korfhage. 1994. BIRD: Browsing Interface for the Retrieval of Documents. *Proceedings of the IEEE Symposium on Visual Languages*, St. Louis, Missouri, pp. 176–177.

Korfhage, Robert R. 1988. Information retrieval in the presence of reference points, Part 1. Research Report LIS001/IS88001, School of Library and Information Science, University of Pittsburgh.

Korfhage, Robert R. 1991a. Information retrieval in the presence of reference points, Part 2. Research Report LIS034/IS91002, School of Library and Information Science, University of Pittsburgh.

Korfhage, Robert R. 1991b. To see, or not to see—Is *that* the query? *Proceedings of the 16th Annual International ACM/SIGIR Conference on Research and Development in Information Retrieval*, Pittsburgh, pp. 134–141.

Korfhage, Robert R., and Kai A. Olsen. 1991. Information display: Control of visual representations. *IEEE Workshop on Visual Languages*, Kobe, Japan, pp. 56–61.

Nuchprayoon, Assadaporn, and Robert R. Korfhage. 1994. GUIDO, a visual tool for retrieving documents. *Proceedings of the IEEE Symposium on Visual Languages*, St. Louis, Missouri, pp. 64–71.

Olsen, Kai A., Robert R. Korfhage, Kenneth M. Sochats, Michael B. Spring, and James G. Williams. 1993a. Visualization of a document collection: The VIBE system. *Information Processing & Management* 29, no. 1:69–81.

Olsen, Kai A., Robert R. Korfhage, Kenneth M. Sochats, Michael B. Spring, and James G. Williams. 1993b. Visualization of a document collection with hypertext links: The VIBE system. *Scandinavian Journal of Information Science* 5:79–95.

EXERCISES

1. Develop the general inequality for retrieval using the Cassini oval model.

2. Investigate the form of the general inequality for retrieval using the conjunctive model. Is it possible to develop a form analogous to that developed for the elliptical model?

3. Investigate the form of the general inequality for retrieval using the disjunctive model. Is it possible to develop a form analogous to that developed for the elliptical model?

4. Show that for the disjunctive and conjunctive retrieval models the bounding lines in GUIDO are parallel to the two axes. What is the difference in the boundaries for the two models?

5. Show that in the Cassini oval model the bounding line in GUIDO is a hyperbola.

6. In the one-point GUIDO model, the boundary of the distance space is the single point representing the query; in the two-point model, it consists of three lines (edges) and two points; and in the three-point model it consists of seven surfaces, nine edges, and three points. Determine what the boundary components are in a four-point GUIDO model, and how many of them there are.

7. Generalize Exercise 6 to an arbitrary number of reference points.

8. Determine the locus (in the document space) of all points such that

$$\|D, R_2\| - \|D, R_1\| = k$$

for a fixed value of k.

9. Show that in VIBE the location of a document point with respect to three reference points can be determined sequentially, beginning with any two reference points. That is, show that we can locate D by first locating D_{12} with respect to R_1 and R_2, then shifting that toward R_3, or by first locating D_{13} with respect to R_1 and R_3, then shifting that toward R_2, or by first locating D_{23} with respect to R_2 and R_3, then shifting that toward R_1. *Hint:* Let the similarity of D_{12} to the (R_1, R_2) pair be the sum of the similarities of D to R_1 and R_2. (This generalizes to an arbitrary number of reference points.)

10. Determine the number of directions to be avoided in Boolean VIBE with n POIs in order to avoid placing one Boolean point on top of another.

11. The principle used in Boolean VIBE to avoid placing one Boolean point on top of another applies equally well to vector VIBE: Two document icons will be superimposed only when the projection direction is that of the line joining the document points (in the document space). Show that this does *not* yield a practical method to avoid superimposing document icons in vector VIBE, by determining the number of directions to be avoided when there are 10, 50, 100, 500, and 1000 documents. (Note that each pair of documents potentially creates a new direction to be avoided.)

CHAPTER 8

Retrieval Effectiveness Measures

A viable information retrieval system must be effective in returning documents in response to an information need. While this generally means that most of the documents retrieved in response to the query should be judged by the user to be appropriate to the information need, such a vague statement of effectiveness provides no solid basis for determining how good a given system is, or for comparing one retrieval system to another. This chapter introduces several ways of measuring effectiveness. The simplest of these depend only on an accept or reject decision for each document. More complex ones may consider several levels of acceptance, the order in which the documents are presented, or other factors. The difficulties in deriving one single measure that adequately describes system performance are also discussed.

8.1 BINARY VERSUS N-ARY MEASURES

There are generally two steps in translating an information need into a query that a given retrieval system can handle. The first of these is to formulate a question that corresponds to the information need. Sometimes this is simple, but often asking the right question is itself a difficult task. Suppose, for example, that the user wishes to select a person for a given position from among a pool of candidates. This may be in any of several contexts:

electing a public official, hiring a staff member, choosing a physician, and so forth. What question or questions should be asked to elicit the information needed to make an informed and intelligent decision? Often it is only by hindsight that the user discovers that the correct question has not been asked, that is, that the information need has not been properly defined.

The second step is to transform the question into a query that is suitable for a given information system. Some information systems can handle natural language questions directly, so that no transformation is needed. Others may require that the query be a logical expression or a list of weighted key terms, use a particular vocabulary, or have some other specific form. If the information system can handle the question directly, then the user must assume that the system can correctly parse the question and understand both its semantics and its pragmatics—a tall order. If the user must transform the question in some way, then she is faced with the task of ensuring that the transformed question still correctly reflects the information need. Are the logical connectives correctly used? Do the weights really convey the proper sense of importance of the various terms? Is the word chosen from the restricted vocabulary an adequate and accurate representation of the word that the user would have preferred?

The *effectiveness* of a retrieval system is an ectosystem measure, related to the user's satisfaction with the system output. In establishing measures of effectiveness, the first decision to be made is the number of levels of judgment allowed the user in this evaluation. The basic choice is between a *binary* and an *n-ary measure* to be used in the user's evaluation of the endosystem output.

A binary measure is the simplest to implement and use but presents only a coarse judgment for the user. Each document is either accepted or rejected. This acceptance or rejection is usually couched in terms of the document's *relevance* to the user. One difficulty with this is that relevance is itself an ill-defined term, whose meaning varies from one user to the next, and even from one situation to another for a given user. Another difficulty is that the user now has three representations—the need, the question, and the query—against which to judge a document. Of these, the judgment vis-à-vis the query is most directly related to system performance. To be more precise, in this chapter the relevance of a document relates to *how well the document responds to the query that was asked.* At the same time the user may also ask *how well the document responds to the information need (or question)*

(Myaeng and Korfhage 1990). Since the query may not exactly describe the information need, this is a different question, which is described as asking for the document's *pertinence.* The distinction between relevance and pertinence, in this sense, provides some indication of how well the information need can be stated in the query language. A clear difference between relevance and pertinence would seem to indicate that the system is imposing constraints on the user that make it difficult to properly express the information need, while the lack of such a difference would indicate that any problem in properly expressing the need may lie in the initial formulation of a question or recognition of the need.

Closely related to relevance and pertinence is the concept of *usefulness.* Almost everyone has had the experience of hunting for one thing and finding something else that is not particularly wanted at the time but that should be remembered for future use. This can happen in using an information system as well. A user may be searching for information related to a given project and come across information appropriate to some other project with which he is involved. This information is not relevant or pertinent to the user's present need, but he does not want to lose it, since it is useful in a different context. Thus, in evaluating a system, another question that can be put to the user is whether any information that is useful in this sense has been found. This is particularly important in systems that involve user interest profiles, since a profile is an expression of a user's general need rather than the specific need of the moment. Another view of usefulness is that the user might judge a retrieved document to be relevant to the need but not useful, since he already knows the information in it. Thus usefulness is independent of relevance: A given document may be useful but not relevant, or relevant but not useful, or neither, or both.

Any of these measures—relevance, pertinence, and usefulness—can be cast into a binary, yes-or-no mode. Alternatively, different levels can also be assigned to the measures. Moving beyond a binary measure to an *n*-ary one allows the user to consider levels or degrees of relevance (or pertinence or usefulness). For example, with $n = 5$, a scale of relevance might be defined as:

4: definitely relevant

3: probably relevant

2: barely relevant, neutral, or not judged

1: probably not relevant

0: definitely not relevant

As a practical matter it is difficult for users to distinguish among a large number of degrees of relevance. Many people are comfortable with three to five different levels but have difficulty in consistently judging documents using a scale with more levels.

While the choice of a scale for relevance is open, the scale for *retrieval* is closed: Either a document is retrieved or it is not. The only reasonable way to extend this scale is to consider a staged retrieval, with documents organized into groups that are retrieved and presented sequentially. This mode is rarely considered in measuring system effectiveness, yet it corresponds to a question of potential significance to the user: Is it worthwhile to retrieve another group of documents, beyond those already seen?

8.2   PRECISION AND RECALL, AND RELATED MEASURES

When binary scales are used for both relevance and retrieval, a 2×2 contingency table can be established showing how the document set is divided by these two measures (Table 8.1).

Among the binary measures, the most widely used are precision and recall. *Precision* is defined as the proportion of retrieved documents that are relevant,

$$P = \frac{w}{n_2} .$$

Recall is defined as the proportion of relevant documents that are retrieved,

$$R = \frac{w}{n_1} .$$

Table 8.1
Contingency Table for Evaluating Retrieval

	Retrieved	Not retrieved	
Relevant	w	x	$n_1 = w + x$
Not relevant	y	z	

$n_2 = w + y$ $N = w + x + y + z$

Precision and recall are both bounded above by 1 (when $y = 0$ and $x = 0$, respectively), and below by 0 (when $w = 0$).

Suppose that a retrieval system is run in response to a query, and measurements are taken as increasing numbers of documents are retrieved, counting the number of relevant documents each time. This yields a series of <precision, recall> pairs that can be plotted on a graph. Consider two extreme responses to a query. First, suppose that only one document is retrieved. If the retrieval system is performing properly, this one document can be expected to be relevant. Hence this retrieval situation has precision of 1.0 and very low recall. At the other extreme, suppose that every document in the database is retrieved. This guarantees retrieval of every relevant document. Recall would be 1.0, but precision would be extremely low. In general there is an inverse relationship between precision and recall.

The number of documents returned in response to a query can be controlled either by specifying that number or by controlling the threshold of similarity to the query required for retrieval. In general, precision falls and recall rises as the number of documents retrieved in response to a query is increased. This relationship is shown in a smoothed *precision-recall graph* (Figure 8.1). (A precision-recall graph that is not smoothed has the same general shape, but a sawtooth appearance. This is because retrieval of a relevant document increases both precision and recall, while retrieval of a nonrelevant document decreases precision but does not affect recall.)

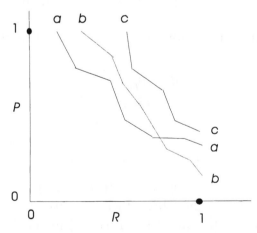

Figure 8.1 Smoothed precision-recall graph.

The major difficulty that arises in using precision and recall to judge a retrieval system is illustrated in this graph. System c is clearly better than either a or b. For any given precision, its recall is higher; for any given recall, its precision is higher. But which of systems a and b is the better one? The answer depends on the criteria for judgment. System b is the better one if the user is interested in high precision, while a is better if high recall is more important. The situation may, of course, be more complicated, with the precision-recall curves for two systems crossing several times.

Two other measures, called fallout and generality, are closely related to precision and recall. *Fallout* is the proportion of nonrelevant documents that are not retrieved,

$$F = \frac{y}{N - n_1} ;$$

generality is the proportion of relevant documents within the entire collection,

$$G = \frac{n_1}{N} .$$

Note that generality relates directly to the query (which determines the relevant documents) rather than to the retrieval process. Note also that "generality" is a misnomer for G. A very general collection is likely to contain many irrelevant documents, so that G will be low. In contrast, a highly specific collection containing only relevant documents has $G = 1$, the highest possible value.

The four quantities—precision, recall, fallout, and generality—are related by the equation

$$\frac{R}{F} = \frac{P/(1 - P)}{G/(1 - G)} ,$$

or

$$RG(1 - P) = FP(1 - G) .$$

From either of these equations, any one of the quantities can easily be expressed in terms of the other three. (See Exercises 1 and 2.)

It is worth noting that the quantities $P/(1 - P)$ and $G/(1 - G)$ also have simple interpretations:

- $P/(1 - P)$ is the ratio of relevant retrieved documents to nonrelevant retrieved documents.
- $G/(1 - G)$ is the ratio of relevant documents in the collection to nonrelevant documents in the collection.

Finally, R/F is the ratio of retrieval performance on relevant documents to retrieval performance on nonrelevant documents. It is desirable to have the first two of these ratios high. That is, the user likely would prefer to work with a collection that is primarily relevant documents (high $G/(1 - G)$) and to have the system retrieve primarily relevant documents (high $P/(1 - P)$). Since R/F is the ratio of these two values, it will be greater than 1 if the system does better locating relevant documents than it does rejecting nonrelevant documents, and less than 1 in the opposite case.

Despite their wide use, there are three major objections to precision and recall as system effectiveness measures. First, while precision can be determined exactly, recall cannot. Obtaining an exact measure of recall requires knowledge of all relevant documents in a collection. This knowledge is available for some special test collections but cannot be obtained in a practical situation. Thus recall can only be estimated, usually by statistical techniques. For this reason recall is an inexact measure.

Second, it is not clear that recall and precision are significant to the user. Cleverdon (1991), for example, suggests that precision is quite important, but that for most users high recall is not very important. That is, while users appreciate output that does not contain many unwanted documents, they are not usually concerned about retrieving every good answer to their query. There are of course exceptions. One situation in which high recall is important is that of an attorney trying to determine all legal precedents to a case. In another study, Su (1994) found that neither precision nor recall were highly significant factors in determining how satisfied a user is with a given retrieval system. If these measures are not important to users, then they are poor measures of system effectiveness.

Third, recall and precision are related to each other, and each alone provides an incomplete picture of the retrieval system's effectiveness. Some people feel that it is important to come up with a single number expressing effectiveness; precision and recall do not readily provide this number. The ratio R/F might be used as a single measure if one had a good estimate of the proportion of relevant documents in the database, n_1/N. However, the poten-

tial weakness of this measure is the same as that of recall—lack of knowledge of the number of relevant documents.

8.3 USER-ORIENTED MEASURES

The measures discussed above all assume that the users form a homogeneous group—that all users have the same response to system output for a
given query. While this is a nice simplifying assumption, it does not match
reality. Thus several *user-oriented measures* have been proposed (Keen
1971). These three are typical:

1. *Coverage ratio:* the proportion of the relevant documents known to
   the user that are actually retrieved.
2. *Novelty ratio:* the proportion of the relevant retrieved documents
   that were previously unknown to the user.
3. *Relative recall:* the ratio of the relevant retrieved documents examined by the user to the number of documents the user would have
   liked to examine.

Suppose, for example, that the user already knows 15 relevant documents
and that the system retrieves 10 relevant documents, including 4 of those
that the user knows. Then the *coverage ratio* would be 4/15, or roughly
26.6%. From this the user would presumably infer that there are a total of
approximately 38 relevant documents—nearly four times the number
retrieved. Since the user has seen 6 new relevant documents, adding these to
the 15 previously known he can estimate that the system database contains
16 or 17 relevant documents that he has never seen, and make a more
informed decision on trying to retrieve those documents.

Using this same example, the *novelty ratio* would be 6/10, or 3/5. A high
coverage ratio would give the user some confidence that the system is locating all of the relevant documents; a high novelty ratio suggests that the system is effective in locating documents previously unknown to the user.
From the novelty ratio in the example, the user might infer that roughly
60% of any group of relevant documents retrieved for this particular query
and database will be previously unknown.

Of course the user is not really interested in being informed about those
documents that are already known, so a high novelty ratio is desirable. The

user of this hypothetical system might be more comfortable with a system that retrieves 50 relevant documents, 10 of which are already known. Then the coverage ratio would be 10/15, or 2/3, and the novelty ratio would be 40/50, or 4/5, both reasonably high numbers.

Relative recall addresses more directly the question of how many documents the user wants. Suppose that the system presents 20 documents to the user and that the user wants 5 relevant documents. If there are only 3 relevant documents among the 20, then the relative recall is 3/5—the user has only 3 of the 5 documents she sought. If, however, there are 5 or more relevant documents among the 20, then presumably the user would quit after finding the desired 5, with a relative recall of 5/5, or 1.

Note that if the relative recall is 1, the measure fails to address the amount of effort required to locate the documents. It could be that the user found the needed documents among the first 5 or 6 examined; it could also be that the user needed to examine all 20 documents to find 5 relevant ones. Thus it is reasonable to define another user-related measure:

> 4. *Recall effort:* the ratio of the number of relevant documents desired to the number of documents examined by the user to find the number of relevant documents desired.

This measure makes two assumptions: that the collection contains the desired number of relevant documents, and that the retrieval system permits the user to search sufficiently far to locate all of them. Thus, this ratio can range from 1, if the desired relevant documents are the first few examined by the user, to nearly 0, if the user would need to examine hundreds of documents to find the desired few.

8.4   AVERAGE PRECISION AND RECALL

All of the measures discussed thus far have been ratios whose values tend to be related to volume. Considering the precision-recall contingency table for a moment, as more documents are retrieved by a system, the numbers in the "retrieved" column increase and those in the "not retrieved" column decrease. It is also reasonable to assume that at low retrieval volumes the numbers in the "relevant" row change more rapidly than those in the "not relevant" row, and that at high retrieval volumes this situation is reversed. Thus all of these ratio measures can be expected to change with retrieval volume.

A similar statement holds for the more personal retrieval ratios. However, the effect of retrieval volume is more difficult to predict, since these measures depend heavily on the perceptions of the individual user.

This dependence on retrieval volume has given impetus to a search for a single number that can characterize the performance of a retrieval system at all levels and for all users. Such a number has proven elusive and is likely to remain so. Nevertheless, it is instructive to examine efforts to find a good single measure.

One group of attempts focuses on two measures, *average precision* and *average recall*. Since both precision and recall change with retrieval volume, and both numbers are bounded by 0 and 1, there is some feeling that average values of these numbers, properly computed, might provide adequate measures by which to judge retrieval systems. Popular methods of doing this are the *three-point averages* and the *eleven-point averages*. A three-point average precision, for example, is computed by averaging the precision of the retrieval system for a given query at three defined recall levels. Typically these recall levels are 0.25, 0.50, and 0.75, although other levels such as 0.20, 0.50, and 0.80 can also be used. (The resulting averages, of course, will differ slightly.) The eleven-point average precision is computed using the recall levels 0.0, 0.1, 0.2, . . . , 0.9, and 1.0. This requires a little more effort to compute than the three-point average but provides a more accurate value. The average recall, less often used, is similarly computed. These averages for single queries can then be averaged over a set of queries to estimate an overall system measure.

Since it is difficult or impossible to determine the recall levels in a practical situation, a related measure is often used when large numbers of relevant documents are available for each query. In this, precision is measured at intervals when a fixed number of relevant documents have been retrieved. For example, precision can be measured when 10, 20, 30, 40, 50, . . . relevant documents have been retrieved. The results can be graphed or averaged as an indication of system performance. Also, the results can be averaged across several queries. The data needed are the numbers of documents retrieved to find the specified numbers of relevant documents.

Example 8.1 Suppose that five queries have been run, with the precision measured at 10, 20, 30, 40, and 50 relevant documents. Table 8.2 shows the resulting computation. The entries are the number of documents retrieved and the precision values.

Table 8.2
Precision at Various Relevant Document Levels

Level	Q1	Q2	Q3	Q4	Q5	Average
10	13, 0.77	15, 0.67	12, 0.83	17, 0.59	15, 0.67	14.4, 0.69
20	28, 0.74	30, 0.67	25, 0.80	29, 0.69	26, 0.77	27.6, 0.72
30	42, 0.71	51, 0.59	43, 0.70	39, 0.77	47, 0.64	44.4, 0.68
40	57, 0.70	65, 0.62	59, 0.68	51, 0.78	62, 0.65	58.8, 0.68
50	71, 0.70	92, 0.54	84, 0.60	103, 0.49	87, 0.57	87.4, 0.57

A completely different way of obtaining averages is the following. Suppose that in a test situation the relevant documents for each of a set of queries are known a priori. Suppose also that each query is run until some predetermined condition is satisfied—for example, a given number of documents has been retrieved. Precision and recall can be measured at that point, obtaining one pair of numbers for each query. From these numbers a table can be constructed, with recall and precision levels at 0.1 increments, say, showing the number of queries that fall into each cell of the table. For example, Table 8.3 is derived from the Cranfield study (Cleverdon 1967). This study includes 1400 documents and 225 queries with known relevant documents. Each query was run 16 times under slightly varying conditions, yielding a total of 3600 query samples. The value 16 in cell <0.2, 0.4>, for example, shows that 16 queries yield a precision value between 0.3 and 0.4, and a recall value between 0.1 and 0.2. From these numbers, the average precision at each recall level and the average recall at each precision level can be computed. If desired, these averages can themselves be averaged to arrive at a single pair of averages for the system.

These two methods of computing average precision and recall generally arrive at different results, since they are portraying the system in different ways. The first method determines averages for the individual queries as each query retrieves increasingly many documents, then averages these; the second fixes on a predefined level of system effort, averaging the effectiveness measures across a set of queries at specified points in that process, then averages these numbers. A system that appears to perform poorly according to one of these measures may appear to be highly effective according to the other.

Table 8.3
Queries at Given Precision-Recall Levels (from Cranfield Experiment)

Recall	PRECISION											Subtotal	Average
	0.0	0.1	0.2	0.3	0.4	0.5	0.6	0.7	0.8	0.9	1.0		
0.0	394	0	0	0	0	0	0	0	0	0	0	394	0.00
0.1	0	3	0	1	7	27	0	0	0	0	102	140	0.85
0.2	0	11	12	2	16	76	15	35	17	0	505	689	0.87
0.3	0	3	2	2	6	43	32	48	58	1	142	337	0.77
0.4	0	5	4	0	8	54	18	90	40	9	382	610	0.85
0.5	0	3	1	2	4	36	63	38	80	8	208	443	0.80
0.6	0	2	0	1	2	11	19	31	41	15	31	153	0.74
0.7	0	7	0	1	5	23	15	67	28	7	73	226	0.74
0.8	0	4	1	0	0	20	19	23	41	20	53	181	0.76
0.9	0	1	2	0	3	5	10	21	58	39	2	141	0.73
1.0	0	5	0	2	2	6	28	43	47	20	133	286	0.82
Subtotal	394	44	22	11	53	301	219	396	410	119	1631	3600	
Average	0.00	0.47	0.30	0.46	0.35	0.36	0.54	0.53	0.59	0.74	0.37		

Average precision = 0.724; average recall = 0.395.

8.5 OPERATING CURVES AND SINGLE MEASURES

Suppose that the document collection is divided into two populations, P_1 and P_2, consisting of relevant and nonrelevant documents (for a given query), respectively. Suppose also that there is some measurable characteristic, C, associated with each document. This characteristic might be the number of times words in a given set appear, or the date of publication, for example. To the extent that C corresponds to the concept of relevance it can be used to distinguish the two populations. If C is fully related to relevance, then P_1 and P_2 can be completely separated on the basis of C; that is, documents in P_1 will have one range of C values, and documents in P_2 will have a completely different range. If C has no relation to relevance, then P_1 and P_2 will be indistinguishable with respect to C. In general, the documents in each population will display some distribution of the values of C. A certain percentage of the documents in each population will have a given value of C.

The values of C can be used to derive an *operating curve* for a given information retrieval system by plotting the points <%P_1, %P_2> corresponding to the values of C. This curve will go from the <0, 0> point to the <100, 100> point, since it covers all retrieval situations—from the initiation of retrieval (none yet retrieved) to the retrieval of the entire database (Figure 8.2). The shape of this curve will depend on the relationship of C to relevance. If high values of C are correlated strongly with relevance, the curve will rise sharply toward high values of %P_1. A characteristic that is strongly associated with nonrelevance will produce an operating curve that is flatter, rising only at the end.

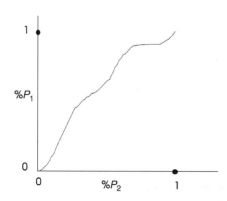

Figure 8.2   Operating curve graph.

If the documents in the two populations P_1 and P_2 each form a normal distribution with respect to the characteristic C, then the operating curve is a straight line whose slope depends on the relationship of the characteristic to relevance. Experimental work by Swets showed that both recall and fallout typically produce normal distributions with respect to the usual query-document similarity measures (Brookes 1968). Thus, by using these measures, a given retrieval system can be represented by a straight-line operating curve.

J.A. Swets (1969) showed that the operating curves can be used to derive a single number, E, as a measure of retrieval system effectiveness. Using straight-line operating curves, that is, those corresponding to measures yielding normally distributed populations, *Swets' E measure* is determined by measuring the distance of the point <50, 50> from the operating curve along the line joining <0, 100> and <50, 50> (Figure 8.3). This number suffices to distinguish between retrieval systems with parallel operating curves but may fail to distinguish between retrieval systems whose operating curves are not parallel. Taking E together with the slope of the operating curve will characterize a system's performance.

8.6   EXPECTED SEARCH LENGTH

The concept of a *weakly ordered set* of retrieved documents can also be introduced in the measurement of a system. Suppose that the set of retrieved documents is divided into k subsets, $S_1, \ldots, S_k$, such that by the retrieval

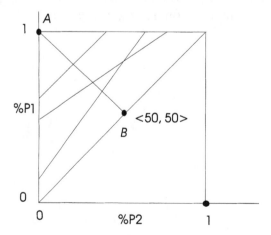

Figure 8.3   Computation of Swets' E measure.

criterion all elements in any one of the subsets are equivalent, but that the documents in subset S_i are better than those in subset S_{i+1}, for $i = 1, \ldots, k - 1$. For example, if Boolean retrieval is done and the query is a disjunction of terms, t_1 or t_2 or $\ldots$ or t_n, then S_1 might consist of those documents containing all n terms, S_2 of those documents containing any $n - 1$ of the terms, S_3 of the documents with only $n - 2$ of the terms, and so forth. By presenting these subsets in order, a weakly ordered set of retrieved documents is developed. That is, all of the documents in any one subset rank equally, but worse than those in preceding subsets and better than those in subsequent subsets. Note that at one extreme there may be only one document in each subset, while at the other extreme all documents may be in the same subset.

In general, even though the documents in one subset all rank equally they may not all be judged to be relevant by the user. The user may need to retrieve several subsets and examine some irrelevant documents in these subsets to obtain all of the relevant documents desired. The *expected search length* is the average number of documents that must be examined to retrieve a given number of relevant documents (Cooper 1968). Thus the expected search length is not a single number but rather a function of the number of relevant documents sought.

Example 8.2 Suppose that the retrieved set of documents divides into three subsets such that S_1 contains three documents, only one of which is actually relevant, S_2 contains four relevant documents and one irrelevant one, and S_3 contains two relevant documents and three irrelevant ones. If just one relevant document is wanted, the user need search only S_1. But that document may be the first, second, or third one examined. Assuming that all combinations are equally likely, the user can expect to examine one document (finding the desired document immediately) one-third of the time, two documents one-third of the time, and three documents one-third of the time. Thus the expected search length to find one relevant document is

$$1 \times \frac{1}{3} + 2 \times \frac{1}{3} + 3 \times \frac{1}{3} = 2.$$

On average the user will need to examine one irrelevant document before she finds the one relevant one that she wants.

Now suppose that she wishes to retrieve six relevant documents. Examining subsets S_1 and S_2 will produce five of the documents. She will find the sixth one in subset S_3. Thus she needs to examine the eight documents in the first two subsets, plus from one to four more documents in S_3, depending on the location of the sixth relevant document. Considering where the two relevant documents occur in S_3, there are four situations in which the first of them (the only one needed) is in the first position, three situations when it is in the second position, two situations when it is third in the subset, and one situation when it is fourth. Thus there are 10 different situations:

4 situations with search length 9,

3 situations with search length 10,

2 situations with search length 11, and

1 situation with search length 12.

The expected search length is thus

$$9 \times \frac{4}{10} + 10 \times \frac{3}{10} + 11 \times \frac{2}{10} + 12 \times \frac{1}{10} = 10.$$

On average, the user will examine four irrelevant documents to find the six that she wants.

The expected search length provides a different measure of retrieval performance, which can be presented either as a table or plotted against the number of relevant documents retrieved (Table 8.4, Figure 8.4). In either form, the measure provides not one value but a series of values showing how

Table 8.4
Expected Search Length Table

Relevant documents	Expected search length
1	2.0
2	4.2
3	5.4
4	6.6
5	7.8
6	10.0
7	12.0

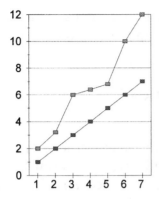

Figure 8.4   Expected search length graph.

the system can be expected to perform for users with different recall require-ments. For our example, the user who wants a single document can expect to examine two documents—twice the desired number—but the user who wants all seven relevant documents will only expect to examine roughly 70% more than desired. In the graphical representation this difference shows up in the deviation of the plot line above the 45° line.

The expected search length can be summarized in a single number repre-senting the average number of documents searched per relevant document found. For the example this is

$$\frac{1}{7}\left(\frac{2}{1} + \frac{4.2}{2} + \frac{5.4}{3} + \frac{6.6}{4} + \frac{7.8}{5} + \frac{10}{6} + \frac{12}{7}\right) \approx 1.78.$$

As with any average, this glosses over a more detailed analysis. However, in this example the individual averages range from 1.36 to 2.1, so the 1.78 over-all average seems to be a reasonably fair representation of system perfor-mance. The user can roughly expect to examine 78% more documents than are desired.

Assuming searches for 1, 2, ..., 7 documents are equally likely, one can also compute an overall expected search length by the weighted average of the individual expected search lengths, using the formula

$$\frac{\sum\limits_{i=1}^{n} i e_i}{\sum\limits_{i=1}^{n} i},$$

where e_i is the expected search length for i documents, and n is the maxi-mum number of relevant documents. In the example, this overall expected search length is 8.43. Since this computation depends on an assumption about usage, the prior computation is perhaps a more accurate reflection of the system performance.

8.7 SATISFACTION AND FRUSTRATION, AND RELATED MEASURES

One of the problems with using recall and precision (or any of the other measures discussed) as single numbers indicative of retrieval system performance is that such measures fail to take into account the sequentiality effect in presenting retrieval results. The typical retrieval system presents results to the user in a linear list. Even with systems that manage to avoid this, the user will examine the documents sequentially. The examination of one document affects the user's judgment of all documents that follow it. Suppose that there are two documents that contain essentially the same information. A user may rate the first of these documents highly but downgrade the second one simply because he feels that it does not present any new information. (In an extreme case, the user may never examine the second one.) Thus the apparent values of the two documents will differ, depending on which one was first examined.

A second effect of sequentiality arises from the mix of relevant and nonrelevant documents typically retrieved. If the user sees many relevant documents first, the fact that the system is also retrieving numerous nonrelevant documents may never be noticed, and the user will be satisfied with the system performance. If, however, the user first encounters numerous nonrelevant documents, then frustration with the system will increase markedly and the user will tend to judge the system more harshly. Thus there is incentive to develop system measures that take into account the sequence in which documents are presented to the user.

The earliest work in this vein is Rocchio's (1966) *normalized recall* measure. An ideal system is defined as one in which all relevant documents are retrieved before any of the nonrelevant ones. A step function graph is developed based on this idea. For an ideal system, the graph will rise one unit as each of the relevant documents is retrieved, to a maximum value equal to the number of relevant documents in the collection. (Since it is assumed that all of the relevant documents are known, the rise in height could be divided by this number, to give a total rise of 1.) For an actual system the graph will rise similarly, but the rises will take place at the points where these documents appear in the output sequence, based on the system's ranking of the documents. For example, there may be five relevant documents in a collection of 200 documents. Supposing that these documents are ranked 1, 3, 5, 10, and 14 by the retrieval system, the ideal and actual graphs for the system can be compared (Figure 8.5). The area between the actual and ideal graphs is a measure of the performance of the retrieval system. This is normalized by dividing by $n_1(N - n_1)$, where n_1 is the number of relevant documents and N is the total number of documents, and subtracting from 1. Thus for an ideal system the measure is 1, and for the worst possible system (all of the nonrelevant documents before any relevant document) it is 0.

A basic problem with normalized recall is that, as with ordinary recall, it assumes knowledge of all relevant documents in a collection. In addition, it is highly sensitive to the placement of the last relevant document in the retrieval sequence. In the example, the area difference is 21, so that the normalized recall is $1 - 21/[5(200 - 5)] = 0.978$. A system that has the same performance except that the last relevant document is the 200th rather than the 16th results in an area of 205, or a measure of 0.790. If, as Cleverdon (1991) suggests, complete recall is not of major importance to the user, this difference in measures probably distorts the perceived difference in performance between the two systems.

A *normalized precision* measure can be defined in an analogous manner. While ordinary precision is an exactly defined measure, normalized precision depends on a knowledge of all of the relevant documents. Thus it suffers from the same basic problem that normalized recall has.

The *sliding ratio* (SR) is a measure similar in concept to normalized recall but different in two significant ways (Pollack 1968):

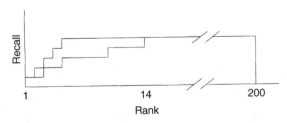

Figure 8.5 Normalized recall graph.

1. It is developed on the basis of weighted relevance judgments.
2. It is based on the retrieval of N documents for some specified value of N, rather than on the full set of relevant documents.

Assume that the ideal system retrieves documents in order of decreasing relevance weight. Suppose that N documents have been retrieved, with weights $w_1, \ldots, w_N$ in sequence. In an ideal system these weights would have been in decreasing order; in an actual system they probably are not. Let $W_1, \ldots, W_N$ be the same set of weights, sorted into decreasing order. For each $n = 1, \ldots, N$ the comparison is then

$$SR(n) = \frac{\sum_{i=1}^{n} w_i}{\sum_{i=1}^{n} W_i}.$$

Observe that SR is computed using only the documents retrieved thus far. However, every document retrieved counts more or less heavily, depending on its relevance weight.

Example 8.3 Suppose that the system has retrieved 10 documents, with relevance weights 7.0, 5.0, 0.0, 2.5, 8.2, 4.5, 3.7, 1.1, 5.2, and 3.1, in the order of retrieval. In an ideal system these documents would have been retrieved and presented in the order 8.2, 7.0, 5.2, 5.0, 4.5, 3.7, 3.1, 2.5, 1.1, and 0.0. These two sequences of weights are then used to compute the table of slid-

Table 8.5
Sliding Ratio Table

n	$\sum w_i$	$\sum W_i$	$SR(n)$
1	7.0	8.2	0.85
2	12.0	15.2	0.79
3	12.0	20.4	0.59
4	14.5	25.4	0.57
5	22.7	29.9	0.76
6	27.2	33.6	0.81
7	30.9	36.7	0.84
8	32.0	39.2	0.82
9	37.2	40.3	0.92
10	40.3	40.3	1.00

ing ratios (Table 8.5). The low values of the sliding ratio for $n = 3, 4$ reflect the low relevance weights of the third and fourth documents.

Since the sliding ratio is based on the documents retrieved up to a certain point, two things happen. First, the ratio will always become 1.00 for the full set of retrieved documents. Second, if the same calculation is performed with a different retrieved document set, for example a larger set, the ratios will be different. Nevertheless, if N is large these ratios present a reasonably accurate picture of the overall retrieval system performance.

Both the normalized recall and the sliding ratio measures attempt to quantify the difference in retrieval sequence between a real system and an ideal one. In doing so, they take into account the positions in which the relevant and irrelevant documents occur in the sequence of retrieved documents. The sliding ratio has two advantages over normalized recall: its use of relevance weights and its dependence only on the documents retrieved. But both measures consider relevant and irrelevant documents as a single group.

The effort to measure the impact of retrieval order has been further refined by Myaeng, who separated out the relevant and irrelevant documents (Myaeng and Korfhage 1990). To do so, he defined three measures similar to the sliding ratio:

1. *Satisfaction*, which considers only the relevant documents

2. *Frustration*, which considers only the nonrelevant documents

3. *Total*, a weighted combination of satisfaction and frustration

When relevance weights are used, the "relevant" documents are defined to be those having certain weights, and the "nonrelevant" documents are those having the remaining weights. For example, if the documents are weighted on a scale of 0 to 4, the user might decide that 0 and 1 represent nonrelevant documents and 2, 3, and 4 represent relevant documents. In computing the satisfaction measure, the nonrelevant documents are counted as having weight 0, but their positions in the sequence are considered. Similarly, for the frustration measure the relevant document weights are counted as 0.

The choice of a weighting scheme in defining the total measure is determined by the user's enjoyment of satisfaction (receiving relevant documents quickly) and tolerance for frustration (having to examine a number of nonrelevant documents). The simplest method is to define the total as the satisfaction minus the frustration, but some users may feel more comfortable with a different definition. One task of a good system designer is to find the combination that is most acceptable to the user.

Example 8.4   Suppose that two retrieval systems are compared, each of which retrieves the same 10 documents. These documents are judged on a five-point scale, with 0 and 1 representing nonrelevant documents and 2, 3, and 4 representing relevant documents. Suppose that System *A* retrieves the documents with weights in the order 3, 4, 2, 0, 2, 3, 3, 4, 1, 0, and System *B* retrieves them in the order 0, 4, 2, 3, 2, 0, 1, 3, 3, 4. To compare the two systems, draw their satisfaction (S), frustration (F), and total (T) graphs, where total is defined as satisfaction minus frustration. The values plotted for the S graph are the weights with the nonrelevant weights replaced by zeros: For System *A* these are 3, 4, 2, 0, 2, 3, 3, 4, 0, 0. For the F graph, only the irrelevant weights are used, and these are plotted as the minimum relevant weight minus the irrelevant weight: For System *A* these are 0, 0, 0, 2, 0, 0, 0, 0, 1, 2. As with the normalized recall and sliding ratio graphs, the values plotted are cumulative. These are compared with the graphs for the ideal system, which would retrieve the documents with weights in the order 4, 4, 3, 3, 3, 2, 2, 1, 0, 0. The area differences for $n = 1, \ldots, 10$ can be computed and compared, as is done for the sliding ratio measure. The graphs for the two systems are shown in Figures 8.6 and 8.7.

The areas for each System *B* graph are larger than those for the corresponding System *A* graph, indicating that on all three scales System *A* provides better performance. This is verified by examining the area computations given in Table 8.6. Observe that these measures behave like the sliding ratio, in that the final values are all the same, independent of the retrieval system being modeled. To complete this example, compare the differences between the ideal system and the two example systems for all three measures. For S and T the calculation shown in Table 8.7 is Ideal – Real; for F it is Real – Ideal. Thus in this example, System *A* is at least as good as System *B*, and generally better, at all levels and by all three measures. Recall that in general the T values are computed by $T = \alpha S - \beta F$, where α and β adjust the relative importance of satisfaction and frustration; in the example, $\alpha = \beta = 1$.

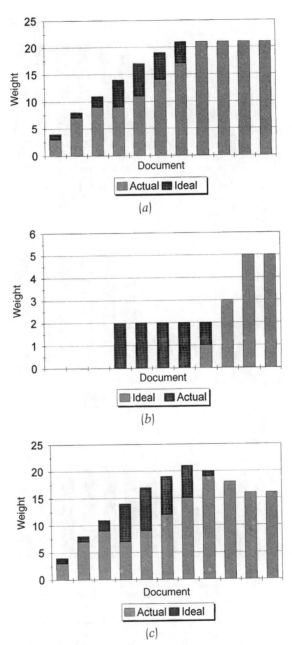

Figure 8.6 *(a) Satisfaction (S), (b) Frustration (F), and (c) total (T) graphs for System* A.

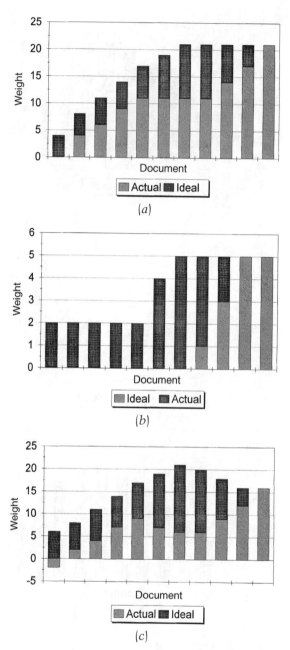

Figure 8.7   (a) Satisfaction (S), (b) Frustration (F), and (c) total (T) graphs for System B.

Table 8.6
Area Computations for the Ideal System and Systems A and B

	IDEAL			SYSTEM A			SYSTEM B		
n	S	F	T	S	F	T	S	F	T
1	4	0	4	3	0	3	0	2	−2
2	8	0	8	7	0	7	4	2	2
3	11	0	11	9	0	9	6	2	4
4	14	0	14	9	2	7	9	2	7
5	17	0	17	11	2	9	11	2	9
6	19	0	19	14	2	12	11	4	7
7	21	0	21	17	2	15	11	5	6
8	21	1	20	21	2	19	14	5	9
9	21	3	18	21	3	18	17	5	12
10	21	5	16	21	5	16	21	5	16

Table 8.7
Area Differences between the Ideal System and Systems A and B

	ΔS		ΔF		ΔT	
n	*A*	*B*	*A*	*B*	*A*	*B*
1	1	4	0	2	1	6
2	1	4	0	2	1	6
3	2	5	0	2	2	7
4	5	5	2	2	7	7
5	6	6	2	2	8	8
6	5	8	2	2	7	12
7	4	10	2	5	6	15
8	0	7	1	4	1	11
9	0	4	0	2	0	6
10	0	0	0	0	0	0

In any of these systems of measurement there is ample room for adjustment of the scores and values according to the preferences of the system designer. Any such scaling, if applied linearly—that is, multiplying by a constant or adding a constant—and consistently across the measures and the systems being studied should not alter the relative results. Scale adjustments that are not linear may affect the relative values, magnifying one aspect or another of a given system.

REFERENCES

Brookes, B.C. 1968. The measure of information retrieval effectiveness proposed by Swets. *Journal of Documentation* 24, no. 1:41–54.

Cleverdon, Cyril W. 1967. The Cranfield tests on index language devices. *Aslib Proceedings* 19, no. 6:173–194.

Cleverdon, Cyril W. 1991. The significance of the Cranfield tests on index languages. *Proceedings of 14th Annual International ACM/SIGIR Conference on Research and Development in Information Retrieval,* ed. Abraham Bookstein, Yves Chiaramella, Gerard Salton, Vijay V. Raghavan, Chicago, pp. 3–12.

Cooper, William S. 1968. Expected search length: A single measure of retrieval effectiveness based on the weak ordering action of retrieval systems. *American Documentation* 19, no. 1:30–41.

Keen, E. Michael. 1971. Evaluation parameters. Chap. 5 in *The SMART retrieval system—Experiments in automatic document processing,* ed. Gerard Salton. Englewood Cliffs, New Jersey: Prentice-Hall.

Myaeng, Sung H., and Robert R. Korfhage. 1990. Integration of user profiles: Models and experiments in information retrieval. *Information Processing & Management* 26, no. 6:719–738.

Pollack, S.M. 1968. Measures for the comparison of information retrieval systems. *American Documentation* 19, no. 4:387–397.

Rocchio, J.J., Jr. 1966. Document retrieval systems—Optimization and evaluation. Ph.D. diss., report no. ISR-10, Harvard Computation Laboratory, Harvard University.

Su, Louise T. 1994. The relevance of recall and precision in user evaluation. *JASIS* 45, no. 3:207–217.

Swets, J.A. 1969. Effectiveness of information retrieval methods. *American Documentation* 20, no. 1:72–89.

EXERCISES

1. Establish the relationship $RG(1 - P) = FP(1 - G)$.

2. Express each of four quantities—precision, recall, fallout, and generality—as a function of the other three.

For the following exercises, assume that there are two retrieval systems (and a given query and database) with the following characteristics. First, the database is known to contain a total of 1000 documents, 15 of them with positive relevance weights for the query. Second, when relevance weights are assigned, they are on a scale of 0 to 10, with documents having a weight of 5 or more considered relevant. Table 8.8 shows the sequential position of documents retrieved by each system, together with their relevance weights. Assume that any document not listed has a weight of 0. Assume also that if no document is listed in a particular sequential position, the document in that position is one of those with weight 0.

3. Draw precision-recall graphs for the two systems.

4. Compute the three-point average precision for each system, and determine which is better by this measure.

5. Draw operating curves for the two systems. If the curves are not straight lines, find the best straight lines you can that approximate the operating curves. (Either "eyeball" this or use a least squares analysis if you have one available.) Then compute Swets' *E* measure for the two systems, determining which is better by this measure.

Table 8.8
Data Table for Exercises 3–8

Document	Relative weight	System 1	System 2
A	10	1	2
B	10	4	1
C	9	2	25
D	8	6	12
E	6	9	19
F	6	3	3
G	6	15	6
H	5	7	5
I	5	10	11
J	4	11	7
K	3	5	14
L	3	13	4
M	2	20	9
N	1	8	8
O	1	12	10

6. Draw the normalized recall graphs for the two systems, and determine which is better by this measure.

7. Compute the sliding ratio for the two systems, and determine which is better by this measure.

8. Draw the satisfaction and frustration graphs for the two systems. Determine which is better by each of these measures. Then determine which system is better by the total measure, using $\alpha = \beta = 1$, $\alpha = 2$ and $\beta = 1$, and $\alpha = 1$ and $\beta = 2$.

9. Why is $n_1(N - n_1)$ an appropriate normalizing factor for normalized recall?

10. Despite the theoretical arguments against recall and precision as system measures, they remain widely used. Discuss the possible reasons behind this. In particular, consider any counters to the arguments raised against precision and recall.

11. Swets attempted to develop a single measure for retrieval system performance; the text argues that this measure does not completely capture performance characteristics. Discuss the value of having a single measure (versus two measures such as precision and recall) and what difficulties there are in developing such a measure.

12. Recall (from Chapter 1) that a system can be measured in terms of its effectiveness, efficiency, and economy. How would one integrate all of these factors into a single measurement system to evaluate information retrieval systems?

Effectiveness Improvement Techniques

It frequently happens that the initial query that a user poses does not really provide a satisfactory basis for information retrieval. The reasons for this are many. The user may have only a vague idea of what information is needed. The user may not know the organization and content of the database. The user's vocabulary may be quite different from that of the database. The user may pose a query that is broader or narrower than what is needed, thus returning either far too many documents or not enough. Whatever the cause, if the user is not satisfied with the results of the first query, then it is reasonable to pose a second query. Ideally, the system should provide help in doing this, beyond the implicit help that occurs because some of the initial set of documents were deemed relevant by the user and others were not. The focus of this chapter is on the problem of creating a dialogue between the user and the information system, enabling the system to be more effective in responding to the user's information need. One portion of this dialogue consists of the system providing information to the user about its parameters, database, and modes of operation. The other portion consists of information that the user can pass back to the system, concerning reactions to the retrieval results thus far.

9.1 Information the User May Find Helpful

The system uses much information that, if made available, can help the user to formulate a good query. Since some users may find a system that bombards them with information about itself rather overwhelming, it is probably best if the system information is made readily available upon demand but is otherwise withheld. Indeed, at the other end of the user spectrum, the sophisticated and steady user may well find it irritating if the system forces her to work through or actively bypass information already known. This phenomenon is common in menu-driven systems that do not have bypasses built in, letting the knowledgeable user skip directly to the menu or function wanted.

Given the restriction of providing information only when requested, there are several types of information that the user may find helpful. For example, a user may want to know the number of documents to be returned by a query. While this information may not be directly helpful, it can guide the user into thinking about query reformulation. The user who knows that his query is producing 579 documents may wish to examine two or three of them, then reformulate the query more tightly. Conversely, the user whose query is producing only three or four documents may wish to broaden the search terms. Some systems provide such suggestions to the user gratis. The system may even initially ask the user to set a limit on the number of documents desired. Then output from the system can be tailored to this number, together with information about how many documents the system would have provided without the limit.

If the system uses a stop list, information about the size of the stop list may be helpful to the user. Extending this idea, the user may want to ask the system whether a particular word is on the stop list, and request a temporary change of status for the word, removing it if it is on the list or adding it if it is not.

Having a thesaurus available to the user is helpful, whether or not the thesaurus is actually used in the retrieval process. If it is used in retrieval, then information about the thesaurus gives the user guidance as to how the system interprets a given query; if the thesaurus is not used directly, it still provides the user with suggestions for rephrasing a query to improve performance.

Other information about the system is perhaps of less direct utility but nevertheless helpful in guiding the user's thinking. The characteristics of the databases tell the user what kind of information to expect in response to a query. Does the system provide bibliographic references only, abstracts, or full text? What fields, years, and journals does each system database cover? Can the user specify which databases are to be used? If the database information is segmented into fields, such as author, title, and source, can the user specify the fields to be used?

Finally, a more general help facility should be provided. The user may not think to ask about some of the above information if he does not know that it is available. Indeed, the beginning user may not even know how to formulate a query.

9.2   RELEVANCE FEEDBACK

The user's response to much of the information discussed in the preceding section is either a manual alteration of the query or an active setting of various system parameters. In another type of dialogue, the user can provide information that the system itself can use to modify its operation. This is known as *relevance feedback,* and consists of the user feeding back into the system decisions on the relevance of retrieved documents. Basically, the system retrieves a set of documents in response to a query and presents these to the user. The user then examines the documents (or document surrogates), and makes decisions on the potential relevance of each document. Normally this decision is that a document is or is not relevant, or that no judgment is being made on a given document. The system uses these judgments to alter its retrieval behavior. A new set of documents is then presented to the user, and the cycle begins again.

There are some obvious practical limitations and rules for such a system, irrespective of its impact on the retrieval process. First, very few users will be willing to sit through endless iterations of the process in hopes of retrieving the "best possible" set of documents. Thus a relevance feedback process, to be successful, must yield results within at most three or four iterations. Second, it should be clear that many users will terminate such a process before it runs to completion, including those users who only want one or two documents. Third, while a user may wish to reevaluate a document in the light of new documents found, it is more likely that a user will become irritated at seeing previously identified relevant documents repeated at each iteration. Thus the process should, as a default, show only new documents at each iteration, with perhaps a summary list when the user indicates that he is through. At the same time, the user must be able to override the default easily and see all of the documents thus far, or at least those that have not been definitely rejected.

Relevance feedback was developed as a viable technique by Salton and his students and colleagues (Rocchio 1965, 1971; Salton 1971a, 1971b). Many experiments have been done over the years, investigating different aspects of a relevance feedback system. The general conclusion from these experiments is that a properly designed and used relevance feedback system can positively alter the retrieval effectiveness of an information system at relatively little additional cost.

One decision in designing a relevance feedback system concerns which relevance judgments—the positive ones or the negative ones—should be used. A system can use only the positive relevance judgments, trying to tailor the retrieval process more toward documents similar to those judged relevant. Alternatively, the system can use only the negative relevance judgments, trying to avoid documents similar to those that the user rejected. Systems that use both the positive and negative judgments can be more finely tuned by weighting the judgments themselves, so that positive judgments, for example, will count twice as heavily as negative ones.

A second decision is where the adjustments should be applied. There are four basic points of application: query, profile, document, and the retrieval algorithm itself. Adjusting the query may seem to be the most natural. This is, after all, the focus of the user's present efforts, and modification of the query directly addresses the question of which documents will be presented to the user now. However, adjustment of the query has no lasting impact on the system. The next time the user approaches the system the whole relevance feedback process must start from scratch.

Modifying the user profile has a more lasting impact on the retrieval process, since the profile survives from one query session to the next. It is likely that any profile a user submits to the system is inaccurate. Thus there are grounds for trying to improve the profile to better match the user's information habits. Against this there is the danger that a modification made on the basis of a single query session may adversely affect future query sessions due to factors peculiar to that one session. Hence modifications to the user profile should probably be made with caution.

The third point of modification is the document description. Whether the description is generated manually or automatically, this description may present an incomplete and inaccurate document representation. This provides motivation to improve the document description. Even when full-text documents are involved, the document itself may not adequately reflect how it fits into a particular document collection or into the literature in general. Once again caution is in order. Changing the document description alters how the entire community of users will see the document. If the user community is highly homogeneous, consisting, for example, of genome researchers, or of stockbrokers, it may be possible to derive document descriptions that will better serve the entire community. But in a heterogeneous community such as the patrons of a public library, it is entirely possible that the view that pleases one user or group of users makes retrieval more difficult for others. Thus if an information system has a highly heterogeneous set of users, relevance feedback is probably better aimed either at individual users or at clearly identifiable subgroups.

A similar comment applies to the fourth type of modification, that of the retrieval algorithm itself. Changing the algorithm affects system performance for all users and thus should be done with extreme caution. Simple changes such as altering parameter values are relatively easy to make and, if necessary, to undo. Significant changes altering the fundamental processing of the algorithm are more difficult to make and should probably not be undertaken automatically. It would, however, be useful to the system manager if suggestions for such modifications could be made automatically from the operation of the system (including relevance feedback).

The changes that can be made in a retrieval system and how they can be made are affected by the underlying model of the system. Most relevance feedback systems focus on one or both of two techniques: modifying term weights, and altering the terms used. The former technique is usable only with systems that permit term weighting, whereas the latter technique can be used with any system.

If term weight modification is possible, the general method involves trying to identify those terms that are closely associated with relevant documents or with nonrelevant documents. Those terms associated with relevant documents are given additional weight in the query, while the terms more tied to nonrelevant documents are given less weight. Assuming a closed weighting scale, such as 0 to 1, the changes can be made proportional to the difference between the present weight and the end value. Suppose, for example, that the user's original query is

chicken: 0.8, pasta: 0.4, spinach: 0.5, crescent rolls: 0.1, rice: 0.3,

where the numbers are the weights for the terms. Suppose that *chicken* and *crescent rolls* are found to be terms associated with relevant documents, while *spinach* and *rice* are associated with nonrelevant documents. If the change to be made is 10% of the difference between the term and the end-point, the modified query will be

chicken: 0.82, pasta: 0.4, spinach: 0.45, crescent rolls: 0.19, rice: 0.27.

Since the term *pasta* was not particularly associated with either group of documents, its weight was not altered. This new query will retrieve a set of documents that is different from the original set but may have many in common with it. The user is interested in seeing the new documents that are thus retrieved.

Altering the terms used can be done in two ways. One involves the use of a thesaurus to find terms that are identified with the original terms. The new terms may either be terms of similar "rank" or terms that are broader or narrower than the original terms. For example, since *chicken* was a good term, we might add the term *turkey;* the term *crescent rolls* might be broadened to *rolls* in general. Since the term *spinach* was not well received, it might be replaced with the more general term *vegetables* or some other specific vegetables, such as *peas* and *broccoli; rice* and *pasta* are in the same general food group, so the decision might simply be to eliminate the term *rice,* which was related to nonrelevant documents.

A second method for altering the terms in a query is to analyze the documents that have been marked relevant or nonrelevant, adding or deleting terms closely associated with those in the query. If it is found, for example, that the relevant documents that refer to *chicken* also frequently mention *basil,* then perhaps that should be added as a new search term. There are many decisions to be made in altering the terms; unless these decisions are carefully considered, adding and deleting terms too freely can quickly lead to disaster. For example, a query involving *telephone* could quickly lead (through generalizing the term) to recovering documents related to any communication medium—telegraph, radio, television, newspaper, signal flags, electronic mail, messenger services, and so forth.

9.3   GENETIC ALGORITHMS

Relevance feedback is a technique for optimizing a query, aiming at the best form of it for use with a given database. As with many optimization procedures, there is the possibility that the method will converge to a result that is only locally optimal. That is, it may lead to a form of the query that is better than the original form but significantly poorer than another, undetected form. This might be the case, for example, if the database contains two rather disparate sets of literature and the query focused on one set, ignoring the other.

Convergence to a local optimum is associated with the methodology called *hill climbing*. This involves trying at each step to make a positive improvement in the query, analogous to always walking uphill. The result of such a stroll will be to reach the top of the hill—but the next hill over might be a higher one, missed because one did not first descend into the valley between the hills. The standard way to guard against finding a local optimum is to begin again from a different point, in effect seeing if the different starting point will lead up a different hill. One may carry out this process several times before becoming reasonably convinced that the optimum, the highest hill, has been found. In an interactive retrieval system the user is unlikely to tolerate such repeated searching for more and better documents.

Several unorthodox algorithms have been developed that aim at rapidly finding optimal problem solutions in a large problem space. (The problem here is in finding the best query form among all possible forms.) One of these techniques, developed by John Holland (1975), is called a *genetic algorithm*. In a genetic algorithm, several possible solutions are generated in parallel. The best few of these solutions are chosen and replicated, while the poorer solutions are discarded. In effect, several hills that might be climbed are identified and examined, with the best few of these hills chosen for further processing. *Replication* of the solutions creates a *breeding population*, from which new solutions will be generated, or bred. The breeding is accomplished by an exchange of some of the characteristics of the chosen solutions in a *crossover* operation. This is analogous to the biological interchange of genes between two chromosomes. Some of the newly created solutions may be poorer than the parents, but some may be better; it is the latter solutions that are sought. Hill climbing is avoided in two ways. One way simply involves pursuing multiple solutions in parallel from different starting points. Hill climbing can still occur, but the lower hills that are only locally optimal are quickly discarded. The other way involves introducing new characteristic values at a low rate through a *mutation* process. In the hill climbing metaphor, this corresponds to just picking a hill at random and trying it. Usually such random attempts fail to produce anything; eventually all trace of them disappears. Occasionally, however, such a mutation will lead to the discovery of a previously unknown solution.

9.4   GENETIC ALGORITHMS FOR RELEVANCE FEEDBACK

The application of genetic algorithm techniques to relevance feedback has focused largely on term weights (Yang and Korfhage 1992). One immediate benefit of the genetic algorithm approach is that it relieves the user of the burden of assigning term weights. To provide good coverage of the solution space, a genetic algorithm begins with unweighted terms chosen by the user and generates a number of *query variants* by assigning term weights randomly. (One could begin by just generating random sets of terms, then mixing, adding, and deleting terms, but this seems a less fruitful approach and has not been investigated.) Each query variant is then simply a vector of weights corresponding to the vector of terms in the query. The number of query variants used in experiments has ranged from 10 to 40. (This is analogous to climbing 10 to 40 hills simultaneously.) There is some evidence that a larger number of variants may produce better results; the penalty paid is computation time and effort.

Each query variant is used to search the database, retrieving sets of documents that are then evaluated. Several different evaluation functions can be used, but all are based on the number of retrieved documents that are relevant, R_r, the number of retrieved documents that are not relevant, R_n, and the number of unretrieved documents that are relevant, N_r. The most general evaluation formula that has been used is

$$\alpha R_r - \beta R_n - \gamma N_r,$$

where the coefficients can be chosen in various ways. Observe that in a practical system the value of N_r is unknown, so that for such situations it is appropriate to set $\gamma = 0$. The specific choice of the three coefficients has a definite influence on system performance.

Both the mean and the median of the evaluation function are calculated, and those query variants with a value at least the larger of these two numbers are retained to seed the next round of processing. The variants are then replicated in proportion to the evaluation measure, with the variants of highest measure generating the most copies. The resulting breeding population is developed to the same size as the original population.

For example, suppose that 10 query variants are used, and that 4 of these rank sufficiently highly to be retained. If these variants each evaluate to a value of 2, then an additional copy of each is made, along with two more copies chosen at random, to bring the total breeding population back to 10. If the variants have values 8, 6, 4, and 2, respectively, then they will receive a total of four, three, two, and one copy each, for a total breeding population of 10.

Since these are the better variants, they should not be discarded. However, simply reprocessing them will not yield any new results. Thus a certain number of random pairs of these variants is chosen for breeding. One way to do this is to randomize the order in which the variants are used and then make the choice of pairs. For example, suppose that the variants are A, A, A, A, B, B, B, C, C, D. A random ordering of these might be A, C, A, B, C, A, A, D, B, B, producing five potential breeding pairs of (A, C), (A, B), (C, A), (A, D), and (B, B).

Breeding is accomplished through a crossover operation that can be performed in several ways. Suppose, for example, that the query contains 15 terms. Then each query variant is a vector of 15 numbers, representing the term weights. A *one-point crossover* is accomplished by choosing one point, breaking the variants at that point, and interchanging the tails of the variants. Thus if the point chosen were between the sixth and seventh weights, one of the new variants would have the first six weights from the first parent and the remainder from the second parent, while the other new variant would have its first six weights from the second parent and the remainder from the first parent.

The *two-point crossover* is similar but involves choosing two points and interchanging the weights between these points. In each method, the break points are chosen at random. Thus even if (A, C) and (C, A) are chosen as breeding pairs, they may generate different offspring due to the random choice of the break points. Obviously, breeding a variant with itself, such as (B, B), will produce nothing new.

Another method of breeding the variants is *uniform crossover*. In this method, each weight position is considered individually and a choice made randomly as to whether to switch the two weights or leave them be. Whichever crossover method is chosen, its use is governed by the *crossover rate*, which dictates how many pairs are actually chosen for breeding. For example, if the crossover rate were 0.6, then 60%, or three of the five pairs of variants, would be randomly chosen for breeding.

Independent of breeding method, mutations are used to introduce new variants. The mutations may be applied either before or after breeding and are governed by the *mutation rate,* which determines the number of variants to be chosen for mutation. The mutation rate is typically kept very low, as a high rate would disrupt the convergence process too much. If, for example, a mutation rate of 0.05 were chosen, then 1 out of every 20 query variants, on average, would be mutated. In other words, on average 1 mutation every other generation would be introduced in the example set of 10 query variants. The mutation consists of choosing randomly one of the weights and replacing it by a randomly chosen value. Such a "wild shot" may or may not produce a good variant.

It appears that the genetic algorithm process is anything but orderly: Initial query weights, breeding pairs, crossover points, mutated queries, mutation points, and mutation values are all chosen randomly. It is a wonder that the process ever produces anything useful. Clearly the choice of crossover rate and mutation rate will have a major impact on the success of the process. The stability and convergence of the process depend on proper choice of these rates, as well as on the replication process and the random choices made. In the example given there are 10 ways to choose three of the five pairs for breeding. Thus, ignoring mutation, some of the variants from one generation are always preserved into the next generation, as shown in Table 9.1.

Suppose, for example, that the first three pairs, (A, C), (A, B), and (C, A), are chosen for breeding. Then the pairs (A, D) and (B, B) are not affected. Thus this particular choice retains one copy each of A and D, and two copies of B. If the breeding choice is the three pairs (A, C), (A, D), and (B, B), then the pairs (A, B) and (C, A) are unaffected, retaining two copies of A, and one each of B and C. However, in this situation, crossing B with itself simply produces two new copies of B. Hence this selection really retains two copies of A, three copies of B, and one copy of C. Note that A and B are never lost, and in only one case, with the breeding pairs (A, C), (C, A), and (A, D), are both C and D lost.

Table 9.1
Copies Made by Breeding Choices

Variant	Original number of copies	NUMBER OF BREEDING CHOICES PRODUCING N COPIES			
		0 copies	1 copy	2 copies	3 copies
A	4	0	4	6	0
B	3	0	0	6	4
C	2	3	6	1	0
D	1	6	4	0	0

However, the indication in a small example that the method is valid is not sufficient reason to use it. Further tests should be, and have been, carried out. The most extensive of these to date involves the Cranfield II database, a database of 1400 documents on aeronautical engineering assembled in the 1960s by Cyril Cleverdon (1967). Included with the database are 225 questions derived from the documents, together with a list of those documents considered relevant to each of the questions. Thus the Cranfield collection, although small and old, is one of the best organized test collections available. Many researchers have used it for a variety of experiments, including several on relevance feedback techniques. A paper summarizing these experiments lists an average precision value of 0.312 as the best attained (Salton and Buckley 1990).

In a series of experiments on the Cranfield collection using weighted key terms to represent the documents, the average precision values shown in Table 9.2 were determined. The columns labeled "increase (%)" show the increase (or decrease) in the average precision value over the 0.312 figure cited in Salton and Buckley. Two things should be noted about the figures shown in this table *for this series of experiments.* First, for most evaluation functions the genetic algorithm relevance feedback technique yielded better results than the best of the standard relevance feedback methods. Second, there is a clear trend in the average precision level as the evaluation function is changed: Higher values of α, up to a maximum of 10 or 20, produce higher precision.

Table 9.2
Relevance Feedback Improvement Using Genetic Algorithms

Evaluations	11 Levels		3 Levels	
	Average precision	Increase (%)	Average precision	Increase (%)
$R_r - 2R_n$	0.322	3.2	0.296	−5.1
$R_r - R_n$	0.344	10.3	0.324	3.8
$R_r - R_n - N_r$	0.389	24.7	0.377	20.8
$2R_r - R_n$	0.389	24.7	0.376	20.5
$3R_r - R_n$	0.405	29.8	0.395	26.6
$4R_r - R_n$	0.414	32.7	0.405	29.8
$5R_r - R_n$	0.422	35.3	0.413	32.4
$10R_r - R_n$	0.429	37.5	0.424	35.8
$20R_r - R_n$	0.428	37.2	0.427	36.8
$30R_r - R_n$	0.423	35.6	0.419	34.3

Similar results have been obtained in a series of experiments using unweighted key terms to represent the documents. Conventional wisdom is that weighted key terms produce better results; this may not be the case when genetic algorithms are used. The genetic algorithm as implemented begins with unweighted terms; to initialize the algorithm with weighted terms might introduce a bias that would prevent the algorithm from locating the globally best form of the query. Research on this has not yet been conducted.

Further experimental evidence suggests that it may be possible to "tune" the system performance to the user's general specifications. The evaluation function used is $P_f = \alpha R_r - \beta R_n$, where R_r is the number of relevant documents returned and R_n is the number of nonrelevant documents returned. If the user selects a specified level of precision or recall, it may be possible to choose the evaluation function to guarantee that the system performs at that level (Table 9.3). In fact, early evidence indicates that the relationship is a broad "S" curve (Figure 9.1). However, much work remains to be done to verify this. If this relationship proves to hold generally across queries and databases, it might provide a new measure by which to evaluate retrieval systems.

One interesting observation can be made, indicating the utility of the genetic algorithm approach to relevance feedback. In many optimization sit-

Table 9.3
Tuning System Performance
by Changing Evaluation Function

$P_f = \alpha R_r - \beta R_n$	Precision	Recall
$R_r - 2R_n$	0.780	0.304
$R_r - R_n$	0.771	0.338
$2R_r - R_n$	0.745	0.413
$3R_r - R_n$	0.704	0.458
$4R_r - R_n$	0.658	0.495
$5R_r - R_n$	0.621	0.527
$10R_r - R_n$	0.500	0.613
$20R_r - R_n$	0.386	0.704
$30R_r - R_n$	0.329	0.750
$40R_r - R_n$	0.300	0.781
$50R_r - R_n$	0.278	0.803
$60R_r - R_n$	0.270	0.816

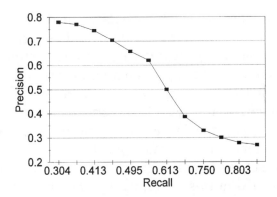

Figure 9.1   Relationship between system performance and evaluation function parameters.

uations, it is reasonable to expect two or more local optima. There may even be multiple global optima, that is, points at which the evaluation function receives its highest value. In genetic algorithm research, the situation in which multiple local optima occur is known as a *rough landscape.* Experiments in information retrieval have shown that this type of situation can arise. For certain queries and databases, the genetic algorithm converges to two solutions rather than one, both producing equally valid lists of documents. Such convergence is not possible using conventional relevance feedback, which follows a single path toward optimality.

Finally, it should be noted that the underlying relevance feedback method used here is term weight modification. Adding or deleting query terms has not been attempted; it seems likely that this will yield further improvements in the results, as it does for standard relevance feedback methods.

9.5   GENETIC ALGORITHMS IN A REALISTIC SITUATION

A long-recognized problem with information retrieval research has been that the databases used are much smaller than those encountered in practice. This has raised questions as to how—and whether—research results would scale up to realistic situations. Recently, however, this state of affairs has changed with a series of TREC (Text REtrieval Conference) experiments sponsored by the U.S. Department of Energy and organized by the National Institute of Standards and Technology. (See Section 9.6.) The use of genetic algorithms for relevance feedback was tested in the first of this series of experiments. The data set for the first round of these experiments consisted of five databases containing nearly 750,000 documents. The documents themselves were full text, ranging in length from a paragraph to several hundred pages. Each of 100 questions was presented as a topic description of roughly a page in length from which a query was to be derived. The documents relevant to each topic were unknown during the experiments and were determined afterwards by a panel of experts.

The performance of the genetic algorithm method was comparable to that of other methods tried in this experiment. It produced better than average results on some of the topics, worse than average on others. This level of performance was achieved despite the fact that the genetic algorithm technique did not make full use of the various relevance feedback techniques for introducing new terms. Two interesting observations arose from this set of experiments. First, the genetic algorithm technique led to different optimal forms of a given query, depending on the database being used. This clearly demonstrates the influence of the individual database characteristics on retrieval performance. Second, the rough landscape phenomenon mentioned in Section 9.4 occurred, with one query optimizing to two distinct forms.

9.6 THE TREC EXPERIMENTS

The TREC experiments provide a new venue for research on improving retrieval effectiveness. A primary result of the experiments is that much has been learned about handling large, full-text databases in a retrieval situation and about how to evaluate the results. Several rounds of these experiments have been conducted, with more scheduled. Research groups throughout the world are participating.

More than 30 university and commercial organizations participated in the first series, TREC-1, using retrieval techniques ranging from simple Boolean to sophisticated natural language processing (Harman 1993). This represented the first effort to conduct experiments on large, full-text databases, with multiple query topics and multiple participating groups. As a result, most groups spent a good part of their effort learning how to handle the amount of data presented within the prescribed time frame.

Twenty-four of the groups produced usable results, from which several observations can be made. First, with one exception all of the groups performed at about the same level. The differences in precision-recall curves, for example, were minimal. Second, this level of performance was achieved despite some obvious differences and inadequacies in various systems. Some experimental groups generated queries automatically from the topic statements; other groups generated the queries manually. Many systems did not incorporate relevance feedback. Some of the topics contained negated terms, for example, asking for a foreign country but not Japan. The level of performance of various systems seemed little affected by whether such negated terms were treated properly, treated as positive terms, or ignored. The computer hardware used ranged from a bank of PCs to a supercomputer. This, too, seemed to have little influence on the level of system performance. Finally, despite the similarity of the precision-recall results, there was an unexpectedly large scatter in the actual documents retrieved. One possible factor in this is that the number of relevant documents almost always differed from the number of documents returned in the experiments. If there were fewer relevant documents, then one might expect a scattering of nonrelevant documents to be included in the returned set; if there were more relevant documents than could have been returned, it seems reasonable that not every system would select the same documents to be returned from among those that are relevant.

Little could be concluded from the first round of TREC experiments except that (a) handling large databases by various techniques is not such a severe problem as some have imagined, and (b) there is still much to learn about designing effective retrieval systems for large text databases. Still, it was deemed a success. A number of interesting minor problems arose. For example, many text processing subsystems converted "AT&T" to "AT T", resulting in two stop words that were subsequently eliminated from the text. Several of the topics involved a numerical evaluation, such as "joint agreements with value in excess of $5,000,000," that traditional text retrieval systems were not equipped to handle. The method of evaluating the search results involved far more work than had been anticipated; yet it was subsequently decided that experimenters had been asked to return too few results, leading to inaccurate evaluations of the retrieval systems.

Each subsequent series of TREC experiments has been based on the experiences and findings of the earlier experiments. In TREC-2, additional databases were incorporated, relevance feedback was made a factor in the experiments (although not every system was required to incorporate it), and the number of documents to be returned was increased from 200 per topic to

1000 (Harman 1994). The total database size increased from roughly 1 gigabyte to 3 gigabytes, and a new set of topics was given to the experimenters. Because many of the experimental groups who participated had also participated in TREC-1 and have since been able to improve their systems, the differences in system performance were clearer in TREC-2. Nevertheless, many of the best systems produced similar overall performances. This led to the conclusion that evaluation was still a problem. Increasing the number of documents returned had eliminated most of the inaccuracies due to the small number of documents per topic; but it became clear that average performance figures are inadequate for understanding system performance, and that more thorough statistical studies of performance are necessary.

TREC-3 introduced new topics with shorter descriptions, allowing for more innovative topic expansion ideas (Harman 1995). In addition, a small group of experimenters worked with a Spanish language collection, while others experimented with interactive query formulation. TREC-4 continued the expanded set of investigations, with groups working on interactive searching and multilingual search tasks. There was increased focus on natural language processing, on merging results from multiple databases, and on information filtering. Finally, a corrupted version of the data, representing the type of data that might come from an OCR system, was introduced to study the effects of this type of data corruption on retrieval.

REFERENCES

Cleverdon, Cyril W. 1967. The Cranfield tests on index language devices. *Aslib Proceedings* 19, no. 6:173–194.

Harman, Donna K., ed. 1993. *The First Text REtrieval Conference (TREC-1)*. Washington, D.C.: NIST Special Publication 500–207.

Harman, Donna K., ed. 1994. *The Second Text REtrieval Conference (TREC-2)*. Washington, D.C.: NIST Special Publication 500–215.

Harman, Donna K., ed. 1995. *Overview of the Third Text REtrieval Conference (TREC-3)*. Washington, D.C.: NIST Special Publication 500–225.

Holland, John H. 1975. *Adaptation in natural and artificial systems*. Ann Arbor, Michigan: University of Michigan Press.

Rocchio, J.J., Jr. 1965. Relevance feedback in information retrieval. Scientific report ISR-9, sec. 23. Harvard Computation Laboratory, Cambridge, Massachusetts.

Rocchio, J.J., Jr. 1971. Relevance feedback in information retrieval. Chap. 14 in *The SMART retrieval system—Experiments in automatic document processing*, ed. G. Salton, pp. 313–323. Englewood Cliffs, New Jersey: Prentice-Hall.

Salton, Gerard, ed. 1971a. *The SMART Retrieval System—Experiments in Automatic Document Processing*. Englewood Cliffs, New Jersey: Prentice-Hall.

Salton, Gerard. 1971b. Relevance feedback and the optimization of retrieval effectiveness. Chap. 15 in *The SMART Retrieval System—Experiments in Automatic Document Processing*, ed. G. Salton, pp. 324–336. Englewood Cliffs, New Jersey: Prentice-Hall.

Salton, Gerard, and Chris Buckley. 1990. Improving retrieval performance by relevance feedback. *JASIS* 41, no. 4:288–297.

Yang, Jing-Jye, and Robert R. Korfhage. 1992. Adaptive information retrieval systems in vector model. *Symposium on Document Analysis and Information Retrieval*, Las Vegas, pp. 134–150.

EXERCISES

1. How do you expect that relevance feedback using only positive judgments will affect the precision and recall of an information retrieval system?

2. How do you expect that relevance feedback using only negative judgments will affect the precision and recall of an information retrieval system?

3. One modification for relevance feedback is to allow the user to "clamp" a term, that is, to fix its value in a query. How do you expect this to influence relevance feedback and the retrieval process?

4. A genetic algorithm classically uses a fixed vector of parameters (terms), modifying only the weights or values assigned. Determine a way to substitute new terms for those currently being used, and still have a reasonable genetic algorithm process.

5. Similarly, determine a way to add new terms to those being used in the genetic algorithm process, that is, to allow the number of components in the vector to change during relevance feedback.

6. The use of random weights to initiate a genetic algorithm allows the algorithm to "explore" the entire document space. What would be the positive and negative effects of permitting the user to bias the initial weights? For example, a user might select a value of 0.7 for one term, with the result that the initial weights for that term in the variants would be normally distributed about 0.7.

CHAPTER 10

Alternative Retrieval Techniques

Up to this point, the focus of this book has been on lexical processing of text—working with individual words and terms to determine whether a document matches an information need. In this chapter, alternative techniques are examined, using some of the other data that are available.

As was suggested in Chapter 5, simply performing a lexical analysis of a natural language query or document misses a good part of the available data. Natural language processing involves techniques to extract information from the manner in which a query or document is written. Other data come from the structure of the text itself. In particular, bibliographic citations provide a means of linking one document to another. Hypertext links in documents are becoming increasingly common, particularly in documents on the World Wide Web. They point very directly to documents related to specific topics within a given document. With the emphasis on processing full-text documents, new ideas have been introduced, including the concept of information filtering as a means of quickly reducing the volume of material to be examined. Both syntactic and semantic approaches to retrieval have gained new vigor with full-text databases. Techniques for combining evidence from multiple approaches have been devised. The chapter closes with a brief look at two advanced areas of information retrieval, the areas of image retrieval and sound retrieval.

10.1   NATURAL LANGUAGE PROCESSING

In the broadest sense, *natural language processing* is involved whenever any textual document is examined. Yet it is common to restrict the term to processing that involves syntactic, semantic, pragmatic, or dialogue processing of documents (Church 1988; Jacobs and Rau 1988; Smeaton 1989; Blair 1990; Harman and Candela 1990). Thus lexical analysis, while it may underlie the more sophisticated techniques, is not of direct interest to natural language processing. These techniques aim at discovering the syntactic and semantic structure of a document.

Syntactic Analysis

The *syntactic structure* of a document is the way in which it is written, following the grammatical or structural rules of the language. Thus the *syntax* of a sentence is focused on its structure rather than its meaning. The sentences "Large red boats move slowly" and "Colorless green ideas sleep furiously" are syntactically the same, although very different in meaning. At the same time, the statements "Grace ate an apple" and "An apple was eaten by Grace" have different syntactic structures but clearly convey much the same meaning. Indeed, a syntactic transformation from the active voice to the passive one changes one sentence into the other, showing their very close relationship. (Note that no syntactic transformation will change "Grace ate an apple" into "A rocket was built by Jane," even though the latter has the same syntactic form as "An apple was eaten by Grace.")

The study of syntax dates back many years, if not centuries. With the advent of computers, increased emphasis was placed on developing formalized syntax rules that would enable a computer to "understand" a natural language sentence. Great strides have been made in this effort. Numerous attempts have been made to develop information retrieval systems based on a syntactic analysis of queries and documents. While these have not failed, they have not been notably more successful than the best lexically based systems. Some researchers argue that this lack of improvement indicates that research should focus on developing better lexical systems; others feel that the lack of improvement shows only that there is much more work needed to understand the syntax of a document.

Syntactic analysis suffers from a number of problems, the first of which is *syntactic ambiguity,* or the existence of sentences that can be assigned more than one syntactic structure. There many examples of this, one of the simplest being "They are visiting relatives." In this sentence, does *visiting* refer to *They*, who are off on a trip to see some relatives, or to *relatives*, the people to whom *They* refers, and who are here on a visit? Just as the ambiguity of a word or phrase can be resolved by the context, so can the ambiguity of a sentence. However, the context needed is larger and more complex.

A second problem is the *deep structure* of a sentence, which underlies the example about Grace. The term refers to the major underlying import of a sentence (the act of Grace devouring an apple), which is preserved through such transformations as the change from active to passive voice. While people have relatively little problem determining whether two sentences have the same deep structure, it is difficult to program complete rules for this determination into a computer.

Third, there is no guarantee that a sentence which is syntactically correct is semantically correct. "Colorless green ideas sleep furiously" may make no sense to anyone except a poet.[1] Yet such sentences cannot be ruled out of documents. They may even appear (largely as examples) in rigorous technical papers.

Finally, a syntactic approach assumes that the language to be handled is syntactically correct. This may not be true, particularly for queries. Furthermore, syntactic rules are constantly changing with language usage, and it is difficult to reach agreement on an adequate and complete set of rules. Some efforts have been made recently to develop analyzers that can handle ill-formed sentences, but this work is still relatively new (Finch and Chater 1992; Grefenstette 1992).

Semantic Analysis

As indicated in the above examples, the syntax of a statement has relatively little to do with its meaning. Yet the goal of a retrieval system is to match the meaning of a document to the meaning of a query. Thus there is also a strong incentive to try to identify the *semantic structure* of a document. Perhaps the strongest argument for this is a philosophical one. When a person is asked to judge how well a document matches the information need identified by a query, it is difficult to believe that the person performs

---

[1] This example is credited to Noam Chomsky, who used it in a 1958 Machine Translation Conference at MIT.

either a lexical or a syntactic analysis of the document. It seems much more reasonable that the person somehow identifies the meaning of the document—that is, its *semantics*—by scanning it (or perhaps by a more careful reading), and then matches that with his or her understanding of the query. The syntactic structure of a document may be difficult to specify completely; the semantic content is even more elusive.

Idiomatic expressions will often slip through a semantic analysis undetected. A term such as *red herring,* for example, will be quite acceptable; but a document containing this term will not generally refer to the fishing industry. Idiomatic expressions such as this one or *carrying coals to Newcastle* have a meaning that has evolved, often from some historical referent, so that the literal interpretation has nothing to do with its current use. Syntactic analysis does not identify the disparity between literal meaning and current usage.

Many attempts are being made to develop information retrieval systems based on the semantics of the documents. Success is at best limited, although a number of different techniques and systems have been developed and are being used for research (Yu and Raghavan 1977; Beghtol 1986; Lesk 1986; Lin, Soergel, and Marchionini 1991; Mauldin 1991; Wendlandt and Driscoll 1991; Rama and Srinivasan 1992). Researchers in this area feel, however, that the results are sufficiently encouraging to warrant further effort and study. (Evans, Ginther-Webster, et al. 1991; Evans, Henderson, et al. 1991; Chen and Lynch 1992; Myaeng and Li 1992; Nie 1992; Evans 1993; Evans et al. 1993; Myaeng and Liddy 1993; Ingwersen 1994).

One of the more notable attempts at semantic analysis is *latent semantic indexing,* a technique that uses *multidimensional scaling* methods to identify the major concepts in a document, in contrast to simply the vocabulary words used (Furnas et al. 1988; Deerwester et al. 1990).

Finally, artificial intelligence techniques that address the problem of creating human-computer dialogues are being applied to information retrieval. Much of the work in natural language processing for information retrieval now focuses on the user interface (Biswas, Bezdek, and Subramanian 1987; Anick et al. 1990). *Dialogue analysis* involves developing a sufficiently accurate interpretation of user input in natural language form that an appropriate response can be presented, thus developing a dialogue that eventually leads to some action—in our case, to document retrieval.

10.2 CITATION PROCESSING

In seeking to retrieve documents from an information system, the goal is to find documents that are closely related, if by no other measure than their common bond to the information need. Yet within many nonfiction documents, including virtually all scholarly papers and books, there is a clear indication of related documents. This indication is the bibliography or list of references that a document cites. Hence *citation processing* is a very easy way to locate a set of related documents. While comparatively easy, citation processing is not completely straightforward. Citations are not always available in the older bibliographic databases. In this situation, the user must identify a document of interest, then locate the document in a library and manually identify the interesting citations. However, with the increasing number of full-text databases, the presence of citations in a database record is more common.

Several researchers have suggested using cited documents to enhance the description of a primary document, or comparing the vocabularies of citing and cited documents as a measure of similarity (Kwok 1984; Salton and Zhang 1986; Trivison 1987). While this does provide some guidance, vocabulary tests of this type should be used with discretion.

Other researchers have examined *co-citations* as a measure of document similarity (Small 1973; White and Griffith 1980). This involves the concept that the similarity of two documents can be measured by the number of papers that cite both of the documents. This may provide a measure that helps identify contemporary documents. Two documents on a given topic written in the same year, for example, may represent independent but closely related work. Yet frequently neither will cite the other, simply because the other had not been published when the one document was written. Thus the strongest link between them may be the fact that they are both cited by the same body of documents.

The same kind of idea applies to *bibliographic coupling*, which occurs when two documents cite the same document. This will frequently happen in contemporary documents on the same topic. In addition, when two documents on the same topic are written at different times, there is a reasonably good chance that the more recent paper will cite the older one, providing a direct link. If a number of years have passed between publication of the two documents, the link may be more indirect, with the recent paper citing another paper that in turn cites the earlier paper.

Small has suggested that these types of linkages can be combined into a similarity measure, counting co-citation and direct bibliographic coupling links twice as heavily as indirect coupling links. Some experimental work indicates that this measure can be used as a basis for defining document clusters.

A bibliographic citation many contain many parts. The following items may or may not be included in a bibliographic citation:

One or more author names

Title

Journal name (if a journal paper)

Journal volume and issue numbers

Journal date of issue

Proceedings name (if in a conference proceedings)

Proceedings year

Sponsoring organization

Date of conference

Book title (if a paper or chapter in a book)

Page numbers (if a journal or proceedings paper, or a chapter in a book)

Book editor

Publisher (if a book or in a book; sometimes for proceedings or journals)

Date of publication

Corporate author (sponsor)

Several problems face the designer of a citation processing system. First is the matter of locating the citations, which may be collected under the title "Bibliography," "References," or some other suitable title. In many disciplines such lists occur commonly at the ends of individual papers; in other disciplines it is common to use footnotes or endnotes as a reference vehicle.

In a book, citations may occur either at the end of the book or at the ends of individual chapters.

In the humanities and related disciplines, explicit lists of cited documents may not exist; citations may be confined to either footnotes or endnotes, which frequently contain commentary on the document in relation to the work at hand. Such commentary provides an important connection between the present document and the cited one but is not of direct concern in citation processing. In fact, it gets in the way, since the citation information must be extracted from the commentary in which it is embedded. In this type of citation, one often faces the standard abbreviations *op. cit.* (*opere citato*, referring to a work previously cited) and *ibid.* (*ibidem*, referring to the work in the immediately previous citation, sometimes written *ib.*). Of course, if the system is seeking the titles and information on cited works, references such as these can be ignored, as the necessary information has already been gleaned from prior notes.

The second problem that the citation system faces is in interpreting the citation itself. Unfortunately, there is no single standard format for citing documents, although standards exist within some fields of study. Yet even when the standard exists, it is often relatively recent and of little use to the person seeking historical documentation. Many citation methods make use of various font enhancements, such as italics and boldface, to indicate various portions of the citation. If this information is available, it can be of help to the user of the citation, but it requires that the retrieval system be capable of recognizing such font changes.

Another problem facing the citation system is that of identifying and eliminating duplicate and useless citations. Suppose that a list of documents has been obtained by one of the standard query techniques. Since these documents are related in some way, the user might expect a degree of commonality among their citations. Thus there is the need to identify duplicate citations when they occur. This would not be difficult if everyone followed one standard; but the lack of a standard means that the same document may be cited in two or three different fashions, including various abbreviations and ordering of the citation elements. Thus one may find an author listed as J.B. Jones, James Jones, James B. Jones, or Jones, J. Such inconsistency may be caused by the manner in which the person writing the citation chooses to represent the name, variations in the way that the author cited has given his name, or different citation standards imposed by journals or book editors.

Similarly, the word "journal" may be spelled out fully or abbreviated "J." or "Jour." A journal citation may give any combination of volume number, issue number, month, and year. Page citations may include the beginning and ending pages or only the beginning page, or may be missing entirely. In addition, there may be errors within the citation. It is possible to find a given paper cited with two or more different sets of page numbers or two different years of publication. The order in which multiple authors of a paper are listed in the citation may not correspond to the order in which they are listed in the cited paper. The title given in the citation may be a modification of the title of the cited paper.

Occasionally a paper or book contains citations that are important to the particular work but are of little or no use to someone seeking to identify similar works. For example, many papers involving statistical work will cite a standard statistics text as the source of the tests that have been used. At other times, a citation will be given simply because a particular quotation has been used as an example. The source of data used in a study is frequently cited. While this is important, the information does little to help the user seeking similar studies. Equipment manuals and standards documentation are frequently cited as sources of specific information used within a paper but provide little help in identifying related papers. Thus such references may be useless in the context of broadening a user's search for information related to a specific need.

By their very nature bibliographic citations point backward in time, to documents that were published before the citation was made. It is impossible for any author to cite papers that have not yet been published. The only exception to this is the occasional citation of an immediately forthcoming document, which is "to appear in" a particular journal or conference proceedings, or "to be published by" a particular publisher. The lack of specific dates and page numbers diminishes the usefulness of such citations.

Fortunately, there exist tools, *citation indexes*, that enable a user to identify and locate documents that cite a given document. These include the well-known *Science Citation Index*, the *Social Science Citation Index*, and other similar indexes published by Information Sciences Institute (Garfield 1954, 1956, 1963, 1964, 1979). A citation index covers a specific set of journals and each year lists all of the publications that were cited in any paper appearing in the covered journals that year. Thus the user who knows of a specific paper published in 1985, for example, can search for that paper in the citation indexes from 1986 through the present. If the paper has been referenced, then the citation index will identify each paper that has cited the given paper. This makes it possible for a user to begin with a single known paper, search backwards in time through its bibliography (and the bibliographies of papers it cites), and forward in time through the citation index (and through citations to any works citing that paper).

One measure of the value of a given paper lies in its relationship to other literature addressing the same or similar problems. The bibliography of a paper provides a good indication of how well the author or authors were acquainted with related work, and how thoroughly the work described in the paper fits into the related work. A citation index provides a measure of how well the paper being cited was received by contemporaries in the field. A check through the citation index will determine the number of papers that have cited a given paper, thus giving a clear indication of its impact on the field of study. It is possible to find that rare gem, a paper with a seminal idea whose author was not aware of related ideas, and that was previously undiscovered because it was published in an obscure journal; but it is more likely that a paper without strong links into the related literature in both directions represents an effort of relatively minor value.

10.3   HYPERTEXT LINKS

Hypertext links provide a means of directly connecting two distinct pieces of text. The concept was developed in the 1960s and enjoyed a certain vogue, particularly among educators who saw it as a means of developing better educational programs. The idea languished for about two decades but has come very much alive with the advent of the World Wide Web. Virtually every Web page contains several hypertext links to other pages, often in parts of the Web developed by somebody else.

A hypertext link consists of an identifier and a pointer. The identifier is often a highlighted word or phrase in the text but can be an explicitly given name. In books using a hypertext style, the pointer is often a page number. In this sense, a hypertext link is much like a "see also" reference. In the Web, the hypertext link is active: when the user clicks on the identifier, a transfer to the linked page occurs.

Because hypertext links are generally created by the author of a document, and because they are explicit pointers to related material, they form a potentially rich source of information. A paper cited in a bibliography may relate strongly to the point in the original text or only peripherally; a hypertext link often focuses more distinctly on material strongly related to the topic in the original text. Thus one enhancement to a retrieval system is a method for using hypertext links to locate and present additional material on a topic. This can be done under user control by providing the user with a list of hypertext links in their contexts and letting the user choose. Alternatively, it can be done automatically, following up each hypertext link as it appears.

Two problems surface in the automatic invocation of hypertext links. One is the problem of organizing the material. In this sense, a hypertext link is much like a footnote: It triggers a break in the flow of the text. The other problem, far more serious, is that unlimited invocation of hypertext links can easily lead to a "lost in cyberspace" feeling, as the material presented at the link sites strays farther and farther from the original textual material. One control on this is to follow only those links that are given in the original text, not those that appear in the texts the links point to. Even this may not provide sufficient control. A more sophisticated retrieval program might try to judge each link with respect to the query and follow only those that appear to have sufficiently high relevance.

10.4   INFORMATION FILTERING AND PASSAGE RETRIEVAL

A significant problem in searching large, full-text databases is that most searches are likely to return large volumes of data, including many non-relevant documents. There are several causes for this. First, when full-text documents are used rather than shorter document surrogates, there is an increased chance of words co-occurring in a document without really being related to each other. Second, in some databases one finds a mix of documents about specific topics, and documents that are essentially pointers to the "real" documents. For example, the first page of the *Wall Street Journal* each day contains a column with one or two sentences about each of the major news stories covered, and a pointer to the actual article. This column is thus likely to be retrieved whenever the newspaper is searched. Third, documents like encyclopedias by their very nature will contain much information that is not about any given topic. Thus it is not appropriate to retrieve the full encyclopedia, but rather a portion of it.

Information filtering refers to techniques used to quickly eliminate large segments of a database from consideration for a given query. The analogy with mining is strong enough that various authors refer to this as *data mining*. Quick and relatively inexpensive techniques are used to "mine the ore" from the database; this concentrated ore can then be processed more thoroughly to yield the final set of documents to be retrieved.

The work with visual information retrieval interfaces can be thought of as contributing to this information filtering effort. Many visual interfaces permit the user to see large portions of a database, then identify within the display a smaller set of documents that seems to be "rich ore."

The concept of *passage retrieval* relates closely to information filtering. The context, however, is not that of eliminating large portions of a database of many documents, but rather that of identifying within one broad document such as an encyclopedia those passages that relate closely to a given query. For this purpose the natural boundaries of a document are heavily used. Thus within an encyclopedia passage, identification can be made at the level of the individual article. A finer cut can be made by identifying sections or paragraphs within each article. Several research efforts have been directed toward this end. Hearst and Plaunt (1993) have developed a method called "Text tiling," with a visual interface called "TileBars." This displays for each document (or, at a finer level, for each section or paragraph) the extent to which the document relates to each of the terms in a query. Salton and Allan (1994) have developed a different display that arranges documents as arcs around an ellipse, with lines joining the documents to show use of the query terms. Much of the research in passage retrieval is based on differential analysis of the key terms in a document. If term A has been used in a query and is significant in document D, then passage retrieval identifies those portions of D where the usage of A differs significantly from its overall usage in the document. Those paragraphs or sections where A is more heavily used are likely to be the ones of most interest to the user. These passages are retrieved, and the remainder of the document is either discarded or held in abeyance until the user decides whether to look at it.

10.5 IMAGE PROCESSING

"Full-text processing" really involves more than simply text, since many documents, particularly technical ones, involve graphics, charts, or images in addition to text. Such documents are now either generated electronically or scanned *in toto* into a computer system. Thus the nontextual parts of a document are present and are significant. Yet the linguistic techniques that can be used for text analysis are of no use with the image portions of a document.

Image processing involves developing techniques for analyzing and manipulating images directly. The techniques that have been used in the past for handling image databases do not suffice. Essentially, these techniques are founded on a textual database with attached images. The processing is done on the textual descriptions of the images in order to retrieve the associated images. There are two reasons why such methods are of very limited utility. First is simply the problem of generating textual representations for the millions of images that could appropriately be placed in databases. (Consider, for example, the fact that virtually all patent applications contain drawings and diagrams that are essential to the patent, in the context of the high and continually growing number of patents.) The second problem is that any textual description of an image is a poor surrogate. The analogous situation within text is that of a document and its abstract. By its nature, even the best abstract does not cover many of the fine points in a paper; a textual description of an image is even more of an abstraction and thus even less satisfactory as a surrogate (Blum 1969; Chang 1986, 1988; Joseph and Cardenas 1988; Conti and Rabitti 1990; Ejiri et al. 1990; Lesk 1990; Rabitti and Savino 1991; Turtur et al. 1991).

Many of the techniques that have been developed for text processing could, in principle, be developed into analogous techniques for processing images. For example, while a number of different similarity measures exist for documents, many of the processes that involve similarity analysis are basically independent of the specific measure: They can be used with any similarity measure. Thus, in principle, if a semantically valid similarity measure could be developed for a set of images, the similarity analysis used for textual documents might be extended easily to handle images.

The other side of the image processing coin comes from computer graphics, where many techniques for image manipulation have been developed. These include edge detection, noise removal, substructure detection, and many others. As with many artificial intelligence techniques, success is somewhat limited and can be heavily domain dependent. That is, techniques developed for analyzing blueprints may be of little or no use for other types of images. Yet enough work has been done in this area that it seems reasonable to expect some of these techniques to find use in image retrieval.

The goal for this work is to develop an image retrieval system that can work directly with the images without invoking textual surrogates. The problem is highly complex. Consider the problem of retrieving photographs of bridges from a box of photographs. People do this with little difficulty. There are many different kinds of bridges—suspension, truss, stone arch, covered, and others—and they can be photographed from different angles and altitudes. There is even a bit of fuzziness in identifying a bridge: Some may question whether a log fallen across a stream is really a bridge. Yet people solve this retrieval problem easily, and aside from logs and stepping stones, most would agree on the set of photographs chosen. To solve the problem with a computer, the user would present a picture of a bridge. This might be a crude sketch, a photograph of a specific bridge, or a blueprint. The transformations required to match a photograph to the query image are complex. First the system must identify a potential bridge. The view in the photograph must be adjusted to match that of the query image, and some kind of transformation or matching process must be applied to account for the fact that the type of bridge in the photograph is not the type shown in the query image.

Research groups are addressing the problem of image retrieval with increasing success, with commercial systems beginning to appear. A research group within IBM has been developing a system, QBIC, that uses sketch matching and graphic characteristics such as color and texture to help identify and retrieve images (Niblack et al. 1993; Faloutsos et al. 1994). Raghavan's group at Louisiana State University has perhaps had more success, albeit in a very limited domain. They have been working on face recognition using frontal views of a face (Gudivada and Raghavan 1995). Myaeng has started an image retrieval project in Korea, with only preliminary results thus far (Han and Myaeng 1996). The concept behind many of these efforts is that of using a pictorial or graphical example directly as a query (Joseph and Cardenas 1988; Hirata and Kato 1992, 1993; Ogle and Stonebraker 1995; Papadias and Sellis 1995). Many of these ideas are finding application in geographic information systems, where maps, satellite images, and other graphical data form the basis for search (Mainguenaud and Portier 1990; Calcinelli and Mainguenaud 1994; Lee and Chin 1995).

10.6 SOUND PROCESSING

A major focus of information processing in this final decade of the century is the development of *multimedia* (or, more accurately, *integrated media*) document systems. Text and images together already constitute a basic form of integrated media documents. However, the term is more often used to designate documents that include animation and sound together with text and still images. Retrieval of such documents can be very simple, based only on textual content, with everything else ignored, or it can be exceedingly complex, involving analysis of the sound and animation components as well as the text and image components. At present, sophisticated retrieval systems based on the content of all components of an integrated media document do not exist. This is an area of active research.

A retrieval system for integrated media documents clearly integrates subsystems for text, image, and sound retrieval. Just as image retrieval ultimately will utilize image queries, so also sound retrieval will use sound as a means of entering queries. One aspect of this is voice recognition. Much progress has been made in this area, albeit in contexts other than information retrieval. The most common context is the use of voice commands. Computers are now on the market that respond to a limited set of spoken commands from the user. There is no doubt that within a few years these systems will be capable of more sophisticated information processing. Another area where progress is being made is in the generation of text from speech. A major driving force in this work is the need to provide computer access to the disabled. Once the technology is developed to permit verbal commands to a computer and to reliably recognize spoken words, the application of this technology to information retrieval is a small step.

A second aspect of sound retrieval is the retrieval of sounds other than voice, ranging from music, through sounds associated with various human activities, to natural sounds. Natural sounds are perhaps the easiest of these to handle. There are large recorded libraries of bird songs, frog calls, and other natural sounds; the retrieval problem is that of matching an input sound to one in the library. This can be done through analysis of the sonograms (sound spectrograms). Sounds associated with human activities present a similar problem and a similar solution. However, the sounds are much more varied, and the libraries of sound samples are not as extensive. In either situation the number of possible sounds is sufficiently large that it will probably pay to develop more sophisticated tools for narrowing in on a set of reasonable candidate sounds.

Music presents a somewhat different challenge, in that it is highly patterned and the patterns are categorized in several ways. One can classify music by its style—baroque, classical romantic, atonal, blues, rock, and so forth—and by its presentation—solo voice, choral, jazz trio, symphony orchestra, string quartet, and so forth. Input to a music retrieval system can be given in several forms. Textual input—the name of a composer, performer, or composition—is only one form. A system might also accept a short recorded segment of music or a few bars whistled or hummed (perhaps off-key). The retrieval system would first classify the music as thoroughly as possible, perhaps through a dialog with the user, then do a detailed search to match the input.

REFERENCES

Anick, Peter G., J.D. Brennan, Rex A. Flynn, David R. Hanssen, B. Alvey, and J.M. Robbins. 1990. A direct manipulation interface for Boolean information retrieval via natural language query. *Proceedings of the 13th Annual International ACM/SIGIR Conference on Research and Development in Information Retrieval,* ed. Jean-Luc Vidick, Brussels, pp. 135–150.

Beghtol, Clare. 1986. Bibliographic classification theory and text linguistics: Aboutness analysis, intertextuality and the cognitive act of classifying documents. *Journal of Documentation* 42, no. 2:84–113.

Biswas, G., J.C. Bezdek, M. Marques, and V. Subramanian. 1987. Knowledge-assisted document retrieval: Part I. The natural language interface. *JASIS* 38, no. 2:83–96.

Blair, David C. 1990. *Language and Representation in Information Retrieval.* New York: Elsevier.

Blum, Bruce I. 1969. An information retrieval system for photographic data. In *The Information Bazaar. Proceedings of the Sixth Annual National Colloquium on Information Retrieval,* ed. Louise Schultz, pp. 133–149. Medical Documentation Service, The College of Physicians of Philadelphia.

Calcinelli, D., and M. Mainguenaud. 1994. Cigales, a visual query language for a geographical information system: The user interface. *Journal of Visual Languages and Computing* 5:113–132.

Chang, Shi-Kuo. 1986. Image information systems. *Proceedings of IEEE* 73, no. 4:757–764.

Chang, Shi-Kuo. 1988. An intelligent image database system. *IEEE Transactions on Software Engineering* 14, no. 5:681–688.

Chen, H., and K. Lynch. 1992. Automatic construction of networks of concepts characterizing document databases. *IEEE Transactions on Systems, Man, and Cybernetics* 22, no. 5:885–902.

Church, Kenneth. 1988. A stochastic parts program and noun phrase parser for unrestricted text. *Proceedings of the Second Conference on Applied Natural Language Processing,* pp. 136–143.

Conti, P., and F. Rabitti. 1990. Image retrieval by semantic content. In *Multimedia Office Filing and Retrieval: The MULTOS Approach,* ed. C. Thanos. North-Holland Series on Human Factors in Information Technology. Amsterdam: North-Holland.

Deerwester, Scott, Susan T. Dumais, George W. Furnas, Thomas K. Landauer, and R. A. Harshman. 1990. Indexing by latent semantic analysis. *JASIS* 41, no. 6:391–407.

Ejiri Masakazu, Shigeru Kakumoto, Takafumi Miyatake, Shigeru Shimada, and Kazuaki Iwamura. 1990. Automatic recognition of engineering drawings and maps. In *Image Analysis Applications,* ed. Rangachar Kasturi and M.M. Trivedi, pp. 73–126. New York: Marcel Dekker.

Evans, David A. 1993. Lessons from the CLARIT project. *Proceedings of the 16th Annual International ACM/SIGIR Conference on Research and Development in Information Retrieval,* Pittsburgh, pp. 224–225.

Evans, David A., K. Ginther-Webster, Mary Hart, Robert G. Lefferts, and Ira A. Monarch. 1991. Automatic indexing using selective NLP and first-order thesauri. In *Proceedings of RIAO 91,* pp. 624–643.

Evans, David A., Steve K. Henderson, Robert G. Lefferts, and Ira A. Monarch. 1991. *A Summary of the CLARIT project.* Technical report CMU-LCI-91-2, Carnegie-Mellon University, Pittsburgh.

Evans, David A., Robert G. Lefferts, Gregory Grefenstette, S. Henderson, William Hersh, and A. Archbold. 1993. CLARIT TREC design, experiments, and results. In *The First Text REtrieval Conference (TREC-1),* ed. Donna K. Harman, pp. 251–286. Washington, D.C.: NIST Special Publication 500–207.

Faloutsos, C., R. Barber, M. Flickner, J. Hafner, W. Niblack, D. Petrovic, and W. Equitz. 1994. Efficient and effective querying by image content. *Journal of Intelligent Information Systems* 3:231–262.

Finch, S., and N. Chater. 1992. Bootstrapping syntactic categories using statistical methods. *Proceedings of the First SHOE Workshop,* Tilburg University, Netherlands, pp. 230–235.

Furnas, George W., Scott C. Deerwester, Susan T. Dumais, Thomas K. Landauer, Richard A. Harshman, Lynn A. Streeter, and Karen E. Lochbaum. 1988. Information retrieval using a singular value decomposition model of latent semantic structure. *Proceedings of the 11th Annual International ACM/SIGIR Conference on Research and Development in Information Retrieval*, Grenoble, France, pp. 465–480.

Garfield, Eugene. 1954. Forms for literature citations. *Science* 120:1030–1040.

Garfield, Eugene. 1956. Citation indexes—New paths to scientific knowledge. *Chemical Bulletin* (Chicago) 43, no. 4:11–12.

Garfield, Eugene. 1963. Citation indexes in sociological and historical research. *American Documentation* 14:289–291.

Garfield, Eugene. 1964. Science Citation Index—A new dimension in indexing. *Science* 144, no. 3619:649–654.

Garfield, Eugene. 1979. *Citation indexing—Its theory and applications in science, technology and humanities.* New York: Wiley.

Grefenstette, Gregory. 1992. Use of syntactic context to produce term association lists for text retrieval. *Proceedings of the 15th Annual International ACM/SIGIR Conference on Research and Development in Information Retrieval*, Copenhagen, pp. 89–97.

Gudivada, Venkat, and Vijay V. Raghavan. 1995. Design and evaluation of algorithms for image retrieval by spatial similarity. *ACM Transactions on Information Systems* 13, no. 2:115–144.

Han, Kyung-Ah, and Sung-Hyun Myaeng. 1996. Image organization and retrieval with automatically constructed feature vectors. *Proceedings of the 19th Annual International ACM/SIGIR Conference on Research and Development in Information Retrieval*, Zurich, Switzerland, pp. 157–165.

Harman, Donna, and Gerald Candela. 1990. Bringing natural language information retrieval out of the closet. *SIGCHI Bulletin* 22, no. 1:42–48.

Hearst, Marti A, and Christian Plaunt. 1993. Subtopic structuring for full-length document access. *Proceedings of the 16th Annual International ACM SIGIR Conference on Research and Development in Information Retrieval*, Pittsburgh, pp. 59–68.

Hirata, K., and T. Kato. 1992. Query by visual example—Content-based image retrieval. In *Advances in Database Technology—EDBT '92, Third Inter-*

national Conference on Extending Database Technology, ed. A. Pirotte, C. Delobel, and G. Gottlob, pp. 56–71. Lecture Notes in Computer Science, vol. 580. Vienna: Springer-Verlag.

Hirata, K., and T. Kato. 1993. Rough sketch-based image information retrieval. *NEC Research and Development* 34, no. 2:263–273.

Ingwersen, Peter. 1994. Polyrepresentation of information needs and semantic entities: Elements of a cognitive theory for information retrieval interaction. *Proceedings of the 17th Annual International ACM/SIGIR Conference on Research and Development in Information Retrieval*, Dublin, pp. 101–110.

Jacobs, Paul S., and Lisa F. Rau. 1988. Natural language techniques for intelligent information retrieval. *Proceedings of the 11th Annual International ACM/SIGIR Conference on Research and Development in Information Retrieval*, Grenoble, France, pp. 85–99.

Joseph, T., and Alfonso F. Cardenas. 1988. Picquery: A high level query language for pictorial database management. *IEEE Transactions on Software Engineering* 14, no. 5:639–650.

Kwok, K.L. 1984. A document-document similarity measure based on cited titles and probability theory, and its application to relevance feedback retrieval. In *Research and Development in Information Retrieval: Proceedings of the Third Joint British Computing Society/ACM SIGIR Symposium*, ed. C.J. van Rijsbergen. Cambridge, England: Cambridge University Press.

Lee, Y.C., and F.L. Chin. 1995. An iconic query language for topological relationships in GIS. *International Journal of Geographical Information Systems* 9, no. 1:25–46.

Lesk, Michael E. 1986. Automatic sense disambiguation using machine readable dictionaries: How to tell a pine cone from an ice-cream cone. *Proceedings of ACM Special Interest Group on DOC*, pp. 24–26.

Lesk, Michael E. 1990. Images in document retrieval: Extraction of figures from pages. In *Proceedings of Anglo-French-U.S. Meeting on Image Databases*, York, England.

Lin, Xia, Dagobert Soergel, and Gary Marchionini. 1991. A self-organizing semantic map for information retrieval. *Proceedings of the 14th Annual International ACM/SIGIR Conference on Research and Development in Information Retrieval*, ed. Abraham Bookstein, Yves Chiaramella, Gerard Salton, and Vijay V. Raghavan, Chicago, pp. 262–269.

Mainguenaud, M., and M.-A. Portier. 1990. Cigales: A graphical query language for geographical information systems. *Fourth International Symposium on Spatial Data Handling,* ed. K. Brassel and H. Kishimoto, Zurich, Switzerland, pp. 393–404.

Mauldin, Michael L. 1991. Retrieval performance in FERRET: A conceptual information retrieval system. *Proceedings of the 14th Annual International ACM/SIGIR Conference on Research and Development in Information Retrieval,* ed. Abraham Bookstein, Yves Chiaramella, Gerard Salton, and Vijay V. Raghavan, Chicago, pp. 347–355.

Myaeng, Sung H., and Ming Li. 1992. Building term clusters by acquiring lexical semantics from a corpus. *Proceedings of the First International Conference in Information and Knowledge Management,* Baltimore.

Myaeng, Sung H., and Elizabeth D. Liddy. 1993. Information retrieval with semantic representation of texts. *Second Annual Symposium on Document Analysis and Information Retrieval,* Las Vegas, pp. 201–215.

Niblack, Wayne, R. Barber, W. Equitz, M. Flickner, E. Glasman, D. Petkovic, P. Yanker, C. Faloutsos, and G. Taubin. 1993. The QBIC project: Querying images by content using color, texture and shape. In *SPIE Storage and Retrieval for Image and Video Databases,* ed. Wayne Niblack, Bellingham, Washington, pp. 173–187.

Nie, Jian-Yun. 1992. Towards a probabilistic modal logic for semantic-based information retrieval. *Proceedings of the 15th Annual International ACM/SIGIR Conference on Research and Development in Information Retrieval,* Copenhagen, pp. 140–151.

Ogle, V., and Michael Stonebraker. 1995. Chabot: Retrieval from a relational database of images. *IEEE Computer* 28, no. 9:40–48.

Papadias, D., and T. Sellis. 1995. A pictorial query-by-example language. *Journal of Visual Languages and Computing* 6, no. 1:53–72.

Rabitti, Fausto, and P. Savino. 1991. Automatic image indexation and retrieval. *Proceedings of RIAO '91,* Barcelona.

Rama, D.V., and Padmini Srinivasan. 1992. An investigation of a conceptual map of a text database for retrieval. *Symposium on Document Analysis and Information Retrieval,* University of Nevada at Las Vegas, pp. 267–282.

Salton, Gerard, and James Allan. 1994. Text retrieval using the vector processing model. *Proceedings of the Third Annual Symposium on Document analysis and Information Retrieval,* Las Vegas, Nevada, pp. 9–22.

Salton, Gerard, and Yong Zhang. 1986. Enhancement of text representations using related document titles. *Information Processing & Management* 22, no. 5:385–394.

Small, H.G. 1973. Co-citation in the scientific literature: A new measure of the relationship between two documents. *JASIS* 24, no. 4:265–269.

Smeaton, Alan F. 1989. Information retrieval and natural language processing. *Informatics* 10:1–14.

Trivison, Donna. 1987. Term co-occurrence in cited/citing journal articles as a measure of document similarity. *Information Processing & Management* 32, no. 3:183–194.

Turtur, A., F. Prampolini, M. Fantini, R. Guarda, and M.A. Imperato. 1991. IDB: An image database system. *IBM Journal of Research and Development* 35, no. 1/2:88–96.

Wendlandt, Edgar B., and James R. Driscoll. 1991. Incorporating a semantic analysis into a document retrieval strategy. *Proceedings of the 14th Annual International ACM/SIGIR Conference on Research and Development in Information Retrieval*, ed. Abraham Bookstein, Yves Chiaramella, Gerard Salton, and Vijay V. Raghavan, Chicago, pp. 270–279.

White, Howard D., and Belver C. Griffith. 1980. Author cocitation: A literature measure of intellectual structure. *JASIS* 31, no. 3:163–171.

Yu, Clement T., and Vijay V. Raghavan. 1977. Single-pass method for determining the semantic relationships between terms. *JASIS* 28, no. 5: 345–354.

EXERCISES

1. Show that the sentence "Time flies like an arrow" can be interpreted in at least five different ways.

2. Find three examples of naturally occurring sentences that are syntactically ambiguous. (Newspaper headlines are a good place to start.)

3. What problems would a syntactically ambiguous sentence create for an information storage and retrieval system?

Output Presentation

The output from an information retrieval system is rarely the exact set of documents desired by the user in response to a query. Even if the documents selected were precisely those that the user wanted, few systems are designed to produce the documents themselves. Rather, the retrieval system produces some indication of the documents, often leaving the user to his or her own resources to locate the actual documents. This chapter examines the organization and content of the items retrieved, and considers the factors that help produce a useful output.

11.1 REFERENCE VERSUS SURROGATE VERSUS DOCUMENT

The output from a retrieval system is limited by the data available in the database, by the programs for manipulating these data, and by the output devices included in the system. Images, for example, cannot be presented unless they either are in the database or can be generated from data in the database. Even when images are present or can be generated, if the only output device available is a character printer, it may not be possible to present a satisfactory image to the user. The focus of this chapter, however, is not on image output, but on a bibliographic database and textual output. There are four distinctive levels of response that an information retrieval system may make to a query:

1. Document reference number
2. Short reference (title, author, source)
3. Full document surrogate (including, for example, abstract and key-words)
4. Full text

The presentation of a *document reference number* is most easily accomplished in a computer-based retrieval system, since this is probably how the system references the document. However, a document reference number is virtually useless to the user; it tells the user nothing about the document other than that one exists. Presentation at this level assumes either a very trusting user who is willing to go to the effort of locating documents simply on this limited basis, or a very knowledgeable one who understands the reference numbering system well enough to make judgments from it.

A *short reference*—title and author, or title, author, and source—is but little better, since titles are frequently vague, opaque, or misleading. However, in the event that a large number of documents has been retrieved, a short reference presentation may be an acceptable first cut. It gives the user an overview of the set of retrieved documents and may permit elimination of the poorest ones or selection of a few that are obviously good.

Presentation of the *full text* of each document retrieved appears to be most desirable, as it eliminates the need for the user to locate the documents elsewhere. However, since most current computer-based retrieval systems do not store full text, this is generally not possible. Moreover, the desirability of full text begins to fade when several dozen documents may be retrieved in response to a query. It would be nice to present the user with full text on demand but not force acceptance of massive amounts of output, some of which will probably be useless.

Presentation of a *full document surrogate* is an effective compromise. Most current bibliographic retrieval systems provide this kind of output. For each document retrieved, the user receives all of the information that is available within the system. The surrogate may contain many kinds of data, such as the following:

Title
Author(s)

Author's location

Source (journal, publisher, university, corporate author)

Date

Abstract

Subject descriptors and categories

Key terms

In addition, a full surrogate may contain other items such as critical commentary and references to related work.

A full surrogate often presents sufficient information about the contents of a document that the reader can make an informed decision about retrieving the full document for use. The value of the full surrogate depends, of course, on what is included in it and the quality of that data. A brief abstract that merely recapitulates the opening paragraph, for example, may be of relatively little value. A well-written abstract that summarizes the main points of the paper and indicates the conclusions that the author reaches, however, often provides an accurate basis for retrieval or rejection of the full document.

The inclusion of standardized subject descriptors and categories can be of major assistance to the user. For example, the requirement by ACM that papers appearing in their journals list the major and secondary *Computing Reviews* subject categories provides a standard applicable to the computer science literature. This helps both the reviewer and the person trying to access a document for retrieval and use. The subject categories are reviewed periodically to assure that they remain current with usage in the field. They are published annually in the reviewing journal.

Even when the retrieval system includes the full text of documents, it may be desirable to present information to the user in two or three easily accessed stages. The first of these would be a short bibliographic reference including the title and perhaps the author's name. The second stage would be the full-text surrogate, the third stage the complete text.

Another option, if the system does not contain the full text of documents, is to provide an automatic means for the user to request complete documents. Such a request could be initiated by a simple click on an option box, with the default being that the complete document is not requested. Any further information necessary for ordering the document could be gleaned either from the system's information about the user or by asking the user a few direct questions.

11.2   GROUPING AND RANKING

The organization of the output from a search is important for its proper interpretation. Since it is virtually certain that the results of a search will include some documents that the user considers relevant and others the user considers irrelevant, the retrieval system is defective if documents are returned in the order in which they are identified rather than in some ranked order. The user will be more satisfied with the effectiveness of the system if the most relevant documents are presented first.

If the documents are evaluated on a two-value scale (acceptable and not acceptable), then there is no way to guarantee that the most significant documents are presented first. One problem with many Boolean retrieval systems is that there are only crude methods for comparing documents and judging their relevance to a query. Presenting the documents in order of the number of terms matched or in reverse chronological order has some benefit for the user. However, since weighting the search terms is generally not permitted, term weights are not available for organizing the output.

Another way to organize the output, in the absence of a ranking function, is by principal author. Users are familiar with bibliographic references in documents, which are often organized in this way. Hence they often find this ordering acceptable. An individual author's works can then be arranged in either chronological or reverse chronological order. The latter seems more reasonable from three points of view. First, the more recent works represent the "state of the art," so they are likely to be of more value to the user. Second, the user is more likely to already know of the older papers and thus not particularly desire them as output from the retrieval system. Third, the newer papers will often reference the older ones, putting them in a context that makes it easier to judge whether to retrieve them.

11.3   QUANTITY VERSUS QUALITY ISSUES

Some consideration should be given to the quantity of output. It is legitimate to ask the user to indicate the approximate number of papers desired. This number may differ widely from one retrieval session to another. The user who is under critical time pressure may be able to handle only one or two papers. She wants the best possible results and will be frustrated by the necessity of examining a longer list of documents to find the best. At the other end of the spectrum is the user who is developing a large bibliography on a topic, perhaps for a survey paper. This person certainly needs all recent references that are relevant and may also want a good representation of the older, more historically significant documents. More typically the user will want a reasonably short but inclusive list of documents, being willing to compromise between precision and recall in that effort. The user may want the list of documents found presented in two or more pieces. A short sampling of the documents may provide the user information on the adequacy of his query, enabling him either to ask for more documents or to rephrase the query.

In the absence of information from the user on the number of documents wanted, the system designer must make some standard judgment about the number to present. If a ranking function is available, then there are two basic choices: Present a fixed number of documents, or present all documents ranked above a stipulated cutoff point. In the absence of a ranking function, only the former choice is available. If this is used, it is useful to inform the user about the number of documents retrieved so that further documents can be requested if the first group presented does not provide an adequate response to the query. In this situation, it is particularly important to try to place the most relevant documents among those presented first rather than scatter them uniformly throughout the retrieved set.

Similarly, if an automatic relevance threshold is applied, the user should be told this and given the opportunity to request further documents. It is possible to use a combination of a fixed number of documents and a threshold level, giving the user all documents above the threshold up to the fixed number specified. In this case also, it is important to present the most highly ranked documents first.

11.4   MEDIA

The output from a search can be presented in three ways. Most commonly, the output is displayed on a computer screen. This has the advantage of immediacy but the drawback of a limited display space, typically about 24 lines. More extensive output can be printed out and given to the user.

Although this lacks the interaction of an on-line system, the user then has the entire output to peruse at leisure. Furthermore, some users are more comfortable with reading paper output than they are with reading from a computer screen. The final way to present the output is of course to retrieve the actual documents and present them to the user. This is generally done only in situations where there is an information professional such as a reference librarian serving as the interface to the system. However, as full-text databases and electronic journals become more popular, it is becoming increasingly easy to download full documents from the system to the user.

When there is a large quantity of output, it is difficult for the user to assimilate it all or to judge how much of it to examine. In this situation it is useful to present a graphic display of the output, indicating to the user the choices between quality and quantity. For example, a simple plot of the ranking of each document (assuming that is available) in decreasing order can indicate distinct breaks in the rankings as well as documents whose rankings are close together (Figure 11.1). In this example, the first five documents are the most relevant. The breaks in rankings show that retrieval should probably include either only those, or also documents 6 through 15. Because of the relative closeness in ranking among successive documents in this second set, retrieving only a few of them seems unwise.

Graphical presentation of retrieval results, if used, must clarify the retrieval for the user. In this respect, it is important to keep the graphics clear and uncluttered to avoid "chart junk" (Tufte 1983, 1990). When this is done it is possible to summarize visually the retrieval of dozens or even hun-

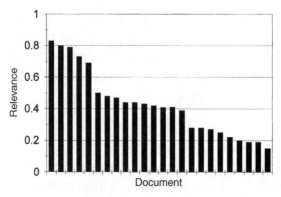

Figure 11.1   Ranked document output.

dreds of documents, allowing the user to make a more informed decision when requesting further information on some of the documents in the retrieved set. A more complete discussion of graphical interfaces for information retrieval is presented in Section 11.6.

Graphical presentation of results is not a full substitute for the original numerical or textual data, since the graphs may lack the detail and accuracy of the data. However, a graph may enable the user to see which of the data are important, to be selected for a more detailed examination. If the graphical display system permits the user to call up the textual or numerical data on demand, then the user has available both the compactness and the structural characteristics of the graphical display and the accuracy and detail of the textual display. Thus a graphical presentation serves an important information filtering function.

In addition to the usual output media of hard copy (paper) and a computer monitor display, the possibility of magnetic computer-readable media such as diskettes and optically readable media such as writable CD-ROMs must also be considered. The option of audio output, either live (presented immediately to the user) or recorded, is also viable when working with voice or sound databases. Finally, a retrieval system can also be linked to a videotape library, so that the result of a search is one or more videotaped documents.

These media differ in their important characteristics. The monitor display provides the most immediate output and is good for direct interaction between the user and the system. Audio output, when appropriate, also provides immediacy but is less well adapted at present to user-system interaction. However, these media lack permanence, which is a feature of the remaining types of media. Hard copy is really the only type listed that is directly useable without some kind of aiding device, but it can be bulky. The remaining media are compact, permanent forms of output, but they require a computer, video player, or audio system for use.

Much can be gained by using a combination of media. The monitor display can be used to scan the data, selecting or deleting various items. The modified output data set can then be transferred to a more permanent medium for future use. If the potential use includes a computer, there is strong reason to select an output and storage medium that is computer readable. However, caution should be exercised in choosing media for long-term storage. Hardware and software technology is changing so rapidly that most of today's computer systems cannot handle some of the media of 5 or 10 years ago.

11.5 CRITIQUE

A major criticism of standard retrieval interfaces is that they tend to place barriers between the user and the desired information. If the information retrieval system is of top quality and the output well organized, then the first few documents retrieved can be expected, in many situations, to provide an adequate answer to the user's query. However, not all information retrieval systems are this effective, and even if the system is effective there remains the question of the quality of the user's query. Users may be quite inaccurate in stating the query and may even present a query that is not, logically, the one that they mean to ask. It cannot be assumed that the response an information retrieval system provides to a query is the best or proper response to the information need.

Yet if the result of a query is not satisfactory, the user is often left without further guidance. The query that was posed failed to produce a good answer: What should be asked next? The basic problem is that information retrieval systems, whether they return a fixed number of documents or all documents with evaluations above a threshold, divide the document set into two classes—those that the user is permitted to see and those that are hidden from the user. The user does not know whether there is anything of interest in the unretrieved part of the set or, if there is, how to find it.

A further criticism can be leveled at those systems that retrieve a fixed number of documents rather than those documents with a high enough evaluation. If there are more relevant documents in the collection than the number retrieved, the user is bound to miss some potentially important documents. If, however, there are fewer relevant documents than the number to be retrieved, the user is bound to receive some unwanted documents, no matter how good the retrieval mechanism itself. Thus retrieval of a fixed number of documents may often produce poor results and leave the user with no guidance in locating further documents of interest.

One final criticism of most retrieval systems is that the documents are presented in a linear list. Even if this list is ordered by some evaluation criterion, that single criterion cannot simultaneously represent the multiple relationships that probably exist among the retrieved documents. Two documents may be closely related, but that fact can be obscured if one receives a much poorer evaluation than the other and hence is placed farther down the list. Conversely, two documents that are close in the list may be about equally related to the query but have relatively little relationship to each other.

All of these criticisms have been addressed in one way or another by various research efforts. Weighting terms to provide the basis for a measure of similarity, and development of relevance feedback and other interactive retrieval mechanisms aim not only at improving the basic output to the user, but also at giving the user more control over the output, albeit indirectly. The development of graphical output systems with multiple windows is another step toward removing barriers between the users and the information. Whether such steps aid the user or simply present more complex systems to be learned is a matter still under study.

11.6   VIRIs (Visual Information Retrieval Interfaces)

The GUIDO, VIBE, and BIRD systems discussed in Chapter 7 provide three examples of *visual information retrieval interfaces*, or VIRIs. Proposals for visualizing the output of an information retrieval system were presented as early as the 1960s (Sammon 1969). However, the technology to make this an attractive output means was not readily available for another 20 years. During the present decade, interest in graphical, or visual, interfaces has blossomed, with the result that more than 50 visual interface systems have been developed. Most of these are still experimental, but several are at the point of commercial viability.

As is frequently the case when a new concept is first explored, there is a bewildering array of visual interfaces with different aims and different graphical presentations. All of the systems share the goal of providing the user with a visual representation of either a single document or a document collection. Thus all of the experimental systems involve some form of document analysis or retrieval capability. The goal of many of these efforts, however, is to provide an interface that can be used with a wide variety of analysis and retrieval tools. Thus the algorithms by which documents are selected and analyzed can often be separated from the remainder of the interface system and other algorithms substituted.

Visual interface systems can be organized according to several criteria related to their purpose, use, and presentation. As each criterion is discussed, example systems will be cited. (These, however, do not constitute a complete list of the systems with that characteristic.)

An interface may focus either on presenting the details of an individual document or on presenting the document as a single element within a document collection. Among the former type of interface, the use of segmented bars is one method of displaying how the keywords and concepts of the query relate to the document structure (TileBars: Hearst and Plaunt 1993; Hearst 1995). Other systems focusing on document details may use network representations to link related parts of documents (Text Relationship Map: Salton and Allen 1994). Systems that focus on the document as an element of a collection may represent the individual document as an icon (VIBE: Olsen et al. 1993), a point in an abstract landscape (Bead: Chalmers 1993), or simply as contributing to the count of documents in an identified subset (InfoCrystal: Spoerri 1993a, 1993b).

Depending on the purpose for which the interface is intended, the objects represented may concentrate on the documents or include elements of a query, classification, or retrieval process. Individual documents can be represented (GUIDO: Nuchprayoon and Korfhage 1994), or sets of documents (ReadingRoom: Lin, Soergel, and Marchionini 1991). Single keywords can be represented (BIRD: Kim and Korfhage 1994), or more complex queries (Information Navigator: Fowler, Fowler, and Wilson 1991). Some displays permit the use of multiple reference points simultaneously (VIBE: Olsen et al. 1993; LyberWorld: Hemmje, Kunkel, and Willett 1994).

The cognitive metaphors and corresponding display structures used in these VIRIs represent a wide range of approaches. There are graphs and networks (Information Navigator), segmented bars (TileBars), scatter plots (VIBE, and the earliest version of Bead: Chalmers and Chitson 1992), landscapes (later versions of Bead), abstract maps (ReadingRoom), clusters (Scatter/Gather: Cutting et al. 1992; Cutting, Karger, and Pedersen 1993; Piles: Rose et al. 1993), and pictorial icons (BookHouse: Pejtersen 1989a, 1989b). Some presentations, such as BookHouse, also use graphic depictions of a library or library stacks.

The processes visualized by these systems include document classification and clustering (VIBE, Piles), browsing (VIBE, Bead, Information Navigator), and document retrieval (GUIDO, BIRD, TileBars).

Most of the visual interfaces are based on a vector model of the document space and retrieval. However, the other models (Boolean, probabilistic, and so forth) can also be used. In particular, both InfoCrystal and Boolean VIBE are based on Boolean retrieval techniques, and BIRD implements a sequential Boolean retrieval process.

Among those interfaces that support searching, support for all types of searching can be found. These include bibliographic search (for example, by specifying title and author), analytical search (based on similarity analysis), analogical search (to find a document like a given one), and browsing. A given interface may support only one or two search types; however, in most cases it is a relatively simple matter to incorporate those search techniques not presently supported into the interface.

Finally, although most of the VIRI work has concentrated on two-dimensional displays, a few efforts have been made at developing three-dimensional interfaces. Specifically, LyberWorld and VR-VIBE (Benford et al. 1995) are three-dimensional interfaces related to VIBE. In each case, however, the "three-dimensional" interface must be projected onto a two-dimensional screen. Perhaps the most advanced effort along these lines is Fowler's Information Navigator, where the user wears stereovision glasses to create a three-dimensional view of the document space.

The value of a visual interface lies in its ability to present a large amount of data in a concise and understandable way, and to enable the user to manipulate that representation in pursuit of his or her individual information objectives. The real test of these interfaces is thus their use with large document collections or (for those focusing on individual documents) lengthy documents. None of these interfaces has yet been tested with more than a few thousand documents; nor has much serious user evaluation of these interfaces been done. As application of these interfaces to larger databases takes place, and as more user testing and experience is gained, a better understanding will develop concerning which interfaces are appropriate to various information-related tasks, and interface design will be adapted to enhance the capabilities of the interfaces.

REFERENCES

Benford, S., David Snowden, C. Greenhalgh, R. Ingram, and I. Knox. 1995. VR-VIBE: A virtual environment for co-operative information retrieval. *Eurographics 95.*

Chalmers, Matthew. 1993. Using a landscape metaphor to represent a corpus of documents. In *Spatial information theory: A theoretical basis for GIS*, ed. Andrew U. Frank and I. Campari, pp. 377–390. Lecture Notes in Computer Science, no. 716. Berlin: Springer-Verlag.

Chalmers, Matthew, and Paul Chitson. 1992. Bead: Explorations in information visualization. *Proceedings of the 15th Annual International ACM/SIGIR Conference on Research and Development in Information Retrieval*, Copenhagen, pp. 330–337.

Cutting, Douglass R., David R. Karger, and Jan O. Pedersen. 1993. Constant interaction-time Scatter/Gather browsing of very large document collections. *Proceedings of the 16th Annual International ACM/SIGIR Conference on Research and Development in Information Retrieval*, Pittsburgh, pp. 126–134.

Cutting, Douglass R., Jan O. Pedersen, David R. Karger, and John W. Tukey. 1992. Scatter/Gather: A cluster-based approach to browsing large document collections. *Proceedings of the 15th Annual International ACM/SIGIR Conference on Research and Development in Information Retrieval*, Copenhagen, pp. 318–329.

Fowler, Richard H., Wendy A.L. Fowler, and Bradley A. Wilson. 1991. Integrating query, thesaurus, and documents through a common visual representation. *Proceedings of the 14th Annual International ACM/ SIGIR Conference on Research and Development in Information Retrieval*, ed. Abraham Bookstein, Yves Chiaramella, Gerard Salton, and Vijay V. Raghavan, Chicago, pp. 142–151.

Hearst, Marti A. 1995. TileBars: Visualization of term distribution information in full text information access. *Proceedings of CHI '95 Human Factors in Computing Systems*, Denver.

Hearst, Marti A., and Christian Plaunt. 1993. Subtopic structuring for full-length document access. *Proceedings of the 16th Annual International ACM/SIGIR Conference on Research and Development in Information Retrieval*, Pittsburgh, pp. 59–68.

Hemmje, Matthais, Clemens Kunkel, and Alexander Willett. 1994. Lyber-World—A visualization user interface supporting fulltext retrieval. *Proceedings of the 17th Annual International ACM/SIGIR Conference on Research and Development in Information Retrieval*, Dublin, pp. 249–259.

Kim, Hanhwe, and Robert R. Korfhage. 1994. BIRD: Browsing interface for the retrieval of documents. *Proceedings of the IEEE Symposium on Visual Languages*, St. Louis, pp. 176–177.

Lin, Xia, Dagobert Soergel, and Gary Marchionini. 1991. A self-organizing semantic map for information retrieval. *Proceedings of the 14th Annual*

International ACM/SIGIR Conference on Research and Development in Information Retrieval, ed. Abraham Bookstein, Yves Chiaramella, Gerard Salton, and Vijay V. Raghavan, Chicago, pp. 262–269.

Nuchprayoon, Assadaporn, and Robert R. Korfhage. 1994. GUIDO, A visual tool for retrieving documents. *Proceedings of IEEE Symposium on Visual Languages*, St. Louis, Missouri, pp. 64–71.

Olsen, Kai A., Robert R. Korfhage, Kenneth M. Sochats, Michael B. Spring, and James G. Williams. 1993. Visualization of a document collection: The VIBE system. *Information Processing & Management* 29, no. 1:69–81.

Pejtersen, Annelise Mark. 1989a. The "Bookhouse": An icon based database system for fiction retrieval in public libraries. *Proceedings of the Seventh Nordic Conference for Information & Documentation*, Aarhus University, Denmark, pp. 1–19.

Pejtersen, Annelise Mark. 1989b. The Book House: Modelling user's needs and search strategies as a basis for system design. Risø-M-2794, Risø National Laboratory, Roskilde, Denmark.

Rose, Daniel Eric, Richard Mander, Tim Oren, Dulce B. Poncéleón, Gitta Salomon, and Yin Yin Wong. 1993. Content awareness in a file system interface: Implementing the 'pile' metaphor for organizing information. *Proceedings of the 16th Annual International ACM/SIGIR Conference on Research and Development in Information Retrieval*, Pittsburgh, pp. 260–269.

Salton, Gerard, and James Allen. 1994. Text retrieval using the vector processing model. *Proceedings of the Third Annual Symposium on Document Analysis and Information Retrieval*, Las Vegas, pp. 9–22.

Sammon, J.W. 1969. A nonlinear mapping for data structure analysis. *IEEE Transactions on Computing* 18, no. 5:401–409.

Spoerri, Anselm. 1993a. InfoCrystal: A visual tool for information retrieval and management. *Proceedings of Information and Knowledge Management '93*, Washington, D.C.

Spoerri, Anselm. 1993b. Visual tools for information retrieval. *Proceedings of IEEE Workshop on Visual Languages*. Bergen, Norway, pp. 160–168.

Tufte, Edward R. 1983. *The visual display of quantitative information*. Cheshire, Connecticut: Graphics Press.

Tufte, Edward R. 1990. *Envisioning information*. Cheshire, Connecticut: Graphics Press.

EXERCISES

1. In using a retrieval system that relates documents to each other through citations or hypertext, one possible output presentation is to list each of the most relevant documents together with some, perhaps five, of the most closely related documents. Discuss the benefits and problems with this type of presentation.

2. In the absence of explicit citation or hypertext links, how might the customary list of documents be reorganized to give a sense of the ranking and at the same time provide more information about how documents in the list relate to each other?

3. One problem with any complex interactive display—hypertext or graphical—is that the user can quickly become disoriented. Discuss methods for alleviating this problem by providing the user with a sense of where exploration of the database has led.

4. A small but significant portion of the population is color blind. Discuss substitutes for color that can be used for such people.

5. Design an output presentation appropriate for a blind user.

6. Most VIRIs are "hard-edged," that is, documents and reference points have very specific locations. How would a fuzzy display, in which the locations are not so firmly fixed, be developed?

CHAPTER 12

Document Access

In a document retrieval system, access to documents is important at two distinct levels. First, the user must have access to the document surrogates upon which the retrieval search is to be performed. Second, the user must also have access to the documents that are the objects of the search. In a fully interactive retrieval system, a necessary condition for this second kind of access—reaching the individual documents for whatever purpose the user has in mind—is that the full documents be available in computer-accessible form. This chapter considers first the problem of entering a full document into a computer system, and second the problem of access to the document by the person who has done a search.

12.1 ELECTRONIC ACCESS

When computer-based information retrieval systems were first developed, access to documents was universally handled outside of the computer system. The user would retire to the nearest library to try to locate the documents on her list. If she was lucky, the system would provide information about which library held the documents and perhaps even their call numbers. In a corporate situation the user might even have been able to order the documents from the library by marking the output list from the computer or by sending back the appropriate punched cards.

Increasingly, access to the full document is being handled by the computer. With the development of on-line systems, it became simple for the user to order a document immediately upon scanning the surrogate. In most cases, however, delivery still relied on some method of getting a printed copy of the document to the user. At the same time, the technical development that began with computer-controlled typesetting and simple word processing has matured, and sophisticated electronic document production systems are now readily available at all levels of computing power. One major result of this is that an increasing number of documents are being generated and made available in electronic form. Some journals now publish electronic editions, and a few have focused on this as the only medium of publication in the future.

Even if publishers were to move to a fully electronic line of books and journals, there would still be a large backlog of hardcopy documents, plus an ongoing stream of less formal documents such as memos, newspapers, and popular magazines that are not directly accessible by computer. Paralleling the development of electronically generated documents has been increasing interest in the conversion of paper documents to electronic form. Document scanners of high resolution and accuracy have been developed, accompanied by *optical character recognition* (OCR) software designed to convert scanned images into character files that can then be processed by customary text processing and information retrieval software.

12.2　PROCESSING SCANNED DOCUMENTS

When a document is scanned into a computer, a *bit map,* or pictorial image, of the document is created. With scanner resolutions of 600 dots per inch or more, this image is a highly accurate representation of the document. Unfortunately, since it is a picture and not a character image, it cannot be processed directly by text processing software. Conversion to a text file format is required first; this is the task of OCR software. Early versions of OCR software were cumbersome to use and had limited capabilities. With the increased resolution of the scanned image, faster computers, and more sophisticated processing algorithms, the capabilities of OCR software have become very impressive. The major drawback now seems to lie in the quality of the original document.

Studies have been conducted at the Information Science Research Institute of the University of Nevada, Las Vegas, comparing the capabilities of various OCR systems with different styles and qualities of text (ISRI 1992, 1993, 1994, 1995). While these studies were initially focused on technical and legal documents, they have been expanded to include newspapers and other, more popular forms of text, and to include documents in Spanish as well as those in English. For these studies, the texts used have been divided into five page-quality levels based on the accuracy of the OCR output. It is not completely clear which factors cause a document to be assigned to one or another of these categories. Obviously, smudged and incomplete printing results in a document being assigned to one of the poorer quality categories. At the same time, errors such as misalignment or skewed printing, which cause the human reader little difficulty, can also result in very poor OCR performance. The differences in results for various categories are clear. At the highest level of document quality, the various OCR systems tested can successfully recognize more than 97% of the characters, while at the lowest level recognition can drop to around 80%. Typical accuracy results, taken from the 1993 report, are shown in Table 12.1. Observe that accuracy for characters is better than that for words, and that accuracy for words in general is better than that for non-stopwords. The results for words depend both on the character recognition capabilities of each system and on the algorithms used to resolve character ambiguities and identify words.

Several distinctive techniques are employed in OCR software to improve the recognition capabilities. One is to make use of context to resolve ambiguities in recognition. For example, the letters c, e, and o can easily be confused with one another if the ink is either too light or heavy enough that it is smeared. By identifying the neighboring letters in a text and using a good dictionary, this confusion can frequently be resolved. Similarly, m and n can be confused. However, among the "words" that can be formed from $\{c, e, o\}$ $\{m, n\}$ $\{c, e, o\}$, only *one* is a common English word and only *eno* is a common Spanish word. Some OCR systems also employ a second level of context, seeking to determine what words are appropriate within a given sentence.

Table 12.1
OCR Accuracy vs. Page Quality (ISRI Tests)

	Group 1	Group 2	Group 3	Group 4	Group 5
Characters (%)	99.3–99.9	98.3–99.7	97.2–99.3	93.9–98.7	81.5–93.2
All words (%)	98.2–99.8	95.9–99.4	92.9–98.7	85.5–96.7	62.1–88.4
Non-stopwords (%)	97.5–99.7	94.5–99.0	90.8–98.0	82.4–96.0	57.3–85.8

Graphical alterations of the characters sometimes help in the recognition process. One problem with applying ink to paper is that because of the unevenness of the paper or the improper application of ink, there can be both missed areas of ink and added speckles. These show up as erroneous bits in the bit map, but the scanner does not know that they are erroneous. Techniques such as adding an extra border of bits to a character, then removing bits or adding missing bits under rules related to the inking of neighboring bits, are useful in eliminating many of these erroneous bits. Even the slightest skewness or misalignment of text can have a deleterious effect on OCR capabilities. However, techniques have been developed to detect and correct skewness or misalignment in characters and in lines of characters, enabling the OCR analysis to proceed.

Highly important in this process of document analysis is *segmentation* of the document image. A text image normally has several different components to it. The title block, for example, is frequently printed in a larger type size and centered on the page. Thus it is appropriate to separate it from the remaining text. It is important to recognize whether the scanned page contains a single column of text or multiple columns, so that the text constituting a sentence or a paragraph can be kept together. Footnotes and figure captions are examples of other textual elements that must be identified and treated separately. Images, graphics, and tables must also be isolated. Many OCR systems are not designed to handle these document elements other than to locate them and exclude them from analysis. Certainly it is not desirable for the OCR system to attempt to decode a photograph as text. At the same time, if a segment can be recognized as an image, then it might be appropriate to encode it in compressed form, using one of the techniques discussed in Chapter 2.

The basic output from OCR processing is an ASCII text file, perhaps with indications of the locations of unanalyzed document elements such as figures and tables. There is, however, increasing interest in the development of software that will incorporate SGML or some similar markup language in the resulting file. If the system can identify and isolate a title block or a paragraph for processing, then there is little reason why the information necessary to perform that isolation cannot be encoded in the final text file for future use. A retrieval system can take advantage of any such encoding to enhance the retrieval process.

Quite clearly, documents appearing in the popular press and handwritten documents present problems that are more difficult to handle than those presented by most technical documents. Newspaper and magazine articles may have unusual type fonts and type oriented at odd angles. They may also have type overlaid on images—easily separable by people but creating difficulties for any computer analysis of the document. Documents in foreign languages present two different problems. One, relatively minor, is the use of a different alphabet or character set; the other is that some languages may be printed vertically rather than horizontally, or read from right to left. OCR systems designed to handle English text in its standard alignment will generally be incapable of properly interpreting texts in these other languages. However, more sophisticated systems, with software to analyze text alignment and a broader range of character sets, can be used to analyze such documents.

The goal of OCR is to provide a document that is electronically accessible. The resulting document will generally be a combination of an ASCII text file, perhaps with markup notation, and an image file. The latter may be the original scanned image or may be reduced to a series of images including the portions of the document that could not be analyzed and converted to text.

12.3   PROCESSING ELECTRONICALLY GENERATED DOCUMENTS

Most electronically generated documents include a variety of control elements that are not part of the text. Even before SGML and other markup systems became widely available, word processors would incorporate their own control codes into a document. Any type of markup within a document, if recognized, can be handled in one of two ways. One way is to eliminate or ignore the markup, in effect treating the document as a straightforward ASCII document. Most systems can then process the document satisfactorily. If the system is designed to recognize the markup and not ignore it, then the information about the document that is contained in the markup can be used not only to properly format the output document but also to direct and control the retrieval process. Many systems have permitted this in a rather informal manner. If a document contains codes indicating specific fields such as title, author, and date, the user can frequently specify which of these fields to search. The use of a markup language formalizes and extends this capability, using the markup to seek out text with specific characteristics, such as italicized or boldface text. To use this capability successfully, the user must have some knowledge about how special text formatting is used within a document collection.

12.4   DISTRIBUTED DOCUMENT SYSTEMS

Cost, efficiency, and the shear number of documents being published are driving information systems to the use of distributed document sets and distributed processing. These developments should have little impact on the user other than to make a larger number of documents available. The user typically is interested in locating and obtaining a document regardless of where it resides either physically or within a computer system. In effect, the user would prefer to view the system as accessing a single logical database in response to a query, even when the system must consult multiple physical databases.

Three major problems arise from this situation. First, it is a virtual certainty that different databases will have different formats and different processing requirements. Hence, the system that accesses these must in some way address the disparities. One way to do this is to rely on individual retrieval systems to handle each of the databases. The system controlling a retrieval process must then be able to mediate among the various database processors, most likely by using a conversion program that will recast a query into the appropriate form for each of the individual retrieval systems.

The second problem is that of data redundancy. Different databases may include copies of the same or equivalent documents. If two retrieved documents are identical, detecting and eliminating the duplication requires relatively little work. However, in some instances the documents may be sufficiently different to cause problems. For example, if the document is a news story, the "original" may have been filed with a news wire service. As this is distributed, individual newspaper editors are free to modify the article, making it fit within the space they have available and perhaps giving it a specific local flavor. Determining that such a document is a modification of the original requires some work; then a decision must be made as to whether the modification warrants inclusion of the second document in a retrieved set. Conceivably, if there is a small limit on the number of documents returned, a substantial portion of the returned set may effectively be copies of one single document.

The third problem is that of matching document evaluations from the distributed systems. Two systems may rate a given document quite differently, either because they are comparing it to different document sets or because they have different evaluation functions. Most probably, however, none of the distributed systems from which the documents are drawn have the specific user focus that the system controlling the search can have. This problem has two parts: A given document may receive two or more distinct evaluations, or a given document may be retrieved and evaluated by some, but not all, of the retrieval systems called upon. In the latter case, a system not retrieving the document may not have recognized it as potentially significant, or may not have the document in its database. A simple solution is to discard the evaluations done by each of the search systems used in the retrieval process and reevaluate the documents on the basis of the users and usage at the controlling system. This, however, discards some evaluations that may be helpful in interpreting a document. A more sophisticated approach is to incorporate individual system evaluations of a document into the new evaluation before showing the document to the user.

12.5   INTERNET AND WEB ACCESS

The development of the Internet and the World Wide Web presents a significant challenge to information retrieval systems everywhere. The popular press periodically cites with appropriate astonishment the number of new Web sites per day and the amount of document traffic across the Web. Buried within this growth are documents that should be retrieved in response to almost any query. Retrieving relevant documents from this vast sea, however, is a daunting task.

There are more than a dozen search engines available on the Web, with more being proposed and developed. Among the better known are AltaVista, Lycos, and Yahoo! Such engines have largely been developed by people with little background or training in information retrieval. As a result, the search methods can be inefficient and ineffective. For example, using 10 different search engines to locate the words *yi xing teapot* retrieved lists of documents ranging in length from 0 to over 54,000. Most, but not all, of the search engines returned the documents in a ranked order. A quick scan of the first 20 retrieved documents (when there were that many) revealed very few that met the search requirements. One search engine returned two clear matches, ranked 18th and 19th in the list. Another returned one relevant document, ranked 18th. This document was, however, about the Chinese tea ceremony rather than about yi xing teapots specifically. A third search engine returned a set of documents that, on the surface, did not match the query, but the first of these was the homepage of a company that had four such teapots for sale. The second document, unfortunately, was a duplicate of the first, pointed to from a different source.

If these results are typical, they indicate that much work needs to be done to improve Web searching. One criticism heard of Web searching techniques is that far too often the user will enter just a single word, resulting in the retrieval of large numbers of matching documents. Of the search engines used in this trial, only one indicated that the search was for all three words. Three of the search engines gave the user some choice: match all the words, match any word, or match the phrase. The other search engines gave no such option, and from the results clearly attempted to match any of the words, effectively taking the disjunction of the search terms. If this is the case, a searcher is better off using a single term, since additional terms will simply increase the number of documents returned. This may improve recall, but it certainly will reduce precision.

The fact that most of the searches found no relevant documents among the first 20, and that two of the search engines placed the only relevant documents well down in the list indicates that the document ranking methods that are used are probably not appropriate. At the very least, further work needs to be done to determine the value of the ranking methods that are used.

It should be noted that there is rapid development of software in this area. Search engines that were developed a few years ago, aimed at an environment that was more directly related to electronic mail and did not yet include the Web, are now obsolescent. Given the quality of current search engines, many companies are trying to develop techniques for improving Web searching. A lack of knowledge and expertise in information retrieval, or even computing in general, does not seem to be a deterrent.

REFERENCES

ISRI. 1992. 1992 Annual Report, UNLV Information Science Research Institute, University of Nevada, Las Vegas.

ISRI. 1993. 1993 Annual Report, UNLV Information Science Research Institute, University of Nevada, Las Vegas.

ISRI. 1994. 1994 Annual Report, UNLV Information Science Research Institute, University of Nevada, Las Vegas.

ISRI. 1995. 1995 Annual Report, UNLV Information Science Research Institute, University of Nevada, Las Vegas.

EXERCISES

1. While English is normally written horizontally, Chinese and some other languages are often written vertically. How could an OCR system determine whether a particular piece of a scanned document was horizontal text, vertical text, or something other than text? (This should be done before trying to match scanned text to known character sets.)

2. Once a scanned document has been converted into ASCII text, it may be desirable to add formatting information to it, identifying the title, author, sections, paragraphs, and so forth. Write a program that will identify these four items within a scanned and OCR-processed text.

3. Determine which other textual elements can be identified by a computer program, and extend your program of Exercise 3 to make these identifications.

4. Write a program that will accept an SGML- or HTML-marked document and use these markings to determine the structural elements of the document.

Web search engines may permit several different kinds of searches, from a general search for documents with words in a given list, to searches using a Boolean expression, to searches constrained within some hierarchy of documents. (For example, a user might limit the search to the college directory of the football directory of the sports directory.) For each of the following queries, investigate the response of at least two different Web search engines, using both open and constrained types of searches. To properly compare the searches, note the following information:

- the name of the search engine,
- the type of search done,
- any special features used,
- the number of documents identified,
- the number of document surrogates you examined,
- the number of documents you examined,

- the number of relevant documents you found,
- the time required to complete the search,
- your impression of the search engine (user satisfaction).

Do you think that other (better) documents were not found? Should the search have been done without using the Web, and why?

5. A person flying from Pittsburgh to the Orient must stop overnight in Los Angeles due to plane connections. Find an inexpensive motel near the Los Angeles airport.

6. Find the schedule for Braathens SAFE flights from Molde, Norway, to Oslo, and the prices.

7. Find information on the diagnosis and treatment of heart disease in the southeastern United States—what is available, where, the cost, and so forth.

8. What international regulations govern the collecting and shipping of rare or endangered plants such as orchids?

9. The user wishes to purchase a new small car, and wants information on those containing dual air bags. Only official information from the manufacturer will be accepted, not magazine or other secondhand reports.

10. Find information about the programs and costs of fitness facilities in or near Keokuk, Iowa.

11. What air fares are available for travel between New York and Oslo? What restrictions apply?

12. The user believes that the University of Washington has a home page on the Web. How does she find the URL for its political science department?

13. The user wants to buy some home financial software. Find information about five good systems, including their capabilities, costs, system requirements, and how they can be purchased.

14. The user is not fully satisfied with his Internet service. Find information about the alternatives that are available, including cost and services offered.

CHAPTER 13

The Ectosystem and Policy Issues

And in conclusion . . . In Chapter 1, the distinction was made between the ectosystem and the endosystem. The process of document analysis and retrieval takes place within the endosystem, but evaluation at all levels must ultimately be done within the ectosystem. This chapter considers the human component of the ectosystem in more detail. Although this part of the information system is not under direct control of the system designer, its characteristics and the decisions made there nevertheless affect the structure and operation of the entire system. We examine also some of the legal and ethical issues that must be considered in the development and use of an information retrieval system.

13.1 THE USER

The user is in one sense external to the system. At the same time, the user is central to the system, for it is the user who has the information need and who ultimately decides whether the system will be used or not. For this reason, the focus of system measurement on the effectiveness of the system is entirely appropriate. However, many of the measures used have been developed without much regard for their applicability to the user. Indeed, there is not much agreement on what the needs of the user are. While Cleverdon (1991) states that recall is of little interest to most users, Su's (1992) work focuses more on recall, presenting evidence that precision is less important. There is some feeling, however, that neither of these measures really addresses the issues that a user might consider important. Measures such as coverage ratio, novelty ratio, and relative recall raise the issue of whether precision and recall are appropriate measures at all.

One aspect of user impact that is often overlooked in system design is the fact that the users as individuals have distinct information needs. Commercial information retrieval systems and even many experimental systems treat the users monolithically. Adjustment for individual needs becomes most critical precisely when it is most difficult to incorporate it into the system. Accounting for individual needs is neither as difficult nor as important in a relatively closed system serving a limited, homogeneous, and stable group of users as it is in an information system of broader scope. The more homogeneous the user group, the more closely the individual needs will conform to a single group model. The more stable the group, the easier it is to identify the needs of each individual within the group. It is within a very broad, open system that individual differences among users become more important. The public library (or on-line information system) must serve many diverse needs; a single user model will probably fit none of these needs well. At the same time, the individual user of such a system tends to be sporadic in his use of the system. The user may come to the system only once or twice a year, providing little opportunity for system designers and managers to develop a model of individual needs. In addition, because of this sporadic use of the system, the user has little opportunity to develop a clear understanding of how the information system can best address his individual information needs.

Another aspect of user behavior is the fact that for many users a formal information system is at best a tertiary source of information. The professional person who needs information will often look first at her own bookshelves, then consult colleagues who are either down the hall or reachable by electronic mail or telephone, and finally, when all else fails, turn to the library or information system. Thus to focus attention on a formal information system is, in a sense, attacking the wrong end of the problem. A more challenging issue is how to help the user locate information within the entire system that she sees—bookshelves, colleagues, *and* the formal information system. This is being recognized in the commercial community as an increasing number of software packages appear that are aimed at helping the individual user develop and organize a personal information collection. The research community, however, has paid only limited attention to such user behavior.

The emergence of the World Wide Web has added an additional layer of complexity to the problem of providing good information access to users. It is estimated that there are more than 50 million Web pages accessible over the Web. New search engines appear seemingly weekly, each claiming to provide better access than its predecessors. Yet without standardization of the Web, there is little that a given search engine can do to avoid lengthy searches through the Web. Most search engines are developed by people with relatively little experience in information retrieval, with the result that the techniques used are relatively simple and primitive. Often the query is simply a list of words. More sophisticated search engines may incorporate Boolean operations; few, if any, permit the weighting of terms. The result is an extension of the relatively weak performance that characterized earlier information retrieval systems: the output may be a lengthy unranked list of Web sites. Certainly there is no attempt to model the user or to enable the user to take dynamic control of the retrieval process.

Providing even a limited set of user stereotypes can help improve system performance. Two or three questions to the user can establish which stereotype to use. However, such stereotypes must be carefully used. Correctly identifying the user as a medical doctor may be either irrelevant or misleading if the user is simply trying to find an interesting concert to attend. Thus one option to be included in any stereotyping system is "general user," and the user needs to be informed about relating the chosen stereotype to the information need.

13.2 THE FUNDER

The funder plays a role in system development only slightly less vital than the user. As noted in Chapter 1, the economic measures of an information system are most important to the funder. It is well to distinguish at least four classes of funders. First, and most traditionally, there are the funders, such as public libraries, who aim at providing a "free" public service. Such service is, of course, not free; rather, it is funded indirectly through tax dollars, bequests, or some other means that remain largely invisible to the user. The disconnection between funding and use allows more flexibility in the provision of service to the user, yet even in this situation inadequacy of service has an impact. A common complaint is that public libraries are among the last items to be included in a municipal budget and among the first to be cut. This perception, whether or not it is valid, arises perhaps from the lack of a visible relationship between the level of funding and the level of service.

The second class of funders includes the corporations, businesses, and other organizations that provide an internal information service for their own employees (and perhaps customers). For this class also, the information service is "free," that is, funded indirectly with no apparent cost to the user. However, since the information system provided is more of a closed system, its effectiveness is more apparent to the people in charge of budgetary policy. While one still hears the complaint that the library is one of the less important and more expendable items in the organizational budget, the fact that its use has a more direct impact on meeting the organizational goals moderates any funding changes.

Particularly with the advent of computers and telecommunication networks, a third class of funders has become significant, namely the funders behind organizations that provide information service for profit. With this class of funders there is a distinct shift: The funding comes largely, if not entirely, from fees for services, charged directly to the user. This provides a strong connection between service and cost: The user no longer has "free" information and must actively decide whether the information provided is worth the cost of using the system. While the funders in this situation may be willing to underwrite start-up costs and perhaps some research and development costs, ultimately the system must pay for itself. Thus there is a strong incentive to provide more effective service to the user, and to provide it more efficiently.

The final class of funders consists of the individual users themselves. Whether the individual user has only a stack of papers on his desk or a full library with on-line access to various information services, the user's individual, personal information system is generally funded by the user. Often this becomes a hidden cost that the user does not consider; yet the cost is real. Bookshelves and filing cabinets cost money. A personal computer costs money. Certainly the user bears part of the cost of various information services that are accessed, whether through user fees or through taxes. Thus the user must make, on a very personal level, the same types of decisions that corporate or governmental budget makers do on whether the information system is cost effective and on how to improve its economics.

13.3   THE SERVER

The information professional plays many different roles in the provision of service, depending on his or her specific skills and the organization of the information system. In all cases, the information professional, more than anyone else involved with the system, is focused on the efficiency of the system, that is, on providing the information service as efficiently as possible. This has a multifaceted impact on acceptance of the system. Efficient service pleases the individual user, giving a very positive impression of the system. At the same time, efficient use of the system permits more users to be served within a given time frame. This, in turn, has a positive impact on the economy of the system, whether this is measured in terms of user fees or simply in terms of the volume of services provided. Finally, the development, maintenance, and operation of an efficient system reflects positively on the information professionals in charge of the system.

Some servers work largely behind the scenes, rarely visible to the users of a system. These include not only the operators of the system, but also the people who develop the information processing algorithms, who design and implement the system, and who have the task of organizing and maintaining the system databases. The impact of these people on the system is not often appreciated by the users, since their work is not directly visible. Only when a system malfunctions, begins to display degraded performance, or cannot provide information that the user reasonably expects do the users become aware of the work of the people behind the scenes.

In systems that do not provide automatic document analysis and classification, these functions become a major role for the information professional. While system designers work to make such functions more fully automatic, in the immediate future it seems certain that most of such work will be done by people on the staff of the information system or its suppliers; even when the analysis is automated, a professional needs to define the algorithms used and determine the specific parameter values for a given system. As the information included in the system grows and changes, algorithms, criteria, and methods that were once appropriate may become outmoded and require updating.

Other servers work more directly with the users. The search intermediary is still an important person in many systems, although the advent of on-line retrieval systems and CD-ROM databases has permitted many users direct access to information. There remain, however, several ancillary services that the information professional can perform, not the least of which is teaching the users how to approach a system effectively. In addition, if the information system does not provide direct access to full-text documents, then some person needs to perform this service. Finally, even if an information system is self-monitoring and usage statistics are gathered automatically, someone must interpret these data and make recommendations and decisions on maintaining the system in sound operating condition.

13.4   COPYRIGHT ISSUES

An issue of major concern to the development and use of any information system is that of copyright, or, more generally, *intellectual property rights.* Increasingly, books and journals carry copyright notices including warnings such as

> All rights reserved. No part of this publication may be reproduced, stored in a retrieval system, or transmitted, in any form or by any means, electronic, mechanical, photocopying, recording, or otherwise, without the prior permission of the publisher.

Taken literally, this virtually excludes any such book or document from inclusion in any database, since it is unlikely that the database developer is going to write for permission for every book or journal in the system. Indeed, taken literally, this phrase prohibits any quotations from the book or paper without obtaining explicit permission.

Against this warning stands the *doctrine of fair use.* Although loosely defined, the doctrine basically asserts (a) that individuals can make any private use of information that they wish and can make limited public, non-profit use of information as long as due credit is given, and (b) the warning notwithstanding, information such as the title, author, and publication data can be freely used in book catalogs, reviews, and bibliographic citations. Related to this is the understanding that limited amounts of material may be quoted from any copyrighted work provided that appropriate citation of the work is made.

A fine balance must be maintained: The purpose of publishing is to place the author's ideas in front of the public, presumably for the benefit of both the author and the public; yet excessively free use of the information may deprive the author of well-deserved recognition and perhaps monetary reward. The point of copyright is that various people, including the author and the publisher of a work, have some identifiable interest in the work, having invested time, effort, and money in bringing the work to fruition, and that hence they should retain some rights in controlling use of the work. Whether such control is feasible with current technology, other than by the goodwill of the users, is debatable. The science fiction short story "Melancholy Elephants," by Spider Robinson (1985), explores the impact of an unlimited extension of copyright protection, beyond that afforded by present law.

For ethical as well as legal reasons, it is prudent to make sure that all citations to previous works are accurate and fall within the fair use doctrine. Whenever there is doubt, writing to obtain formal permission to use the work is not an onerous chore.

With on-line databases, the question of copyright arises in another guise. It would certainly seem efficient and cost-effective for the user of such a system to be able to download a group of retrieved documents from the system onto his own private system for subsequent analysis and use. Yet if the on-line system holds the copyright to these documents, or worse, if someone else holds the copyright and has given the on-line system limited use of the documents, then downloading the documents to a private system may violate copyright. This is of particular concern when full-text documents, rather than simply bibliographic citations, are involved.

The latest twist on the copyright issue is that increasingly journals are publishing electronic editions, either in addition to paper editions or as replacements. This movement raises a number of interesting issues related to author and publisher compensation, appropriate interpretation of copyright laws, and acceptable use of the documents. At one end of the spectrum, the author or holder of the document could encrypt it and require a user fee or some other well-defined form of authorization for the potential user to gain access. At the other end, a document might be freely available and might even be altered by attached annotations made by various users. In at least one instance, a list server that provides free exchange of informal information among its users also on occasion contains extensive copyrighted material, provided with a copyright notice but without cost by the author and publisher. Clearly, in this case the author has decided that making the information available to this particular audience is more important than charging a fee for access to it.

13.5   PRIVACY ISSUES

Another issue directly affecting use of an information system is the user's right to privacy. Instances have arisen in which law enforcement agencies have tried to determine library usage patterns of various people; this has led some library systems to maintain only records of books and journals currently on loan, destroying such records once a document has been returned. In a system that maintains user profiles, the possibility of improper access to such information, or of court-ordered access, must be carefully considered, with precautionary safeguards built into the system design.

One idea that has been explored in working with user profiles is to have the system update the profile on the basis of use of the system and reaction to documents retrieved. This would ostensibly improve performance of the system but raises difficult questions of user control. Carried to an extreme, such automatic profile upgrading could reveal facets of use that the user would rather keep private, or might even reveal facets that are unknown to the user but evident from the usage pattern. It seems clear that such sophisticated upgrading of the user profile should not be implemented without a clear and effective policy for user control, including the right of the user to decline to permit any upgrading of the profile even though this might result in poorer system performance for that particular user.

13.6   SECURITY ISSUES

Security issues are closely allied with both copyright issues and privacy issues. It is almost an axiom that the security of a computer-based system is imperfect—that the best that can be done is to make it extremely difficult and expensive to gain illegal access either to information within the system or to information about the system. Having said this, it is nevertheless incumbent on the system owners to develop and maintain as effective a security system as is feasible.

The system itself loses if someone can illegally access information. For private information systems such access may amount to personal or corporate espionage; for a commercial information system it may mean a real loss of potential revenue. For any system, illegal access raises the possibility of corruption of the data in the system.

In addition, the individual user of the system faces a potential loss if the system security is lax. Not only can intruders determine the usage patterns of the individual system patron, but they can also create an economic loss for the users by illegally charging system use to various account numbers.

These concerns are of course not unique to information storage and retrieval systems. They are of concern in any information system and no doubt have a more significant impact in information systems dealing with medical, credit, and criminal justice information. This fact has, unfortunately, sometimes stifled research on such issues, as funding agencies fail to see copyright, privacy, and security or information retrieval systems as issues of major concern.

REFERENCES

Cleverdon, Cyril W. 1991. The significance of the Cranfield tests on index languages. In *Proceedings of the 14th Annual International ACM/SIGIR Conference on Research and Development in Information Retrieval*, ed. Abraham Bookstein, Yves Chiaramella, Gerard Salton, and Vijay V. Raghavan, Chicago, pp. 3–12.

Robinson, Spider. 1985. Melancholy elephants. Tor. New York.

Su, Louise T. 1992. Evaluation measures for interactive information retrieval. *Information Processing & Management* 28, no. 4:503–516.

EXERCISES

1. Read Spider Robinson's "Melancholy Elephants." Relate the ideas in the story to intellectual property rights in the context of the World Wide Web. Is the problem that Robinson poses a significant one? Is his solution an appropriate one?

String Matching Techniques

The essence of the retrieval process lies in matching a subset of the documents to the query. While more advanced techniques attempt to extract or infer the "meaning" of a document or the "concepts" behind it, most standard retrieval techniques ultimately come down to matching one string of characters against another. This seems simple enough: Lay out the pattern string, for example, a keyword from the query, against the text string and try to match it, character by character. If it matches, fine; if not, move the pattern string along one position and try again. While this brute force technique will work, it involves an unnecessarily large amount of work. If the pattern string contains m characters and the text string n characters, then in the worst case mn comparisons are necessary (see the exercises).

There are four different string matching techniques that require much less work. Each has its advantages and disadvantages. *String differencing*—deciding which string comes closest to matching a given string, assuming that there is no exact match—is also described.

A.1 KNUTH-MORRIS-PRATT MATCHING

Different examples of string matching show that the reason that the brute force technique requires so much work is that it may repeat many comparisons: There is no memory of the comparisons that have been made. If there were some way to remember the comparisons that have already been made and to use that information, it might reduce the number of comparisons needed. All of the techniques to be discussed attempt to do precisely this.

Whenever a character in the pattern string is compared with a character in the text string, one of two things happens: either they match or they do not. If they match, the examination continues with the next character. However, if they do not match, the character that was encountered in the text string is known. The problem is to relate that information to the pattern string.

The *Knuth-Morris-Pratt algorithm* (KMP) (Knuth, Morris, and Pratt 1977) is built around the concept of remembering the initial sequences, or *heads*, of the pattern string. For example, if the pattern string is *throw*, then any *t* that is met in the text string might be a match for the first character of the pattern. If, however, the pattern is *catch*, then any *c* that is met might match either the first or fourth character of this pattern. There is no way to decide unambiguously which character of *catch* to use in the match. However, it is clear that *ca* will match the first two characters, *ch* the last two characters, and *c* followed by anything else will not match the pattern.

KMP operates by constructing a *finite state recognizer* for a given pattern string. This machine has an initial state, plus one state for each character in the pattern string. The transitions the machine makes from one state to the next correspond to the characters seen in the text string. Each state may be thought of as "remembering" the head of the pattern string up to and including the character that it represents. An informal construction of these recognizers is given here.

The informal construction consists of four steps leading to a *state transition diagram* for the recognizer. First, a *spine* is constructed, representing a correct match of the pattern. Second, a *default bus* is constructed, representing the action in the event that there is no other defined match for a given state. Third, an *initial bus* is constructed, to be used when the character in the text string is the first character in the pattern string. Finally, *links* are added, representing substrings within the pattern that match heads of the pattern string.

As an aside, note that decisions must be made about locating single or multiple occurrences of the pattern and about handling overlapping pattern instances. These issues are discussed after the basic construction.

The first example uses the pattern *throw*. The spine consists of six states: an initial state conventionally numbered 0, and states 1, 2, . . . , 5, representing the characters *t, h, r, o,* and *w,* respectively. A transition is made from state *i* – 1 to state *i* whenever the *i*th character is matched. Thus upon seeing *t* the machine changes into state 1. If this is followed by *h,* it changes to state 2; thus arriving at state 2 means that the pair *th* has been seen. If the next character is *r,* so that *thr* has been seen, the recognizer changes to state 3, and so forth. If the entire string *throw* is matched, the machine ends up in state 5 with a successful match. Conventionally, success states are shown in the diagram by double circles. The spine of the recognizer is shown in Figure A.1.

Remember that the only way to transfer from one state to another is by recognizing a specific character. The arrow representing each transition is labeled with the character that activates that transition. What if a different character is seen? Depending on what that character is, one of several other transitions is taken. However, the recognizer generally must allow for seeing a character that has nothing to do with the pattern string, or that does not meet a character to be seen at a particular state. This is the purpose of the default bus. The character ? is used to denote *any character other than those specifically identified with transitions from a state.* Note that this is a *context-dependent* definition, as the interpretation of ? will change from state to state. However, the default bus can be defined without fully knowing the meaning of ? at each state. Adding this to the example produces Figure A.2.

The loop on state 0 indicates that as long as any character other than *t* (the head of the pattern) is seen the machine remains in state 0. At the same time, the pattern is advanced along the text string to examine the next character. Similarly, the default transitions from the other states each show that

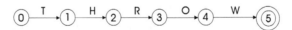

Figure A.1   The spine for throw.

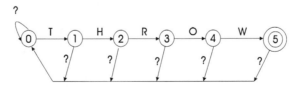

Figure A.2   Recognizer for throw, *default bus attached.*

whenever there is not a proper match, the recognizer begins again in state 0, moving the pattern along one character in the text string.

Now consider the text string *thrthrow*. The recognizer that has been defined to this point will match *thr*, then fail on the second *t* because it is looking for an *o*. However, the default bus will return the recognizer to state 0, looking for a *t*, but *move the pattern along*. Thus the machine tries to match the *t* in the pattern to the second *h* in the text string, thereby missing the pattern occurrence. For this reason, the initial bus is added, representing the transitions when the initial letter of the pattern is located. The interpretation for this pattern would be that the machine failed to match the *o* but did locate a *t*. Thus it should next try to match the second pattern character, *h*, against the next text character. In this way it can successfully locate the pattern occurrence within the text. The recognizer now has the diagram shown in Figure A.3.

Note that from each state in the pattern other than the initial state, the initial bus leads back to state 1, the state that recognizes a *t*.

For this particular pattern, construction of the recognizer is finished: There are no further links to add to the machine. The reason for this is that there is no repetition of the initial character in the pattern string. Observe that the definition of ? now changes from state to state. For state 1 it means any character other than *h* or *t* (since there are transitions for these characters), for state 2 any character other than *r* or *t*, and so forth.

Now consider a second example pattern, *catch*. This is similar to the first example except that the initial character, *c*, is repeated as the fourth character within the pattern. This means that there is a transition from state 3 to state 4 upon locating a *c*. However, the initial bus construction suggests that there should be a transition from state 3 to state 1 upon locating a *c*. Thus there would be two transitions out of state 3 defined for the one character *c*. How does such a recognizer, called *nondeterministic*, determine which tran-

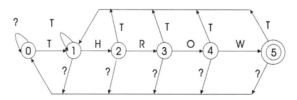

Figure A.3   Recognizer for throw, *initial bus added.*

sition to follow? Fortunately, there is no need to make this decision, as constructing the recognizer allows for it.

Begin the construction of the recognizer for *catch* as was done for *throw*, by defining the spine and default bus. Also construct the initial bus, but do not connect state 3 to this, since there must be the transition from state 3 to state 4 for *c* (Figure A.4).

Now carry out the fourth step of the construction, the addition of links to the recognizer. To understand this, consider the following text strings: *catch, catcocatch, catccatch, catcatch*, and *catcacatch*. The first of these is obviously the pattern to be matched, and the recognizer should succeed in identifying this. It does. In the second text string there is also a match, but it does not begin with the second *c* in the string. However, the recognizer cannot know this until the *o* that follows this *c* is examined. At this point the machine is in state 4. Recognizing an *h* would pass the machine successfully into state 5, but the *o*, matching nothing in the string, sends it back to state 0, where it can then identify the next character as *c* and carry on. The situation is similar for the third text string, but in this case the initial bus out of state 4 will place the machine back in state 1 (having recognized the third *c*), leading to a successful recognition. The fourth text string raises a case that has not yet been addressed, matching the (second) initial *ca*. The recognizer is in state 4, having seen a *c*, and now seeing an *a*. This is not the *h* that is desired, but *ca* does match a head of the pattern string. Thus a transition is needed back to the state that "remembers" *ca*, state 2. Adding this transition link produces the desired recognizer, shown in Figure A.5.

The reader can verify that this recognizer properly identifies the occurrence of *catch* in the final example text string.

The informal design of finite state recognizers is concluded with one for the pattern *cocoa* (Figure A.6), leaving it to the reader to verify that the recognizer works properly in all cases.

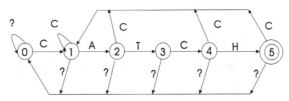

Figure A.4   Recognizer for catch, *after the initial bus.*

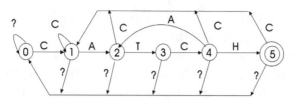

Figure A.5   Recognizer for catch, *final form.*

Consider next the question of multiple occurrences of the pattern string. The recognizers that have been shown each have both a default bus and an initial bus transition out of the success state. Thus if there is still text beyond the recognized word such a recognizer will continue to process it, searching for the next occurrence of the word. If only one occurrence of the word is to be found, the recognizers can be modified by removing the default and initial buses from the success state. A finite state recognizer can either halt after finding the first occurrence of a word, or continue to look for other occurrences.

If there are overlapping patterns, a decision must be made on identifying them. For example, suppose that the pattern is *aba* and the text string is *abababa*. The text then contains two occurrences of the pattern if overlapping occurrences are not allowed, or three if overlaps are allowed. If overlaps are not allowed, there is no problem in adapting the *aba* recognizer to locate both occurrences. If overlaps are allowed, the final *a* of one pattern occurrence must serve also as the initial *a* of another possible occurrence. Thus leaving the success state there must also be a *b* transition, recognizing the overlapping *ab* occurrence.

Formal construction of the KMP recognizer can now be discussed. Observe that the advantage of this recognizer over the brute force comparison method is that *each character of the text string is examined only once.*

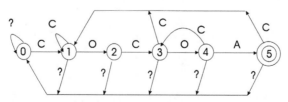

Figure A.6   Recognizer for cocoa.

Thus in the worst case there are only *n* comparisons made for a text string of length *n*, regardless of the pattern length. This advantage would be lost, of course, if it were difficult and costly to construct the recognizer. Fortunately, the effort to construct the recognizer is proportional to the length of the pattern string. Thus the total effort is of the order *m* + *n* rather than the *mn* required for the brute force method. (In most situations *n* is very large compared to *m*, so that the work to construct the recognizer is negligible.)

The KMP recognizer can be constructed in two steps. First, a set of *failure links* is defined, representing the need for transitions to prior states in the event of a match failure. These links are then used to construct a *state transition table*. It is this table, rather than the state transition diagram, that is used in the computer algorithm for recognition. (They are fully equivalent representations.)

A.2 BOYER-MOORE-GALIL MATCHING

In 1977 Boyer and Moore presented a different finite state recognizer that can accomplish more rapid searches than are possible with the KMP algorithms. The worst-case performance of this model was subsequently improved in a modification by Galil (1979). The final algorithm is called the *Boyer-Moore-Galil algorithm* (BMG). The basic idea behind this algorithm is the same as that for the KMP algorithm—to use the states of a finite state recognizer to remember portions of the pattern that have already been recognized. However, in contrast to KMP, BMG begins at the right-hand end of the pattern string. The principal result of this is that whenever the text string character fails to match any character in the pattern string, the pattern can be advanced by its full length. Consider, for example, the following text string, to match against the pattern *throw*:

```
the quick brown fox jumps over the lazy dog
throw
```

The KMP algorithm would match the *th* and fail on the *e*, advancing the pattern so that the *t* is beneath the first space in the text string. However, the BMG algorithm first compares the *q* to the pattern characters. Since it does not match any character in the pattern, the pattern is advanced its full length, aligning the *w* beneath the second space in the text string. In this way, the pattern advances rapidly against the text string:

```
the quick brown fox jumps over the lazy dog
    throw

the quick brown fox jumps over the lazy dog
      throw

the quick brown fox jumps over the lazy dog
        throw

the quick brown fox jumps over the lazy dog
          throw

the quick brown fox jumps over the lazy dog
            throw
```

At this point, the *r* in the text string fails to match the *w* but does match the *r* in the pattern, so the pattern is advanced to align that match. Then the *t* in the text fails to match the *w*, but does match the *t* in the pattern, so once again the pattern is advanced to the proper alignment.

```
the quick brown fox jumps over the lazy dog
              throw

the quick brown fox jumps over the lazy dog
                throw
```

As can be seen, the pattern advances against the text string in relatively large jumps. Worst-case performance for the BMG algorithm involves *n* comparisons, while the best-case performance involves only *n/m* comparisons.

If this is such a good algorithm, why is it not always used? The answer lies in the construction of the finite state recognizer. The recognizer for the KMP algorithm needs to remember the various heads of the pattern string, the *t*, *th*, *thr*, *thro*, and *throw* in our example. But the recognizer for the BMG algorithm must remember various substrings that may occur anywhere within the pattern. (Remember that in the example both *r* and *t* were matched, neither of which involve the right-hand end of the pattern.) Furthermore, if the substring occurs at various points within the pattern, the algorithm must choose the correct move to match an alignment. For example, if the text contains a *c* and the pattern is *catch*, then we want to align the second *c* of the pattern (before the *h*)—not the first one—with the character in the text string. The result of this is that construction of the finite state recognizer for BMG is more costly. A complete analysis of the algorithm suggests that BMG is excellent in situations where a pattern can be defined that will be involved in many repeated searches, but that for a pattern that will be involved in only a few searches the KMP algorithm is more cost effective.

A.3 Aho-Corasick Matching

The *Aho-Corasick algorithm* (Aho and Corasick 1975) for string matching is also based on finite state recognizers. This method differs from the previous ones in that it uses multiple recognizers to speed up the search process.

A.4 Rabin-Karp Matching

The final string matching technique to be considered, the *Rabin-Karp algorithm*, is based on an entirely different concept. Rather than rely on the states of a finite state recognizer to remember substrings of the pattern, it relies on the ability to define a *signature* for the pattern string that is unlikely to be matched by the signature of any other string of the same length. The method strongly resembles hash coding.

In hash coding, each data item has an associated key. By defining a key-to-address transformation, a storage address that depends on the key for the data item can be calculated. If the hash code is well designed, then it is unlikely that any two data items have the same calculated address. (If they do, a collision results, and one of the items must be stored elsewhere.)

The Rabin-Karp algorithm begins by using the pattern string as a "key" and calculating a signature value for the pattern in the same way that one would calculate a key-to-address transformation. The interest, of course, is in this value, not in storing the pattern at a location defined by the value. Next, the algorithm calculates a signature value for a substring of the text string having the same length as the pattern string. If this value is different from the signature for the pattern, then clearly the substring does not match the pattern, and the next substring can be considered. However, if the signature of the substring in the text matches that of the pattern, then it may be a match for the pattern, or it may have be a different string that happens to have the same signature (a "collision" in the hash coding sense). The only way to know is to then compare the pattern and the substring character by character.

The success of the Rabin-Karp algorithm is based on two facts: It is easy to calculate the signatures for the text substrings, and false matches requiring a character-by-character comparison are relatively rare. As a result, the performance of this algorithm is similar to that of the KMP algorithm. The ease of computation of the signatures relies on calculating each signature from the previous one in three easy steps: Drop the lead character, shift the remaining characters over one, and add the new trailing character. Thus if the text string is *the quick brown fox jumped* . . . and the signature for *ick b* has just been computed, the process is:

$$ick\ b \rightarrow \_ck\ b \rightarrow ck\ b\_ \rightarrow ck\ br,$$

where the underscore represents a dropped or missing character. The corresponding numerical calculation involves a subtraction, a multiplication (or shift), and an addition. For example, one of the calculations in the string 49270354 would be

$$92703 \rightarrow ((92703 - 90000) \times 10) + 5 = 27035.$$

A.5   STRING DIFFERENCING

The algorithms discussed thus far all aim at finding an exact match for a given pattern string. In some circumstances this either cannot be done or represents too narrow a search focus. For example, suppose that the user is unsure of the exact spelling of a word or wishes to search for related words whose spellings may differ. She might be looking for papers on the convergence of a given process and be interested in both of the words *converge* and *convergence*. If she is interested in papers on *color* display screens, she is unlikely to find any in the British literature unless she also looks for the British spelling, *colour*.

One way to handle this problem is to search explicitly for the several variants known. This, however, involves either multiple search passes or the use of multiple search "machines" in parallel. In addition, it does not allow sufficient search flexibility in situations where all possible variants are not known.

Another method of handling the search is to introduce *wild cards*, characters that can be matched by anything. A version of this concept has been used in the default bus of the finite state recognizers, where the character ? is matched by anything that does not match a character specified on another transition line. The de facto standard for wild cards in string matching is to use a question mark (?) to denote a match by at most one character, and an asterisk (*) to denote a match by an arbitrary number of characters. Thus by specifying the string *colo?r* both *color* and *colour* are matched (and also the unlikely strings *coloar, colobr,* . . .), and by specifying *converge** both *con-*

verge and *convergence* are matched, along with *convergent* and other variations. One minor problem with this method is the fact that a wild card will
also match undesired characters, as in *coloar.* A more significant problem
arises from the fact that * represents a substring of unspecified length. Thus
its use in the middle of a pattern string might result in a "hung" search, as
the algorithm searches past strings of increasing length, all of which are
potential matches to *. Without some sort of limitation on the search there
is the risk of matching *gor*ing,* for example, in the text *algorithm searches
past strings.* Two possible ways to limit the search are to use the blank space
as an absolute search terminator, overriding the asterisk, or to limit the
scope of the asterisk to a specified number of characters, say at most 5, or 10.
Such limitations may or may not be appropriate in a given situation.

A third method of handling variation in matching is to search for the nearest match rather than an exact match. This method can be used, for example, in spelling correctors. Within a text there is a string (the "pattern" for
the search) that does not match any word in the spelling dictionary (the
"text" for the search). Rather than return a complete failure, the spelling
corrector suggests to the user one or more words that are, in some sense,
close to the pattern word and may be the correct spelling. In information
retrieval the user may be uncertain of the spelling of a person's name; the
system should return all instances of names that are close to what the user
specifies. The use of wild cards will permit this but will not give any measure of "close."

One algorithm that does provide a closeness measure is the *string-to-
string correction algorithm.* Suppose that the problem is to transform a
string *A* into another string *B.* This can always be done by using some characters from *A,* dropping some, and substituting some characters from *B:*

$$long \rightarrow slong \rightarrow shong \rightarrow shorg \rightarrow short.$$

The problem is to find a transformation involving a minimal number of
changes. The number of changes is in some sense a measure of the closeness
of the two strings. Suppose that a cost of 0 is associated with every character of *A* that can retained in the transformation, and a cost of 1 with every
character of *A* that is dropped and with every character of *B* that is added.
Then, for example, it costs one unit to transform *bring* to *brig* (since one letter is dropped) and two units to change it to *brung* (since one letter is
dropped and a different one is substituted). By this measure, *long* and *short*

are rather far apart, since the transformation costs seven units. This cost is sometimes called the *edit distance.*

This problem can be viewed as that of finding a shortest path in a graph associated with the two strings A and B. If these strings have m and n characters, respectively, construct an $(m + 1) \times (n + 1)$ grid. The horizontal edges of the grid represent the introduction of characters from B, and the vertical edges represent deletion of characters from A. Add a diagonal edge to the grid wherever the characters of A and B match. Costs of 1 are associated with every horizontal or vertical edge, costs of 0 with every diagonal edge. The string A is associated with the upper left corner of this grid (as no character in A has been replaced by characters from B), and B is associated with the lower right corner (where the replacement is complete).

Begin at the upper left corner of the grid and move toward the lower right corner, first finding all points that can be reached by paths of length 0, then by paths of length 1 (from the upper left corner), paths of length 2, and so forth, until we reach the lower right corner. Here are three examples:

- *long* to *short* (Figure A.7, cost 7)
- *brig* to *bring* (Figure A.8, cost 1)
- *alabama* to *malabar* (Figure A.9, cost 4)

The string-to-string correction algorithm is not limited to use with character strings. For example, the same type of algorithm has been applied to the problem of updating a computer screen. In a graphic display, the updating often consists of changing one small portion of the screen while leaving

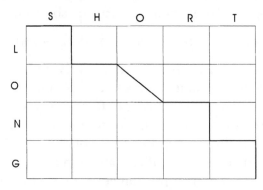

Figure A.7   Changing long *to* short.

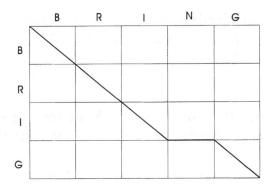

Figure A.8   Changing brig *to* bring.

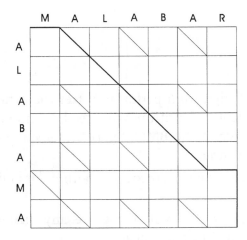

Figure A.9   Changing alabama *to* malabar.

the remainder unchanged. The string-to-string correction algorithm can be used to identify the most efficient way to accomplish this update.

REFERENCES

Aho, A.V., and M.J. Corasick. 1975. Efficient string matching. An aid to bibliographic search. *Communications of the ACM* 18, no. 6:333–340.

Boyer, R.S., and J.S. Moore. 1977. A fast string searching algorithm. *Communications of the ACM* 20, no. 10:762–772.

Galil, Zvi. 1979. On improving the worst case running time of the Boyer-Moore string matching algorithm. *Communications of the ACM* 22, no. 9:505–508.

Knuth, Donald E., J.H. Morris, and V.R. Pratt. 1977. Fast pattern matching in strings. *SIAM Journal of Computing* 6, no. 2:323–350.

EXERCISES

1. Show that in the worst case the brute force matching technique requires *mn* comparisons. *Hint:* Assume that the text string is *aaa . . . aa.*

2. Develop a finite state recognizer for each of the following strings.

    onion

    oconomowoc

    nononondagan

    abracadabra

    abcadabdabcdabcax

3. Find a case in which the KMP algorithm performs better than the BMG algorithm. *Hint:* The KMP algorithm will need to move quickly along the text string while the BMG algorithm advances only one or two characters at a time.

4. Develop a finite state recognizer that will recognize both *color* and *colour.*

5. Develop a finite state recognizer that will recognize any string beginning in *converge* and ending in a blank space.

6. Find the minimal cost of each of the following string-to-string transformations.

    banana to *tannin*

    purpose to *propose*

    algorithm to *logarithm*

    abracadabra to *arbadacarba*

File Structures

The documents used in information retrieval are organized into collections that have some coherence. A given collection of documents may be very closely linked in concept, such as all of the piano music of Beethoven, or highly diverse, such as the collection of the Library of Congress. This collection of documents is called a *file*, and each document is called a *record*. The success of any retrieval process depends to a large extent on the manner in which the collection of documents to be used is organized, since the efficiency of various search processes is closely linked to the data file structure. There are four basic search techniques: sequential, binary, linked list, and direct, each related to a particular data organization.

A *sequential search* assumes only that the records (or documents) of a file are located in consecutive "cells" of memory. The search begins at one location, usually the first document record, and proceeds to examine each record in turn. Sequential search is an $O(n)$ process. That is, the length of time that a sequential search takes is proportional to the number of records in the file.

A *binary search* assumes both that the records are located in consecutive cells and that they are in some sorted order. The search starts at the middle of the file; it determines whether the desired record matches the data at that location or is in the first half or the second half of the file. The process is iterated on the appropriate half of the file. Because half of the remaining portion of the file is eliminated from the search at each cycle, binary search is an $O(lg\ n)$ process, where lg denotes the logarithm to the base 2. That is, the time required is proportional to the logarithm of the number of records. For a very large file the difference in search times is substantial.

While it requires time and effort to maintain a list in sorted order, unless the list is constantly changing the time is worth it. Consider a list of 1,000,000 documents. If these are not sorted, then in the worst case all 1,000,000 documents will be examined to determine that the one wanted is not there. To find a document that is in the list will require, on average, roughly 500,000 probes into the list. However, if the list is sorted and stored so that we can use binary search, then a maximum of 20 probes into the list will either find the desired document or determine that it is not there, since lg 1,000,000 < 20.

Linked list search is basically sequential, with the location of each record determined by a specific link address given in its predecessor. Thus the records do not have to be sequentially stored. However, sorting the file does not improve the search time, since there is no way to locate the middle of the file. Thus linked list search is an $O(n)$ process, just as sequential search is. If a sorted linked list is *doubly linked,* that is, each datum has pointers to both its predecessor and its successor, the search time can be reduced by heading in the correct direction from the starting point, but it is still a linear search.

Direct search depends on the ability to go directly to the location of the desired record. For this to succeed, the location at which a record is stored must depend in some way on the contents of the record. While this is not often used in information retrieval systems, when it is applicable, a well-designed direct search system will require only one or two accesses to locate a given record. Direct search is an $O(1)$ process, meaning that the time to execute a search is independent of the amount of data in the file.

Since the search process is thus tied to the file structure, the types of file structures used for textual material affect the performance. There are five major types. When working with images, other file structures more appropriate to two- and three-dimensional objects are often used.

Common examples of file organization include an office filing system, a computer disk, a recipe file, and the card catalog of a library. The latter two examples usually hold individual records organized into various categories. The office filing cabinet and the computer disk often contain several files, each having its own set of data. They are thus files of files, or *second-order filing systems.*

An important point is that access to a given record is through the appropriate filing system: A user does not look for a business letter in the recipe file, nor (usually) a favorite recipe in one of the office files. Note also that the data within a file have their own structure, *independent of the file structure.* A business letter has a given form, no matter how the secretary organizes the files.

Each record in a file is assumed to have one or more keys that can be used to identify it. These may be specific numbers or names assigned to the files and their records, or something characteristic of the contents of the record. A well-designed filing system allows quick access to the keys without reading each file completely.

B.1   SEQUENTIAL FILES

A *sequential file* is a file in which the records are considered to be stored sequentially. Access is fundamentally to one record at a time, sequentially in the order in which they occur in the file. Binary search may be possible if the file is sorted and stored on disk or in the main memory of a computer. If, however, the file is stored on magnetic tape, the access mechanism for the tape precludes efficient binary searching.

The basic *key* for records in a sequential file is the *record number,* identifying the sequential position of the record in the file. Other keys may exist, which can be used to determine if a given record is to be examined or passed.

The *record size* determines the location of the next record for sequentially stored files. If all records are the same size, this location is easily calculated; if the records differ in size, then either the size or the location of the next record must be a field in each record, or each record must be fully scanned to locate its end and the beginning of the next one.

Because of their nature, sequential files are generally good for *updating* and *listing* but poor for *content search,* since there may be no way to access records with a specified content directly.

B.2   HASHED FILES

A *hashed file* is organized on the basis of the individual *key values* for each record in the file. From each key value, an address for the record is computed by using a *key-to-address transformation.* Each keyword or key phrase is transformed into a numerical equivalent, from which an address is computed. Properly done, this has the effect of scattering records uniformly throughout the computer memory. This structure enables very rapid access to each record. From the record key the system can compute the address at which the record should be stored, if it is in the file.

Unfortunately, there is always the possibility that the computations from two different key values will yield the same address, resulting in a *collision*. When this occurs, obviously some other location must be found for one of the records. Several techniques exist for doing the key-to-address transformation—and for handling collisions when they do occur—to minimize the effect of any collision.

When a data file is fixed and will not be updated, it is possible to define a *perfect hash function* that guarantees there will be no collisions. This idea can be extended to a *minimal perfect hash function*, which also guarantees no wasted storage space, and even to an *ordered minimal perfect hash function*, in which the records occur in sorted order. Such functions are sometimes used to create files of indexes into a data file (Witten, Moffat, and Bell 1994).

Although hashed files have excellent retrieval properties for individual records, since the records are scattered throughout memory it is very difficult to produce a sorted list of the records. In addition, it is very difficult to locate records similar to a given one. Because the addresses assigned depend heavily on the specific content of the records, similar records may be scattered widely throughout the memory. Since locating similar records is an important technique in information retrieval, hashed files find relatively little use here.

B.3   INDEXED FILES

An *indexed file* imposes an additional structure on the records in a file, with the aim of improving access to the file. There is thus a tradeoff—creating or updating a file requires additional processing, while searching and accessing the file requires less processing. The basic purposes of an index (from the system point of view) are

- to identify file sections of a manageable size, and
- to reduce the amount of work involved in a process.

The *index structure* divides a file into locatable sections. Although indexes may be anything that can be identified with the records, typical indexes include names, section numbers or headings, and dates.

The choice of an index is dictated by the logic of use and by a balance among the section sizes. The logic of use requires that records that will be used together should be placed within the same section. Yet if these sections vary widely in size, then effectiveness of indexing the file is reduced.

For example, consider an $O(n^2)$ process, in which time is proportional to the square of the number of records. (Several common sorting routines, inefficient for large quantities of data, are of this nature.) If this process is applied to a file of size 1000, the number of units of work involved will be roughly 1,000,000 (that is, n^2) units. If the file is broken into 10 sections each of size 100, the amount of work will be approximately 10,000 units per section, or a total of 100,000 units. This eliminates 900,000 units of work, some of which will be used to decide the section to which the process should be applied.

To show the effect of balancing the sections, suppose that the same file were broken into one section of 550 records and nine sections of 50 records each. The large section would then require 302,500 units of work, and each of the small ones 2500 units, for a total of 325,000 units of work. While this is better than the original 1,000,000 units, it is worse than the work required by the balanced division by a factor of 3.25.

For a very large file, *multiple indexing levels* are frequently desirable. In this way each section size can be kept relatively small, yet the sections are organized in such a way that only a few of them need be handled at any one time. Suppose, for example, that a file has 1,048,576 (or 2^{20}) records but that only 256 records can be handled at a time. Breaking the file into 4096 sections would require 4096 index terms to identify these sections. Alternatively, if these sections were divided into 64 groups of 64 sections each, then only 64 index terms would be required to identify the various groups, and another 64 index terms would be required within each group to access a section. If the same index terms are used in various groups (just as the same house numbers are used on various streets), this *two-level index* permits organization of the entire file with only 128 index terms. Similarly, a *three-level index* will permit use of only 16 index terms at each level, and a *four-level index* will permit only 8 index terms per level. This may be much easier for a user to understand.

A *direct file* is one in which the only access to records is via the records themselves. An *inverted file* is a file with an associated *inverted index*, which specifies those records in the file containing each of the index terms. Normally a file is only *partially inverted*, with only certain key terms in the inverted index. A *concordance* is a fully inverted file and its associated index, with the location of each term in the file fully specified, even down to the page, paragraph, or sentence in the case of text files.

As an example, suppose that the user wishes to locate all records containing the term *digital computer*. In a direct file he must examine each record to see if it contains this term. In an inverted file, the inverted index specifies exactly those records that contain this term (assuming *digital computer* was used as an index term). The user can thus access these records without a search of the file.

A considerable amount of effort is necessary to create and maintain an inverted file. However, the reduction in search time is generally considered worth the extra effort. In effect, the search for a term such as *digital computer* is done once and the results remembered for future search use.

B.4 TREE-STRUCTURED FILES

A *tree-structured file,* or *hierarchical file,* has its records arranged in a tree. This logical structure generally corresponds to some conceptual organization of the data. The *branching factor* in a tree-structured file is the maximum number of "children" a record can have. As with multilevel index structures, it is desirable to keep the branching factor reasonably low. However, because of the match to a conceptual structure it is not always possible to control the branching factor.

Examples.   The records associated with a genealogy file might reasonably be arranged in a tree structure corresponding to the family tree. The branching factor may be as large as 15, 20, or more because of the existence of families with many children.

The records in a file of research literature might be arranged in a tree corresponding to the citation structure. The branching factor is controlled by the most influential paper, since it will have the most citations.

The records in a file of paleontology literature might be organized in a tree corresponding to an hypothesized pattern of evolution. For this file, the branching factor depends upon the hypothesized pattern.

The *storage structure* of a tree-structured file generally cannot correspond exactly to the tree structure, since storage has an inherently linear structure. Because the records in the file may have various sizes, particularly in a text or image file, there is no completely satisfactory way to force the storage structure to mirror the logical structure of the tree.

B.5   CLUSTERED FILES

The records in a *clustered file* are organized so that those records that are similar, according to some specified criteria, are located close together and readily accessible as a group. Because retrieval from a bibliographic or image file is inexact and relies on similarity judgments, this clustered structure is widely used in information retrieval work.

Development of a clustered file depends on the selection of a *clustering technique,* or classification technique. Several of these have been developed, based on statistical, set theoretic, or graph theoretic concepts. *Statistical techniques* try to assess, on the basis of record characteristics, the probability that a group of records all relate to the same topic sufficiently to be clustered together. *Set theoretic techniques* may be simpler. In a text file, for example, set theoretic clustering may be based on the number of keywords that records have in common. *Graph theoretic techniques* depend on representing interrecord relationships as lines in a graph, and looking for complete subgraphs or other specific graph structures.

A fundamental decision in forming a clustered file is whether the clusters are disjoint or may have common members. In the latter case, organization of the file is more difficult and may require multiple copies of records or multiple pointers to each record. Maintenance of a file with overlapping clusters is difficult because of the need to coordinate the multiple copies or reference pointers.

The clusters in this type of file may or may not correspond to categories that are understandable to the user. While there is a natural tendency to develop understandable clusters, a more efficient file structure may be realized if the clusters are allowed to develop more freely. As with other "divide and conquer" techniques, it is appropriate to keep the clusters of relatively uniform size.

One can approach the clustering task by assuming that the entire file is one large cluster and looking for the best way to split the file into smaller clusters. The opposite approach is to consider each record in the file as an individual file and find good criteria for grouping records together into larger clusters. Both methods work but may result in quite different structures for a given file.

B.6 NETTED FILES

A *netted file* is similar to a clustered file, except that there are no clearly defined criteria for similarity. Instead, an explicit network is used to link together records that relate to some given concept. The result can be a very complex semantic net defining the organization of the file. Because of the complexity of a netted file, there is often no correspondence between the logical net structure and the physical storage structure of the file.

REFERENCES

Witten, Ian H., Alistair Moffat, and Timothy C. Bell. 1994. *Managing gigabytes: compressing and indexing documents and images.* New York: Van Nostrand Reinhold.

FURTHER READING

Dimsdale, J.J., and H.S. Heaps. 1973. File structure for an on-line catalog of one million titles. *Journal of Library Automation* 6:37–55.

Lefkowitz, D. 1964. *File structures for on-line systems.* Rochelle Park, New York: Spartan Books.

Long, P.L., K.B.L. Rastogi, J.E. Rush, and J.A. Wyckoff. 1972. Large on-line files of bibliographic data: An efficient design and a mathematical predictor of retrieval behavior. *Information Processing* 71:473–478.

Lum, V.Y. 1973. General performance analysis of key-to-address transformation methods using an abstract file concept. *Communications of ACM* 16:603–612.

Lum, V.Y., and P.S.T. Yuen. 1972. Additional results on key-to-address transformation techniques: A fundamental performance study on large existing formatted files. *Communications of ACM* 15:996–997.

Lum, V.Y., P.S.T. Yuen, and M. Dodd. 1971. Key-to-address transformation techniques: A fundamental performance study on large existing formatted files. *Communications of ACM* 14:228–239.

Salton, Gerard, and A. Wong. 1978. Generation and search of clustered files. *ACM Transactions on Data Base Systems* 3, no. 4:321–346.

Stellhorn, W.H. 1977. An inverted file processor for information retrieval. *IEEE Transactions on Computers* C-26, no. 12:1258–1267.

Glossary

An online version of this glossary is available at http://www.pitt.edu/~korfhage/glossary. html. Modifications and additions to the glossary are made first in the electronic version.

0-1 vector A vector each of whose components is either 0 or 1.

Absolute Term Frequency The raw count of the number of times that a term occurs in a document or document collection.

Abstract A brief one or two paragraph description of the contents of a document, usually by the author.

ACM Association for Computing Machinery, a professional organization.

Ad Hoc Query A query that is asked once, requiring search of an entire database.

Adaptive Model A data compression method in which the encoding changes or adapts as the statistical properties of an individual document are determined.

Agglutinative Language A language in which syntactic relationships are expressed by distinct suffixes.

Aho-Corasick Algorithm A string matching algorithm that uses multiple finite state recognizers for simultaneous matching of several substrings.

Algorithm The specification of a method by which an information system accomplishes a given task.

Animation The presence of motion in a document such as a videotape.

ANSI American National Standards Institute, the U.S. authority for data encoding and other standards.

Antonym A word meaning the opposite of a given word.

Approximate Match   A matching technique retrieving documents that are similar to, but may not exactly match, the query specification.

Arithmetic Code   A data compression method that represents an entire document by a single number computed adaptively from the frequencies of letters or pixels within the document.

Arithmetic Mean Coefficient   A similarity measure based on the arithmetic mean.

Array   A rectangular array of data, usually of numbers.

ASCII   American Standard Code for Information Interchange, a method for encoding alphanumeric data.

Atomic Data   Data that are not subdivided into smaller units.

Automatic Indexing   Indexing that is performed according to an algorithm, without human intervention.

Average Information Content   A measure of how much information is contained in a typical message from a given set of messages.

Average Precision   A value computed by averaging the precision values at several different recall levels, typically three or eleven levels.

Average Recall   A value computed by averaging the recall values at several different precision levels, typically three or eleven levels.

Average Similarity   The average of the similarities of document pairs within a collection.

Balance   In an indexing method, assuring that the subcollections identified by index terms are of approximately uniform size.

Base Representation   Representation of a document as a vector of numbers related to every term in the vocabulary used for a collection of documents.

Basis Vector   One of a set of vectors from which all vectors within a given vector space can be defined.

Bead   A visual information retrieval interface using a landscape metaphor.

Bibliography   The list of documents cited by a given document.

Bilevel Image   An image in which a pixel has only two values, typically black or white.

Binary Measure   A measure having only two values.

Binary Search   A search technique that iteratively discards half of a given set in an effort to locate a desired item. The technique requires a sorted set.

BIRD   A visual information retrieval interface utilizing a separator array to effect sequential development of a Boolean query two terms at a time.

Bit   The smallest unit of data, having only two possible values.

Bit Map   A representation of a 0,1-vector in which each component is represented by a single bit.

BMG Algorithm   *See* Boyer-Moore-Galil algorithm.

BookHouse   A visual information retrieval interface using a library metaphor.

Boolean Algebra   An algebra based on a certain set of arithmetic rules, used for logical computations. The number of elements in a finite Boolean algebra is always a power of 2. The most common Boolean algebra has only two elements, 0 and 1, and differs from ordinary algebra in that $1 + 1 = 1$.

Boolean Point   In a visual information retrieval interface, a point representing a Boolean combination of reference terms.

Boolean Query   A query in which the individual terms are combined with Boolean or logical connectives.

Boolean Retrieval System   A retrieval system using Boolean queries.

Boyer-Moore-Galil Algorithm   A string matching algorithm based on matching substrings from the right-hand end, rather than the left-hand end. This is an $O(n)$ algorithm that in the best case may be faster than other $O(n)$ algorithms by a factor of five or more.

Branching Factor   In a tree or hierarchical file organization, the maximum number of subunits that a given unit can have.

Breeding Pair   In a genetic algorithm, two variants that are associated for possible crossover operations.

Breeding Population   In a genetic algorithm, the replicated population from which the population of variants for the next generation is formed.

Broader Term   In a thesaurus, a term whose interpretation includes a given term and similar or related terms.

Brown corpus   A well-known frequency study of American texts of various types.

Byte   A sequence of eight bits, hence a unit of data having 256 possible values.

Caption   A brief text describing a figure in a document.

Cassini Oval Model   A model of interaction among query terms, in which the similarity of two documents is computed using the product of the distances of each reference term from the document.

Cell   In general, an element position in an array. Specifically, one of four element positions in the separate array for BIRD.

Characteristic Function   A function whose value is 1 for elements of a given set and 0 for elements not in the set. It is used, for example, to separate documents satisfying a query (1) from those not satisfying it (0).

Citation Index   An index that lists documents citing a given document.

Citation Processing   A retrieval technique in which documentary citations are traced to identify documents related to a given one.

City Block Distance   A distance computed using the sum of the absolute values of distance changes in each direction, so called because it counts the number of blocks traversed in moving from one location to another in a city.

Classification Bin   In BIRD, a bin in which a selected subset of documents can be stored.

Cluster Point   A point that represents a cluster of documents.

Clustered File   A file in which the data elements are organized by a clustering technique.

Clustering Technique   A technique by which relationships among data elements such as documents are determined and closely related elements are grouped into clusters.

CNF   *See* conjunctive normal form.

Co-citation   The phenomenon of two documents being cited by a given document, used as a measure of similarity of the two documents.

Coefficient of Association   A measure of similarity between two documents.

Co-filter   Use of a user profile as a second reference point in conjunction with a query.

Collision   In hashing, the situation in which two data items are assigned to the same location.

Communication Theory   *See* transmission theory.

Component   An individual element in a vector.

Concept   An idea within a document, in contrast to the specific terms used to express that idea.

Concordance   An inverted index identifying all occurrences of each term within a body of text.

Conditional Probability   The probability that a given event occurs, assuming that another specified event has occurred.

Conditional Probability Coefficient   A similarity measure based on conditional probability.

Conjunct In the disjunctive normal form, a group of individual terms joined by AND; in the conjunctive normal form, a group of disjuncts joined by AND.

Conjunctive Model A model of interaction among query terms, in which the similarity of two documents is computed using the maximum of the distances of each reference term from the document.

Conjunctive Normal Form A standard form for logical expressions, in which individual terms are joined by OR, and such groups of terms are joined by AND.

Conjunctive Query A Boolean query using only AND and NOT.

Content-bearing Words Words that are deemed to relate to the concepts in a document. *See also* stop list.

Content Search A search to locate a record or document having a specific content.

Context-Dependent Any character or term whose interpretation depends on the context within which it occurs.

Context Encoding An encoding method in which the code for a given symbol depends on the context within which it occurs.

Contingency Table An array in which the cells represent specific combinations of conditions, often a 2×2 table in which each of two conditions may or may not occur.

Continuous Tone Image An image in which each pixel may have any of a range of values. Typically the value of an individual pixel is closely related to the values of surrounding pixels.

Contour Within a document space, the boundary of a region containing documents to be retrieved.

Controlled Vocabulary A restricted set of words and phrases that are used to describe documents within a given set.

Copyright The right of an individual or corporation to receive credit for, and benefit from, published works.

Cosine Coefficient A similarity measure based on the cosine of the angle between two documents.

Cosine Measure The vector angle between two documents, used as a measure of similarity.

Coverage Ratio The proportion of the relevant documents known to the user that are actually retrieved.

Cross Referencing   In a thesaurus, reference to terms related to the given term.

Crossover   In a genetic algorithm, the method of exchanging portions of two variants to create two new variants.

Crossover Rate   In a genetic algorithm, the fraction of breeding pairs that are chosen for a crossover operation.

Current Awareness System   An information retrieval system in which users are automatically notified of any new documents that may relate to their interests; also called **selective dissemination of information**, and **routing system**.

Data   The documents received, stored, and retrieved by an information endosystem.

Data Compression   The encoding data in less than one byte per character for text, and in as little as one or two bits per pixel for images.

Data Fusion   The merging of search results from several different databases, possibly using several different search techniques.

Data Model   In data compression, the model, adaptive or static, used to represent the data.

Deep Structure   The structure of a sentence related to its meaning, independent of the specific syntax used.

Default Bus   In a finite state recognizer, a bus that is used for any unspecified character.

Deleted Average Similarity   Average similarity of documents within a collection, computed on the assumption that occurrences of a given term have been deleted from the computation.

DeMorgan's Laws   Logical laws governing the interaction of AND, OR, and NOT.

Deterministic   An algorithm or automaton such that for any given set of data each step has only one possible successor.

Device   A computer or other tool used to process information.

Dewey Decimal Classification   A system of classifying documents according to contents.

Dice's Coefficient   A similarity measure developed by Dice.

Dimensional Compatibility   In an abbreviated vector representation of documents, the concept that a given position must refer to the same term in each of the documents, whether or not that term occurs.

Direct File   A file of documents without an index into it.

Direct Search A search of each document within a file to locate those containing a given term.

Discriminant Function In probabilistic retrieval, a function that determines whether a given document should be retrieved.

Disjunct In the conjunctive normal form, a group of individual terms joined by OR; in the disjunctive normal form, a group of disjuncts joined by OR.

Disjunctive Model A model of interaction among query terms, in which the similarity of two documents is computed using the minimum of the distances of each reference term from the document.

Disjunctive Normal Form A standard form for logical expressions, in which individual terms are joined by AND, and such groups of terms are joined by OR.

Dissimilarity Measure A measure in which high values represent documents that are dissimilar and low values, such as 0 represent documents that are similar.

Distance Measure A measure relating two entities that satisfies certain conditions: zero distance only between an entity and itself, non-negativity, symmetry, and the triangle inequality.

Distance Space A space in which documents are positioned according to their distances from given reference points.

DNF *See* disjunctive normal form.

Doctrine of Fair Use The concept in copyright law that limited individual use of any document is permitted without specific permission of the copyright holder.

Document A stored data record in any form.

Document Analysis The process of analyzing a scanned document to determine its components such as headings, paragraphs, and figures.

Document Cluster A group of related documents.

Document-Document Matrix An array used to compare documents within a collection according to a given criterion.

Document Identifier A number or other code uniquely identifying a document.

Document Reference Number The identifier by which an information system refers to a document.

Document Space A conceptual space in which documents are distributed according to given characteristics, often term occurrences.

Document Surrogate A limited representation of a full document.

EBCDIC   Extended Binary Coded Decimal Information Code, a method for encoding alphanumeric data, now largely obsolete.

Economy   How well the information system meets the economic goals of the funder.

Ectosystem   Those system factors that are not under the control of the designer, including the people who are involved with the system, the forms in which information is available, and the equipment and technology available for the system.

Effectiveness   The quality of the information system response to the information need.

Efficiency   The time and effort required for the information system to respond to the information need.

Eleven-point Average   Computation of average precision or average recall from the values at eleven recall or precision points, respectively, namely, at 0.0, 0.1, . . . , 1.0.

Ellipsoidal Model   A model of interaction among query terms, in which the similarity of two documents is computed using the sum of the distances of each reference term from the documents.

Endosystem   Those system factors that the designer can specify and control, such as the equipment, algorithms, and procedures used.

Euclidean Distance   Ordinary straight-line distance.

Exact Match   A document that exactly matches the terms and criteria in a query.

Exclusive OR   Interpretation of "or" as meaning either one or the other but not both.

Exhaustivity   The extent to which a given set of index terms covers all topics and concepts met in a document set.

Expected Search Length   The average number of documents to be examined to locate a given number of relevant documents.

Expert System   An inferential information system built on a knowledge base.

Extended Boolean Query   A modification of Boolean queries to include weighting of the terms.

Extended User Profile   Any user profile that includes user characteristics that cannot be directly related to terms in documents, such as levels of education and experience.

Extract   A brief description of a document formed by selecting certain sentences from the document.

Extrinsic Measure   A document similarity measure that depends on reference to some point independent of the two documents.

Failure Link   In the KMP algorithm, a link to be taken when a required character is not present.

Fallout   The proportion of nonrelevant documents that are not retrieved.

Feedback   The passing of information between components of a system in response to some action of the system.

File   A collection of documents or other entities organized into a single unit.

Fine Structure   The detailed representation of data, including encoding methods used.

Finite State Recognizer   An automaton or algorithm that recognizes a given string of characters.

Frustration Measure   A performance measure based on the positions of nonrelevant documents in the retrieved set.

Full Disjunctive Normal Form   A disjunctive normal form in which each disjunct contains all of the terms or their negations.

Full Document Surrogate   An extended representation of a document, possibly including title, author, author's location, source, date, abstract, subject descriptors and categories, and key terms.

Full Text   The entire text of a document.

Funder   The person or organization who underwrites the cost of operating the information system.

Fuzzy Matching   A matching process based on the concept of a fuzzy set.

Fuzzy Query   A query based on the concept of a fuzzy set.

Fuzzy Set   A set for which each element of the space, rather than being in or out of the set, has an associated membership function representing the belief that that element should be in the set.

Generality   The proportion of relevant documents within the entire collection.

Genetic Algorithm   An iterative process of simultaneously solving many variants of a complex problem, leading to the identification of a near-optimal solution to the problem, so-called because of the analogy to breeding within a population of plants or animals.

Graph Theoretic Clustering   A clustering method based on concepts from graph theory.

Grayscale Image   A monochrome image having several, usually eight, levels of intensity.

Gross Structure   The extent and type of formatting that the document exhibits.

GUIDO   A visual information retrieval interface based on the distances of a document from given reference points.

Hash Function   A function used for key-to-address transformation in hashing.

Hashed File   A file whose organization is based on a hashing technique.

Hashing   A method of assigning items to computer storage where the storage location is computed from the characteristics of the individual items. In theory hashing permits one step access to any data item.

Hierarchical File   A file whose contents are organized in a hierarchical or tree-like manner.

Highly Dissimilar Documents   Documents that conceptually have very little in common.

Highly Similar Documents   Documents that are very close conceptually.

Hill Climbing   An optimization technique that moves at each step toward a better solution to a problem. The flaw in the technique is that such a direct move may miss the best possible solution, which is reachable only be moving away from a good solution, or by starting at a different point.

Home Page   In the World Wide Web, a site identified with an individual user or organization.

Homograph   A word that is spelled the same as a given word, but has a different meaning.

Homonym   A word that sounds the same as a given word, but has a different meaning.

HTML   Hypertext Markup Language, a method for encoding the format of a document on the World Wide Web, including hypertext links.

Huffman Code   A static data compression code, widely used because of its ease of development and application.

Hypertext   A system of linking a portion of a document to related portions of the same or different documents through direct pointers.

Ib.   *See* ibid.

Ibid.   A reference in a footnote or endnote to a document cited in the immediately preceding reference.

Ibidem   *See* ibid.

Idf   *See* inverse document frequency.

Idiomatic Expression   A phrase that has a conventional meaning seemingly unrelated to the literal meaning of the words.

Image Database   A collection of images, organized for information processing and retrieval.

Image Processing   The processing of an image to store it in a computer or to analyze its contents and components.

Inclusive OR   Interpretation of "or" as meaning either one or the other or possibly both.

Independence Value   A base value used in some similarity measures, related to the statistical independence of two terms or documents.

Index of Independence Coefficient   A similarity measure based on statistical independence.

Index Structure   The organization of an index system, particularly with reference to the number of levels in the index.

Index Term   A term used to identify a concept in a document.

Indexed File   A file with an associated set of index terms.

Indexer-User Mismatch   The fact that indexers and users may use different terms to denote a given concept.

Indexing   The act of creating an index for a document or a document collection.

Indexing Language   The language, particularly the set of terms, used to create an index.

InfoCrystal   A visual information retrieval interface based on displaying all Boolean combinations of the reference terms.

Information   Data that have been matched to a particular information need, having both personal and time-dependent components that are not present in the concept of data.

Information Content   A measure of the information inherent in a given message or document.

Information Filtering   The concept of utilizing inexpensive techniques to eliminate most of a document collection from further consideration in relation to a given information need.

Information Navigator   A visual information retrieval interface based on the concept of navigating a document space.

Information Need   The requirement to store information (data) in anticipation of future use, or to find information (data) in response to a current problem.

Information Retrieval   The location and presentation to a user of information relevant to an information need expressed as a query.

Information Retrieval System   Any system, usually involving computers, that performs information retrieval.

Information Theory   *See* transmission theory.

Initial Bus   In a finite state recognizer, a bus used when the initial symbol of a substring is recognized.

Initial State   The starting state for a finite state recognizer.

Inner Product   A value computed from two vectors by multiplying corresponding components and adding the results.

Integrated Media Document   A document that may contain text, images, and sound.

Integrated Media Systems   An information system for handling integrated media documents.

Intellectual Property Right   The right of the creator of a document to recognition and benefit from his or her work.

Internet   The worldwide system linking computers through telecommunications.

Intrinsic Measure   A similarity measure that refers only to the documents being compared, not to any external point.

Inverse Document Frequency   The logarithm of the reciprocal of the number of documents in a collection that contain a given term.

Inverse Document Frequency Weight   A term weight computed from term frequency and inverse document frequency.

Inverse Relationship   A relationship between two values such that as one value increases the other decreases.

Inverted File   A file accessible through an inverted index.

Inverted Index   An index into a file arranged so that each term in the index directly identifies the documents containing that term.

Iterative Affix Removal   A stemming method in which compound affixes are removed iteratively. For example, *tionally* is shortened to *tional*, then to *tion*, then removed entirely.

Jaccard's Coefficient   A similarity measure developed by Jaccard.

JBIG   Joint Bilevel Image Experts Group, a standard for encoding bilevel images.

JPEG   Joint Photographic Experts Group, a standard for encoding continuous tone images.

Judging Dilemma The problem associated with having a fixed range of judgment values. If a given document is assigned a value near the maximum and a subsequent document is clearly superior, that superiority cannot be accurately represented without reassessing all prior documents.

Key A term used to access or organize a data file; in hashing, a term used to identify an individual data item.

Key Phrase A phrase chosen to represent the content of a document.

Key-to-Address Transformation In hashing, the computation of the address for a data item from its key.

Key Value The value of a key.

Keyword One of a set of individual words chosen to represent the content of a document.

KMP Algorithm *See* Knuth-Morris-Pratt algorithm.

Knowledge Information integrated to form a large, coherent view of a portion of reality.

Knowledge Base The stored data, algorithms, facts, concepts, and rules that are representative of one or more selected experts in a particular area.

Knuth-Morris-Pratt Algorithm An $O(n)$ substring matching algorithm based on the use of a finite state recognizer.

Lack of Consistency The fact that a given indexer or information system user may not be consistent in the use of terms over a period of time.

Latent Semantic Indexing A technique based on multidimensional scaling for identifying the major concepts in a document or document collection.

Law of Double Negation The logical rule that states that a second negation cancels out a first negation: NOT NOT A is the same as A.

Lempel-Ziv Code *See* Ziv-Lempel code.

Level of Compression The degree to which a document has been compressed.

Lexical Similarity Document similarity based solely on the occurrence of words.

Lg A notation for the logarithm to the base 2.

Library of Congress Classification A system of classifying documents according to contents.

Linear Correlation Coefficient A similarity measure based on the linear correlation between two documents.

Linear Transformation A transformation defined by a linear equation.

Linearly Independent Vectors A set of vectors such that no linear combination adds up to the zero vector.

Link In documentation, a relationship between two terms; in the KMP algorithm, a path to be followed in a given circumstance.

Linked List Search Search through items organized into a linked list.

List of References The documents cited by a given document.

List of Terms The terms used in a given document or document collection.

Listing The process of creating a list of documents in a file.

Logic A method for reasoning about the relationships among terms.

Logic of Use The concept that closely related documents should be within the same section of an indexed file.

Logical Connective One of the operators, typically AND, OR, and NOT, used to express the co-occurrence relationships among terms.

Logical Structure The conceptual organization of a file, in contrast to its physical organization in a storage system.

L_p **Metric** One of a family of metrics developed using the pth root of the sum of the pth powers of absolute differences in components.

LSI *See* latent semantic indexing.

LyberWorld A three-dimensional visual information retrieval interface with document placement based on the ratio of similarities of the document to given reference points.

Machine Readable Medium Any document storage medium that can be read by a computer.

Manhattan Distance *See* city block distance.

Manual Indexing Indexing that is done directly by a person, rather than by an algorithm.

Mapping If documents and queries are regarded as having distinct forms, the process of transforming a document into an entity that can be matched to the query.

Markup Language A notation used to add to text information about its formatting.

Matching If documents and queries are regarded as having similar forms, the process of identifying documents that are similar to a given query.

Matrix A rectangular array, generally of numbers.

Maximal Direction Distance A distance measure that utilizes only that largest of the distances in any coordinate direction; L_∞

Measure   A numerical value used for evaluation. A measure may be applied to terms, documents, pairs of documents, retrieval systems, and so forth. The measure may be such that the actual value is important, the relative values are important, or only the ordinal values are important.

Medium   Any material used to store a document.

Membership Grade   In fuzzy set theory, the degree of belief that a given element belongs to a given set.

Metric   *See* distance measure.

MIDI   Musical Instrument Digital Interface, a standard for encoding for music.

Minimal Perfect Hash Function   A perfect hash function that utilizes minimal space.

Minimization   A technique for determining a Boolean function that is logically equivalent to a given one and contains a minimum number of operator occurrences.

Monotone Nondecreasing Function   A function f of one variable with the property that if $x_2 > x_1$ then $f(x_2) \geq f(x_1)$.

MPEG   Moving Picture Experts Group, a standard for encoding motion pictures and video.

Multidimensional Scaling   A statistical technique for determining the best set of coordinates or dimensions to represent a given set of data.

Multimedia Document   *See* integrated media document.

Multimedia System   Any information system that can process multimedia documents.

Mutation   In genetic algorithms, the technique of randomly replacing a parameter value with a new, randomly chosen value.

Mutation Rate   In genetic algorithms, the rate at which mutations are applied.

Narrower Term   In a thesaurus, a term that is more specific than a given term. Entities identified by the narrower term are among those identified by the original term.

***n*-ary Measure**   A measure that takes on n different values.

Natural Language Processing   Text processing that includes syntactic, semantic, and sometimes pragmatic interpretation techniques.

Natural Language Query   A query stated in English or some other natural language.

Natural Order   An ordering of entities that people commonly use: numerical order for numbers, alphabetic order for letters and words, calendar order for month and days of the week, and so forth.

Negative Dictionary   *See* stop list.

NetScape   One of the most widely used systems for accessing the World Wide Web.

Netted File   A file whose structure is based on a network of relationship.

Noise   Transmission errors that corrupt the original signal; any portion of a document that is not appropriate in response to a given information need.

Nondeterministic   Any algorithm or automaton which may include a step involving several possibilities with no method of deciding among the possibilities.

Normalization   In logic, the process of converting a logical expression to a canonical form such as CNF or DNF.

Normalized Precision   A measure in which precision is normalized against all relevant documents.

Normalized Recall   A measure in which recall is normalized against all relevant documents.

Normalized Similarity Measure   A similarity measure that has been adjusted so that the similarity of a document to itself is 1.

Novelty Ratio   The proportion of the relevant retrieved documents that were previously unknown to the user.

***n*-simplex**   A n-dimensional polyhedron with $n + 1$ vertices.

OCR   *See* optical character recognition.

One-Point Crossover   In genetic algorithms, a breeding technique using one randomly chosen point, interchanging the portions of the two breeding individuals to the right of that point.

op. cit.   Reference in a footnote or endnote to a previously cited document.

Operating Curve   For an information retrieval system, a curve plotting the fraction of relevant documents retrieved against the fraction of irrelevant documents retrieved, as the system retrieves increasing numbers of documents. In general, a curve plotting one system characteristic against another as the system carries out its function.

Opere Citato   *See* op. cit.

Optical Character Recognition   A technique for identifying the distinct segments of a scanned document and for converting the textual portions to ASCII or some other text code.

Order of Precedence   The order in which a given set of operators is to be processed in the absence of parentheses or other indications to the contrary. For arithmetic this is conventionally unary minus (negative number) before multiplication and division before addition and subtraction, with left-to-right ordering among operators of equal precedence. For logic it is conventionally NOT before AND before OR, with left-to-right order among operators of equal precedence.

Ordered Minimal Perfect Hash Function   A minimal perfect hash function that also preserves the sorted order of a set of entities.

Ordered Proximity   A proximity measure in which the order of the words is taken into account.

Overlap Coefficient   A similarity measure based on the overlap in terms between two documents.

Partially Inverted File   A file with an associated index that includes some, but not all, words.

Perfect Hash Function   A hash function that produces no collisions.

Pertinence   A measure of how well a document matches an information need.

Phrase   A contiguous set of words within a sentence.

Piecewise Linear Transformation   A transformation that is defined by different linear equations over different ranges of its variables.

Piles   A visual information retrieval interface based on the metaphor of piles of papers on a desk.

POI   *See* point of interest.

Point of Interest   A reference point, such as a term, phrase, user profile, or known document; a POI.

Post-filter   Application of a user profile to a set of retrieved documents to alter its characteristics, either by excluding some documents or by changing the order in which they are presented.

Postscript   A widely used markup language.

Pragmatic Factor   Any factor involving the specifics of an information seeking situation, such as known documents, user background, and time constraints.

Precision   The proportion of retrieved documents that are relevant.

Precision-recall Graph   A graph plotting precision against recall.

Pre-coordinated Indexing Language   An indexing language in which the terms to be used have been chosen a priori, along with the set of terms that each chosen term is to represent.

Pre-filter Application of a user profile to a query before retrieval, to alter the characteristics of the query.

Prefix Property The property of an encoding system that no code is the prefix of any other code.

Pretrieval A technique for attempting to retrieve the one document most relevant to an information need before a query is posed.

Probabilistic Matching A document-query matching based on the probability that the document will satisfy the query.

Probabilistic Query A query with term weightings interpreted as probabilities that the given terms will identify relevant documents.

Probability Difference Coefficient I A similarity measure based on probability.

Probability Difference Coefficient II A similarity measure based on probability.

Process The operation of a system.

Product The result of the operation of a system.

Proportion of Overlap Coefficient A similarity measure based on the overlap in terms between two documents.

Proximity A measure of the nearness of two term occurrences in a document, usually in terms of the number of intervening terms, or of co-occurrence within a sentence.

Proximity Operator A function that identifies pairs of terms satisfying specified proximity conditions.

Pseudo-metric A measure that behaves like a metric, except that two distinct entities may be at a "distance" of 0.

QBIC An image query system based on color, texture, and rough sketches.

Query The formal expression of an information need.

Query-Profile Interaction The way in which a query and a user profile are used jointly to identify relevant documents.

Query Variant In genetic algorithms, one of a set of query representations differing only in the term weights.

Rabin-Karp Algorithm A substring matching algorithm based on a hash function.

Range Match A matching process in which a specified range of values, such as numbers or names, is acceptable.

ReadingRoom A visual information retrieval interface presenting a self-organizing semantic map of a document set.

Recall   The proportion of relevant documents that are retrieved.

Recall Effort   The ratio of the number of relevant documents desired to the number of documents examined by the user to find the number of relevant documents desired.

Record   An individual entity within a file.

Record Number   The identifier for a record.

Record Size   The size of a record, usually in bytes or computer words.

Rectangular Distance   *See* city block distance.

Rectangular Distance Coefficient   A similarity measure based on the rectangular or city block distance between two documents.

Reference List   *See* bibliography.

Reference Point   A point by which a document can be judged; a POI.

Related Term   In a thesaurus, a term whose meaning bears some relationship to that of a given term.

Relative Recall   The ratio of the relevant retrieved documents examined by the user to the number of documents the user would have liked to examine.

Relative Term Frequency   Term frequency normalized by the length of a document or by the number of documents in a collection.

Relevance   A measure of how well a document matches a query.

Relevance Feedback   An iterative process in which the user indicates the relevance of documents within a sample retrieval and the system utilizes this information to modify the query.

Relevant Document   A document that matches a query according to some specified measure.

Replication   In a genetic algorithm, the process of duplicating the best of the query variants in one generation in preparation for defining the succeeding generation.

Retrieval   *See* information retrieval.

Retrospective Search System   A search system that responds to an ad hoc query by searching the entire database for relevant documents.

Review   A brief description of a document, written by someone other than the author, often including critical remarks relating the document to the literature of an area.

Role   The way in which a given term is used in a document.

Routing Query   A query that is permanently on file, to be matched against any new documents entered into the system.

Routing System   *See* current awareness system.

RTF   Rich Text Format, a method for encoding textual data.

Run Length Encoding   An encoding method based on the lengths of sequences of characters in a document. Most often used for image encoding, where the characters are individual black or white pixels.

Satisfaction Measure   A performance measure based on the positions of relevant documents in the retrieved set.

Scaling Effect   The effect that increasing the size of a database has on information processing.

Scanner   A device for generating a digital image of a document and entering it into a computer or telecommunication system.

Scatter/Gather   A visual information retrieval interface based on the metaphor of iteratively scattering documents into groups, gathering desired documents together, and rescattering them into new groups.

Search Technique   A method used to locate a record within a file.

Second Order Filing System   A two-level filing system, with the entities in each main file being files.

See Reference   In a thesaurus, a reference to a term that is used in place of the given term.

See Also Reference   In a thesaurus, a reference to a related term.

Segmentation   In optical character recognition, the process of identifying the distinct portions of a document, such as headings, sections, paragraphs, and figures.

Selective Dissemination of Information   *See* current awareness system.

Semantic Structure   The structure of a sentence based on its meaning, rather than on the order in which the words appear in the sentence.

Semantic Analysis   Analysis of a text to determine its meaning.

Semantics   The study of the meaning of text.

Semi-static Model   In data compression, a model that is basically static, but is reinitiated periodically to better fit the data.

Separable Verb   In German, a verb whose prefix can be separated from the main portion of the verb, often appearing at the end of the sentence.

Separation Coefficient   A similarity measure based on the separation between two documents.

Separator Array   In BIRD, the cell array used to separate documents according to the presence or absence of two specified terms.

Sequential File   A file whose order is sequential.

Sequential Search   A search technique that begins at the beginning of a file and sequentially processes the entities in the file.

Server   Any information professional who operates the system and provides service to the users.

Set Theoretic Clustering   Any clustering method based on set theory.

SGML   Standard Generalized Markup Language, a widely used markup language.

Short Reference   A document reference that includes only title, author, and source.

Signal   The bit stream or electromagnetic wave form must be transmitted from one place to another during information processing.

Signal-to-Noise Ratio   A method of weighting term frequencies based on information content.

Signature   A function, often a short string of bits, designed to characterize a particular string or other textual element.

Similarity   A comparison of two documents, or a document and a query, to determine how much they relate to the same concepts.

Similarity Measure   A measure of similarity.

Simple Linear Transformation   *See* linear transformation.

Simple User Profile   A user profile stated entirely in terms of keywords.

Sliding Scale   A measure of recall based on the retrieval of a specific set of documents.

Sound Processing   The processing of voice, music, and other sound data.

Sparse Matrix   A matrix containing many zeros or empty cells. Typically fewer than 10% of the cells contain non-zero data.

Special Index   An index of special characteristics of a text, such as figures, cited authors, or mathematical proofs.

Specificity   The depth of coverage of an index. The extent to which specific topic ideas are indexed in detail.

Spine   In a finite state recognizer, the sequence of states that recognizes a correct string of characters.

Standards   Agreed upon rules for the specification, design, and development of entities within a given class.

State   In a finite state recognizer, one of several conditions of the automaton that corresponds to recognition of a specific sequence of characters.

State Transition Diagram   A diagram showing the states of a finite state recognizer and the conditions from switching from one state to another.

State Transition Table   A table showing the states of a finite state recognizer and the conditions for switching from one state to another.

Static Model   A data compression method using an encoding that is fixed a priori and does not adapt to the characteristics of an individual document.

Statistical Clustering   A method of clustering based on statistics.

Stemming   The removal of suffixes, and sometimes prefixes from words to arrive at a core that can represent any of a set of related words.

Stemming Algorithm   An algorithm to perform stemming.

Stop List   A list of words to be ignored in information processing. A stop list usually contains the most common words in text, and may include from 15 to approximately 500 words.

Storage Structure   The way in which a file is stored in computer memory, in contrast to the logical or conceptual structure of the file.

String-to-String Correction   The process of identifying a minimal set of changes necessary to replace one string of characters by another.

Summary   A section at the end of a document providing an overview of the document contents.

Swets' E measure   A measure of effectiveness for an information retrieval system, proposed by Swets and based on the operating curve.

Synchronization Point   In data compression, a point at which a semi-static encoding is reinitialized.

Synonym   A word having the same meaning as a given word.

Syntactic Ambiguity   The property of natural language that a given sentence may be parsed in two or more distinct ways.

Syntactic Analysis   Analysis of a text to determine its syntactic structure.

Syntactic Structure   The textual structure imposed by the syntax of a language.

Syntax   Linguistic rules for composing well-formed sentences.

Term   A word or phrase having a distinct meaning.

Term Discrimination Value   A measure of how much a given term contributes to separating a set of documents into distinct subsets.

Term-Document Matrix   An array matching terms to documents, usually containing similarity values.

Term-Term Matrix   An array matching term to term, usually related to documents that contain each pair of terms.

Text Relationship Map   A visual information retrieval interface based on identifying and matching the occurrences of terms within documents.

Text Tiling   The process of dividing a text into paragraphs or other units, and identifying the occurrences of terms within these units.

Tf.idf   A term weighting based on term frequency and inverse document frequency.

Thesaurus   A document identifying relationships among terms. Classically these relationships are based on term meanings, but they can also be based on term co-occurrences.

Three-point Average   Computation of average precision or average recall from the values at three recall or precision points, respectively, usually 0.25, 0.5, and 0.75, or 0.2, 0.5, and 0.8.

Threshold   A set value of a similarity or other measure. Documents for which the measure value is below the threshold will not be considered.

TileBars   A visual information retrieval interface based on text tiling.

Topicality   The extent to which a document relates to a given topic.

Total Measure   A weighted sum of the satisfaction and frustration measures.

Transmission Theory   The study of signal processing.

TREC   Text REtrieval Conference, an on-going series of information retrieval experiments with very large databases, involving research groups around the world.

Tree-structured File   A file whose conceptual structure is a tree or hierarchy.

Triangle Inequality   The statement that the sum of the lengths of any two sides of a triangle is at least equal to the length of the third side. A key property of metrics or distance measures.

Trie   From retrieval, a tree structure whose vertices are letters in the words of a vocabulary. Used for rapid matching of words in a text.

Trigger Phrase   A phrase in a text that identifies specific features of the text, such as figures, examples, or conclusions.

Truth Table   An array used for representing or determining the truth or falsity of a logical proposition.

Two-point Crossover   In genetic algorithms, a breeding technique using two randomly chosen points, interchanging the portions of the two breeding individuals between the two points.

Uncontrolled Vocabulary   The use of unrestricted terms in indexing.

Uniform Crossover   In genetic algorithms, a breeding technique in which it is randomly decided for each element of a breeding pair of individuals whether they should be switched.

Unit Circle   The set of points at distance 1 from a given point.

Updating   The process of changing entries in a file to make them current.

Usefulness   The concept that a retrieved document may be relevant to an information need other than the present one, or that a document relevant to the present need may not useful since the information in it is already known.

User   The person who either wishes to store information in the system, or to retrieve information from the system.

User-oriented Measure   A measure taking into account the individual situation and characteristics of the user, in contrast to one that is uniform for all users.

User Profile   A description of the user's interest and background in relation to the information need.

Vector   An ordered list of elements, in information retrieval either terms or term weights. The elements are called components.

Vector Angle Coefficient   A similarity measure based on the angle between two documents.

Vector Model   A retrieval model based on viewing documents and queries as term or term weight vectors.

Vector of Terms   A vector whose components are terms.

VIBE   A visual information retrieval interface based on the ratios of similarities between a document and multiple reference points.

View   An abstracted and organized subset of data.

VIRI   *See* visual information retrieval interface.

Visual Information Retrieval Interface   Any two- or three-dimensional graphic display showing some of the relationships among documents, or among terms within a given document; a VIRI.

Vocabulary   The set of words used in an information system.

VR-VIBE   A visual information retrieval interface based on VIBE, but introducing a third dimension and virtual reality techniques.

Weakly Ordered Set   A set in which there is an order relation defined between some, but not all, elements. The set can be partitioned into subsets each consisting of elements that have no order relationship among themselves.

Weight Vector   A vector whose components are term weights.

Weighted Boolean Query   A modified Boolean query with weights applied to the terms or the Boolean operators.

Weighting of Terms   The assignment of numerical values to terms, representing their importance in a document or query.

Wild Card   In a character string representation, a special character indicating that one or more arbitrary characters may be substituted.

Wisdom   A broad view, encompassing all of known reality, governing the use of the information that has been obtained and the knowledge that has been developed, and involving the capacity to make balanced judgments in the light of certain value criteria.

Word Order   The order in which words occur in a phrase or sentence.

World Wide Web   A development of the Internet permitting individuals and organizations to make information publicly available, and to access information that others have made publically available.

WWW   *See* World Wide Web.

Yule Auxiliary Quantity   A similarity measure developed by Yule.

Yule Coefficient of Colligation   A similarity measure developed by Yule.

Zipf's Law   The observation, due to Zipf, that the frequency with which a term occurs in a document collection and its position in a frequency-ranked list of words are approximately inversely related.

Ziv-Lempel Code   In data compression, an encoding method in which each occurrence of a substring is encoded by a pointer to a prior substring plus an additional character.

Index

Absolute term frequency, 115
Abstract, 23
Abstraction principles, 2–3
Ad hoc query, 146, 148
Aho-Corasick, 299
Algorithm(s):
  Aho-Corasick, 299
  Boyer-Moore-Galil, 297–298. *See also*
    Knuth-Morris-Pratt
  choice of for efficiency, 5–6
  as endosystem component, 5, 23
  genetic, 225, 226–231. *See also* TREC
    experiments
  Knuth-Morris-Pratt, 292–297
  performance of, 8
  Rabin-Karp, 299
  retrieval use in relevance feedback, 223
  stemming, 28–29, 135–137. *See also* Data
    compression, stemming technique
  string-to-string correction type, 301–303
  use in automatic indexing, 109–110
  use in knowledge base, 9
AltaVista, 277
ANSI, 26–27
Arithmetic coding, 36–38
ASCII:
  conversion of codes for, 27
  limitations of, 26–27
  in OCR processing, 274
  standards of, 26–27
  use in personal computers, 26–27
Atomic datum, 25

Base representation, 125
Basis vectors, 87–88
Bead, 266
Bibliographic coupling, 241–242
Bibliographic retrieval system, 258
Binary measures, 192–198
  fallout, 196–198, 208
  generality, 196–198, 208
  precision, 194–196, 197, 199–202, 208
  recall, 192–196, 197, 199–202, 208
Binary search, 135, 305–306
  in sequential files, 307
Binary tree, 31
BIRD (Browsing Interface for Retrieval
  of Documents), 183–187. *See also*
  VIRI
bitmap, 272, 274
BookHouse, 266
Boolean algebra, 53
Boolean points, 180, 182
Boolean query(ies), 53–63, 65–69, 205, 266

Boolean query(ies) *(Continued)*:
  conjunctive normal form (CNF), 57, 58, 60–61, 180
  disjunctive normal form (DNF), 57, 58–60, 61. *See also* Query(ies), disjunctive
  extended, 65–69
  full disjunctive normal form, 57, 58–60
  incorporation of search engines, 283
  Law of Double Negation, 60
  modifications for retrieving documents, 82
  problems with, 55–62
  reducing processing size, 61–62
  use in BIRD, 185
  use of connectives AND, OR, and NOT, 53–63. *See also* Boolean VIBE
  use of parentheses, 55–56
  weight assignment methods, 65–68
Boolean retrieval system:
  document space, 80
  noncompliance with document structure, 18
  origins, 81
Boolean VIBE, 181–182, 186–187, 266
  coincidence of points, 182
  determining number of documents and location, 181–182
Boyer-Moore-Galil, 297–298
Branching factor, 310
Breeding pairs, *see* Query, variants
Byte(s), 25–26

Citation index(es), 244–245
Citation processing, 241–245. *See also* Document surrogates
  parts of bibliography, 242
  problems in identifying useless citations, 243–244
  problems in interpreting citations, 243
  problems in locating citations, 242–243
Citations, bibliographic, 286–287
Classification bins, 184–185
Clustered files, 311
Clustering techniques, 311
Cluster point(s), 164, 266
Co-citations, 241, 242

Code, adaptive, *see* Model(s), adaptive
Codes, arithmetic, 31–34, 36–38
Code(s), formatting, *see* Markup language(s)
Coefficient of association, 127–131
  Arithmetic Mean, 128, 129, 130, 131
  Conditional Probability, 128, 129, 130, 131
  Dice's Coefficient, 130–131
  Index of Independence, 129, 130
  Linear Correlation, 129, 130
  Probability Difference I, 128, 129, 130
  Probability Difference II, 128, 129, 130
  Proportion of Overlap, 128, 129, 130
  Rectangular Distance, 128, 129, 130
  Separation Coefficient, 128
  Vector Angle, 128, 129, 130, 131
  Yule Auxiliary Quantity, 129,130
  Yule Coefficient of Colligation, 129, 130
Collision, 299, 308
Communication theory, *see* Information theory
Compression, *see* Compression, image; Data compression
Compression, image, 39–41, 274
Computer graphics, *see* Image processing
Computing Review, 23
Context encoding, 41
Contingency table, 126–127
Copyright, 286–288
  electronically generated documents, 287
  purpose of, 287
Cosine Coefficient, *see* Coefficient of association, Vector Angle
Cosine measure, 84–87
Cosine transforms, 85
Coverage ratio, 198, 208
Cranfield II database, 229. *See also* Relevance feedback
Crossover:
  one-point, 227
  rate, 227
  two-point, 227
  uniform, 227
Cross-referencing, 109
Current awareness (CA) system, 145, 147–148

Data:
    atomic, *see* Data structure, atomic data
    components of, 9
    compressed, *see* Data compression
    organization of, 8
    relation to signal, 9
    use in endosystem, 8
Database(s):
    indexing for, 105–110
    object-oriented, 73
    problem with data fusion, 98
    redundancy of natural languages, 29
Database(s), full-text:
    data compression methods, 28–30
    problems in searching, 246
    query importance in, 73
    stemming of, 28–29, 137
Database(s), hierarchical, 20, 24
Database(s), network, 20, 24
Database(s), relational, 20, 21, 24
Data compression, 27–38. *See also*
    Model(s), data
    arithmetic coding in, 36–38
    Huffman coding in, 31–34
    level of compression, 29
    stemming technique, 28
    use of adaptive model in, 30, 31–34
    use of data model in, 29–30
    use in document surrogates, 27–38
    use of semi-static model in, 30
    use in sound databases, 41–42
    Ziv-Lempel, coding in, 31, 34–35
Data fusion, 97–98
Data mining, 13. *See also* Information
    filtering
Data structure:
    atomic data, 25
    standards of, 25–27
Default bus, 292–296, 300
DeMorgan's law, 60, 180
Devices, 5
Dimensional compatibility, 64
Direct search technique, 306
Discriminant function, 90–91
Discrimination value, 121–122
Dissimilarity measures, *see* Metrics

Distance measures, 83
Distributed document sets, 276–277
Distributed processing, 276–277
Doctrine of fair use, 286–287
Document(s):
    analysis of, 12
    binary search technique, 305–306
    citation processing, 241–245
    comparing problems with Boolean
      system, 260
    copyright interpretation, 287
    database, 11
    definition, 17
    definition of similarity, 120–122
    description modification for relevance
      feedback, 222–223
    determining location in Boolean VIBE,
      181–182
    development of additional classes, 19
    direct search technique, 306
    effect of scaling on, 97
    electronic form availability, 272
    expected search lengths, 205–208
    file organization, *see* File structure
    fully formatted, 20, 53
    fully unformatted, 20
    gross structure of, 20–21
    information filtering, 97
    linked list search technique, 306
    mapping onto queries, 19
    multimedia, *see* Integrated media
    quality in OCR systems, 273
    query pertinence, 193
    query relevance, 192–193
    query usefulness, 193
    relationship to query(ies), 18
    searching techniques, 305–307. *See also*
      Search process
    semantic structure, 239–240
    sequential search technique, 305
    storage of, 19
    structure for storage, 20–21
    subsets, 205–206
    syntactic structure, 238–239
    textual, 11, 20
    use in reference points, 164, 165

Document(s) *(Continued)*:
  use of index terms, 120
  visual interfaces on vector-based model, 266
Document cluster(s):
  caution for use of, 165
  methods of defining, 164
Document clustering, 266. *See also* VIBE
Document identifiers, 22, 24
Document image, 274
Document reference number, 258
Documents, foreign language, 275
Document(s), full-text, 258
  server role, 286
  surrogates, 105
  violation of copyright, 287
Document space, 80, 266. *See also* Query(ies), relationship to document(s)
  in Boolean-based matching, 81–82, 266
  use in profile modification, 150
Document surrogate, full:
  inclusion of subject categories, 259
  output for bibliographic retrieval, 258–259
  value of, 259
Document surrogates, *see also* Indexing, manual
  accessibility to full document, 272
  difficulties in use, 21
  as a form of data compression, 28
  usefulness, 22–24
Document vocabulary, 134–139
  problems with common terms, 134–135
  problems with similar/related terms, 138–139
  problems with variations of terms, 135–138
Doubly linked list search, 306

Ectosystem, 4–5. *See also* Query(ies), language of
Edit distance, 301–312
Encoding:
  of Chinese characters, 27
  use in compression, 40–42
Encoding system:
  American Standard Code for Information Interchange (ASCII), 25

Extended Binary Coded Decimal Information Code (EBCDIC), 25
  Rich Text Format, 26
Endosystem, *see also* Query(ies), language of
  components of, 5–6
  internal use of document surrogate, 23
  sorting documents in Boolean queries, 62
  user familiarity with, 4
Expected search length, 205–208
Expert system, 9
Extract(s), 23

Failure links, 297
Feedback, 10, 12–13. *See also* Relevance feedback
File structure:
  clustered file, 311
  common examples of, 306
  direct, 309
  hashed file, 307–308
  indexed file, 308–310
  inverted, 309–310
  netted file, 312
  sequential file, 307
  tree-structured file, 310–311
Finite state recognizer, 292, 296, 297–298, 299, 300
  in Aho-Corasick matching, 299
  in Boyer-Moore-Galil matching, 297–298
  in Knuth-Morris-Pratt matching, 292–296
Funder:
  business organizations as, 4
  corporate class of, 284
  economy of ectosystem, 7, 285
  as ectosystem component, 4
  importance to ectosystem, 283
  individual user, class of, 284–285
  public service class of, 283–284
  role of, 4, 5
  services-for-profit class of, 284
Fuzzy information retrieval, 70
Fuzzy judgment, 92–93
Fuzzy set, *see* Query(ies), fuzzy
Fuzzy set theory, 70

Genetic algorithm, 225–232. *See also* Relevance feedback; TREC experiments
Geographic information systems, 40
Graph, *see* Output, graphic display of
Graph theoretic techniques, 311
GUIDO (Graphical User Interface for Document Organization), 168–173, 177, 185–187. *See also* VIRI

Hash coding, 299. *See also* File structure, hashed file
Hash function, 308
Hashing techniques, 135
Hierarchical file, 310
Hill climbing, 225
Homographs, 139
Homonyms, 139
HTML, 39
Huffman encoding, 31–34
Hypertext links, 245–246

Image compression, 39–42. *See also* OCR
    geographic information systems, 40
    standards of, 40–41
    use of multimedia systems, 40
Image processing, 248–249. *See also* OCR
    use of string-to-string algorithm in, 302–303
Index:
    use of, 110
    where used, 105–106
Indexer-user mismatch, 108
Indexing, 105–114
    automatic, 109–113, 114
    cross-referencing in, 109
    language characteristics, 107, 108. *See also* Indexing, automatic
    language development, 113–114, 115
    lexical, 123. *See also* Similarity, document
    linked terms, 108
    manual, 106–107, 108
    purpose of, 106
    roles of terms in, 108
    sources for, 124
    trigger phrases, 124
Index term(s):
    association with other, 113–114, 122

defining of, 112–113
    determining term frequency, 115–116
    phrase frequency, 122–123. *See also* Index term(s), determining term frequency
    proximity as a criterion for, 123
    use of, 120
InfoCrystal, 266
Information, 8. *See also* Data
Information filtering, 246–247
    description of, 97
    use in effective retrieval, 13
Information Navigator, 266, 267
Information retrieval system:
    components of, 11
    profile and query for, 156–157
    research for broadening use, 19
    tests used in design of, 11
    user significance to, 12
Information storage and retrieval:
    document surrogate problems, 21–22
    key concept of similarity, 125–133
    use of, by user, 10
Information theory, 117–120
    area of study, 9
    properties of, 9
Initial bus, 292–296
Integrated media, 249–251. *See also* Image processing
    retrieval of musical patterns, 250–251
    retrieval of non-human sounds, 250
    voice recognition in, 250
Intellectual property rights, *see* Copyright
Inverse document frequency weight, 116–117
Inversion transform, 83
Inverted file, 110
Inverted index, 309
Iterative affix removal stemmer, 28

Jaccard's Coefficient, 131. *See also* Coefficient of association
JBIG (Joint Bilevel Image Experts Group), 41
JPEG (Joint Photographic Experts Group), 41

Key phrase, *see* Document surrogates, usefulness

Key-to-address transformation, 307–308
Keyword, 23
Knowledge base(s), 9
Knuth-Morris-Pratt (KMP):
  basic construction of recognizer,
    292–295
  concept of, 292
  cost effectiveness, 298
  formal construction of recognizer,
    296–297
  multiple occurrences of pattern strings,
    296
  overlapping patterns in pattern strings,
    296

Latent semantic indexing, 240
Lempel-Ziv, *see* Ziv-Lempel code
lexical similarity, 81
Linked list search technique, 306
Links, 108, 292–297
LyberWorld, 267
Lycos, 277

Mapping, 62, 80, 82, 182
  abstract, 266
Markup language(s):
  types of, 38
  use of, in electronically generated
    documents, 275
  use of, in OCR, 274–275
Matching:
  Aho-Corasick, *see* Aho-Corasick
  Boolean-based, 81–82, 88. *See also*
    Matching, probabilistic
  Boyer-Moore-Galil (BMG), *see* Boyer-
    Moore-Galil
  cosine measure in vector-based, 84,
    86–87
  document and query, 80–95, 110
  fuzzy, 92–93
  Knuth-Morris-Pratt (KMP), *see* Knuth-
    Morris-Pratt
  pattern string differences, 300–303
  probabilistic, 89–91, 92. *See also*
    Information theory
  proximity, 94–95. *See also* Index term(s),
    phrase frequency

Rabin-Karp, *see* Rabin-Karp
  use of wild cards, 300–301
  vector-based, 82–86, 88. *See also* Query,
    vector
Matrix, 110
Matrix, document-document, D, 111
Matrix, term-document, A, 110–111, 115
Matrix, term-term, T, 111. *See also* Similarity, document
Measures:
  average precision, 200–202, 208. *See also*
    Binary measures, precision
  average recall, 200–202, 208. *See also*
    Binary measures, recall
  coverage ratio, 198
  methods of computing, 200–202
  normalized precision, 209, 215
  normalized recall, 208–209, 211, 212
  novelty ratio, 198–199
  precision and recall, 194–198
  recall effort, 199
  relative recall, 198, 199
  sliding ratio (SR), 209–211, 212, 215
  use in word proximity, 122–123
  user-oriented, 198. *See also* Binary mea-
    sures
  value of a term, 117–120
  word and term counts in lexically based,
    125–133
Media, 5
Methods, document cluster, 165
Metrics, 83, 86, 131–133, 164
  application to reference points, 164
  city block distance, 86, 132, 133
  definition of, 131
  Euclidean distance, 86, 132, 133
  maximal direction distance, 86, 132, 133
  properties of, 83
Model(s):
  adaptive, 31, 34
  Cassini oval, 155, 156, 165–167
  conjunctive, 154, 165–168
  data, 30, 31
  disjunctive, 154, 165–168
  ellipsoidal, 154–155, 165–168, 171–172.
    See also Query(ies), models of combin-
    ing to profile

semi-static, 30
static, 30, 34
vector-based. *See* GUIDO; VIBE; VIBE, Boolean
MPEG (Moving Picture Experts Group), 41
Multilingual retrieval systems, 138
Multimedia, *see* Integrated media
Multiple indexing levels, 309
Music retrieval system, 251
Mutation rate, 228

n-ary measure, 193–194
Natural language(s):
    aiding user interpretation, 38. *See also* Markup language(s)
    query model, 71–72
    redundancy of, 29
    semantic structure, 239–240
    syntactic structure of, 238–239
    techniques for processing, 238
Negative dictionary, *see* Document vocabulary
Noise, 9
Normalization:
    within Boolean query, 58
    within vector query, 65
Novelty ratio, 198–199, 208
n-simplex, 179

OCR (optical character recognition), 272–275
    document components, 274
    document quality, 273
    effects of misalignment, 273, 274
    goal of, 275
    improving character recognition, 273–274
    output as ASCII file, 274
    problems with foreign languages, 275
O(n) process, 165
Operating curve, 203–204
Optima, 231
Output:
    advantages to multimedia use, 263
    audio, 263
    automatic relevancy, 261, 262, 264
    graphic display of, 262–263

how information is presented, 261–262
manual relevancy, 261, 262, 264
OCR processing, 274
organizing output, 260
quality of user's query, 264
quantity, 260–261
VIRI, 265–267
Overlap Coefficient, *see* Coefficient of association, Conditional Probability

Passage retrieval, 247
Pattern string, 292–299, 300
    constructing recognizers, 292–295, 297–298
    construction of Boyer-Moore-Galil, 297–298
    construction of recognizers, 292, 297
    multiple occurrences of, 296
    overlapping patterns in, 296
    problems in string differencing, 301
    use of, in Rabin-Karp algorithm, 299
Phrase frequency counts, 122
Piecewise linear transformation, 152, 157
Piles, 266
Point of interest (POI), 179–183. *See also* Reference point(s)
Precision-recall graph, 195–196, 199–202
Precision-recall measure, *see* Binary measures
Probability theory, 89–92, 118–120
Profile(s), user, 145–159
    combining query and profile distances, 153–154
    current awareness system for user, 147–148. *See also* Retrospective search system
    ethical concerns, 158–159
    extended profiles, 146–147
    modifying queries, 150
    query modification formulas, 151–153
    retrospective search systems, 148–149
    right to privacy, 288
    as separate reference point, 153
    simple, 145–146
    use in relevance feedback, 222
Profile(s), user:
    use of Cassini oval model in, 155

Profile(s), user *(Continued)*:
  use of conjunctive model in, 154
  use of disjunctive model in, 154
  use of ellipsoidal model in, 154–155
  weighting profile/query, 156–157
Pseudo-metric, 131–132

Query(ies):
  ad hoc, 146. *See also* Retrospective
    search system
  altering terms in, for relevance feedback,
    224
  Boolean, *see* Boolean query(ies)
  disjunctive, 180–181
  document mapping, 19
  effectiveness of language used for, 193
  full text response, 258
  fuzzy, 69–70, 249. *See also* Matching,
    fuzzy; Query(ies), probabilistic
  images used as, 249
  integration with profiles, *see* Profile(s),
    user
  language of, 51–52
  matching criteria, 52–53
  models of combining to profile, 153
  modification of, with profile as co-filter,
    153–154, 157
  modification of, with profile as post-
    filter, 150
  modification of, with profile as pre-filter,
    150–153, 157
  natural language, 72
  probabilistic, 71, 266
  problems with Boolean system, 260
  reference points as addition to, 153–158
  relationship to document(s), 18
  response by information retrieval
    system, 258–260
  routing, 145–147
  short reference, 258
  similarities of, 71
  storage of, 19
  topic form, 18
  user profile use as, 145–146
  value of stemming, 136
  variants, 226–228

Query, vector, 150
  differences between Boolean query and,
    63–64, 65
  practicality, 64
  problems with, 65, 86
  weighted, *see* Boolean query(ies),
    extended
  0,1-vector evaluation method, 63–64

Rabin-Karp, 299–300. *See also* Knuth-
    Morris-Pratt
ReadingRoom, 266
Recall effort, 199, 208
Recognizer, 292–297
  nondeterministic, 294–295
Record, *see* Document(s)
Reference point(s):
  definition, 163–164. *See also* Profile(s),
    user; Query(ies)
  documents used as, 164–165
  use in BIRD, 183–185
  use in Boolean VIBE, 179–183
  use in GUIDO, 168–179
  use in retrieval process, 12
Relative recall, 198, 199, 208
Relative term frequency, 115–116
Relevance feedback, 13, 221–231, 232
Retrieval process:
  mapping, 19
  multiple reference points, 12
Retrieval system(s), 13–14
Retrieval system, Boolean:
  difficulties with, 81–82
  use of document space, 80. *See also*
    Matching, Boolean-based
Retrospective search system, 148–149
Review, 23
Roles, 108–109
Routing query, 145–147

Scaling, 96–97, 215
Scaling, multidimensional, 240
Scatter/Gather, 266
Science Citation Index, 244
SDI (selective dissemination of informa-
    tion) system, 145

Search engines, 277–278, 283
    development of, for data fusion, 98
    weighting of, 283
Search process, 306–312
Second-order filing system, 306
Security of computer-based systems,
    288–289
Segmentation, 39
Sequential file, 307
Sequential search technique, 305
Server:
    as ectosystem component, 4
    efficiency of ectosystem, 6–7
    interaction with user, 286
    role of, 4–5, 285–286
Set theoretic techniques, 311
SGML, 39
Short reference, 258
Signal(s):
    forms of, 9
    information content of, 117–120
Signal-to-noise ratio, 119–120
Signature value, 299
Similarity:
    average, 120–121
    definitions of, 125–133
    deleted average, 121–122
    document, 120, 125–133, 241
    document ratio of in VIBE, 173–179
    measures, 120–122, 125–133, 168
    use of, in metrics, 132
    in vector-based matching: cosine
        measure, 84–86
    in vector-based matching: metrics, 82–83
Simple linear transformation, 151, 157
SMART system, 82. *See also* Matching,
    vector-based; Metrics
Social Science Citation Index, 244
Sound databases, 41
Sound retrieval, *see* Integrated media
Spine, 292–293
State transition diagram, 292, 297
State transition table, 297
Statistical techniques, 311
Stemming, *see* Data compression,
    stemming technique

    in Boolean queries, 53
    in document vocabulary, 135–137
    in natural language queries, 72
Stop list, 134–135, 220
String differencing, 291, 300–303
    construction of graph, 302
    searching for variants, 300–301
String matching, 300
    Aho-Corasick techniques, *see* Aho-
        Corasick
    Boyer-Moore-Galil (BMG) techniques,
        see Boyer-Moore-Galil
    Knuth-Morris-Pratt (KMP) techniques,
        see Knuth-Morris-Pratt
    Rabin-Karp techniques, *see* Rabin-
        Karp
String-to-string correction algorithm,
    301–303
Suffix, 28
Surrogates, *see* Document surrogates
Swets' E measure, 204, 208
Synchronization point(s), *see* Model(s),
    data
System(s):
    measuring economy, 7
    measuring effectiveness, 6, 7
    measuring efficiency, 6
System designer:
    control of system factors, 4–6, 11
    endosystem effect on ectosystem,
        6–7
    problem in data fusion, 98
    role in ectosystem, 4–6
    role in endosystem, 4–6

Term(s):
    altering for use in relevance feedback,
        224
    array matching, 115
    discrimination value, 120
    importance in a query, 95
    problem with vector space models,
        86–87
    significance of punctuation, 114
    value, 12
    weighting of, 95–96, 117, 226

Term discrimination value, 120
Term value, 12
Term weight(s):
 availability for output, 260
 in a document, 117
 generating query variants, 226
 modification in relevance feedback,
  223–224
Text Relationship Map, 266
Text tiling, 114–115, 247
Thesaurus, 62, 138, 220
TileBars, 247, 266
Transforms, 83
TREC experiments, 18, 73, 232–234
Trie, 135
Trigger phrases, 124
Truth table, 58–59

User:
 behavior, 282–283
 as ectosystem component, 4, 281–283
 effectiveness of ectosystem, 6
 identifying for ectosystem performance,
  283
 information used in extended profiles,
  146–147
 law enforcement agencies, 288
 presentation of output to, 261–262
 problems with system interaction, 98
 profiles, *see* Profile(s), user
 right to privacy, 288
 role of, 4, 5, 10, 124, 149, 158–159, 193,
  208
 suggestions for proficient querying,
  219–232
 use of controlled vocabulary, 24
 use of relevance feedback, 221–224
User profiles, *see* Profile(s), user

Vector-based matching, *see* Matching,
  vector-based
Vector models, *see* Query, vector
Venn diagram, 127–128
VIBE (Visual Information Browsing Envi-
  ronment), 173–187, 266. *See also* VIRI
 Boolean, 179–183

use of two-point model in, 174, 175, 177
 use of three-point model in, 174–175
VIRI (visual information retrieval
  interfaces), 265–267. *See also* BIRD;
  GUIDO; VIBE
 purpose criteria, 266
 use criteria, 266
Vocabulary, *see also* Index; Indexing
 control of, in queries and documents,
  24–25
 controlled, in indexing, 107, 108, 110
 use of Brown Corpus in indexing, 123
Vocabulary, uncontrolled, 24–25, 110,
  133–140
 impact on information retrieval systems,
  134
 multilanguage retrieval systems, 137–138
 stemming, 135–137
 use of stop lists, 134
VR-VIBE, 267

Weighted Boolean queries, 65–69
Weighting, 134
 disallowance of fractions, 69
 in extended Boolean query, 65–69. *See
  also* Matching, fuzzy
 for interactive retrieval systems, 265
 of phrase frequency, 122
 profile and query for information
  retrieval, 156–157
 of search engines, 283
 of terms, 95–96, 117, 226
 use in relevance feedback, 223–224, 227,
  230, 231
Weights:
 application to reference points, 164
 relevance, 211
Weight vector:
 assigning weights, 64–65, 150–151, 153
 similarity value in retrieval, 65
Wild cards, 300–301
Wisdom:
 components of, 9
 incorporation of into endosystem, 10
Word frequency counts, 51, 110, 114, 115,
  122, 125

method of definition, 116
use in lexically based measure, 125–133
World Wide Web, *see* Hypertext links
accessibility to user, 283
effectively access data, 97
importance of hypertext links, 13
retrieving relevant documents, 277
search criticism, 278

search engines, 277–278
use of HTML, 39

Yahoo!, 277

0-1 vectors, 126
Zipf's law, 112, 113
Ziv-Lempel code, 31, 34–35